Dictionary

of

Correct
Spelling

Books by Norman Lewis

See, Say, and Write! Books I, II
RSVP—Reading, Spelling, Vocabulary, Pronunciation,
Books 1, 2, 3
RSVP for College English Power, Books I, II, III
RSVP with Etymology, Books 1, 2, 3
Instant Spelling Power for College Students
Instant Word Power
Rapid Vocabulary Builder, revised edition
Word Power Made Easy, revised edition
The New Roget's Thesaurus in Dictionary Form,
revised edition
How to Read Better and Faster, fourth edition
Thirty Days to a More Powerful Vocabulary
(with Wilfred Funk), revised edition
The Modern Thesaurus of Synonyms
The New Power with Words
Thirty Days to Better English
How to Become a Better Reader
New Guide to Word Power
Dictionary of Modern Pronunciation
Correct Spelling Made Easy
Better English
Twenty Days to Better Spelling
How to Get More Out of Your Reading
How to Speak Better English
The Lewis English Refresher and Vocabulary Builder
Power with Words

Dictionary

of

Correct
Spelling

• A HANDY REFERENCE GUIDE •

Norman Lewis

BARNES & NOBLE BOOKS
A DIVISION OF HARPER & ROW, PUBLISHERS
New York, Cambridge, Philadelphia
San Francisco, London, Mexico City
São Paulo, Sydney

A hardcover edition of this book was published by Funk & Wagnalls Company.

DICTIONARY OF CORRECT SPELLING. Copyright © 1962 by Norman Lewis. All rights reserved. Printed in the United States of America. No part of this book may be used or reproduced in any manner whatsoever without written permission except in the case of brief quotations embodied in critical articles and reviews. For information address Harper & Row, Publishers, Inc., 10 East 53rd Street, New York, N.Y. 10022. Published simultaneously in Canada by Fitzhenry & Whiteside Limited, Toronto.

First BARNES & NOBLE BOOKS edition published 1983.

Library of Congress Cataloging in Publication Data

Lewis, Norman, 1912-
    Dictionary of correct spelling.

    (Everyday handbook ; EH/584)
    1. Spellers.   I. Title.
PE1145.2.L49   1983   423'.1   83-47595
ISBN 0-06-463584-8 (pbk.)

83 84 85 86 10 9 8 7 6 5 4 3 2 1

for Mary, Margie, Debbie,
David, and Holly

Rules for hyphenating compounds
> See HYPHENATING, or either the first or last part of the compound in its alphabetical position.

Rules for forming irregular plurals
> See PLURALIZING

Rules for dividing words at ends of lines
> See SYLLABICATING

Rules for doubling final consonants before adding a suffix
> See DOUBLING

PLAN OF THE BOOK

The *Dictionary of Correct Spelling* is designed for quick and convenient reference whenever you have a problem in spelling. It not only shows you how to remember the correct patterns of those words that are most frequently misspelled, but it also explains the principle behind each spelling.

The author has used as his final authority on correct spellings, preferable forms, and hyphenated or unhyphenated compounds his favorite reference work—*Webster's New World Dictionary of the American Language—College Edition.*

GENERAL FEATURES

1. *Conciseness*

This book is concerned solely and exclusively with the correct spelling of English words.

Which words most lend themselves to misspelling? Which does the poor speller invariably get wrong? Which is even the educated person insecure about? Which present thorny problems that only an expert can solve without doubt or hesitation? Such words, and only such, are listed and explained.

2. *Completeness*

And yet (and this is an indication of how difficult, complicated, contradictory, and baffling our system of spelling is) there are over five thousand entries—from *aardvark,* with its untypical double *-a;* through *cozy* (which has five other acceptable spellings), *improvise* (ending in *-ise*), *modernize* (ending in *-ize*), and *paralyze* (ending in *-yze*); *to zwieback,* which comes from German *zwei,* twice, and *backen,* baked, but is nevertheless spelled *-ie,* not *-ei.*

You will find much more here than just the thousands of demons that can plague anyone who is not absolutely sure of his spelling. In infinite detail and with a wealth of clarifying examples the book explores and efficiently unravels every knotty problem that can possibly come up:

When to use *-able* or *-ible; ac-* or *acc-; -acious, -aceous,* or *-atious; -ance* or *-ence; -cede, -ceed,* or *-sede; -ie* or *-ei;* and so on, right through

the whole body of principles that govern the system of spelling under which we operate
When and where to use the apostrophe
When to hyphenate compounds
How to divide words at the ends of lines
How to pluralize irregular nouns
How to make a correct choice between words that sound alike but are spelled differently.

3. *Convenience*

Locating what you want in these pages is as easy as using a dictionary. Everything in the book—individual entries, preferable forms where two or more spellings are acceptable, spelling rules, principles of pluralizing and of word division, contractions, possessives, compounds, homonyms—appears *in one continuous alphabetical arrangement.*

SPECIAL FEATURES

1. *Individual Entries*

Every word listed in this book is prone to misspelling—largely because two or more patterns may seem equally logical to anyone but an expert. For example, is it—

> *coolly* or *cooly?*
> *definately* or *definitely?*
> *dessicate* or *desiccate?*
> *drunkeness* or *drunkenness?*
> *embarassment, embarassement,* or *embarrassment?*
> *exhilerate, exhillarate,* or *exhilarate?*
> *friccasee, fricazee,* or *fricassee?*
> *indispensible, indespensable,* or *indispensable?*
> *innoculate, inocculate,* or *inoculate?*
> *irresistable, irrisistible,* or *irresistible?*
> *irridescent, irredescent,* or *iridescent?*
> *liquify* or *liquefy?*
> *occurence, occurrance,* or *occurrence?*
> *sacreligious* or *sacrilegious?*
> *seperate* or *separate?*
> *sieze* or *seize?*

These are typical of the words many people might have occasion to use in their writing—words they are as likely as not to misspell. If you were not absolutely sure of any one of them and decided to look it up, you would find not only the correct spelling (which any good dictionary will give you) but also, and more important, why it's spelled the way it is (there's always a reason, even if not necessarily a supremely sensible one, for the exact pattern of letters in a word) ; what specific rule applies; what category to turn to for more information on, and additional examples of, this rule; and how best to avoid the insidious pitfalls the word contains, so that you won't ever have to check on the spelling a second time.

Here are some instances of how a few of the words in the preceding list are dealt with.

coolly. Note the double -l, since the adverbial suffix *-ly* is added to the adjective *cool*. (See -LY, 7.)

desiccate. This spelling may look insane, but it's the only correct one— one *-s,* two *-c*'s. From Latin *siccus,* dry, plus the prefix *de-*.

drunkenness. The adjective *drunken* (as in a *drunken bum*) plus *-ness,* hence two *-n*'s toward the end. No such word, or spelling, as *drunkeness, drunkardness,* or *drunkedness.* (See -NESS AFTER N-.)

2. *Deliberate Misspellings*

But, you may ask, if I don't know how to spell a word in the first place, how am I going to look it up?

And this is a fair question. The people who can't spell *psychiatry* may logically look under the *S*'s—and, as we know, they can hunt all day through a dictionary without finding it. If they're in doubt about *supersede* they might sensibly start their search at *superc-,* again to be met only with irritating frustration.

So misspelled words are also listed in the book—*under the patterns in which they are commonly misspelled.*

Poor spellers, looking for *psychiatry* under the *S*'s, will find *sy-* and the following note: *For words that seem to start with this syllable, see PS-, S-.* They will find *supercede* and be directed to the correct listing, *supersede.* If they think the words are spelled *innoculate, kahki, Kruschchev,* or *seige* (as, of course, they are not), they will, in each instance, find what they want where they think it might logically be, and will then be guided to the proper entry.

3. *Major Categories*

The rules of English spelling are vastly complicated and riddled with exceptions. By breaking them down into short and simple parts, we can understand them more easily and remember them far better.

In this book you will find all the principles that govern our inefficient and cumbersome system of spelling neatly fragmented into 136 major categories. For example:

-ABLE, -EABLE. When do we drop final -e before -able, when may we retain it?

-ABLE, -IBLE. Eight simple classifications of words that end in -able, seven equally simple classifications of -ible words, and how to remember which is which.

-ANCE, -ENCE. Ten separate categories devoted to this confusing ending, depending on whether the preceding letter is c-, d-, g-, i-, l-, n-, r-, t-, u-, or v-.

-ARY, -ERY. What simple keys are there for choosing correctly between these two confusing endings?

-CEED, -SEDE, -CEDE. What are the only three English words ending in -ceed? What is the only one ending in -sede?

-Y PLUS A SUFFIX. When do we change -y to -i, when do we keep it as is?

4. Homonyms

The book contains almost 200 categories of homonyms—words of similar sound but different meanings and spellings, such as affect—effect; council—counsel; stationary—stationery; there—they're—their; who's—whose, etc.

The distinction in meaning and use between the confusing words is briefly and clearly explained, and illustrative phrases or sentences are supplied where necessary.

5. Compounds

When do we hyphenate a compound, when do we write it solid, when do we spell it as two separate words? Under HYPHENATING will be found the few basic principles that govern hyphenating, plus forty or so specific groups, such as ante-, anti-, co-, pre-, well-, etc. Throughout the book are 260 additional categories of compounds, each in its alphabetical position, each clearly indicating when to hyphenate, when to separate, and when to combine into a solid word.

6. Word Division

When and where do we divide a word that runs over from one line to the next? When or in what ways may we not divide a word? Under SYLLABICATING, you will find the simple rules illustrated with hundreds of clarifying examples.

7. *Pluralization*

Adding an -s to a noun to form the plural presents no problem. But what if the word ends in -a (*alumna, formula, stigma,* for example)? Or -eau (*beau, bureau,* etc.)? Or -ful (*spoonfuls, spoonsful,* or *spoons full*)? Or -o (*echos* or *echoes, buffalos* or *buffaloes, cellos, celloes,* or *celli*)? A dozen categories under PLURALIZING headings give you the exact forms, as well as the fundamental principles that apply to all words with the same endings.

Dictionary

of

Correct

Spelling

A

aardvark. Double -*a* for this African animal.

Aaron. Double -*a*.

abacus. Not *abacous*. (See -US, -OUS.)

abhorrence. Note the double -*r* and the -*ence* ending. (See -ANCE, -ENCE, AFTER R-, 3.)

abhorrent. Note the -*ent* ending. (See -ANCE, -ENCE, AFTER R-, 3A.)

-ABLE, -EABLE

1. Generally, drop the final -*e* of a word before adding -*able*.

argue—arguable
desire—desirable
pleasure—pleasurable
prove—provable
use—usable
value—valuable

2. In a very few instances the -*e* may be retained, though the far preferable spelling drops it.

blame—blamable *or* blameable
like—likable *or* likeable
love—lovable *or* loveable
move—movable *or* moveable
sale—salable *or* saleable
size—sizable *or* sizeable

3. If a word ends in -*ee* both -*e*'s are retained.

agree—agreeable
decree—decreeable
free—freeable
see—seeable

See also -CEABLE; -GEABLE.

-ABLE, -IBLE

(For words ending in -*ible,* see -IBLE, -ABLE.)

1. If the root to which the suffix is to be added is a full word in its own right, the correct ending is -*able* rather than -*ible*. (There are,

however, a number of exceptions, which you will find under -IBLE, -ABLE.)

accept—acceptable
avail—available
break—breakable
correct—correctable
credit—creditable
depend—dependable
detect—detectable
detest—detestable
dispense—dispensable
expend—expendable
mail—mailable
pass—passable
perish—perishable
person—personable
predict—predictable
present—presentable
profit—profitable
remark—remarkable
surmount—surmountable

2. If the root to which the suffix is to be added is a full word lacking only final -*e,* the correct ending is again -*able*.

ador(e)—adorable
argu(e)—arguable
blam(e)—blamable
debat(e)—debatable
deplor(e)—deplorable
describ(e)—describable
desir(e)—desirable
excit(e)—excitable
excus(e)—excusable
lov(e)—lovable
mov(e)—movable
pleasur(e)—pleasurable
presum(e)—presumable
siz(e)—sizable
us(e)—usable
valu(e)—valuable

3. If the letter preceding the suffix is an -*i,* again -*able*.

amiable	classifiable
appreciable	enviable

insatiable   reliable
justifiable   satisfiable
       sociable

4. Or if the preceding letters are *-ee.*

agreeable   freeable
disagreeable   seeable

5. If other forms of the word contain *-a* as a principal vowel, the suffix is *-able.*

abomination—abominable
capacity—capable
commendation—commendable
delectation—delectable
demonstrate—demonstrable
duration—durable
enumerate—innumerable
estimate—estimable
hospitality—hospitable
imitate—imitable
inflammation—flammable
irritate—irritable
penetrate—penetrable
pregnant—pregnable
reparation—reparable
separate—separable
tolerate—tolerable
violate—violable

6. When the root ends in a "hard" *-c* (sounding like *-k*) or "hard" *-g* (as in *gay*), only *-able* will maintain the correct sound.

amicable   explicable
applicable   navigable
indefatigable   placable
despicable   practicable
educable   revocable

7. Certain *-able* words do not fit into any useful categories. These you must become so familiar with visually that only the correct suffix looks right.

affable   inevitable
arable   inexorable
culpable   inscrutable
equitable   insuperable
formidable   malleable
indomitable   memorable
ineffable   palpable

portable   probable
potable   unconscionable

8. When an *-e* is retained after *c-* or *g-* to keep the consonant "soft," the ending is always *-able,* as in *noticeable, manageable,* etc. For a full list of these see -CEABLE; -GEABLE.
See also -ABLE, -EABLE; -CEABLE; -GEABLE; -IBLE, -ABLE.

---

abominable. Since *-a* is the principal vowel in another form of the word (*abomination*), the correct ending is *-able.* (See -ABLE, -IBLE, 5.)

abridgeable. The *-e* of *abridge* is retained before *-able* in order to preserve the original "soft" (or *-j*) sound of the preceding *-g.* (See -GEABLE.)

abridgment. When a word ends in *-dge,* the *-e* is preferably dropped before *-ment.* (See -DGMENT, -DGEMENT.)

abscence. Misspelling of *absence.*

abscess. Note the *-c.*

absence. No *-c* directly after the *s-;* think of the adjective *absent,* which is usually spelled correctly.

absess. Misspelling of *abscess.*

absorption. The *-b* of *absorb* is a *-p* in the noun form.

abstention. Ends in *-ention.* (See -ENSION, -ENTION.)

abstinence. Somewhat more words end in *-nence* than *-nance,* this one among others. (See -ANCE, -ENCE, AFTER N-, 1.)

abstinent. Ending is *-ent.*

abundance. One of the few words in which *-ance,* not *-ence,* follows a *d-.* (See -ANCE, -ENCE, AFTER D-, 3.)

abundant. Ending is *-ant.*

abuttal. Because *abut* is accented on the last syllable, the final *-t* is doubled before a suffix beginning with a vowel. (See DOUBLING FINAL -T, 2.)

abutted. See *abuttal.*

AC-, ACC-. See ACC-, AC-.

---

academically. Note the *-ally* ending, common to adverbs formed from adjectives ending in *-ic.* (See -LY, ALLY, 1.)

academy. Letter following the *d-* is *-e,* not *-a.*

ACC-, AC-
   1. The following often misspelled words start with *acc-,* the two *-c's* producing the sound of *-k.*

acclaim	accouchement
acclimate	account
acclivity	accouter
accolade	accredit
accommodate	accretion
accompany	accrue
accomplice	accumbent
accomplish	accumulate
accord	accurate
according	accursed
accordion	accuse
accost	accustom

   2. It will thus be seen that before *-l, -o, -r,* and *-u, acc-,* rather than *ac-,* is the common spelling. However, note these important exceptions:

acolyte	acronym
acorn	acropolis
acoustics	across
acrid	acrostic
acrimony	acumen
acrobat	acute

   3. Words like *accede, accident, accessory,* etc., in which each *-c* is pronounced separately, generally present no problems.

---

accede. *-Cede* is the common ending for such verbs, but there are exceptions. (See -CEED, -SEDE, -CEDE, 3.)

accelerate. Note the single *-l,* as in the related noun *celerity.*

accelerator. Be careful of the *-or* ending. (See -ER, -OR, 5.)

ACCELERATOR, EXHILARATOR
   An *accelerator* (ak-SEL-er-ay-ter) makes something go faster, and is the correct word for the so-called gas pedal on an automobile. The word is confused by some with *exhilarator,* which cheers up, enlivens, or stimulates, and is pronounced eg-ZIL-a-ray-ter.

ACCEPT, EXCEPT
   Accept is a *verb* meaning *to receive, take,* etc.
      Will you *accept* this gift?
      She *accepted* his proposal.
   Except is either a preposition or a verb showing exclusion.
      Everyone smiled *except* her.
      In making these remarks I *except* present company.
      This is true in general, present company *excepted.*

---

acceptable. The ending is *-able,* not *-ible.* (See -ABLE, -IBLE, 1.)

accessary. See *accessory.*

accessible. If the root forms its noun by the immediate addition of *-ion* (*accession*), the correct ending is likely to be *-ible.* (See -IBLE, -ABLE, 2.)

accessory, accessary. In present usage the *-ory* ending is preferable here whether the word is a noun or adjective.

accidence. Almost always, with only a few exceptions, *-ence,* not *-ance,* follows a *d-.* (See -ANCE, -ENCE, AFTER D-, 1.)

accidentally. Note that *-ly* is added to the adjective *accidental,* hence the *-ally* ending. (See -LY, -ALLY, 3.)

acclamation. Double *-c,* one *-m.*

accommodate. Both *-c* and *-m* are doubled.

accompanied. The *-y* of *accompany* changes to *-ie* before *-d* or *-s.* (See -Y PLUS A SUFFIX, 1.)

accompanies. See *accompanied.*

accompaniment. The -*y* of *accompany* changes to -*i* before -*ment*. (See -Y PLUS A SUFFIX, 6.)

accomplish. Double -*c*.

account. Double -*c*.

accumulate. Double -*c*, one -*m*.

accuracy. Double -*c*; -*acy* at end.

accurate. Double -*c*; -*ate* at end.

accusatory. The ending is -*ory*, not -*ary*. (See -ARY, -ORY, 2.)

accustom. Double -*c*.

-ACEOUS, -ATIOUS, -ACIOUS. See -ACIOUS, -ACEOUS, -ATIOUS.

---

acetic. See ASCETIC, ACETIC.

ache. Note the -*h*.

achieve. -*I* before -*e*, except after *c*-. (See -IE, -EI, 1.)

aching. The -*e* of *ache* is dropped before a suffix beginning with a vowel. (See DROPPED -E.)

-ACIOUS, -ACEOUS, -ATIOUS

This confusing ending is pronounced the same in all three spellings.

1. The most frequent form is -*acious: audacious, gracious, pugnacious*, etc.

2. Of the common words, only *curvaceous* ends in -*aceous*. But a great many technical terms from botany, zoology, chemistry, medicine, etc., have this spelling: *herbaceous, sebaceous, setaceous*, etc.

3. The following end in -*atious:*
disputatious   ostentatious
flirtatious   vexatious

You will note that for each of these there is a corresponding noun in -*ation: disputation, flirtation, ostentation, vexation*.

4. So, if you are in any serious doubt, -*acious* is more than likely to be the correct ending.

See also -ICIOUS, -ITIOUS; -OCIOUS.

acknowledge. Think of this demon as *know* with the prefix *ac*- and ending with the word *ledge*.

acknowledgeable. The *e* of *acknowledge* is retained before -*able* in order to preserve the original "soft" (or *j*) pronunciation of the preceding -*g*. (See -GEABLE.)

acknowledgment. When a word ends in -*dge*, the -*e* is preferably dropped before -*ment*. (See -DGMENT, -DGEMENT.)

acolyte. Starts with *ac*-, not *acc*. (See ACC-, AC-, 2.)

acorn. Starts with *ac*-, not *acc*-. (See ACC-, AC-, 2.)

acoustics. Starts with *ac*-, not *acc*-. (See ACC-, AC-, 2.)

acquaintance. Ends in -*ance*, not -*ence*. (See -ANCE, -ENCE, AFTER T-, 1.)

acquiesce. Note the -*esce* ending. (See -ESCE, -ESCENT, -ESCENCE, 1.)

acquiescence. Note the -*sc* and also the -*ence* ending. (See -ANCE, -ENCE, AFTER C-, 5.)

acquire. Remember the -*c*.

acquittal. Because *acquit* is accented on the last syllable, the final *t* is doubled before a suffix beginning with a vowel. (See DOUBLING FINAL -T, 2.)

acquitted. See *acquittal*.

acre. The ending is -*re* to keep the -*c* "hard." (See -ER, -RE, 2.)

acreage. Final -*e* of *acre* is retained before the suffix -*age*. (See -AGE AFTER FINAL -E, 2; -ER, -RE, 4.)

acred. See -ER, -RE, 3.

across. *Cross* plus *a*-. (See ACC-, AC-, 2.)

actor. Only spelling for both a doer and a Thespian. (See -ER, -OR, 3.)

actually. *Actual* plus the adverbial suffix -*ly*; hence two *l*'s. (See -LY, 7.)

ADAPT, ADOPT

To *adapt* is to change or modify;

to *adopt* is to take and use as one's own.

> He could not *adapt* himself to primitive society.
> He has *adopted* many of his brother's characteristics.
> He was an *adopted* child.

adapter. Ends in *-er.* (See -ER, -OR, 1.)

addendum. The plural is *addenda.* (See PLURALIZING WORDS IN TERMINAL -UM, 1.)

address. Two *-d*'s always.

adherence. Note the *-ence* ending. (See -ANCE, -ENCE, AFTER R-, 4.)

adherent. Note the *-ent* ending. (See -ANCE, -ENCE, AFTER R-, 4A.)

adjective compounds. See HYPHEN-ATING, 2, 11.

ADJOIN, ADJOURN

> To *adjoin* is to be or lie next to; to *adjourn* is to suspend a meeting until a future time.
> The hospital *adjoins* the cemetery.
> They live in *adjoining* houses.
> The meeting was *adjourned.*

adjudication. Note the first *-d.*

administrator. Ends in *-or.* (See -ER, -OR, 5.)

admissible. When the root ends in *-miss,* the correct ending is *ible.* (See -IBLE, -ABLE, 4.)

admittance. Because *admit* is accented on the last syllable, the final *-t* is doubled before a suffix beginning with a vowel. And notice that the ending is *-ance,* not *-ence.* (See -ANCE, -ENCE, AFTER T-, 1; DOUBLING FINAL -T, 2.)

admitted. See *admittance.*

adolescence. Note the *-sc* and also the *-ence* ending. (See -ANCE, -ENCE, AFTER C-, 5; -ESCE, -ESCENT, -ESCENCE.)

adolescent. See *adolescence.*

adopt. See **ADAPT, ADOPT.**

adorable. The ending is *-able,* not *-ible.* (See -ABLE, -IBLE, 2.)

adress. Misspelling of *address.*

adscititious. Ends in *-itious,* not *-icious.* (See -ICIOUS, -ITIOUS, 3.)

adventitious. Ends in *-itious,* not *-icious.* (See -ICIOUS, -ITIOUS, 3.)

adverbs with participles. See HY-PHENATING, 13.

adversary. Most words with both a primary and secondary accent end in *-ary* rather than *-ery.* (See -ARY, -ERY, 1, 2.)

advertise. Ends in *-ise.* (See -ISE, 8.)

ADVICE, ADVISE

> *Advice* is a noun, *advise* a verb.
> Thank you for your *advice.*
> I don't need you to *advise* me.

advisable. Ends in *-able.* (See -ABLE, -IBLE, 2.)

advise. Note the *-ise* ending, common to all words ending in *-vise.*

adviser, advisor. Either spelling correct, the *-er* form more prevalent. (See -ER, -OR, 2.)

adz, adze. Both forms correct and current.

aegis, egis. The former is more popular—both are correct.

aeon, eon. The shorter form is more modern, but the longer one is more popular. Both correct.

aerate. Pronounced in a number of ways, some not fully acceptable, but spelled only as shown.

aerial. Pronounced AIR-ee-'l, but not spelled that way.

aeroplane. See *airplane.*

aesthetic, esthetic. The second is the more modern form, but the first is commoner. Both correct.

AFF-, AF-

1. Before a vowel, or the consonants *-l* and *-r, aff-* is more commonly found than *af-.* For example:

affable
affair
affect
affectation
affection
affiance
affidavit
affiliate
affinity
affirm
affix
afflatus

afflict
affluent
afflux
afford
afforest
affranchise
affray
affricate
affright
affront
affusion

2. Where *a-* is simply a prefix tacked on to a full word beginning with *f-, af-* is of course the correct spelling: *afar, afebrile, afield, afire, aflame, afloat, aflutter, afoot, aforementioned, aforesaid, aforethought, afoul, afresh.*

3. The following are also spelled *af-: aficionado, afraid, Africa.*

---

affable. Ends in *-able.* (See -ABLE, -IBLE, 7.)

AFFECT, EFFECT

Affect is generally a *verb,* and has the usual verbal forms: *affected, affects, affecting.*

> This *affected* him deeply.
> He often *affects* a Southern accent.
> How will a Republican victory *affect* business policy?
> He was not a bit *affected* by her tears.
> It was an *affecting* sight.
> Can her tears *affect* your decision?

Affect is a noun only as a technical term in psychology, and with the special meaning of *mood, feeling,* or *emotion as a factor in behavior.* It is then pronounced AF-fekt.

Effect is, with one exception, a *noun.*

> What a stunning *effect!*
> He has an unusual *effect* on his patients.

What will the *effect* of a Republican victory be?
> Her tears had no *effect* on him.
> The scenic *effects* are breathtaking.

In the one exception, *effect* is a verb if it means to *bring about, produce,* or *cause.*

> He was unable to *effect* (i.e., *bring about*) a settlement of the steel strike.
> Psychoanalysis often *effects* (i.e., *brings about*) a radical change in personality.
> Research scientists have been trying for years to *effect* (i.e., *bring about*) a cure for cancer.
> They *effected* (i.e., *brought about*) their escape by bribing the guard.

However (and note that the verb does *not* mean *bring about*):

> The steel strike has strongly *affected* the economic picture.
> Psychoanalysis *affected* him strangely.
> Antibiotic drugs do not seem to *affect* the course of cancer.

Affect (except as a technical term in psychology) and *effect* are pronounced identically. The first syllable has the sound of the *-a* in *sofa* or *ago,* or the *-e* in *agent,* and the second syllable receives the accent.

---

affectible. If the root forms its noun by the immediate addition of *-ion* (*affection*), the correct ending is likely to be *-ible.* (See -IBLE, -ABLE, 2.)

AFFECTING, AFFECTIVE, EFFECTIVE. See EFFECTIVE, AFFECTIVE, AFFECTING.

---

affiance. Ending is *-ance.* (See -ANCE, -ENCE, AFTER I-, 3.)

affluence. Always *-ence,* not *-ance,* after

fl-. (See -ANCE, -ENCE, AFTER U-, 2.)

aficionado. One *-f.* (See AFF-, AF-, 3.)

AG-, AGG-. See AGG-, AG-.

-age. See HYPHENATING, 49B, 49C.

-AGE AFTER FINAL -E

1. In the following words, final *-e* is dropped before the suffix *-age.*
anecdote—anecdotage
concubine—concubinage
line—linage
(i.e., the number of lines on a page, pronounced *LY-nij.* A variant spelling, *lineage,* with unchanged pronunciation, is also acceptable.)
2. In the following words, the *-e* is retained.
acre—acreage
line—lineage
(i.e., ancestry, pronounced *LIN-ee-ij*)
mile—mileage

ageing. See *aging.*

agendum. The plural is *agenda.* (See PLURALIZING WORDS IN TERMINAL -UM, 1.)

AGG-, AG-

1. The following words (and their derivatives) start with *agg-:*
agglomerate   aggregate
agglutinate   aggressive
aggrandize   aggrieve
aggravate
It will thus be seen that *agg-* precedes only *-l* or *-r.*
2. When *a-* is a prefix attached to a full word in its own right—*agleam, aglimmer, aglitter, aglow*—we also have *ag-* preceding *-l.*
3. *Ag-* precedes *-r* in the following words (and their derivatives).
agrarian   agriculture
agree   aground
4. Also in any words built on

Latin *agro-,* field: *agrology, agronomy,* etc.

aging. This spelling is preferable to *ageing.*

agitator. End in *-or.* (See -ER, -OR, 5.)

aglomerate. Misspelling of *agglomerate.* (See AGG-, AG-, 1.)

aglutinate. Misspelling of *agglutinate.* (See AGG-, AG-, 1.)

agrandize. Misspelling of *aggrandize.* (See AGG-, AG-, 1.)

agravate. Misspelling of *aggravate.* (See AGG-, AG-, 1.)

agree. Only one *-g* in this word or any of its derived forms. (See AGG-, AG-, 3.)

agreeable. Always *-able* after *ee-.* (See -ABLE, -EABLE, 3; -ABLE, -IBLE, 4.)

agreement. See *agree.*

agreer. Two *-e*'s only, even though it's *agree* plus *-er.* (See -EER.)

agregate. Misspelling of *aggregate.* (See AGG-, AG-, 1.)

agressive. Misspelling of *aggressive.* (See AGG-, AG-, 1.)

agrieve. Misspelling of *aggrieve.* (See AGG-, AG-, 1.)

-AID, -AYED. See -AYED, -AID.

aide-de-camp. The principal part of a compound word is pluralized: *aides-de-camp.* Also spelled, but less commonly, *aid-de-camp, aids-de-camp.*

airial. Misspelling of *aerial.*

airplane, aeroplane. The first is the more modern, and far preferable, spelling. *Airoplane* is incorrect.

AISLE, ISLE

Though identical in pronunciation, the two words are totally unrelated in every other way. *Aisle* is a passageway or corridor (a narrow *aisle* between two rows of seats); *isle* is a small island.

Isle, like *island,* contains an *-s*

because of its derivation from the Latin *insula*, an island (and English words like *insular* and *insulate* are less adulterated examples of this Latin ancestry). *Aisle* is spelled and pronounced the way it is because of early confusion with *isle*—it derives from the Latin *ala*, a wing.

AL-, ALL-. See ALL-, AL-.

-AL, -ALL

1. With very few exceptions, a verb will end in *-all* rather than *-al*. For example, *call, recall, befall, install*, etc.

2. The double *-l* of these verbs, then, is retained in derived forms— *called, recalling; installation*, etc. (*Installment*, with double *-l*, is the preferable spelling of this noun, but *instalment*, with one *-l*, is also correct.)

3. Two of the exceptions are *cabal* and *corral*. Since in both instances the accent is on the final syllable, derived forms will contain a double *-l*: *caballed, caballing; corralled, corralling*.

4. Two other exceptions are *appall* and *enthrall*, for which there are also the rarely used variants *appal* and *enthral*. Derived forms contain two *-l*'s: *appalling, appalled; enthralling, enthralled*. And the preferable *enthrallment* may also be spelled *enthralment*.

See also ALL-, AL-; DOUBLING FINAL -L; -EL, -ELL; -IL, -ILL; -OL, -OLL.

Aladdin. One *-l*, two *-d*'s, not the other way around.

albeit. One *-l*, though pronounced as if there were two (awl-BEE-it).

albino. Pluralize by adding *-s* only; *albinos*. (See PLURALIZING WORDS IN TERMINAL -O, 2.)

alga. Plural is *algae*. (See PLURAL-

IZING WORDS IN TERMINAL -A, 1.)

ALL-

Compounds with this prefix are generally hyphenated: *all-American, all-inclusive, all-seeing, all-wise,* etc.

ALL-, AL-

Deciding whether to start a word with *al-* or *all-* presents a problem to some spellers, though most of us can rely successfully on our visual memory. The following *all-* forms, occasionally misspelled, are worth noting.

allege	allot
allegiance	allow
allegro	alloy
allergy	allude
alleviate	allure
alley	ally
alligator	

If in serious doubt, start other words with *al-*.

See also -AL, -ALL.

-ALL, -AL. See -AL, -ALL.

Alladin. Misspelling of *Aladdin*.

allayed. Since the terminal *-y* of *allay* follows a vowel, it does *not* change to *-i* before a suffix. (See -Y PLUS A SUFFIX, 9.)

allayer. See *allayed*.

allaying. See *allayed*.

allege. No *-d* anywhere in this word.

allegiance. One of the few instances in which *-ance*, rather than *-ence*, follows *i*-. (See -ANCE, -ENCE, AFTER I-, 4.)

alleys. A word ending in *-ey* is pluralized by the simple addition of *-s*. (See -EYS, -IES, -YS, 1.)

alliance. Ending is *-ance*. (See -ANCE, -ENCE, AFTER I-, 2.)

all mighty. See ALMIGHTY, ALL MIGHTY.

all most. See ALMOST, ALL MOST.

allmost. Misspelling of *almost*.

allotment. Final *-t* of *allot* is not doubled since the suffix *-ment* starts with a consonant.

allotted. Because *allot* is accented on the last syllable, the final *-t* is doubled before a suffix beginning with a vowel. (See DOUBLING FINAL -T, 2.)

allotting. See *allotted.*

all ready. See ALREADY, ALL READY.

ALL RIGHT, ALRIGHT, ALL-RIGHT

With one exception, *all right* (two words) is the only fully acceptable spelling, no matter what it means.

> We're *all right.* (all of us)
> We're *all right,* now. (we're fine)
> *All right,* I'll give in. (O.K.)
> *All-right* (hyphenated) is the spelling for the slang adjective— He's an *all-right* guy.
> *Alright,* though much used by the unsophisticated, is still considered substandard.

---

all so. See ALSO, ALL SO.

all together. See ALTOGETHER, ALL TOGETHER.

ALLUDE, ELUDE

To *allude* is to refer indirectly; to *elude* is to avoid, escape from, etc.

> Are you *alluding* to my religion?
> He *eluded* capture.
> The exact word *eludes* me.

ALLUSION, ILLUSION

An *allusion* is an indirect reference; an *illusion* is a false, though often pleasant, notion, a deceptive appearance, etc.

> He made some unpleasant *allusions* to my role.
> You have some strange *illusions* about life.

---

all ways. See ALWAYS, ALL WAYS.

-ALLY, -LY. See -LY, -ALLY.

ALMIGHTY, ALL MIGHTY

The distinction can best be seen in the following sentences:

> God is *almighty.* (all-powerful)
> We're *all mighty* glad to see you. (all of us are mighty glad)
> You and your *almighty* snobbery! (extreme)
> We're *almighty* glad. (extremely glad)

ALMOST, ALL MOST

The one-word form means *nearly* —We're *almost* there; He's *almost* happy it happened; etc.

Two separate words are used in a sentence like *We're all most happy to see you,* meaning *all of us are most happy.*

—ALOGY, —OLOGY

Thousands of words end in *-ology* (*biology, geology, meteorology, physiology,* etc.), so the few that terminate in *-alogy* are often misspelled. Guard against substituting *-o* for *-a* in the following.

analogy   mammalogy
genealogy   mineralogy
             tetralogy

The *-a* is found also in derived forms: *analogous, genealogist,* etc.

ALREADY, ALL READY

Whether you use one or two words depends on your meaning.

> It is *already* late. (*by now*)
> He was *already* dead. (*by then*)
> We're *all ready.* (*all of us*)
> The books are *all ready.* (*completely*)

---

alright. See ALL RIGHT, ALRIGHT, ALL-RIGHT.

ALSO, ALL SO

The spelling depends on the meaning.

He *also* serves. (too, in addition)

It's *all so* confusing. (all of it is so confusing)

ALTAR, ALTER

The first is a stand or platform in a church; it's what spinsters hope to be lead to. The second is a verb meaning *to change*. They're pronounced identically.

although, altho. The latter spelling not acceptable in formal writing. (See -OUGH, -O.)

alto. Pluralize by adding -*s* only: *altos.* (See PLURALIZING WORDS IN TERMINAL -O, 2.)

ALTOGETHER, ALL TOGETHER

The spelling depends on the meaning.

He's *altogether* confused. (totally)

We're *all together* in this. (all of us are together)

aluminum, aluminium. The latter spelling, with the extra -*i*, is British.

alumna. A female graduate—plural is *alumnae,* the last syllable rhyming with *see.* (See PLURALIZING WORDS IN TERMINAL -A, 4.)

alumni. Plural of *alumnus,* pronounced *a-LUM-nye.*

alumnus. A male graduate—the plural is *alumni,* the last syllable rhyming with *sigh.* (See PLURALIZING WORDS IN TERMINAL -US, 12.)

ALWAYS, ALL WAYS

The spelling depends on the meaning.

He's *always* complaining. (forever)

In *all ways* it's different. (every way)

AM-, AMM-. See AMM-, AM-.

amanuensis. Plural is *amanuenses.* (See PLURALIZING WORDS IN TERMINAL -IS.)

amateur. Ends in -*eur.*

ambassador. Ends in -*or.* (See -ER, -OR, 5.)

ambition. Ends in -*ition,* not -*icion.* (See -ICIOUS, -ITIOUS, 4.)

ambitious. Ends in -*itious,* not -*icious.* (See -ICIOUS, -ITIOUS, 3.)

ambulance. One of the comparatively few words in which -*ance* rather than -*ence,* follows *l-.* (See -ANCE, -ENCE, AFTER L-, 3.)

amiable. -*Able* is the correct suffix after the letter *i-.* (See -ABLE, -IBLE, 3.)

amicable. Only the -*able* ending will keep the preceding -*c* "hard." (See -ABLE, -IBLE, 6.)

AMM-, AM-

Few words of any consequence start with *amm-* rather than *am-;* if in doubt, use a single -*m.* Noteworthy are *ammeter, ammonia,* and *ammunition.*

among. Not *amoung,* a common misspelling in students' compositions.

amount. One -*m.* (See AMM-, AM-.)

amulet. Ends in -*et,* not -*ette.* (See -ET, -ETTE, 4.)

anachronism. The -*ch* is a stumbling block for some unsophisticated spellers, and all derived forms are spelled similarly. It's from Greek *chronos,* time, plus *ana-,* not.

analogous. Preceding the -*l* is -*a,* not -*o.* (See -ALOGY, -OLOGY.)

analogue, analog. The longer spelling is preferable. (See -OGUE, -OG, 1.)

analogy. The ending is -*alogy,* not -*ology.* (See -ALOGY, -OLOGY.)

analysis. Plural is *analyses.* (See PLURALIZING WORDS IN TERMINAL -IS.)

analyst. Note the *-y* after the *l-*, as in the verb *analyze.*

analytic. See *analyst.*

analyze. This and *paralyze* are the only two common verbs ending in *-yze.* (See -IZE, -YZE, 2.)

-ANCE, -ENCE, AFTER C-

1. If the *-c* is "soft" (pronounced *s*), the ending must be *-ence.*

beneficence maleficence
innocence munificence
magnificence reticence

2. The adjectives follow suit.

beneficent maleficent
innocent munificent
magnificent reticent

3. If the *-c* is "hard" (pronounced *k*), the ending must be *-ance.*

insignificance significance

4. The adjectives also end in *-ant.*

insignificant significant

5. After *-sc* in a large number of words, the ending is *-ence,* so long as the *-c* is "soft," as it invariably is. Among many others:

acquiescence iridescence
adolescence obsolescence
convalescence opalescence
effervescence phosphorescence
evanescence quiescence

6. The adjectives of such nouns will of course end in *-ent: acquiescent, adolescent,* etc.

-ANCE, ENCE, AFTER D-

1. Most such words will end in *-ence:*

accidence impudence
antecedence incidence
coincidence independence
confidence jurisprudence
credence precedence
dependence providence
diffidence prudence
dissidence residence
evidence subsidence
improvidence superintendence
imprudence

2. The adjective or alternate noun

form will of course end in *-ent: accident, antecedent,* etc.

3. A very few words end in *-ance* following *d-.* Among them:

abundance guidance
attendance misguidance
forbiddance riddance

4. Again, the adjective or alternative noun follows suit: *abundant, attendant.*

-ANCE, -ENCE, AFTER G-

1. If the *-g* is "hard," as in *girl,* the ending is of course *-ance.* There are only a few of these, among them:

arrogance elegance
extravagance

2. The adjectives, similarly, are *arrogant, elegant, extravagant.* In the nouns *litigant* and *termagant,* the "hard" *-g* again determines the *-ant* ending.

3. In *intransigeance,* the *-g* is "soft," but the *-ance* ending is inherited from the French; to compensate, we use the *-e* also. (Likewise, *intransigeant.*) The modern *intransigence* and *intransigent* are correct also, but not half as sophisticated.

4. The "soft" *-g* (as in *gem*) is more common in this pattern, and is followed by *-ence* or *-ency.* For example, among others:

diligence
emergence (emergency)
exigence (exigency)
indigence
intelligence
negligence

5. The adjectives are the same: *diligent, emergent,* etc.

-ANCE, -ENCE, AFTER I-

1. Generally *-ence,* rather than *-ance,* follows *-i.*

conscience experience
convenience incipience
disobedience inconvenience
ebullience inexpedience
expedience inexperience

insipience
nescience
obedience
omniscience
percipience
prescience

prurience
resilience
salience
sapience
science
subservience

2. Nouns from verbs ending in *-y* (*apply*, etc.) end in *-ance*.

alliance (*ally*)
appliance (*apply*)
compliance (*comply*)
defiance (*defy*)
reliance (*rely*)
variance (*vary*)

3. Derivative or similar nouns also end in *-ance*.

affiance
misalliance

noncompliance
self-reliance

4. Also the following:

allegiance
brilliance
radiance

insouciance
luxuriance

5. Adjectives follow the pattern of their nouns: *convenient, disobedient, ebullient,* etc.; *brilliant, compliant, defiant,* etc.

-ANCE, -ENCE, AFTER L-

1. Generally, with some exceptions noted in Section 3, below, *-ence* is the ending after *-l*. For example:

benevolence
condolence
corpulence
equivalence
excellence
flatulence
fraudulence
indolence
insolence
malevolence

opulence
pestilence
prevalence
redolence
somnolence
succulence
truculence
turbulence
violence
virulence

2. The adjectives are similar: *benevolent, corpulent, equivalent,* etc.

3. A few words do end in *-ance*, among them:

ambulance
jubilance
nonchalance

petulance
sibilance
vigilance

4. The adjectives, too, end in *-ant: petulant, vigilant,* etc. *Stimulant* and *undulant* have noun forms in *-ation: stimulation, undulation.*

-ANCE, -ENCE, AFTER N-

1. The statistically safer ending after *n-* is *-ence*. For example:

abstinence
continence
eminence
immanence
imminence
impermanence
impertinence

incontinence
permanence
pertinence
pre-eminence
prominence
supereminence

2. The adjectives are similar: *abstinent, continent,* etc.

3. A number of words *are* spelled *-ance* after *n-*. Among them:

appurtenance
consonance
countenance
determinance
discountenance
dissonance
dominance

maintenance
ordinance
predominance
repugnance
resonance
sustenance

4. Again, the adjectives are similar: *apurtenant, consonant.*

-ANCE, -ENCE, AFTER R-

1. If a two-syllable verb ends in *-r* and is accented on the *last* syllable, the noun will end in *-ence.*

con-FER—conference
de-FER—deference
in-FER—inference
pre-FER—preference
re-FER—reference

(Note that in the nouns above the accent has shifted to the *first* syllable—IN-fer-ence, etc., hence only one *-r*.)

2. Observe, also, the following.

trans-FER *or* TRANS-fer—transference

(Although the verb may be accented on either syllable, and the noun likewise, only one *-r* may be used.)

3. Consider these:

ab-HOR—abhorrence
con-CUR—concurrence

de-TER—deterrence
in-CUR—incurrence
oc-CUR—occurrence
re-CUR—recurrence

(Note that in nouns above the accent *remains* on what was the final syllable of the verb, hence double -*r*.)

3A. Adjective forms of the nouns above will end in -*ent*.

abhorrent   occurrent
deterrent   recurrent

4. Note that if a verb ends in -*ere* the noun is likely to end in -*rence*.

adhere—adherence
cohere—coherence, incoherence
inhere—inherence
interfere—interference
revere—reverence, irreverence

4A. Adjective forms or variant noun forms of the nouns in Section 4 also end in -*ent*.

adherent   inherent
coherent   irreverent
incoherent   reverent

5. An important exception is *persevere—perseverance*.

6. If a two-syllable verb ending in -*er* is accented on the first syllable, the noun ending is likely to be -*ance*.

sever—severance
sunder—sunderance
suffer—sufferance
temper—temperance, intemperance
utter—utterance

7. The important exception is:
differ—difference, indifference

7A. The adjectives are *different* and *indifferent*.

8. If a verb ends in -*ear,* the likely ending is -*ance*.

appear—appearance
clear—clearance
disappear—disappearance
reappear—reappearance
forbear—forbearance

8A. From *appear,* however, the adjective *apparent* ends, contrariwise, in -*ent*.

9. If a verb ends in -*ure,* the noun will end in -*rance*.

assure—assurance
endure—endurance
ensure—ensurance
insure—insurance
procure—procurance
reassure—reassurance
reinsure—reinsurance
secure—securance

10. Certain special words end in -*ance*—watch the following particularly.

exuberance (the verb is exuber*a*te)
ignorance
preponderance (verb: preponder*a*te)
protuberance (verb: protuber*a*te)
tolerance, intolerance (verb: toler*a*te)

10A. The adjectives, all with -*ant* endings, are:

exuberant   preponderant
ignorant   protuberant
intolerant   tolerant

-ANCE, -ENCE, AFTER T-

1. After *t-,* -*ance* is somewhat more common. The following are worth noting:

admittance   pittance
assistance   precipitance
circumstance   reluctance
concomitance   remittance
hesitance   repentance
inhabitance   resistance
inheritance   transmittance

2. The corresponding adjectives or variant nouns end, of course, in -*ant*.

concomitant   reluctant
hesitant   repentant
inhabitant   resistant
precipitant   unrepentant

3. But -*ence* does occur after *t-,* as in the following:

competence   intermittence
existence   penitence
impenitence   persistence
inadvertence   sentence
incompetence   subsistence
insistence

4. The adjectives of the nouns above end similarly in -*ent*.

competent
existent
impenitent
inadvertent
incompetent

insistent
intermittent
penitent
persistent
subsistent

5. Nouns built on the adjective *potent* will, of course, end in *-ence* (or *-ency*).

impotence
omnipotence

impotency
potency

6. And the adjectives will end in *-ent: impotent, omnipotent.*

-ANCE, -ENCE, AFTER U-

1. After *qu-* the correct suffix is always *-ence.*

consequence
eloquence
grandiloquence
inconsequence

magniloquence
sequence
subsequence

2. If the preceding letters are *-fl,* the correct suffix is again *-ence.*

affluence
confluence
effluence

influence
mellifluence
refluence

3. Other *-ence* words following *u-* are:

congruence
incongruence

constituence

4. All adjectives follow the same form: *affluent, confluent; congruent, constituent; consequent, eloquent;* etc.

5. Nouns formed from verbs ending in *-ue* have the *-ance,* rather than *-ence,* suffix.

continue—continuance
discontinue—discontinuance
issue—issuance
pursue—pursuance

-ANCE, -ENCE, AFTER V-

1. Generally after *v-,* the correct suffix is *-ance.*

connivance
contrivance
relevance

irrelevance
observance

2. Adjectives follow the same form: *relevant, irrelevant,* etc.

---

ancestor. Ends in *-or.* (See -ER, -OR, 5.)

ancient. The combination *-ie,* rather than *-ei,* is always used when the preceding *-c* has the sound of *-sh.* (See -IE, -EI, 12.)

anecdotage. Final *-e* of *anecdote* is dropped before the suffix *-age.* (See -AGE AFTER FINAL -E, 1.)

anemia, anaemia. The latter spelling is old-fashioned and rarely seen.

angel. See ANGLE, ANGEL.

Angelus. Not *Angelous.* (See -US, -OUS.)

ANGLE, ANGEL

You'd be amazed at how often students in mathematics courses write *angel* (spiritual being) for *angle* (as of a triangle).

---

animus. Not *animous.* (See -US, -OUS.)

anisette. Only the *-ette* ending is fully acceptable here. (See -ET, -ETTE, 3.)

annotator. Ends in *-or.* (See -ER, -OR, 5.)

annually. *Annual* plus the adverbial ending *-ly,* hence two *-l's.* (See -LY, 7.)

annul. Two *-n's,* one *-l;* but see *annulled.*

annulled. Because *annul* is accented on the last syllable, final *-l* is *doubled* before a suffix starting with a vowel. (See DOUBLING FINAL -L, 1.)

annulling. See *annulled.*

annulment. Back to one *-l,* since the suffix now starts with a consonant. (See DOUBLING FINAL -L, 3.)

anoint. If you have an impulse to double the first *-n,* resist it. One is *anointed* with *an oil*—this mnemonic will remind you to start with *anoi-.*

anonymous. A very tricky word— watch the single *-n's,* the *-o* after the first *n-,* and the *-y* after the second *n-.* The noun is *anonymity.*

answer. The *-w* is silent, but must appear.

-ant after c-. See -ANCE, -ENCE, AFTER C-.

-ant after d-. See -ANCE, -ENCE, AFTER D-.

-ant after g-. See -ANCE, -ENCE, AFTER G-.

-ant after i-. See -ANCE, -ENCE, AFTER I-.

-ant after l-. See -ANCE, -ENCE, AFTER L-.

ant after n-. See -ANCE, -ENCE, AFTER N-.

-ant after r-. See -ANCE, -ENCE, AFTER R-.

-ant after t-. See -ANCE, -ENCE, AFTER T-.

-ant after u-. See -ANCE, -ENCE, AFTER U-.

-ant after v-. See -ANCE, -ENCE, AFTER V-.

antalope. Misspelling of *antelope*.

ANTE-, ANTI-

In some words the prefix *anti* (against or contrary) has a pronunciation so close to, or almost identical with, the prefix *ante-* (before) that confusion in spelling can easily result. (Of course, there are those who pronounce *anti-*, as in *antisocial*, AN-tye, and for them no spelling problem occurs.)

If, however, you keep in mind the different meanings of these prefixes, and analyze your word accordingly, you can easily avoid error.

Remember: *anti-* against, etc.; *ante-* before.

Note the following:

ANTI- (against)	*ANTE-* (before)
antibiotic	antecedent
antibody	antechamber
anticlimax	antedate
antidote	antediluvian
antifreeze	antemeridian
anti-Semitic	antenatal
antiseptic	antepenult
antisocial	anteroom
antitoxin	

See also HYPHENATING, 20, 21.

ante bellum. No hyphen. (See HYPHENATING, 21.)

antecede. *-Cede* is the common ending for such verbs, but there are exceptions. (See -CEED, -SEDE, -CEED, 3.)

antecedence. Almost always, with only a few exceptions, *-ence*, not *-ance*, follows a *d-*. (See -ANCE, -ENCE, AFTER D-, 1.)

antecedent. See *antecedence*.

anteceed. Misspelling of *antecede*.

antediluvian. Note that the prefix is *ante-* (before), not *anti-* (against), and that the vowel following *d* is *-i*, not *-e*.

anteloap. Misspelling of *antelope*. (See -OPE, -OAP.)

antelope. Not *antalope*. (See -OPE, -OAP.)

ante-mortem. Always hyphenated. (See HYPHENATING, 21.)

antenna. For plural see PLURALIZING WORDS IN TERMINAL -A, 2.

ante-Norman. Hyphenated because the root word starts with a capital. (See HYPHENATING, 21.)

antenuptial. No hyphen. (See HYPHENATING, 21.)

anteroom. No hyphen. (See HYPHENATING, 21.)

ante-Victorian. Hyphenated because the root word starts with a capital. (See HYPHENATING, 21.)

ANTI-, ANTE-. See ANTE-, ANTI-.

---

anti-American. Hyphenated because the root word starts with a capital. (See HYPHENATING, 20.)

anti-English. Hyphenated because the root word starts with a capital. (See HYPHENATING, 20.)

anti-immigration. Hyphenated to separate the two *-i*'s. (See HYPHENATING, 20.)

anti-integration. Hyphenated to separate the two *-i*'s. (See HYPHENATING, 20.)

antilabor. No hyphen. (See HYPHEN-ATING, 20.)

antimacassar. *Macassar* was once an oil used as a hair pomade; the doily placed on the back or arms of a chair was used to prevent penetration of the oil to the upholstery. Note, also the single *-c* and double *-s.*

anti-Semitic. Hyphenated because the root word starts with a capital. (See HYPHENATING, 20.)

antislavery. No hyphen. (See HYPHENATING, 20.)

antithesis. Plural is *antitheses.* (See PLURALIZING WORDS IN TERMINAL -IS.)

antiwar. No hyphen. (See HYPHEN-ATING, 20.)

ANY-

As pronouns or adverbs, compounds with *any-* are solid words. Otherwise, if *any* is an adjective, two separate words are used.

solid—pronoun or adverb
Is *anyone* here?
I'll talk to *anybody.*
I can't go *anyhow.* (always solid)
I'll take *anything.*
Anyway, I don't believe him.
I'll go *anywhere.* (always solid)

separate—adjective plus noun or pronoun
I'll take *any one* of the two books.
Are there *any bodies* in the morgue?
Are there *any things* on the table?
Can you find *any place* to park? (always separate)
I'll do it *any way* you wish.
See also EVERY-, NO-, SOME-.

any time. Always two words, no matter how used.

anywhere, anywheres. Good style avoids the final *-s* here and in words like *somewhere, nowhere,* etc.

AP-, APP-. See APP-, AP.

apartment. One *-p,* as in *apart.*

apex. For plural see PLURALIZING WORDS IN TERMINAL -X, 1.

aplomb. Note the *-b.*

apocryphal. Even the most literate of spellers wonder whether or not to slip an *-h* in after the *c-. Don't.*

apologize. Note the *-o* after *l-,* and the *-ize* ending. (See -IZE, -YZE, 1.)

apologue. Not acceptable as *apolog.* (See -OGUE, -OG, 2.)

apology. Not *apolagy.*

apostasy. The ending is *-sy,* not *-cy.* (See -CY, -SY, 4.)

apostrophe. Only the first vowel is *a-,* and there are two *-o's.*

APOSTROPHE TO SHOW POSSESSION. See POSSESSIVES.

APOSTROPHE, USE OF

1. The apostrophe is used in contractions in place of missing letters: *doesn't* (does not); *I'll* (I will); *I'm* (I am); *it's* (it is); *o'clock* (of the clock); *you're* (you are).
2. Figures or letters are generally pluralized by the addition of *'s.*

5's	A's
6's	B's
10's	O.K.'s or OK's

(But recently, according to the house rules of some publishers, the apostrophe is omitted: *5s, 6s, As, Bs, OKs,* etc.)
3. If the figure is written out as a word, no apostrophe is necessary: *fives, sixes, tens,* etc.
4. Though no real possession is indicated, expressions referring to value, time, or distance usually contain an apostrophe: *arm's length, cent's worth, day's pay, dollar's worth, five cents' worth, hour's delay, nickel's worth, penny's worth, stone's throw.*
See also POSSESSIVES.

apothecary. It's the *-e* after the *h-* that causes all the trouble.

APP-, AP-

A common source of error is the omission of the second -*p* in words that start with *app*-. Note the following:

appall	appoint
apparatus	apportion
apparel	appraise
apparent	appreciate
appeal	apprehend
appear	apprentice
appease	apprise
append	approach
appendectomy	approbation
appendix	appropriate
appetite	approve
applaud	approximate
apply	appurtenance

If in doubt, start other words with *ap*-.

---

apparent. Ends in -*ent*.

appearance. Ends in -*ance*. (See -ANCE, -ENCE, AFTER R-, 8.)

appellation. Two -*p*'s, two -*l*'s.

appendix. For plural see PLURALIZING WORDS IN TERMINAL -X, 1.

appliance. Ending is -*ance*. (See -ANCE, -ENCE, AFTER I-, 2.)

applicable. Only the -*able* ending will keep the preceding -*c* "hard." (See -ABLE, -IBLE, 6.)

application. Two -*p*'s.

applied. The -*y* of *apply* changes to -*i* before a suffix.

applies. See *applied*.

appologize. Misspelling of *apologize*.

appreciable. -*Able* is the correct suffix after the letter *i*-. (See -ABLE, -IBLE, 3.)

apprehension. Ends in -*ension*. (See -ENSION, -ENTION.)

apprise. Note the -*ise* ending, common to words ending in -*prise*. (See -ISE, 4.)

approval. The -*e* of *approve* is dropped before a suffix starting with a vowel. (See DROPPED -E.)

appurtenance. One of a group of words ending in -*ance*, rather than -*ence*, after *n*-. (See -ANCE, -ENCE, AFTER N-, 3.)

AR-, ARR-. See ARR-, AR-.

---

arable. Note the -*able* ending. (See (See -ABLE, -IBLE, 7.)

arbiter. Ends in -*er*. (See -ER, -OR, 1.)

arc, ark. With -*c* it's a curve; with -*k* it's a clumsy boat, or the famous one captained by Noah.

arcanum. The plural is either *arcana* or *arcanums*. (See PLURALIZING WORDS IN TERMINAL -UM, 1.)

arctic. The first -*c* is often not pronounced, but must be written.

-ARD, -ARDS

In words like *frontward, backward, downward,* etc., the *ard* ending (the non -*s* spelling) is the *adjective* form: *a frontward glance, a backward child, a downward thrust.*

As an *adverb*, such a word may be spelled either with or without the -*s*. The choice can be entirely capricious or be determined by sentence euphony—neither spelling is by itself superior to the other. Thus: *facing frontward, frontwards; walking backward, backwards; dropping downward, downwards;* etc.

The words illustrating this principle are:

backward, backwards
downward, downwards
forward, forwards
frontward, frontwards
homeward, homewards
sideward, sidewards
toward, towards
upward, upwards

As a *preposition,* either *toward* or *towards* may be used: *He walked slowly toward (or towards) the girl.*

-ARDS, -ARD. See -ARD, -ARDS.

arduous. Make sure to get in that *-u* before *-ous.* (See -UOUS.)

arguable. The final *-e* of *argue* is dropped before a suffix that starts with a vowel; and the ending is *-able.* (See -ABLE, -EABLE, 1; -ABLE, -IBLE, 2; DROPPED -E.)

arguing. See *arguable.*

argument. A glaring but important exception to the usual pattern of adding *-ment* directly to a verb. Note that the *-e* of *argue* has been dropped. (See -MENT, 2; RE-TAINED -E, 2.)

arise. Note the *-ise* ending, common to all words built on *rise* as a base. (See -ISE, 3.)

aristocratically. Note the *-ally* ending, common to adverbs formed from adjectives ending in *-ic.* (See -LY, -ALLY, 1.)

ark. See ARC, ARK.

armadillo. Pluralize by adding *-s* only; *armadillos.* (See PLURALIZING WORDS IN TERMINAL -O, 2.)

armistice. The ending is *-ce.*

armor, armour. The first spelling is American, the second British. (See -OR, -OUR, 1.)

arm's length. Note the apostrophe. (See APOSTROPHE, USE OF, 4.)

around. One *-r.*

arouse. One *-r.*

ARR-, AR-
    The *arr-* beginning is found in the following words that are occasionally misspelled:

arraign	arrest
arrange	arrive
arrant	arrogant
array	arrow
arrears	arroyo

If in serious doubt, start other words with *ar-.*

---

arrival. The final *-e* of *arrive* is dropped before a suffix that starts with a vowel. (See DROPPED -E.)

arrogance. Because of the "hard" *-g,*

-ance, not *-ence.* (See -ANCE, -ENCE, AFTER G-, 1.)

artistically. Note the *-ally* ending, common to adverbs formed from adjectives ending in *-ic.* (See -LY, -ALLY, 1.)

-ARY, -ERY
    1. Note that the word *dictionary* has *two* accents. A primary, strong accent is heard on the first syllable; a secondary, weaker accent on the third syllable—DIC-tion-ar-y. (In British pronunciation, on the other hand, only the primary accent is used.) Of the hundreds of words in the *-ary, -ery* category that contain a secondary accent on the next to the last syllable (i.e., on the *-ar* or *-er*), most, *by far,* end in *-ary.* If in any doubt, then, this is the ending of choice. Here is a random sampling.

adversary	sanctuary
beneficiary	secondary
commentary	secretary
culinary	sedentary
dictionary	stationary
dignitary	(*motionless*)
disciplinary	statuary
discretionary	temporary

    2. Only six important words of this type end in *-ery.*

cemetery	millinery
confectionery	monastery
dysentery	stationery*
lamasery	(paper, etc.)

    3. Other words ending in *-ery* have only a primary accent.
    bakery (BAK-er-y)
    brewery (BREW-er-y)
    bribery (BRIB-er-y)
    finery (FIN-er-y)
    flattery (FLAT-er-y)
    thievery (THIEV-er-y)

---

* For the distinction between *stationery* and *stationary,* see STATIONERY, STATIONARY.

-ARY, -ORY

These two endings are not pronounced the same, but a number of words sometimes cause confusion.

1. Note that the following end in *-ary.*

complementary	momentary
complimentary	monetary
evolutionary	proprietary
fragmentary	pulmonary
hereditary	salutary
honorary	

2. And that the following end in *-ory.*

accusatory	explanatory
auditory	migratory
circulatory	obligatory
conciliatory	peremptory
congratulatory	promissory
contributory	propitiatory
depilatory	reformatory
derogatory	repository
desultory	signatory
dilatory	transitory
discriminatory	

3. And consider particularly the following pairs:

A. *accessory, accessary.* The two spellings now refer to the same word, whether noun or adjective, with the latter less and less used.

B. *depository, depositary.* These spellings are actually interchangeable, although some people prefer to use the *-ory* ending for the *place* where something is deposited, the *-ary* ending for the *person* or *firm* entrusted with something of value.

C. *sanatory, sanitary, sanitory.* We can dispose of the third spelling quickly—it does not exist except as an error. The all-inclusive term is *sanitary,* which means both (a) clean, disease-free, hygienic, etc., and (b) pertaining to, or promoting, health, healthful surroundings or conditions, etc. *Sanatory* means only promoting,

or conducive to, health, or, less often, curative. There is, then, an overlapping of the two words, each, in addition, with an individual, specialized meaning.

D. *sanatorium, sanitarium.* (Though not containing the endings under discussion, these words might profitably be considered at this point.) Both spellings are correct and refer to the same institution, *sanitarium* being the commoner form. However, some people in the field of health maintain that a *sanitarium* has more of a hospital atmosphere, function, and clientele, while a *sanatorium* is more of a convalescent home, is likely to be situated in healthful surroundings (mountains, seashore, etc.), and is less involved in medical or surgical treatment. (Either word, incidentally, is sometimes used as a euphemism for a mental hospital). In the final analysis, of course, the sign on the particular institution involved determines the proper spelling in each case.

E. *tributary, tributory.* The latter spelling is now obsolete.

See also -ARY, -ERY.

AS-, ASS-. See ASS-, AS-.

---

asbestos. Ends in *-os,* not *-us.*

ascend. Either the *-s* or the *-c* is often gaily omitted by poor spellers in this word and in *ascension, ascent, ascertain, ascetic, descend, descent, condescend,* etc.

ascension. See *ascend.*

ascertain. See *ascend.*

ASCETIC, ACETIC.

An *ascetic* leads a life of rigorous self-discipline and self-denial. The word is also an adjective.

Acetic is an adjective only, referring to vinegar, etc., as in *acetic acid.*

asma. Misspelling of *asthma.*

ASS-, AS-

Make sure to use a double -*s* in the following:

assail	assiduous
assassin	assign
assault	assimilate
assay	assist
assemble	associate
assent	assort
assert	assuage
assess	assume
asset	assure
asseverate	

If in serious doubt, start other words with *as-.*

---

assassin. Two sets of double -*s*'s.
assassinate. See *assassin.*
assess. Again two sets of double -*s*'s.
assessor. Ends in -*or.* (See -ER, -OR, 5.)
assiduous. Make sure to get in that -*u* before -*ous.* (See -UOUS.)
assinine. Misspelling of *asinine.*
assist. Two -*s*'s first, then a single -*s.*
assistance. Ends in -*ance.* (See -ANCE, -ENCE, AFTER T-, 1.)
assistant. Ends in -*ant.*
assistant professor. No hyphen. (See HYPHENATING 5A.)
assurance. The suffix -*ance* invariably attaches to a noun formed from a verb ending in -*ure.* (See -ANCE, -ENCE, AFTER R-, 9.)
asthma. The -*sth* sounds like *z*, but there's no *z* in the word.

AT-, ATT-. See ATT-, AT-.

---

athenaeum, atheneum. The second spelling is more modern, the first somewhat commoner.
athlete. Not *athalete.*
athletic. Not *athaletic.*

-ATIOUS, -ACIOUS. -ACEOUS. See -ACIOUS, -ACEOUS, -ATIOUS.

---

atrocious. Ends in -*cious,* not -*tious.* (See -OCIOUS.)

ATT-, AT-

1. It is worth noting that the following verbs are all accented on the second syllable—and all start with *att-:*

attach	attenuate
attack	attest
attain	attire
attemper	attract
attempt	attribute
attend	attune

2. Noun and other derived forms of these verbs would similarly start with *att-.*

3. The only other words of any consequence so starting are:

attar	attorney
attic	attrition
attitude	

4. It would be safe, then, to start any words not enumerated above with *at-* rather than *att-.*

---

attendance. One of the few words in which -*ance* not -*ence,* follows a *d-.* (See -ANCE, -ENCE, AFTER D-, 3.)
attendant. See *attendance.*
attention. Ends in -*ention.* (See -ENSION, -ENTION.)
attorney at law. Preferably not hyphenated. (See HYPHENATING, 5B.)
attorney general. No hyphen. (See HYPHENATING, 5A.)
attorneys. A word ending in -*ey* is pluralized by the simple addition of -*s.* (See -EYS, -IES, -YS, 1.)
audible. The ending is -*ible,* not -*able.* (See -IBLE, -ABLE, 1.)
audience. After an *i-,* -*ence* is commoner than -*ance.* (See -ANCE, -ENCE, AFTER I-, 1.)
auditor. Ends in -*or.* (See -ER, -OR, 5.)
auditory. The ending is -*ory,* not -*ary.* (See -ARY, -ORY, 2.)

-AUER, -OWER, -OUR. See -OUR, -OWER, -AUER.

AUGER, AUGUR
An *auger* is a tool for boring holes. To *augur* (pronounced the same as *auger*) is to foretell, or be an omen of. The word is also a noun, meaning prophet.

The noun *augury* similarly contains a *-u* after the *g-*.

AUGHT, OUGHT
Either spelling may be used with the meaning of *zero; aught,* however, is preferable.

In archaic phraseology *(for aught I care,* etc.), *aught* is again the preferable spelling.

However, as a verb *(I ought to go), ought* is the only spelling. See also *naught, nought.*

-AUGHT, -OUGHT
Words so ending are pronounced alike, and it is a matter of training your visual memory to remember which is which. Study these:

-AUGHT	bought
caught	brought
distraught	dreadnought
fraught	forethought
onslaught	fought
taught	ought (i.e., should)
untaught	overwrought
-OUGHT	sought
besought	thought
bethought	wrought

augur. See AUGER, AUGUR.
augury. Note the *-u* after *g-*.
aural. See ORAL, AURAL.
auspicious. Ends in *-icious,* not *-itious.* (See -ICIOUS, -ITIOUS, 1.)
austerity. The *-e* of *austere* is dropped before a suffix beginning with a vowel. (See DROPPED -E.)
author. Ends in *-or.* (See -ER, -OR, 5.)

-AUTIOUS
Note that the following end in *-tious: cautious, incautious, precautious.* The corresponding noun forms end in *-tion: caution, incaution, precaution.*

auto. Pluralize by adding *-s* only: *autos.* (See PLURALIZING WORDS IN TERMINAL -O, 2.)
automatically. Note the *-ally* ending, common to adverbs formed from adjectives ending in *-ic.* (See -LY, -ALLY, 1.)
automaton. Plural is either *automata* or *automatons.* (See PLURALIZING WORDS IN TERMINAL -ON.)
auxiliary. Though sometimes glossed over carelessly in pronunciation, the *i-* must precede *-ary.*
available. The ending is *-able,* not *-ible.* (See -ABLE, -IBLE, 1.)
avaricious. Ends in *-icious,* not *-itious.* (See -ICIOUS, -ITIOUS, 1.)

AVERT, EVERT
To *avert* is to prevent, turn away, or avoid something.

To *evert* is to turn inside out, as an eyelid or any saclike object.

aviator. Ends in *-or.* (See -ER, -OR, 5.)
avocado. The plural is *avocados.* (See PLURALIZING WORDS IN TERMINAL -O, 2.)
awesome. The suffix *-some* is added directly to *awe;* hence the first *-e.*
awe-stricken, awe-struck. Hyphenate both of these.
awful. An exception to the general rule: final *-e* of *awe* is dropped before the suffix *-ful.* (See RETAINED -E, 2.)

AWHILE, A WHILE
The solid word is an adverb.
He stayed *awhile.*

Let's rest *awhile.*

In the two-word combination we're using *while* as a noun, preceded by *a.* This is the proper form after a preposition, especially *for.*

He stayed for *a while.*

Let's rest for *a while.*

If *while* is clearly a noun, it is separated from *a* even if there is no preposition.

He took quite *a while* to finish.

He needs *a while* to finish it.

He listened *a* little *while,* then left.

awkward. Some spellers carelessly omit the first *-w.*

ax, axe. Both correct, the latter commoner in England.

axis. Plural is *axes.* (See PLURALIZING WORDS IN TERMINAL -IS.)

aye, ay. Either spelling correct, but the first much commoner.

-AYED, -AID

1. If a verb ends in *-ay* (*play, stray, betray,* etc.), the past tense is formed by adding *-ed* (*played, strayed, betrayed*).

2. The past tenses of *pay, say,* and *lay,* however, are spelled *paid* (but see **paid**) *said, laid. Slay* is, of course, *slew* in the past, though in slang usage *slayed* is often heard ("I slayed them.").

3. All combinations with the verb *lay* (*mislay, waylay, outlay,* etc.) are also spelled *-laid* in the past (*mislaid, waylaid, outlaid*). The spelling *layed* is never acceptable, not even for hens that *lay* eggs, though the form is often found for the vulgar use of the word.

4. *Relay,* i.e., *re-lay,* or lay again, is spelled *relaid* in the past tense; but *relay,* to send, which is not a derived form of *lay,* is *relayed* in the past.

azma. Misspelling of *asthma.*

B

(Rules for double -b: see DOUBLING FINAL -B.)

baboon. One *-b.*

baccalaureate. Think of *laureate,* as in *poet laureate,* to remember the one *-l,* double *-c.* Or if that's too much trouble, substitute *bachelor's degree,* which is what the word means.

baccarat. This card game has two *-c's,* one *-r.*

bacchanalian. Two *-c's,* and ends in *-ian,* not *-ion.*

bachelor. Ends in *-or,* and there's no *-t* anywhere. (See -ER, -OR, 5.)

back-. See HYPHENATING, 24.

backbiting. No hyphen. (See HYPHENATING, 24A.)

backdoor. Solid as an adjective. (See HYPHENATING, 24A.)

back down. Separate when *back* is used as a verb, as in *He won't back down.*

backdown. Solid when used as a noun, as in *His backdown surprised us.*

-backed. See HYPHENATING, 25.

back end. No hyphen. (See HYPHENATING, 24C.)

backfire. No hyphen. (See HYPHENATING, 24A.)

backhanded. No hyphen. (See HYPHENATING, 24A.)

backlash. No hyphen. (See HYPHENATING, 24A.)

back-paddle (verb). Hyphenated. (See HYPHENATING, 24B.)

back page. No hyphen. (See HYPHENATING, 24C.)

back rest. No hyphen. (See HYPHENATING, 24C.)

back-scratcher. Hyphenated. (See HYPHENATING, 24B.)

back seat. No hyphen, except as an adjective in *back-seat driver.* (See HYPHENATING, 24C.)

back-seat driver. Hyphenated. (See HYPHENATING, 24B.)

backslapper. No hyphen. (See HYPHENATING, 24A.)

back stairs. Separate words when used as a noun. (See HYPHENATING, 24C.)

backstairs. Solid word when used as an adjective.

back street. No hyphen. (See HYPHENATING, 24C.)

backstroke. Solid word. (See HYPHENATING, 24A.)

backswept. Solid word. (See HYPHENATING, 24A.)

backswing. Solid word. (See HYPHENATING, 24A.)

back talk. No hyphen, two words. (See HYPHENATING, 24C.)

backtrack (verb). Solid word. (See HYPHENATING, 24A.)

back up. Separate words when *back* is a verb (Please *back up.*), solid when a noun (His sudden *backup* surprised me.).

backup. See *back up.*

backwash. Solid word. (See HYPHENATING, 24A.)

backward, backwards. Use only the first spelling as an *adjective;* use either form as an *adverb.* (See -ARD, -ARDS.)

back yard. Separate words. (See HYPHENATING, 24C.)

bacterium. The plural is *bacteria.* (See PLURALIZING WORDS IN TERMINAL -UM, 1.)

bagette. Misspelling of *baguette.*

bagged. Double the *-g* of *bag* before adding a suffix starting with a vowel. (See DOUBLING FINAL -G.)

baggy. See *bagged.*

baguette, baguet. The longer spelling is preferable. (See -ET, -ETTE, 2.)

BAIL, BALE

Restrict *bale* to the meaning of bundle, package, etc., noun or verb, and use *bail* for anything else and you'll avoid all confusion.

A *bale* of hay.

Let's *bale* the cotton.

He wants to *bail* out his friend.

Can you provide *bail* for him?

He *bailed* out the boat.

baleful. The first syllable is the poetic term *bale,* harm or evil, hence *a baleful* (not *bailful*) *glance.*

BALLAD, BALLADE

A *ballad* is a song or poem, usually of a sentimental or romantic nature.

A *ballade* (accent on the second syllable) is either a verse form or pattern, or musical composition usually for piano or orchestra.

ballistics. Two *-l*'s.

balloon. Round, like a *ball,* hence two *-l*'s. Some people even get hung up on the double *-o.*

banana. No double *-n*'s.

bandeau. The plural is *bandeaux.* (See PLURALIZING WORDS IN TERMINAL -EAU, 1.)

bandit. The Anglicized plural, *bandits,* is the commoner form; the Italian *banditti* may be used to lend a continental flavor or to indicate bandits as a group or class.

banjo. Pluralize by adding *-s* only: *banjos.* (See PLURALIZING WORDS IN TERMINAL -O, 2.)

banneret, bannerette. For the small flag, the simpler spelling is preferable, both are correct. For a kind of knight, or degree of knighthood, only *banneret* is correct. (See -ET, -ETTE, 1.)

BANQUET, BANQUETTE

Noun or verb, the shorter form refers to an elaborate meal.

Banquette, on the other hand, may mean: (a) a bench, (b) a sidewalk, or (c) a gunner's platform.

banqueted. Because *banquet* is *not* accented on the last syllable, final *-t* is *not* doubled before a suffix beginning with a vowel. (See DOUBLING FINAL -T, 3.)

banqueter. See *banqueted.*

banqueting. See *banqueted.*

baratone. Misspelling of *baritone.*

barcarole, barcarolle. Either spelling acceptable.

bare. See BEAR, BARE.

barebacked. No hyphen. (See HYPHENATING, 25.)

bared. Past tense of *bare,* to expose.

barely. The final *-e* of *bare* is retained preceding the adverbial suffix *-ly.* (See -LY, 10.)

baring. Participle of the verb *bare,* to expose.

baritone. One *r-,* followed by *-i.*

bark, barque. Either spelling acceptable for the sailing vessel.

baronet. Ends in *-et,* not *-ette.* (See -ET, -ETTE, 4.)

barred. The *-r* of *bar* is doubled before a suffix beginning with a vowel. (See DOUBLING FINAL R, 1.)

barrenness. *Barren* plus *-ness,* hence the double *-n.* (See -NESS AFTER N-.)

barring. See *barred.*

base. See BASS, BASE.

BASS, BASE

Pronounced BAYSS, *bass* is the musical term meaning low; pronounced BASS, it's a species of fish or wood. Otherwise, the proper word, noun or adjective, is *base* (bottom, low, mean, etc.).

bassinet. Unlike *bathinette,* this word ends in *-et.* (See -ET, -ETTE, 4.)

basso. Pluralize by adding *-s* only: *bassos.* (See PLURALIZING WORDS IN TERMINAL -O, 2.)

bassoon. Note the double *-s* and double *-o.*

batchelor. Misspelling of *bachelor.*

bateau. The plural is *bateaux.* (See PLURALIZING WORDS IN TERMINAL -EAU, 1.)

bathinette. Only the *-ette* ending fully acceptable. (See -ET, -ETTE, 3.)

battalion. A battalion is equipped for *battle*—in both words two *-t*'s, one *-l.* And note that the ending is *-ion,* not *-ian.*

baught. Misspelling of *bought.*

bayonet. Ends in *-et,* not *-ette.* (See -ET, -ETTE, 4.)

bazaar. One *-z,* two *-a*'s, though the uncommon *bazar* is technically also correct. This is a market place, store, etc., not to be confused with the adjective *bizarre.*

BE-

Write all compounds with *be-* as solid words: *bedaub, bedazzle, bedevil, becharm, bestir, bespeak,* etc.

BEACH, BEECH

Beach refers to the shore, sand, etc., and is both noun and verb; *beech* is a kind of tree.

BEAR, BARE

Bear is the animal, or a verb meaning to carry, tolerate, etc.; *bare* is an adjective meaning naked, or a verb meaning to expose, as *bare one's bosom, bare one's secret,* etc. Past of *bear* is *bore,* the past participle is *borne.* The past and past participle of *bare* are *bared,* the present participle *baring.*

beat. See BEET, BEAT.

beau. The plural is either *beaus* or *beaux.* (See PLURALIZING WORDS IN TERMINAL -EAU, 3.)

beaureau. Misspelling of *bureau.*

beauteous. Ends in *-eous.*

beauties. The plural of *beauty.* When a word ends in *-y* preceded by a consonant, the plural ends in *-ies.* (See -EYS, -IES, -YS, 3.)

beautifully. Note the double *-l* since the adverbial suffix *-ly* is added to the adjective *beautiful.*

BED-

1. Most compounds with this word are written solid:

bedbug	bedrock
bedchamber	bedroll
bedclothes	bedroom
bedcover	bedside
bedfast	bedsore
bedfellow	bedspread
bedmate	bedspring
bedpan	bedstead
bedpost	bedstraw
bedridden	bedtime

2. The following are hyphenated:

bed-wetter	bed-wetting

3. The following are separate words:

bed companion	bed linen
bed jacket	bed rest

bedded. Note that the *-d* of *bed* is doubled when a suffix beginning with a vowel is added. (See DOUBLING FINAL -D, 1.)

bedding. See *bedded*.

bedimmed. The *-m* of *bedim* is doubled before a vowel. (See DOUBLING FINAL -M, 2.)

bedimming. See *bedimmed*.

BEE-

The following compounds with *bee-* are written solid: *beehive, beekeeper, beeline, beeswax*.

beech. See BEACH, BEECH.

beef. For plural see PLURALIZING WORDS IN TERMINAL -F OR -FE, 4A.

BEET, BEAT

Beet is the plant or vegetable; otherwise, for a score of different meanings, whether noun or verb, *beat* is the form to use.

befriend. Note the *-ie* combination. (See -IE, -EI, 13.)

beggar. Double final *-g* of *beg* before

adding a suffix that starts with a vowel. The ending is *-ar,* not *-er.* (See DOUBLING FINAL -G.)

begged. See *beggar*.

begging. See *beggar*.

beginner. See *beginning*.

beginning. Double final *-n* of *begin* before adding a suffix that starts with a vowel.

behavior, behaviour. The first spelling is American, the second British. (See -OR, -OUR, 1.)

belie. The participle is spelled *belying*. (See -IE TO -Y.)

belief. The plural is *beliefs*. (See PLURALIZING WORDS IN TERMINAL -F OR -FE, 2.)

believe. The rule is *-i* before *-e* except after *c-*. (See -IE, -EI, 1.)

bellboy. No hyphen. (See HYPHENATING, 3A.)

belligerence. Double *-l* and *-ence* ending. (See -ANCE, -ENCE, AFTER R-.)

belligerent. See *belligerence*.

bellyache. No hyphen. (See HYPHENATING, 3A.)

belying. Participle of *belie, -ie* changing to *-y* before *-ing*. (See -IE TO -Y.)

benefactor. The letter after *n-* is *-e,* not *-a;* the ending is *-or,* not *-er.*

beneficence. *-Ence,* rather than *-ance,* to keep the preceding *-c* "soft." (See -ANCE, -ENCE, AFTER C-, 1.)

beneficent. See *beneficence*.

beneficial. The letter after the *n-* is *-e,* not *-i.*

beneficiary. Most words with both a primary and secondary accent end in *-ary* rather than *-ery.* (See -ARY, -ERY, 1, 2.)

benefit. As in *beneficial, -e* after the *n-*.

benefited. Because *benefit* is *not* accented on the last syllable, final *-t* is *not* doubled before a suffix beginning with a vowel. (See DOUBLING FINAL -T, 3.)

benefiting. See *benefited*.

benevolence. Generally, *l-* is followed

by *-ence* rather than *-ance.* There are a few exceptions, however, worth studying. (See -ANCE, -ENCE, AFTER L-, 1, 3.)

benevolent. See *benevolence.*

bequeath. This sounds as if there should be an *-e* at the end, since it rhymes with *breathe*—but there isn't.

BERTH, BIRTH

A *berth* is a place, compartment, space, office, sleeping arrangement on a train, etc.

Birth refers to descent, the process of being born, etc.

besaught. Misspelling of *besought.*
beseige. Misspelling of *besiege.*

BESIDE, BESIDES

Beside is a *preposition* meaning *next to.*

He sat *beside* his wife.

Besides means *also, in addition, what's more, moreover,* etc.

Besides arsenic, you'll need a pinch of cyanide.

Besides, he has no money.

besiege. The rule is *-i* before *-e* except after *c-.* There are, of course, exceptions, but this isn't one of them. (See -IE, -EI, 1.)

besought. Ends in *-ought.* (See -AUGHT, -OUGHT.)

bethought. Ends in *-ought.* (See -AUGHT, -OUGHT.)

betrayed. Since the terminal *-y* of *betray* follows a vowel, it does *not* change to *-i* before a suffix. (See -Y PLUS A SUFFIX, 9.)

better. The comparative of *good.* Also, one who bets, but *bettor* is more common for this meaning.

bettor. One who bets. *Better* also acceptable for this meaning, but less common. (See -ER, -OR, 4.)

bewigged. Double final *-g* of *bewig* before a suffix starting with a vowel. (See DOUBLING FINAL -G.)

BI-

Compounds with this prefix are written solid: *biannual, biplane, bilateral,* etc.

BIANNUAL, BIENNIAL

Biannual describes events that occur *twice a year.*

Biennial describes events that occurr *every two years.*

biased. Single *-s* preferable in all derived forms of the verb *bias.*
biases. See *biased.*
biasing. See *biased.*
bicycle. This is a vehicle of two (*bi-*) wheels (*cycle*)—hence not *bycicle.*
bidder. Note that the *-d* of *bid* is doubled when a suffix is added. (See DOUBLING FINAL -D, 1.)
bidding. See *bidder.*
biennial. See BIANNUAL, BIENNIAL.
bigger, biggest. Double final *-g* of *big* before a suffix starting with a vowel. (See DOUBLING FINAL -G.)
bild, bilt. Misspellings of *build, built.*
binoculars. One *-n.*
bird cage. No hyphen. (See HYPHENATING, 3B.)
birth. See BERTH, BIRTH.
bivouacked. The *-k* must be inserted in the derived forms of *bivouac* in order to preserve the original pronunciation of final *-c.* (See -C, -CK, 1.)
bivouacking. See *bivouacked.*
bizarre. Not to be confused with *bazaar.* This is an adjective meaning strange, odd, weird, etc. Only one *-z,* two *-r*'s.

BLACK-

1. The following compounds with *black-* are written solid:

blackberry	blackjack
blackbird	blackleg
blackboard	blackmail
blackface	blackout
blackhead	blacksmith

2. These are hyphenated:
black-and-blue
black-eyed
black-hearted
black-letter (*adjective*)
black-list (*verb*)

3. Other combinations are written as two words: *black belt, black flag, Black Death, Black Friday,* etc.

---

blamable. *Blameable* is also correct, but the preferable spelling omits the unnecessary *-e*. And note that the ending is *-able.* (See -ABLE, -IBLE, 2.)

blatant. Ends in *-ant,* not *-ent.*

bleu. The French spelling of *blue,* correct in *bleu cheese.*

blithely, blithesome. The suffix is added to *blithe,* so keep the *-e.*

BLOC, BLOCK
    Bloc is the spelling for a group of people combined into some sort of political or racial unit—otherwise, for any other meaning, *block.*

BLOND, BLONDE
    As an adjective, either spelling may be used. As a noun, *blond* denotes a male, *blonde* a female.

---

blousy. Misspelling of *blowzy.*

BLOW-
    Compounds with *blow-* are written solid: *blowfish, blowhole, blowout, blowoff, blowup,* etc.; except for *blow-hard* (a boaster), which is hyphenated.

---

blowzy. This is the only spelling, and has nothing to do with *blouse.*

bludgeon. The *-e* keeps the *-g* "soft."

bluing, blueing. The first spelling is preferable.

bluish. The *-e* of *blue* is dropped before *-ish.*

blunderbuss. Ends in double *-s.*

blurred, blurring, blurry. Note the double *-r* in all derived forms of *blur.* (See DOUBLING FINAL R, 1.)

bogy, bogey, bogie. All these spellings are correct, the first somewhat commoner than the others.

bokay. Misspelling of *bouquet.*

bolero. Pluralize by adding *-s* only: *boleros.* (See PLURALIZING WORDS IN TERMINAL -O, 2.)

bony. The *-e* of *bone* is dropped before the suffix *-y.* (See DROPPED -E; -Y, -EY, 1.)

BOOK-
    1. Most compounds with *book-* are written solid: *bookcase, bookkeeper, bookmark, bookrack, bookstore, bookworm,* etc.
    2. *Book-learned* is the only important hyphenated combination.
    3. The following are separate words:

book club	book matches
book end	book review
book jacket	book section
book learning	book value

---

bookkeeper. Two *-k*'s, since this is *book* plus *keeper.* Likewise *bookkeeping.* Never use a hyphen in either word.

boozy. No *-e.*

boquet. Misspelling of *bouquet.*

BORN, BORNE
    With the *-e* the word is the past participle of *bear,* as in *He has borne this burden long enough,* or *She has borne the unborn child for six months* (i.e., she was pregnant with).
    Born refers to birth, as in *He was born in 1949.*

---

borough, boro. See -OUGH, -O.

BOUGH, BOW
    The first word rhymes with *how* and is the branch of a tree; for any other meanings *bow,* which may

rhyme either with *how* or with *so*, depending on the context, is the correct spelling.

---

bought. Ends in *-ought.* (See -AUGHT, -OUGHT.)

bouillabaisse. This chowder has two *-l*'s, two *-s*'s.

BOUILLON, BULLION

Pronounced approximately the same by many people, but the first word is a clear broth, the second is gold or silver in bars or ingots.

---

boulder. Pronounced the same as the adjective *bolder,* but spelled *-ou.* (See -O, -OU, 2.)

bounceable. The *-e* of *bounce* is retained before *-able* in order to preserve the original "soft" pronunciation of the preceding *-c.* (See -CEABLE.)

boundary. Not *boundry.*

bounteous. Not *bountious.*

bouquet. Though the first syllable is often pronounced *bo,* it must be spelled *bou-.*

bourgeois. The *-e* is necessary to keep the *-g* "soft." This is an adjective or is a noun denoting an individual (*bourgeoise* is the feminine); the group or class is *bourgeoisie.*

bow. See BOUGH, BOW.

BOW-

Most compounds are solid (*bowknot, bowline, bowstring*), but *bow hand* and *bow tie* are separated. *Bow-shaped* is hyphenated.

---

bower. See -OUR, -OWER, -AUER, 2.

boxcar. No hyphen. (See HYPHENATING, 3A.)

box seat. No hyphen. (See HYPHENATING, 3B.)

boy (verb). See BUOY, BOY.

braggadocio. Two *-g*'s.

braggart. Again two *-g*'s.

brassiere, brassière. First spelling preferable; note the double *-s.*

braught. Misspelling of *brought.*

brayed. Since the terminal *-y* of *bray* follows a vowel, it does *not* change to *-i* before a suffix. (See -Y PLUS A SUFFIX, 9.)

brazenness. *Brazen* plus *-ness,* hence the double *-n.* (See -NESS AFTER N-.)

BREACH, BREECH

A *breach* is a break or a breaking; to *breach* is to break.

Breech is the rump; also part of a gun.

BREAD, BRED

Bread, noun or verb, refers to the food; *bred* is the past participle of *breed,* as in *well bred,* etc.

---

breadth. Not *bredth.*

breakable. The ending is *-able,* not *-ible.* (See -ABLE, -IBLE, 1.)

breathe, breath. The first is a verb (*to breathe*), the second a noun (*a deep breath*).

bred. See BREAD, BRED.

bredth. Misspelling of *breadth.*

breech. See BREACH, BREECH.

breeches. Colloquial term for *trousers,* pronounced *britches.*

briar. See *brier.*

briary. See *briery.*

bric-a-brac. No *-k*'s.

BRIDAL, BRIDLE

Bridal, as an adjective, refers to a wedding or a bride; as a noun it is a synonym for *wedding.*

Bridle is a noun (horse's *bridle,* etc.) or verb (*bridle* your tongue, *bridle* in anger).

---

bridgeable. The *-e* of *bridge* is retained before *-able* in order to preserve the original "soft" (or *-j*) pronunciation of the preceding *-g.* (See -GEABLE.)

bridle. See BRIDAL, BRIDLE.

brief. *-I* before *-e,* except after *c-.* (See -IE, -EI, 1.)

briefs. This is the plural of the noun *brief.* (See PLURALIZING WORDS IN TERMINAL -F OR -FE, 2.)

brier, briar. Either spelling equally good.

briery, briary. Again you have a free choice.

brigadier general. No hyphen. (See HYPHENATING, 5A.)

brilliance. Ending is *-ance.* (See -ANCE, -ENCE, AFTER I-, 4.)

brilliant. Ends in *-ant.*

britches. Misspelling of *breeches.*

broach. See BROOCH, BROACH.

BROAD-

Adjective compounds with this word are hyphenated: *broad-backed, broad-brimmed, broad-minded, broad-shouldered,* etc.

The nouns *broadcloth* and *broadtail* are solid.

broag. Misspelling of *brogue.*

brocatel, brocatelle. Spell it either way, but use only one *-c.*

broccoli. Two *-c*'s, one *-l.*

brochette. Ends in *-ette.* (See -ET, -ETTE, 3.)

brogue. Ends in *-gue.* (See -OGUE, -OG, 2.)

brokenness. *Broken* plus *-ness,* hence the double *-n.* (See -NESS AFTER N-.)

bronco, broncho. Pluralize by adding *-s* only: *broncos, bronchos.* (See PLURALIZING WORDS IN TERMINAL -O, 2.)

BROOCH, BROACH

The *-oo* spelling is generally used for the word denoting an ornamental pin, *-oa* for all other meanings. (Technically, the pin may also be spelled *broach,* but rarely is.)

brother-in-law. Always hyphenated; plural is *brothers-in-law.* (See HYPHENATING, 6A.)

brought. Ends in *-ought.* (See -AUGHT, -OUGHT.)

BRUNET, BRUNETTE

Use either spelling for the adjective, but the shorter form as a masculine noun, the longer as a feminine noun.

buccaneer. Two *-c*'s, one *-n.*

bucketful. The plural is *bucketfuls.* (See PLURALIZING WORDS IN TERMINAL -FUL.)

buffaloes, buffalos. The former is the preferable plural; both are correct. Note the double *-f.* (See PLURALIZING WORDS IN TERMINAL -O, 4.)

buffoon. Two *-f*'s, two *-o*'s.

build-up. Hyphenated when used as a noun.

built. Not *bilt.* And the noun, incidentally, is *build,* not *built* (He has a stocky *build*).

built-in. Hyphenated when used as an adjective preceding the noun. (See HYPHENATING, 11.)

built-up. Hyphenated when used as an adjective preceding the noun. (See HYPHENATING, 11.)

buisness. Misspelling of *business.*

bulletin. Two *-l*'s, followed by *-e,* not *-a.*

bullion. See BOUILLON, BULLION.

bumpkin. Don't ignore the *-p.*

BUOY, BOY

Buoy is a noun or verb (moored to the *buoy*—to *buoy* up one's spirits); *boy* is a noun only, and denotes, of course, a young male.

bureau. The only vowel in the first syllable is *-u;* the plural is either *bureaus* or *bureaux.* (See PLURALIZING WORDS IN TERMINAL -EAU, 3.)

burgeon. The *-e* keeps the *-g* "soft."

burro. Pluralize by adding *-s* only; *burros.* (See PLURALIZING WORDS IN TERMINAL -O, 2.)

buses. This is the preferable plural of the noun *bus.* When the word is used as a verb, double the *-s* before adding a suffix: *bussed, busses, bussing.* (See DOUBLING FINAL CONSONANTS — ONE-SYLLABLE WORDS, 3, 4.)

bushelful. The plural is *bushelfuls.* (See PLURALIZING WORDS IN TERMINAL -FUL.)

busied. The *-y* of *busy* changes to *-i* in all derived forms except *busybody.* But check *busyness.*

busier, busiest. See *busied.*

busies. See *busied.*

busily. See *busied.*

business. *Busy* plus *-ness,* the *-y* changing to *-i;* but see *busyness.* (Not *buisness,* the common misspelling.)

business-wise. Note the *-ise* ending, common to all words built on the base *-wise.* (See -ISE, 1.)

busses. A variant plural of the noun *bus—buses* is preferable.

busyness. When the *quality or state of being busy* is meant, this spelling may be used, or, variantly, *busyness.*

buy. Some poor spellers forget the *-u.*

by-. For compounds with this prefix see HYPHENATING, 46.

bycicle. Misspelling of *bicycle.*

C

-C, -CK

Final *-c* has a "hard," or *k,* sound, as in *panic, frolic, traffic,* etc. Preceding *-e, -i,* or *-y,* however, *-c* has a "soft," or *s,* pronunciation, as in *cent, city,* or *cybernetics.*

1. Therefore, to preserve the original pronunciation of final *-c* when adding *-ed, -er, -ing,* or *-y,* a *-k* must be inserted. For example:

bivouac—bivouacked, bivouacker, bivouacking
colic—colicky
frolic—frolicked, frolicking
mimic—mimicked, mimicker, mimicking
panic—panicked, panicking, panicky
physic—physicked, physicking
picnic—picnicked, picnicker, picnicking
politic—politicked, politicking
shellac—shellacked, shellacker, shellacking
traffic—trafficked, trafficker, trafficking
zinc—zincked, zincking, zincky

2. In *politicize,* however, since the *-c* is pronounced "soft" (po-LIT-i-size), no *-k* is necessary.

3. When a suffix starting with any letter other than *-e, -i,* or *-y* is added, again no *-k* is required, as in *frolicsome, political, maniacal,* etc.
See also -CEABLE.

-----

cabal. Noun or verb, ends in one *-l* only. (See -AL, -ALL, 3.)

caballed. The *-l* of *cabal* is doubled before a suffix that starts with a vowel. (See -AL, -ALL, 3.)

caballing. See *caballed.*

cabinetmaker. No hyphen. (See HYPHENATING, 3A.)

cacophony. The pattern of vowels is *a-o-o.*

cadet. Ends in *-et,* not *-ette.* (See -ET, -ETTE, 4.)

caduceus. Not *caduceous.* (See -US, -OUS.)

cafeteria. One *f-,* followed by *-e.*

caffeine. Two *-f*'s, plus *-ei.* (See -IE, -EI, 4A.)

cagey, cagy. Though both correct, the former spelling is preferable. (See -Y, -EY, 2.)

cajole. Ends in *-e.*

calculus. A noun, so the ending is *-us*, not *-ous*. (See -US, -OUS.)

CALENDAR, CALENDER, CO-LANDER

For dates, it's a *calendar; calender* is a machine that smooths out paper or cloth; a *colander* is a large sieve or strainer. Each of the three words is spelled with only one *-l*.

calf. The plural is *calves*. (See PLURALIZING WORDS IN TERMINAL -F OR -FE, 1.)

caliber, calibre. The latter spelling is now old-fashioned, though still current in Great Britain. (See -ER, -RE.)

calisthenics. The second vowel is an *-i*.

calk, caulk. Spelled either way, the first preferable.

CALLOUS, CALLUS

Callous is the adjective, meaning covered with *calluses* (the noun), or cold and unfeeling.

Callus is the noun, the actual thickened growth on the skin.

The verb *callous* means to make insensitive; the verb *callus* to form calluses.

Calvary. See CAVALRY, CALVARY.

camaraderie. This comes directly from the French and keeps its Gallic spelling. The Anglicized *comradery* is also correct.

cameo. A word ending in *-o* preceded by a vowel is pluralized by the addition of *-s* only: *cameos*. (See PLURALIZING WORDS IN TERMINAL -O, 3.)

-CANCE, -CENCE. See -ANCE, -ENCE, AFTER C-.

canceled. Because *cancel* is *not* accented on the last syllable, final *-l* is *not* doubled before a suffix beginning with a vowel. Double *-l* is

acceptable in this word, but single *-l* is preferable. (See DOUBLING FINAL -L, 2.)

canceling. See *canceled*.

cancellation. Double *-l* required. (See DOUBLING FINAL -L, 4.)

candelabra. The plural of *candelabrum*, but also commonly used as a singular, for which the plural form is *candelabras*. (See PLURALIZING WORDS IN TERMINAL -UM, 1.)

candor, candour. The first spelling is American, the second British. (See -OR, -OUR, 1.)

canister. One *-n*.

CANNON, CANON

With the double *-n*, the word means either military guns or part of a bell; with a single *-n*, it's a law of the church; a clergyman; or a standard of judgment.

cannonade, cannoneer. These words are formed by adding the suffix *-ade* or *-eer* to *cannon*—hence double *-n* first, then single *-n*.

cannot, can not. Generally written as a solid word, but also correct as two words.

canoed. The correct spelling for the past of the verb *canoe*—note the single *-e*. (See -OE, TERMINAL, 3.)

canoeing. Final *-e* of *canoe* retained before *-ing*. (See -OE, TERMINAL, 3.)

canoeist. Final *-e* of *canoe* retained before *-ist*. (See -OE, TERMINAL, 3.)

canoer. One who paddles a canoe—note the single *-e;* some prefer the term *canoeist*. (See -OE, TERMINAL, 3.)

canon. See CANNON, CANON.

cañon. See *canyon, cañon*.

-CANT, -CENT. See -ANCE, -ENCE, AFTER C-.

can't. Contraction of *cannot,* the apostrophe appearing in place of the missing *-no.* (See APOSTROPHE, USE OF, 1.)

cantaloupe, cantaloup. Either spelling correct, but watch the *-a* after the *t-,* and the *-ou* at the end. (See -OPE, -OAP; -OOP, -OUP, -UPE, 3F.)

CANVAS, CANVASS

With one *-s* it's the cloth; with two it's the verb for soliciting orders, votes, opinions, etc., or the noun with the same meaning.

They lived under *canvas* for two weeks.

He *canvassed* the neighborhood.

He made a *canvass* of public opinion.

canyon, cañon. The first spelling is preferable, since it's English; but the second pattern, a Spanish import, is also correct.

capable. Since *-a* is the principal vowel in another form of the word (*capacity*), the correct ending is *-able.* (See -ABLE, -IBLE, 5.)

capful. The plural is *capfuls.* (See PLURALIZING WORDS IN TERMINAL -FUL.)

CAPITAL, CAPITOL

The *-ol* form is the *building* in which a state legislature sits, or, when capitalized, the building in Washington, D.C., in which Congress meets.

The *-al* spelling is used for all other meanings, including the city that is the seat of government—Albany is the *capital* of New York State.

capricious. Ends in *-icious,* not *-itious.* (See -ICIOUS, -ITIOUS, 1.)

caracul. See *karakul.*

caramel. Some people pronounce the *-a* after the *r-,* some don't; but it has to appear in the spelling of the word.

CARAT, KARAT, CARET, CARROT

Technically, *carat* and *karat* are interchangeable—either may be used as a unit of weight of precious stones or pearls, or to show relative purity of gold. However, for gold, *karat* is the word more commonly used.

A *caret* is a symbol (an inverted V) to show omission of a letter, word, or words.

And *carrot,* of course, is the vegetable.

carcass, carcase. The former is the preferable spelling.

caress. One *-r.*

caret. See CARAT, KARAT, CARET, CARROT.

cargoes, cargos. The former is the preferable plural; both are correct. (See PLURALIZING WORDS IN TERMINAL -O, 4.)

carom, carrom. Both correct, the single *-r* preferable.

caromed, caroming. Only one *-m* before suffixes since the accent is *not* on the last syllable of *carom.* (See DOUBLING FINAL CONSONANTS—WORDS OF MORE THAN ONE SYLLABLE, 2.)

carousel. See *carrousel.*

carried, carrier, carries. The *-y* of carry changes to *-i* before *-ed, -er,* or *-es.* (See -Y PLUS A SUFFIX, 1, 3.)

carrom. See *carom.*

carrot. See CARAT, KARAT, CARET, CARROT.

carrousel, carousel. Both correct, the double *-r* preferable. Note the single *-s.*

carryall. No hyphen. (See HYPHENATING, 3A.)

casino. Pluralize by adding *-s* only: *casinos.* (See PLURALIZING

WORDS IN TERMINAL -O, 2.)

cast. See CASTE, CAST.

castanets. Ends in *-ets,* not *ettes.* Note that the first two vowels are *-a.* (See -ET, -ETTE, 4.)

CASTE, CAST

Caste is the spelling for the social, economic, or occupational class, group, or distinction.

Cast is used for all other meanings.

CASUAL, CAUSAL

The two words are entirely different, and are confused only through carelessness.

Casual is offhand, informal, planless, indifferent, etc.

Causal is the adjective from the noun *cause.*

---

catagory. Common misspelling for *category.*

catalogue, catalog. The longer spelling is preferable. (See -OGUE, -OG, 1.)

catalyst, catalytic, catalysis. Note the *-y* after the *l-,* as in the verb *catalyze.* (See -IZE, -YZE, 6.)

catalyze. One of the rare verbs ending in *-yze.* (See -IZE, -YZE, 5.)

catarrh. One *-t,* two *-r*'s.

catchup. See KETCHUP, CATCHUP, CATSUP.

category. Not *catagory.*

cater-cornered. The variant *catty-cornered* is also correct, though less frequent in writing than in speech, and the inevitable corruption, *kitty-cornered,* is not completely unacceptable. The traditional spelling, and therefore the most sanctioned, is, of course, *cater-cornered.*

cat's-eye. Use both the apostrophe and the hyphen. (See HYPHENATING, 1.)

cat's-paw. Apostrophe and hyphen, as in *cat's-eye.* (See HYPHENATING, 1.)

catsup. See KETCHUP, CATCHUP, CATSUP.

catty-cornered. See *cater-cornered.*

caught. Note that the pattern is *-aught.* (See -AUGHT, -OUGHT, 1.)

caulk. See *calk.*

causal. See CASUAL, CAUSAL.

caution. Ends in *-tion.* (See -AUTIOUS.)

cautious. Ends in *-tious.* (See -AUTIOUS.)

CAVALRY, CALVARY

No reason to confuse these words except pure carelessness.

The *cavalry* is made up of mounted troops in an army; *Calvary* (capitalized) is the place where Jesus was crucified.

-CEABLE

Before *-a,* the letter *-c* is regularly "hard" (i.e., pronounced like *k*), as in *cable, cat, recant,* etc. For this reason, the final *-e* of words ending in *-ce* (*notice, service,* etc.) is retained before *-able,* thus assuring the preservation of the original "soft," or *s,* sound.

 bounce—bounceable
 embrace—embraceable
 enforce—enforceable
 lace—laceable
 notice—noticeable
 peace—peaceable
 pronounce—pronounceable
 replace—replaceable
 service—serviceable
 trace—traceable

See also -ABLE, -EABLE; -C, -CK; -GEABLE.

---

cede. See -CEED, -SEDE, -CEDE, 3.

ceed. Misspelling of *cede.*

-CEED, -SEDE, -CEDE

1. Only *three* words end in *-ceed: exceed, proceed, succeed.* (Note, however, that the noun of *proceed* is spelled *procedure.*)

2. Only *one* word ends in *-sede:* supersede.

3. All others end in *-cede: accede, antecede, cede, concede, intercede, precede, recede, secede.*

---

ceiling. *-E* before *-i* after *c-*. (See -IE, -EI, 2.)

cellaret. Ends in *-et*, not *-ette*. (See -ET, -ETTE, 2.)

cello. Plural is *cellos*, or, in musical circles, the Italian-derived *celli.* (See PLURALIZING WORDS IN TERMINAL -O, 2.)

cemetery. One of the few words with both a primary and secondary accent ending in *-ery* rather than *-ary.* (See -ARY, -ERY, 2.)

censer. See CENSOR, CENSURE, CENSER.

CENSOR, CENSURE, CENSER

A *censor* is a person; *censure,* both noun and verb, refers to disapproval; and a *censer* is a container for incense.

The verb *to censor* means to subject to censorship—i.e., examine or review and change, edit, cut, delete, etc., before permitting publication or exhibition.

He is a moving-picture *censor.*
He *censors* mail at the prison.
He feared his wife's *censure.*
The child was *censured* for lying.
What an odd-shaped *censer!*

---

censure. See CENSOR, CENSURE, CENSER.

CENT, SCENT

A *cent* is a penny.

Scent, noun or verb, refers to smell, usually pleasant.

---

centenary. One *-n,* ends in *-ary.*

centennial. Two *-n's.*

center, centre. The latter spelling is now old-fashioned, though still current in Great Britain and in certain street names in America. (See -ER, -RE.)

cent's worth. Note the apostrophe. (See APOSTROPHE, USE OF, 4.)

certain. Ends in *-ain.*

certificate. Ends in *-ate.*

chagrined. One *-n* in all derived forms of *chagrin,* though it may look funny and all logic cries out against it. (See DOUBLE VS. SINGLE CONSONANTS.)

chagrining. See *chagrined.*

chancellery. Double *-l* required. (See DOUBLING FINAL -L, 4.)

chancellor. See *chancellery.*

chancre. The ending is *-re* to keep the *-c* "hard." (See -ER, -RE, 2.)

chancroid. See -ER, -RE, 3.

chancrous. See -ER, -RE, 3.

changeable. The *-e* of *change* is retained before *-able* in order to preserve the original "soft" (or *-j*) pronunciation of the preceding *-g.* (See -GEABLE.)

chapeau. The plural is either *chapeaux* or *chapeaus.* (See PLURALIZING WORDS IN TERMINAL -EAU, 2.)

chapel. Not *chaple* or *chapple.*

character. The *-h* comes after the first *c-* only.

characteristic. See *character.*

charlatan. Begins with *ch-*, even though we pronounce it *sh-*, and all the vowels are *-a.*

charred. Double *-r* in all derived forms of *char.* (See DOUBLING FINAL -R, 1.)

charring. See *charred.*

chartreuse. Note the French ending *-euse.*

chassis. Spelled only as indicated, even though it's pronounced *shassy* to rhyme with *classy.*

chastise. Note the *-ise* ending. (See -ISE, 8.)

château. The plural is *châteaux.* (See PLURALIZING WORDS IN TERMINAL -EAU, 1.)

chauffeur. Double -*f* and the French ending, -*eur*.

check, cheque. The second is the British spelling of a bank draft.

checker, chequer. For the game, or the tokens used in the game, the second is the British form.

chef. The plural is *chefs*. (See PLURALIZING WORDS IN TERMINAL -F OR -FE, 2.)

chemisette. Only the -*ette* ending fully acceptable. (See -ET, -ETTE, 3.)

cheque. See *check*.

chequer. See *checker*.

cherub. The plural for this word when it means an angel is commonly *cherubim;* otherwise, as for a rosy-faced child, *cherubs*.

chief. The plural is *chiefs*. And -*i* before -*e* except after *c*-. (See -IE, -EI, 1; PLURALIZING WORDS IN TERMINAL -F OR -FE, 2.)

chock-full. Hyphenate, and use a double -*l* on *full*. Also spelled *chuck-full* and *choke-full*.

choir. Ends in -*oir*, even though pronounced *quire*.

choke-full. See *chock-full*.

CHORAL, CHORALE

Without the -*e*, and accented on the first syllable (KOR-'l), the word is an adjective referring to a choir or chorus.

With the -*e*, and accented on the second syllable (ko-RAL), the word is a noun meaning a hymn sung by the choir and congregation. The noun may, however, also be spelled *choral,* though less commonly, and is still accented on the second syllable.

chord. See CORD, CHORD.

chow mein. When sounded as *ay*, the spelling -*ei*, rather than -*ie*, is always correct. (See -IE, -EI, 6.)

chrysanthemum. If you break the word into syllables you'll have no real trouble with it—provided you don't forget the -*h*: *chry-san-the-mum*. Understandably, most people prefer to call them *mums*.

chuck-full. See *chock-full*.

churchgoer. No hyphen (See HYPHENATING, 3A.)

cigarette, cigaret. The longer spelling is preferable. (See -ET, -ETTE, 2.)

cilynder. Misspelling of *cylinder*.

cinema. The second vowel is an -*e*.

cinnamon. Double -*n* in the middle.

circulatory. Note that the ending is -*ory*, not -*ary*. (See -ARY, -ORY, 2.)

circumcise. One of five verbs ending in -*cise* rather than -*cize*. (See -ISE, 6.)

circumstance. -*Ance* is found somewhat more often than -*ence* after *t*-. (See -ANCE, -ENCE, AFTER T-, 1.)

circumvention. Ends in -*ention*. (See -ENSION, -ENTION.)

cirrhosis. Double *r*- followed by -*h*, as in *catarrh*.

CITE, SITE

Cite is a verb only. It means any of the following: summon to appear in court; mention officially for a praiseworthy action; refer to for example or proof; quote from.

Site is a noun only, meaning either a place or a piece of land.

-CK, -C. See -C, -CK.

clamor, clamour. The first spelling is American, the second British. (See -OR, -OUR, 1.)

clangor, clangour. The first spelling is American, the second British. (See -OR, -OUR, 1.)

clarinet. Ends in -*et*, not -*ette*. (See -ET, -ETTE, 4.)

clarinetist, clarinettist. Preferable spelling has one -*t* after the *e*-.

classifiable. -*Able* is the correct suffix after the letter *i*-. (See -ABLE, -IBLE, 3.)

CLEAN-

Clean-cut, clean-limbed, and *clean-shaven* are hyphenated; *clean-handed* and *cleanup* (as a noun) are written solid.

cleanness. *Clean* plus *-ness,* hence the double *-n.* (-NESS AFTER N-.)

CLEAR-

Clear-cut and *clear-sighted* are hyphenated; *cleareyed* and *clearheaded* are written solid.

clearance. Note the *-ance* ending. (See -ANCE, -ENCE, AFTER R-, 8.)

clerestory, clearstory. Both spellings correct, the first commoner.

CLEW, CLUE

Both spellings correct, the first preferable for all meanings except one, i.e., a hint or help in solving a problem, puzzle, mystery, crime, etc., in which instance *clue* is preferable.

client. Ends in *-ent,* not *-ant.*

CLOSE-

Most adjectives combined with *close-* are hyphenated: *close-lipped, close-mouthed, close-cut, close-shaven,* etc.

However, *closefisted* is solid.

Nouns with *close* are generally separate words: *close call, close quarters, close harmony,* etc.

But the noun *close-up* is hyphenated.

CLOTHES-

The following compounds with *clothes-* are solid: *clothesbag, clothesbasket, clothesbrush, clotheshorse, clothesline, clothespin.*

Most other combinations are separate words: *clothes closet, clothes pole, clothes rack,* etc.

CLOTHS, CLOTHES

Cloths are pieces or kinds of material; *clothes* are garments, wearing apparel, etc.

clubhouse. No hyphen. (See HYPHENATING, 3A.)

clue. See CLEW, CLUE.

CO-

For compounds with *co-* see HYPHENATING, 14.

COAL-

Most combinations with *coal-* are separate words: *coal car, coal field, coal mine, coal tar, coal truck,* etc.

However, these are solid: *coalbag, coalbin, coalbox, coalyard.*

As an adjective preceding its noun, *coal-black* is hyphenated.

coalesce. Note the *-esce* ending. (See -ESCE, -ESCENT, -ESCENCE, 1, 2.)

coalescent. See *coalesce.*

COARSE, COURSE

Coarse is an adjective only. It means rough, unrefined, vulgar, etc.

Course is a noun with scores of meanings (movement, way, series, subject in school, etc.), or a verb meaning run, flow, etc.

coat hanger. Separate words.

coatroom. Solid word.

coattail. Solid word.

cocaine, cocain. First spelling preferable.

cockeyed. Solid word. (See -EYED, 2.)

coconut, cocoanut. First spelling preferable.

coeducation. No hyphen. (See HYPHENATING, 14B.)

coercible. The ending is *-ible* to keep the preceding *-c* "soft." (See -IBLE, -ABLE, 5.)

coercion. From the verb *coerce,* hence the uncommon ending *-cion.*

coherence. Note the *-ence* ending. (See -ANCE, -ENCE AFTER R-, 4.)

coherent. See *coherence.*

coily. Misspelling of *coyly.*

COINCIDENCE, COINCIDENT

Coincidence is a noun, *coincident* an adjective that is a variant form of the commoner *coincidental.* Because *coincidence* sounds like a plural, some people fall into the error of thinking that *coincident* must be the singular form and say, in all innocence, "What an amazing coincident!"

coincidentally. Note that *-ly* is added to the adjective *coincidental,* hence the *-ally* ending. (See -LY, -ALLY, 3.)

coinsurance. No hyphen. (See HYPHENATING, 14B.)

COL- COLL-

1. Before a vowel, *coll-* is far more common than *col-.* The following are the only *col-* words likely to be misspelled:

colic	colony
coliseum	colophon
colitis	colossal
colonist	Colosseum
colonize	colossus
colonnade	

2. In other common words, then, double the *-l* after *co-* when the next letter is a vowel: *collaborate, collapse, collar, collect, college, collide,* etc.

colander. See CALENDAR, CALENDER, COLANDER.

COLD-

Cold-blooded and *cold-hearted* are hyphenated, as is also the verb to *cold-shoulder.*

Nouns combined with *cold-* are invariably separate words: *cold*

cream, cold front, cold shoulder, cold wave, cold war, etc.

coldslaw. Misspelling of *coleslaw.*

coleslaw, cole slaw. Preferably a solid word. The fact that it's served cold does not govern the spelling—this is a slaw made of *cole,* which is a family of plants including cabbage.

colicky. The *-k* must be inserted in the derived form of *colic* in order to preserve the original pronunciation of final *-c.* (See -C, CK, 1.)

COLISEUM, COLOSSEUM

The two words are interchangeable—they are pronounced identically and mean the same thing.

Generally, however, though not necessarily, a building erected in modern times is spelled *coliseum*—the famous one of ancient Rome is spelled *Colosseum.*

When a specific *coliseum* is meant (There's a business show at the *Coliseum*), *c-* is capitalized. And for the building in Rome, no matter how spelled, always a capital *C-.*

colitis. One *-l* only. (See COL-, COLL-, 1.)

COLL-, COL-. See COL-, COLL-.

collaborate. Two *-l's.*

collapsible. Note the *-ible* ending. (See -IBLE, -ABLE, 7.)

collar. Ends in *-ar.*

collectible. If the root forms its noun by the immediate addition of *-ion* (*collection*), the correct ending is likely to be *-ible.* (See -IBLE, -ABLE, 2.)

collector. Ends in *-or.* (See -ER, -OR, 5.)

collage. This is a kind of surrealist art, pronounced ko-LAHZH; also a misspelling of *college.*

college. No *-a,* no *-d.*

collosal. Misspelling of *colossal.*

colloseum. Misspelling of either *coliseum* or *colosseum.*

collosus. Misspelling of *colossus.*

cologne. Note the silent *-g.*

colonnade. One *-l,* two *-n's.* (See COL-, COLL-, 1.)

color, colour. The first spelling is American, the second British. (See -OR, -OUR, 1.)

colors. See HYPHENATING, 47.

colossal. One *-l,* two *-s's.* (See COL-, COLL-, 1.)

colosseum, coliseum. See COLISEUM, COLOSSEUM.

colossus. One *-l,* double *-s.* Plural is *colossi* or *colossuses.* (See COL-, COLL-, 1.)

column. The *-n* is silent but must appear in spelling.

COM-, COMM-

The following are the only words of any consequence that are spelled *com-,* rather than *comm-,* before a vowel.

coma (unconsciousness)
comatose
comedian
comedy
comely
comestible
comet
comic
comity (politeness)

Also, of course, derivatives of, or compounds with, the verb *come: coming, comeback,* etc.

If in any doubt, then, double the *-m* after *co-* when the next letter is a vowel: *command, commemorate, commend,* etc.

---

coma. See COMMA, COMA.

combatant. Single *-t,* the only allowable pattern, since the word is accented on the first syllable. (See DOUBLE VS. SINGLE CONSONANT; DOUBLING FINAL -T, 4.)

combated. Preferably spelled with one

-t, and preferably pronounced with the accent on the first syllable. (See DOUBLE VS. SINGLE CONSONANT; DOUBLING FINAL -T, 4.)

combating. See *combated.*

combative. See *combatant.*

combustible. Note that the ending is *-ible,* not *-able.* (See -IBLE, -ABLE, 1.)

comedown. Written solid as a noun (That was quite a *comedown*), separate as verb and adverb (He has *come down* in the world).

coming. The final *-e* of *come* is dropped before a suffix that starts with a vowel. (See DROPPED -E.)

COMM-, COM-. See COM-, COMM-.

COMMA, COMA

Comma is the punctuation mark (,), *coma* (pronounced KOE-ma) a state of deep unconsciousness.

---

commander in chief. Preferably not hyphenated. (See HYPHENATING, 5B.)

commemorate. The pattern is double *-m,* then single *-m*—the word is built on the same Latin root from which *memory* comes, plus the prefix *com-.*

commendable. Since *-a* is the principal vowel in another form of the word (*commendation*), the correct ending is *-able.* (See -ABLE, -IBLE, 5.)

commentary. Most words with both a primary and secondary accent end in *-ary* rather than *-ery.* (See -ARY, -ERY, 1, 2.)

commentator. Ends in *-or.* (See -ER, -OR, 5.)

commission. Double *-m.*

commit. Double *-m* here and in all derived forms. The word is built on the Latin root *-mit,* plus the prefix *com-.*

committal. See *committed.*

committed. Because *commit* is accented on the last syllable, the final

-*t* is doubled before a suffix beginning with a vowel. (See DOUBLING FINAL -T, 2.)

committee. Note the double -*m* and double -*t*. See *committed.*

committing. See *committed.*

commodity. Double -*m*.

commonness. *Common* plus -*ness,* hence the double -*n*. (See -NESS AFTER N-.)

communicate. Double -*m*.

community. Double -*m*.

comparative. An *a*- after the *r*-, even though *comparison* is different.

comparison. An *i*- after the *r*-, even though *comparative* is different.

compass points. See HYPHENATING, 41.)

compatible. Note that the ending is -*ible,* not -*able.* (See -IBLE, -ABLE, 1.)

compel. Ends in one -*l,* not two. (See -EL, -ELL, 2.)

compelled. Because *compel* is accented on the last syllable, final -*l* is *doubled* before a suffix starting with a vowel. (See DOUBLING FINAL -L, 1.)

compelling. See *compelled.*

competence. Note the -*ence* ending. (See -ANCE, -ENCE, AFTER T-, 3.)

competent. Ends in -*ent,* not -*ant.* (See -ANCE, -ENCE, AFTER T-, 4.)

competition. Vowel after the *p*- is -*e,* not -*i.* Think of the verb *compete.*

competitor. Ends in -*or.* (See -ER, -OR, 5.)

complainant. Ends in -*ant.*

complected. *Complexioned* is considered better, as in *dark-complexioned.*

complection. Misspelling of *complexion.*

complement. See COMPLIMENT, COMPLEMENT.

complementary. See COMPLIMENTARY, COMPLEMENTARY.

complexion. Note the -*xion* ending. (See -ECTION, -EXION.)

compliance. Ending is -*ance.* (See -ANCE, -ENCE, AFTER I-, 2.)

COMPLIMENT, COMPLEMENT

Compliment, verb or noun, refers to praise, admiration, etc.

A *complement* is something that completes a whole or is added to something else; the verb *complement* means to make complete, or be a *complement* to.

COMPLIMENTARY, COMPLEMENTARY

With the -*i* the adjective means expressing praise, admiration, etc., or given without charge, as a *complimentary* ticket.

With the -*e* the adjective means serving to complete, as a *complementary* color, angle, etc.

---

comportment. *Comport* plus -*ment,* hence no -*e* after the *t*-.

comprehensible. If the root ends in -*ns,* the likely ending is -*ible,* not -*able.* (See -IBLE, -ABLE, 3.)

comprehension. Ends in -*ension.* (See -ENSION, -ENTION.)

compressible. If the root forms its noun by the immediate addition of -*ion* (*compression*), the correct ending is likely to be -*ible.* (See -IBLE, -ABLE, 2.)

comprise. Note the -*ise* ending, common to words ending in -*prise.* (See -ISE, 4.)

compromise. One of three words that end in -*mise* rather than -*mize.* (See -ISE, 5.)

COMPTROLLER. See CONTROLLER, COMPTROLLER.

---

comradery. See *camaraderie.*

CON-, CONN-

The following are the only words of any consequence spelled *con-,* rather than *conn-,* before a vowel.

conation	conical
conative	conifer
conatus	conundrum
cone	

If in any doubt, then, double the -*n* after *co-* when the next letter is a vowel: *connect, connive*, etc.

---

conasseur. Misspelling of *connoisseur*.

concede. -*Cede* is the common ending for such verbs, but there are exceptions. (See -CEED, -SEDE, -CEDE, 3.)

conceed. Misspelling of *concede*.

conceit. -*E* before -*i* after *c*-. (See -IE, -EI, 2.)

conceive. -*E* before -*i* after *c*-. (See -IE, -EI, 2.)

concensus. Misspelling of *consensus*.

concerto. The commoner plural is *concertos*, but people in musical circles prefer the Italian-derived *concerti*.

conciliatory. Note that the ending is -*ory*, not -*ary*. (See -ARY, -ORY, 2.)

concomitance -*Ance* is found somewhat more often than -*ence* after *t*-. This word is not related to *commit*— only one -*m* in the middle. (See -ANCE, -ENCE, AFTER T-, 1.)

concomitant. -*Ant* slightly more common than -*ent* after *t*-. (See -ANCE, -ENCE, AFTER T-, 2.)

concubinage. Final -*e* of *concubine* is dropped before the suffix -*age*. (See -AGE AFTER FINAL -E, 1.)

concurred. The final -*r* of *concur* is doubled before -*ed*, -*ence*, and -*ing*, since the accent falls on the last syllable (*cur*) and remains there in the derived forms. (See DOUBLING FINAL -R, 2, 3.)

concurrence. See *concurred*. Note also that the ending is -*ence*, not -*ance*. (See -ANCE, -ENCE, AFTER R-, 3.)

concurring. See *concurred*.

condenser. Ends in -*er*.

condescend. See *descend*.

condescension. Ends in -*ension*. (See -ENSION, -ENTION.)

condolence. After *l*-, -*ence* is likely to be the correct ending. (See -ANCE, -ENCE, AFTER L-, 1.)

conductor. Ends in -*or*. (See -ER, -OR, 5.)

confectionery. One of the few words with both a primary and secondary accent ending in -*ery* rather than -*ary*. (See -ARY, -ERY, 2.)

conferee, conferree. The spelling with one -*r* is better, both are correct.

conference. Only one -*r;* and notice the -*ence* ending. (See -ANCE, -ENCE, AFTER R-, 1; DOUBLING FINAL -R, 3.)

conferrable. See *conferred*.

conferred. The final -*r* of *confer* is doubled before -*able*, -*er*, -*ed*, and -*ing*, since the accent falls on the last syllable (*fer*) and remains there in the derived forms *conferrable*, *conferrer, conferred, conferring*. (See DOUBLING FINAL -R, 2, 3.)

conferrer. See *conferred*.

conferring. See *conferred*.

confessor, confesser. Both spellings correct, and no distinction as to whether it is the person confessing or the priest being confessed to. However, the -*or* is commoner for both.

CONFIDANT, CONFIDANTE, CONFIDENT

A *confidant* is a close and trusted friend (in whom one confides) of either sex; *confidante* emphasizes that this friend is a female.

Although the spelling *confident* is technically an acceptable variant of *confidant*, this is such a rare usage that it is best to keep the -*ent* ending restricted to the adjective (He feels *confident* of success, etc.).

---

confidence. Almost always, with only a few exceptions, -*ence*, not -*ance*, follows a *d*-. (See -ANCE, -ENCE, AFTER D-, 1.)

confident. See *confidence*.

confidentially. The adverbial ending -*ly* is added to the adjective *confidential*, hence the double -*l*. (See -LY, -ALLY, 4.)

confluence. Always -*ence*, not -*ance*, after *fl*-. (See -ANCE, -ENCE, AFTER U-, 2.)

congratulatory. The ending is -*ory*, not -*ary*. (See -ARY, -ORY, 2.)

congruence. With very few exceptions, -*ence*, rather than -*ance*, follows *u*-. (See -ANCE, -ENCE, AFTER U-, 3.)

conisseur. Misspelling of *connoisseur*.

CONN-, CON-. See CON-, CONN-.

---

connasseur. Misspelling of *connoisseur*.

connectible. If the root forms its noun by the immediate addition of -*ion* (*connection*), the correct ending is likely to be -*ible*. (See -IBLE, -ABLE, 2.)

connection, connexion. The latter spelling is British. (See -ECTION, -EXION.)

connivance. Generally after *v*- the correct suffix is -*ance*, not -*ence*. (See -ANCE, -ENCE, AFTER V-, 1.)

connoisseur. This word is full of pitfalls, so get a strong visual image of it. Double -*n*, -*oi* in the middle, -*eur* at the end.

conqueror. Ends in -*or*. (See -ER, -OR, 5.)

conscience. The combination -*ie*, rather than -*ei*, is always used when the preceding -*c* has the sound of *sh*. Or think of the word as *con*- plus *science*. (See -IE, -EI, 12.)

conscientious. The -*sc* combination produces the *sh* sound.

conscious. See *conscientious*.

consensus. The letter after the first *n*- is -*s*, not -*c*.

consequence. Always -*ence*, not -*ance*, after *qu*-. (See -ANCE, -ENCE, AFTER U-, 1.)

consequent. See *consequence*.

consh-. For words that seem to start this way, try *consc*-.

consistent. Ends in -*ent*, as do also *insistent* and *persistent*.

consonance. One of a group of words ending in -*ance* rather than -*ence*, after *n*-. (See -ANCE, -ENCE, AFTER N-, 3.)

consonant. See *consonance*.

conspicuous. Make sure to get in that -*u* before -*ous*. (See -UOUS.)

conspirator. Ends in -*or*. (See -ER, -OR, 5.)

constituence. With very few exceptions, -*ence*, rather than -*ance*, follows *u*-. (See -ANCE, -ENCE, AFTER U-, 3.)

constituent. See *constituence*.

constructor. Ends in -*or*. (See -ER, -OR, 5.)

consul. A member of the ambassadorial staff of a nation—not to be confused with the word *council* or *counsel*. The adjective is *consular*, the office or position is *consulate*. *Consul*, by the way, is also the word for a chief magistrate of ancient Rome. (See COUNCIL, COUNSEL.)

contagion. Ends in -*ion*.

contagious. Ends in -*ious*, not -*eous*.

contemporaneous. Ends in -*eous*, not -*ious*.

contemptible. Note the -*ible* ending. (See -IBLE, -ABLE, 7.)

contemptuous. Note the -*u* before -*ous*. (See -UOUS.)

contention. Ends in -*ention*. (See -ENSION, -ENTION.)

contiguous. Note the -*u* before -*ous* (See -UOUS.)

continence. Somewhat more words end in -*nence* than -*nance*, this among others. (See -ANCE, -ENCE, AFTER N-, 1.)

continent. See *continence*.

CONTINUAL. See CONTINUOUS, CONTINUAL.

---

continuance. Nouns formed from verbs ending in -*ue* have the -*ance*, rather than -*ence*, suffix. (See -ANCE, -ENCE, AFTER U-, 5.)

CONTINUOUS, CONTINUAL

These words are close in meaning, and are often used interchangeably. Strictly, however, *continuous* indicates action or circumstance that continues for a period without stop or interruption. *Continuous rain* suggests that there is no letup; *continuous work* that there is no pause; *continuous talking* that there is no moment of silence; *continuous warfare* that there is not a day of peace.

Continual, on the other hand, describes frequently repeated occurrence. *Continual reminders* are given over and over; *continual rain* comes down intermittently, i.e., interrupted by occasional dry spells; a woman nags, criticizes, or scolds her husband *continually*, i.e., again and again, at frequent intervals during the day, week, or month—but *continuously* (if you can imagine such an unlikely situation) if she does nothing all day or all week but nag, criticize, or scold.

Of the two words, only *continuous* may refer to space—*a continuous* (i.e., *unbroken*) *line, expanse, boundary*, etc.

---

contractible. If the root forms its noun by the immediate addition of *-ion* (*contraction*), the correct ending is likely to be *-ible*. (See -IBLE, -ABLE, 2.)

contractor. Ends in *-or*. (See -ER, -OR, 5.)

contralto. Pluralize by adding *-s: contraltos*. In musical circles, *contralti* is sometimes used. (See PLURALIZING WORDS IN TERMINAL -O, 2.)

contrariwise. Note the *-ise* ending, common to all words built on the base *-wise*. (See -ISE, 1.)

contravention. Ends in *-ention*. (See -ENSION, -ENTION.)

contributor. Ends in *-or*. (See -ER, -OR, 5.)

contributory. Note that the ending is *-ory*, not *-ary*. (See -ARY, -ORY, 2.)

contrivance. Generally after *v-* the correct suffix is *-ance*, not *-ence*. (See -ANCE, -ENCE, AFTER V-, 1.)

control. Ends in a single *-l*. (See -OL, -OLL, 4.)

controlled. Because *control* is accented on the last syllable, final *-l* is *doubled* before a suffix starting with a vowel. (See DOUBLING FINAL -L, 1.)

CONTROLLER, COMPTROLLER

Two forms of the same word, and whichever spelling is used the pronunciation is the same: kon-TROL-er. The title of the government official who directs the finances of a city or state is often written *comptroller;* in a private corporation, *controller* is the more usual pattern.

---

controlling. See *controlled*.

convalesce. Note the *-esce* ending. (See -ESCE, -ESCENT, -ESCENCE, 1.)

convalescence. Note the *-sc* and the *-ence* ending. (See -ANCE, -ENCE, AFTER C-, 5.)

convalescent. Note the *-sc*. (See -ANCE, -ENCE, AFTER C-, 5; -ESCE, -ESCENT, -ESCENCE, 2.)

convenience. Most often, as here, *-ence*, rather than *-ance* follows *i-*. (See -ANCE, -ENCE, AFTER I-, 1.)

convenient. See *convenience*.

convention. Ends in *-ention*. (See -ENSION, -ENTION.)

convertible. Ends in *-ible*. (See -IBLE, -ABLE, 2.)

convincible. The ending is *-ible* to keep the preceding *-c* "soft." (See -IBLE, -ABLE, 5.)

convocation. Note that the *-k* of *convoke* has changed to *-c* before the vowel *-a*. (See -K TO -C.)

coockoo. Misspelling of *cuckoo*.

cooed, cooing. These derived forms of *coo* are corectly spelled, although the three successive vowels may look strange at first. (See -OO, TERMI-NAL.)

coolie, coolly. A *coolie* is a Chinese laborer, for which *cooly* (one -*l*) is a variant spelling; *coolly* is the adverbial form of *cool*.

coolly. Note the double -*l*, since the adverbial suffix -*ly* is added to the adjective *cool*. (See -LY, 7.)

cooly. Misspelling of *coolly*.

coop. See -OOP, -OUP, -UPE, 1.

co-operate. The most practical way to write this word and any of its derivatives is with a hyphen. (See HYPHENATING, 14A.)

co-ordinate. Here, too, the most practical way to write the word and any of its derivatives is with a hyphen. (See HYPHENATING, 14A.)

copied. The -*y* of *copy* changes to -*i* before -*ed*, -*er*, and -*es*. (See -Y PLUS A SUFFIX, 1, 3.)

copier. See *copied*.

copies. See *copied*.

copyright. This is *copy* plus a government-granted *right*—nothing to do with *writing*.

copywriter. One who *writes* copy, as in an advertising firm.

coquet, coquette. The verb is preferably spelled with one -*t*, is also correct with two. The noun, probably to emphasize the feminine, is correct only with the double -*t*.

coquettish. Correct with two -*t*'s only.

COR-, CORR-

1. Before a vowel *corr*- is commoner than *cor*-. The following are the only *cor*- words likely to be misspelled.

coral (i.e., the	corollary
marine form, or	coronary
the color)	coronation
coralline	coroner
Corinne	coronet
corolla	coruscate

2. In other common words, then, double the -*r* after *co*- when the next letter is a vowel: *correct, correlate,* *correspond, corridor, corroborate, corrupt,* etc.

CORAL, CORRAL

With one -*r* it's the color or the marine organism. With two -*r*'s, and accented on the second syllable, it's an enclosure, or a verb meaning to enclose, confine, capture, etc.

---

coralline. One -*r*, two -*l*'s (See COR-, CORR-, 1.)

CORD, CHORD

Most things shaped, or acting, like a kind of string or thin rope or twine, are spelled *cord,* including the *vocal cords.*

Chord, on the other hand, is one of the strings of a musical instrument, a combination of musical tones, an emotion, or a geometric line.

He played a series of melancholy *chords.*

What you say hits a sympathetic *chord* in the audience.

Chord AB intersects arc F at X.

---

corduroy. It's the -*u* that most people have trouble with.

core. See CORPS, CORPSE, CORE.

corelate. misspelling of *correlate*.

corespond. Misspelling of *correspond*.

CORESPONDENT, CORRESPONDENT

With one -*r* (first syllable pronounced KOE), this is the person named in a divorce proceeding as having committed adultery with the spouse being sued. With two -*r*'s it's one who corresponds, i.e., writes letters, or conducts a column for a paper.

---

coridor. Misspelling of *corridor*.

Corinne. One -*r*. (See COR-, CORR-, 1.)

coroborate. Misspelling of *corroborate*.

corode. Misspelling of *corrode*.

corolla. One *-r*. (See COR-, CORR-, 1.)

corollary. One *-r*, two *-l*'s. (See COR-, CORR-, 1.)

coronary. Only one *-r*. (See COR-, CORR, 1.)

coronation. Only one *-r*. (See COR-, CORR, 1.)

coroner. Only one *-r* after the *o-*. (See COR-, CORR-, 1.)

coronet. Only one *-r*. (See COR-, CORR-, 1.)

CORPS, CORPSE, CORE

A *corps* (pronounced KORE) is a group of people, as the Marine *Corps,* diplomatic *corps,* etc.

A *corpse* (pronunced KORPS) is a dead body.

Core is the innermost part of anything.

---

corpulence. Generally *-l* is followed by *-ence* rather than *-ance*. There are a few exceptions, however, worth studying. (See -ANCE, -ENCE, AFTER L-, 1, 3.)

CORR-, COR-. See COR-, CORR-.

---

corral. See CORAL, CORRAL.

corralled. The *-l* of *corral* is doubled before a suffix beginning with a vowel. (See -AL, -ALL, 3.)

corralling. See *corralled*.

correct. Two *-r*'s. (See COR- CORR-, 2.)

correctable. Note that the ending is *-able,* not *-ible*. (See -ABLE, -IBLE, 1.)

correlate. Two *-r*'s. (See COR-, CORR-, 2.)

correspond. Two *-r*'s. (See COR-, CORR-, 2.)

correspondent. See CORESPOND-ENT, CORRESPONDENT.

corroborate. Two *-r*'s in the middle, one *-b*. (See COR-, CORR-, 2.)

corridor. Double *-r* in the middle, and ends in *-or*. (See COR-, CORR-, 2; -ER, -OR, 5.)

corrode. Two *-r*'s. (See COR-, CORR-, 2.)

corrodible. Ends in *-ible*. (See -IBLE, -ABLE, 2.)

corronary. Misspelling of *coronary*.

corronation. Misspelling of *coronation*.

corroner. Misspelling of *coroner*.

corrugate. Two *-r*'s followed by *-u*. (See COR-, CORR-, 2.)

corruptible. If the root forms its noun by the immediate addition of *-ion* (*corruption*), the correct ending is likely to be *-ible*. (See -IBLE, -ABLE, 2.)

corruscate. Misspelling of *coruscate*.

corseted. Because *corset* not accented on the last syllabl . final *-t* is *not* doubled before a suffix beginning with a vowel. (See DOUBLING FINAL -T, 3.)

cortesian. Misspelling of *courtesan*.

cortex. The plural is *cortices*. (See PLURALIZING WORDS IN TERMINAL -X.)

corugate. Misspelling of *corrugate*.

coruscate. Only one *-r*. (See COR-, CORR-, 1.)

corvette, corvet. The longer spelling is preferable. (See -ET, -ETTE, 2.)

cosey, cosie. See *cozy*.

COSTUME, CUSTOM

Costume, noun or verb, refers to clothing, or style or type of dress. *Custom,* a noun only, is habit, convention, established usage, etc.

---

cosy. See *cozy*.

cough. Ends in *-ough,* even though *caught* ends in *-aught*.

cought. Misspelling of *caught*.

couldn't. Contraction of *could not,* the apostrophe appearing in place of the missing *-o*. (See APOSTROPHE, USE OF, 1.)

COUNCIL, COUNSEL

A *council* is a legislative or discussion group, or, less commonly, the deliberations of such a group; the word is a noun only.

Counsel, both noun and verb, involves the concept of advice. To *counsel* is to give advice, or to urge or recommend a plan of action; *counsel*, as a noun, is either the advice or recommendation itself, or a legal adviser, i.e., an attorney, as in *counsel for the defense*. With a plural significance the word may refer to a group of lawyers involved on the same side of a lawsuit or other cause.

See also COUNCILOR, COUNSELOR.

councilor. Because *council* is *not* accented on the last syllable, final *-l* is *not* doubled before a suffix beginning with a vowel. *Councillor* is also correct, but the one *-l* spelling is preferable. (See DOUBLING FINAL *-L*, 2.)

COUNCILOR, COUNSELOR

A *councilor* is a member of a *council*, i.e., of a discussion group, legislative assembly, etc. If he belongs to the lawmaking body of a city or town, he is generally called a *councilman*.

A *counselor*, on the other hand, gives *counsel*, or advice and help, hence he is a legal *counselor*, or attorney, a children's *counselor* at camp, etc.

Both words may also be spelled with a double *-l*, but the single *-l* form is preferable.

See also COUNCIL, COUNSEL.

counsel. See COUNCIL, COUNSEL.
counseled. Because *counsel* is *not* accented on the last syllable, final *-l* is *not* doubled before a suffix beginning with a vowel. *Counselled* is also correct, but the single *-l* spelling is far preferable. (See DOUBLING FINAL *-L*, 2.)

counseling. See *counseled*.
counselor. See COUNCILOR, COUNSELOR; also *counseled*.
countenance. One of a group of words ending in *-ance* rather than *-ence*, after *n-*.
counter-. See HYPHENATING, 36.
counterfeit. Note the *-ei* combination. (See -IE, -EI, 9.)
coupé. See -OOP, -OUP, -UPE, 31.
course. See COARSE, COURSE.
courtesan, courtezan. Both spellings correct, but the latter uncommon.
courtesy. Practiced at the royal *court*, so to speak, hence the odd first syllable. Note that the ending is *-sy*, not *-cy*.
court-martial. The principal part of a compound word is pluralized: *courts-martial;* and note the hyphen. (See HYPHENATING, 1.)
coverlet. Ends in *-et*, not *-ette*. (See -ET, -ETTE, 4.)
coveted. Because *covet* is *not* accented on the last syllable, final *-t* is *not* doubled before a suffix beginning with a vowel. (See DOUBLING FINAL *-T*, 3.)
coveting. See *coveted*.
covetous. See *coveted*.

COW-

Compounds with *cow-* are generally written solid: *cowbell, cowboy, cowcatcher, cowgirl, cowhand* (also *cow hand*), *cowherd, cowpuncher,* etc.

But *cow-eyed* is hyphenated, and *cow barn* and *cow pony* are written separate.

cower. See -OUR, -OWER, -AUER, 2.
coyer, coyest. Comparative and superlative of *coy*. (See -IER, -IEST, 6.)
coyly. Since the terminal *-y* of *coy*

follows a vowel, it does *not* change to -*i* before a suffix. (See -Y PLUS A SUFFIX, 9.)

coyness. See *coyly.*

cozy. As an adjective this word can be spelled in every way imaginable, and they're all acceptable: *cosy, cozey, cosey, cozie, cosie.* (However, *cozy* is by far the preferable and commonest form.) As a noun, *cosy* and *cosey* are also correct, *cozy* again preferable.

craziness. The -*y* of *crazy* changes to -*i* before -*ness.* (See -Y PLUS A SUFFIX, 6.)

CREAK, CREEK
    Creak, noun or verb, refers to sound—The chair *creaks.*
    Creek, noun only, is a small stream.

---

credence. Almost always, with only a few exceptions, -*ence,* not -*ance,* follows a *d*-. (See -ANCE, -ENCE, AFTER D-, 1.)

credible. Note that the ending is -*ible,* not -*able.* (See -IBLE, -ABLE, 1.)

CREDIBLE, CREDITABLE
    Something *credible* is believable— a *credible* story.
    Something *creditable* is worthy of credit or praise—That was a *creditable* attempt.

---

creditable. Note that the ending is -*able,* not -*ible.* (See -ABLE, -IBLE, 1.)

creek. See CREAK, CREEK.

crescendo. Note the -*sc.*

crescent. Note the -*sc.* (See -ESCE, -ESCENT, -ESCENCE, 3.)

cretonne. One -*t,* two -*n*'s.

cried. The -*y* of *cry* changes to -*i* before -*ed,* -*er,* -*es.* (See -Y PLUS A SUFFIX, 1, 3.)

crier. See *cried.*

cries. See *cried.*

crisis. Plural is *crises.* (See PLURALIZING WORDS IN TERMINAL -IS.)

criterion. Plural is either *criteria* or *criterions.* (See PLURALIZING WORDS IN TERMINAL -ON.)

crocheted. The -*t* of *crochet* is *never* doubled before a suffix. (See DOUBLING FINAL -T, 5.)

crocheting. See *crocheted.*

croop, croup. See -OOP, -OUP, -UPE, 3A.

croquet, croquette. Pronounced kro-KAY, the first is the game; pronounced kro-KET, the second is the food. (See -ET, -ETTE, 3, 4.)

cross-. See HYPHENATING, 32.

croup, croop. See -OOP, -OUP, -UPE, 3A.

crying. Final -*y* is unchanged before -*ing.*

crysanthemum. Misspelling for *chrysanthemum.*

crystalline. Double -*l* required in derived forms of *crystal.* (See DOUBLING FINAL -L, 4.)

crystallize. See *crystalline.*

cubbard. Misspelling of *cupboard.*

cuckoo. Not *coockoo.*

cue. See QUEUE, CUE.

culinary. Most words with both a primary and secondary accent end in -*ary* rather than -*ery.* (See -ARY, -ERY, 1, 2.)

culpable. Note the -*able* ending. (See -ABLE, -IBLE, 7.)

cumulous. Not *cumulous.* (See -US, -OUS.) For plural see PLURALIZING WORDS IN TERMINAL -US, 1.

cupboard. The -*p* is silent, but appears in the spelling.

cupful. The plural is *cupfuls.* (See PLURALIZING WORDS IN TERMINAL -FUL.)

cupped. Final -*p* of a one-syllable word is doubled before a suffix beginning with a vowel. (See DOUBLING FINAL -P, 1.)

cupping. See *cupped.*

curator. Ends in -or. (See -ER, -OR, 5.)

curb, kerb. The second spelling is British.

cure-all. Hyphenated.

curlicue, curlycue. The first spelling is preferable.

curly. Not *curley*.

CURRANT, CURRENT

Currant is a kind of berry or dried grape. The spelling *current* is used for all other meanings.

---

curriculum. The plural is either *curricula* or *curriculums*. (See PLURALIZING WORDS IN TERMINAL -UM, 1.)

curvaceous. The only nontechnical word ending in *-aceous*. (See -ACIOUS, -ACEOUS, -ATIOUS, 2.)

cushion. Note the *-i.*

custom. See COSTUME, CUSTOM.

customary. Ends in *-ary.*

CUT-

Most noun compounds with *cut-* are solid: *cutaway, cutback, cutoff, cutout, cutthroat, cutup,* etc.

Cut glass, cut price, and *cut rate* are two-word nouns.

As adjectives, *cut-price* and *cut-rate* are hyphenated.

When *cut* is a verb, its adverb is, of course, separated from it: *cut away, cut back,* etc.

-CY, -SY

1. When doubt exists as to a choice between *-cy* and *-sy* as an ending, *-cy* is more likely to be the proper form (*consistency, constancy, fluency, frequency, infancy, legacy, leniency, literacy, lunacy,* etc.).

2. It will be noticed that *-cy* indicates the noun form especially of adjectives that end in *-nt:*

    constant—constancy
    fluent—fluency

    frequent—frequency
    insurgent—insurgency
    sufficient—sufficiency

3. The same ending characterizes nouns formed from words ending in *-t, -te,* or *-tic:*

    democratic—democracy
    literate—literacy
    lunatic—lunacy
    prelate—prelacy
    private—privacy
    prophetic—prophecy
    regenerate—regeneracy
    secret—secrecy

4. Because of the abundance of *-cy* words, the common error is to use this ending where *-sy* is required. Note especially the following: *ecstasy, idiosyncrasy, hypocrisy, apostasy, heresy, jealousy.*

---

cylinder. Note that the *-y* precedes the *-i.*

czar, tsar, tzar. Any of these spellings for a Russian or other Slavic ruler of former times, the first being the commonest form. As an American word (*movie czar, baseball czar,* etc.), only the first spelling.

Czech. A native of Czechoslovakia; not spelled *Check* or *Czeck.*

D

(Rules for double -d: See Doubling Final -D.)

dachshund. Pronounced in a number of ways, but spelled along strictly German lines; note the *-chsh* combination, and that the second syllable is *-hund,* not *-hound.*

daguerreotype. A favorite in spelling bees because of the *-rre* preceding the *-o.* Named after the inventor, Louis Daguerre.

dairy. See DIARY, DAIRY.

dairy, dairies. When a word ends in

-*y* preceded by a consonant, the plural ends in -*ies*. (See -EYS, -IES, -YS, 3.)

damageable. The -*e* of *damage* is retained before -*able*. (See -GEABLE.)

damask. The fabric ends in -*k*, not -*c*.

DAMMED, DAMNED

These words are pronounced the same, but *dammed* means held or kept back, *damned* means condemned, criticized, or cursed. *I'll be damned!* is the way to spell the expression of surprise, though there are some who hesitate to put the word into writing.

-DANCE, -DENCE. See -ANCE, -ENCE, AFTER D-.

-DANT, -DENT. See -ANCE, -ENCE, AFTER D-.

datum. The plural is *data*. (See PLURALIZING WORDS IN TERMINAL -UM, 1.)

daughter-in-law. Always hyphenated; the plural is *daughters-in-law*. (See HYPHENATING, 6A.)

DAY-

The following noun compounds of *day-* are written solid:

daybreak   daytime
daydream   daywork
daylight

The following are separate.

day bed   day letter
day coach   day nursery
day in court   day room
day laborer   day school

Also solid are the adjective *day-long* and the verb *daydream*.

Daylight-saving time is hyphenated as shown, as are most adjectives (*day-weary*, etc.).

day's pay. Note the apostrophe. (See APOSTROPHE, USE OF, 4.)

DEAD-

Most noun compounds with *dead-* are written solid (*deadfall, deadhead, deadline, deadwood*, etc.).

The following nouns are separate:

dead beat (*slang*)   dead letter
dead center   dead pan
dead end   dead weight
dead heat

Adjectives are generally hyphenated (*dead-beat, dead-end, dead-letter, dead-set*, etc.).

deaf-and-dumb. Hyphenated when an adjective (*deaf-and-dumb* language) preceding its noun.

deaf-mute. Hyphenated.

DEAR, DEER

Deer is the animal from which we get venison; *dear* is expensive, loved, precious, etc.

DEATH-

Adjective compounds with *death-* are hyphenated: *death-dealing, death-defying*, etc.

Some noun compounds are solid words: *deathbed, deathblow, deathtrap, deathwatch*.

Most others are written separate: *death mask, death rate, death rattle, death warrant*, etc.

Death's-head is hyphenated; *death-like*, in common with most -*like* words, is solid.

See also HYPHENATING, 40.

debatable. Note that the ending is -*able*, not -*ible*. (See -ABLE, -IBLE, 2.)

debtor. Ends in -*or*. (See -ER, -OR, 5.)

Decalogue, Decalog. The longer spelling is preferable. (See -OGUE, -OG, 1.)

decayed. Since the terminal -*y* of *decay* follows a vowel, it does *not* change to -*i* before a suffix. (See -Y PLUS A SUFFIX, 9.)

decaying. See *decayed*.

deceit. *-E* before *-i* after *c-*. (See -IE, -EI, 2.)

deceive. *-E* before *-i* after *c-*. (See -IE, EI, 2.)

decide, decided. The second consonant is *-c*, though *-s* is usually found in students' compositions.

declension. Ends in *-ension*. (See -ENSION, -ENTION.)

décolleté. If you use accents on this French import, they go on the first and last *-e*'s. Leave them out completely if you prefer, though most often they appear.

decorator. Ends in *-or*. (See -ER, -OR, 5.)

decreer. Two *-e*'s only, even though it's *decree* plus *-er*. (See -EER.)

deer. See DEAR, DEER.

defendant. Ends in *-ant*.

defense. This American spelling is preferable to the British *defence*. (See -ENCE, -ENSE, 2.)

defensible. If the root ends in *-ns*, the likely ending is *-ible*, not *-able*. (See -IBLE, -ABLE, 3.)

deference. Only one *-r*, since the accent of *defer* has shifted back to the first syllable. And note the *-ence* ending. (See -ANCE, -ENCE, AFTER R-, 1; DOUBLING FINAL -R, 3.)

deferred. The final *-r* of *defer* is doubled before *-ed*, and *-ing* (*deferring*), since the accent falls on the last syllable (*-fer*) and remains there in these derived forms. (See DOUBLING FINAL -R, 2, 3.)

deferring. See *deferred*.

defiance. Ending is *-ance*. (See -ANCE, -ENCE, AFTER I-, 2.)

deficient. The combination *-ie*, rather than *-ei*, is always used when the preceding *-c* has the sound of *sh*. (See -IE, -EI, 12.)

defied. The *-y* of *defy* changes to *-i* before *-ed*, *-er*, or *-es*. (See -Y PLUS A SUFFIX, 1, 3.)

defier. See *defied*.

defies. See *defied*.

definitely. This is built on the root *finite*, hence the *-i*, *-i*, *-e* pattern in the body of the word. Likewise *indefinitely*.

deflection, deflexion. The latter is British. (See -ECTION, -EXION.)

deflower. See -OUR, -OWER, -AUER, 2.

delayed. Since the terminal *-y* of *delay* follows a vowel, it does *not* change to *-i* before a suffix. (See -Y PLUS A SUFFIX, 9.)

delaying. See *delayed*.

delectable. Since *-a* is the principal vowel in another form of the word (*delectation*), the correct ending is *-able*. (See -ABLE, -IBLE, 5.)

delicious. Ends in *-icious*, not *-itious*. (See -ICIOUS, -ITIOUS, 1.)

deliverance. Note the *-ance* ending. (See -ANCE, -ENCE, AFTER R-, 6.)

deliveries. Since *delivery* ends in *-y* preceded by a consonant, the plural ends in *-ies*. (See -EYS, -IES, -YS, 3.)

de luxe. Two words.

demagogue, demagog. The longer spelling is preferable. (See -OGUE, -OG, 1.)

demeanor, demeanour. The first spelling is American, the second British. (See -OR, -OUR, 1.)

DEMI-
Compounds with this prefix are generally written solid: *demigod, demimonde*, etc.

---

demise. One of three words ending in *-mise*, rather than *-mize*. (See -ISE, 5.)

demogogue. Misspelling of *demagogue*.

demonstrable. Since *-a* is the principal vowel in another form of the word (*demonstrate*), the correct ending is *-able*. (See -ABLE, -IBLE, 5.)

demurral. The final *-r* of *demur* is doubled before *-al*, *-ed*, and *-ing*, since the accent falls on the last syllable (*mur*) and remains there in the derived forms. (See DOUBLING FINAL -R, 2, 3.)

demurred. See *demurral.*

demurring. See *demurral.*

denial, denied, denies. The *-y* of *deny* changes to *-i* before *-al, -ed,* or *-es.* (See -Y PLUS A SUFFIX, 1.)

denominator. Ends in *-or.* (See -ER, -OR, 5.)

deodorant. Ends in *-ant.*

dependable. Note that the ending is *-able,* not *-ible.* (See -ABLE, -IBLE, 1.)

dependence. Almost always, with only a few exceptions, *-ence,* not *-ance,* follows a *d-.* (See -ANCE, -ENCE, AFTER D-, 1.)

dependent. Not *dependant.* (See *dependence.*)

depilatory. *-Ory,* not *-ary.* (See -ARY, -ORY, 2.)

deplorable. *-Able,* not *-ible.* (See -ABLE, -IBLE, 2.)

depositary. See -ARY, -ORY, 3B.

depositor. Ends in *-or.* (See -ER, -OR, 5.)

depository. See -ARY, -ORY, 3B.

depravation, deprivation. The first noun is from the verb *deprave,* the second from *deprive.*

deputy mayor. No hyphen. (See HYPHENATING, 5A.)

derelict. Not *deralict.*

derivative. Not *derivitive*—think of the noun *derivation.*

derogatory. One *-r* at the beginning, and ends in *-ory,* not *-ary.* (See -ARY, -ORY, 2.)

descend. Either the *-s* or the *-c* is often gaily omitted by poor spellers in this word, and also in *ascend, ascension, ascertain, ascetic, condescend, descent,* etc.

descendant. As a noun, i.e., one who descends from an ancestor, the word ends in *-ant* (think of the *an-* in ancestor). The adjective may be spelled either *-ant* or *-ent;* to be

efficient, spell the word *-ant* no matter how used.

descent. See *descend.*

describable. *-Able,* not *-ible.* (See -ABLE, -IBLE, 2.)

describe. Starts with *de-,* not *di-.*

discriminate. Misspelling of *discriminate.*

description. As in describe, *de-,* not *di-.*

DESERT, DESSERT

With one *-s* it's a verb (Don't *desert* me) or a barren stretch of land (the Mojave Desert—note the one *-s* in *sand* and in *desert*).

With two *-s*'s it tops off a meal (Let's have ice cream for *dessert*).

---

deshabille. See *dishabille.*

desiccate. This spelling may look insane, but it's the only correct one—one *-s,* two *-c*'s. From Latin *siccus,* dry, plus the prefix *de-.*

desideratum. The plural is *desiderata.* (See PLURALIZING WORDS IN TERMINAL -UM, 1.)

desirable. Drop final *-e* of *desire* before adding *-able.* (See -ABLE, -EABLE, 1; -ABLE, -IBLE, 2.)

desiring, desirous. The *-e* of *desire* is dropped before a suffix beginning with a vowel. (See DROPPED -E.)

desolate. One *-s.*

despair. If you think of the adjective *desperate,* you won't be tempted to write *dis-.*

despatch. See *dispatch, despatch.*

despatcher. See *dispatcher.*

desperadoes, desperados. The former is the preferable plural; both are correct. (See PLURALIZING WORDS IN TERMINAL -O, 4.)

desperate. Unlike *separate,* has *-e,* not *-a,* following the *p-.*

despicable. Only the *-able* ending will keep the preceding *-c* "hard." (See -ABLE, -IBLE, 6.)

despise. Note the *-ise* ending. (See -ISE, 8.)

despondent. Ends in *-ent.*

dessert. See DESERT, DESSERT.

dessicate. Misspelling of *desiccate.*

destroyed, destroyer, destroying. Since the terminal *-y* of *destroy* follows a vowel, it does *not* change to *-i* before a suffix (See -Y PLUS A SUFFIX, 9.)

destructible. If the root forms its noun by the immediate addition of *-ion* (*destruction*), the correct ending is likely to be *-ible.* (See -IBLE, -ABLE, 2.)

desultory. *-Ory,* not *-ary.* (See -ARY, -ORY, 2.)

detectable. *-Able,* not *-ible* (See -ABLE, -IBLE, 1.)

detention. Ends in *-ention.* (See -ENSION, -ENTION.)

determinance. One of a group of words ending in *-ance* rather than *-ence,* after *n-.* (See -ANCE, -ENCE, AFTER N-, 3.)

determinant. See *determinance.*

deterred, deterrence, deterring. The final *-r* of *deter* is doubled before *-ed, -ence,* and *-ing,* since the accent falls on the last syllable (*ter*) and remains there in the derived forms. (See DOUBLING FINAL -R, 2, 3.)

deterrence. Note the double *-r* and the *-ence* ending. (See -ANCE, -ENCE, AFTER R-, 3.)

deterrent. Note the *-ent* ending. (See -ANCE, -ENCE, AFTER R-, 3A.)

detestable. *-Able,* not *-ible.* (See -ABLE, -IBLE, 1.)

develop, developed, developer, developing. Single *-p* in these derived forms, since the accent does *not* fall on the last syllable of *develop.* (See DOUBLING FINAL -P, 4.)

development. Note that this word is a combination of the verb *develop* plus the suffix *-ment;* hence no *-e* after the *p-.* (See -MENT, 1.)

DEVICE, DEVISE

With the *-c* it's a noun (a strange *device*), with the *-s,* a verb (to *devise* new methods). Note, also, that both words start with *de-* (as does the related adjective *devious*), not *di-;* and that the verb ends in *-ise,* not *-ize.*

See also -ISE, 2.

---

devide, Misspelling of *divide.*

devine. Misspelling of *divine.*

dexterous, dextrous. Either spelling, the first preferable. The noun is *dexterity.*

-DGMENT, -DGEMENT

Final *-e* is generally retained before the suffix *-ment* (*manage—management; place—placement,* etc.), but in words ending in *-dge* (*judge, lodge,* etc.) the *-e* is preferably dropped:

abridge—abridgment
acknowledge—acknowledgement
judge—judgment
lodge—lodgment

The variant, and less common, spellings — *abridgement, acknowledgement, judgement, lodgement,* are not incorrect but are generally avoided.

---

diaeresis. See *dieresis.*

diagramed, diagraming. The single *-m* spelling is theoretically correct, but *diagrammed* and *diagramming* are more popular and are fully acceptable.

diagrammatic. Despite the point made in the preceding entry, only the double *-m* spelling is permitted here.

dialogue, dialog. The longer form is preferable. (See -OGUE, -OG, 1.)

dialysis, dialytic. Note the *-y* after the *l-,* as in the verb *dialyze.* (See -IZE, -YZE, 6.)

dialyze. One of the rare verbs ending in *-yze.* (See -IZE, -YZE, 5.)

diaphragm. The *-g* is silent here, but pronounced in the adjective *diaphragmatic.*

diaries. When a word like *diary* ends in *-y* preceded by a consonant, the plural ends in *-ies.* (See -EYS, -IES, -YS, 3.)

diarrhea. The *-rrh* pattern is frequent in medical terms. *Diarrhoea* also correct, but old-fashioned.

DIARY, DAIRY

Diary is a record of daily happenings or a book or calendar for keeping such a record; a dairy is a place where milk products are processed or sold. The words have nothing in common but the same letters in different order.

---

dictionary. Most words with both a primary and secondary accent and in *-ary* rather than *-ery.* (See -ARY, -ERY, 1, 2.)

didn't. The apostrophe shows the omission of *-o.* Not *diden't.*

die. The participle is spelled *dying.* (See -IE TO -Y.)

DIE, DYE. See DYE, DIE.

---

dieresis, diaeresis. The complicated second spelling, though correct, is old-fashioned.

dietitian, dietician. The first spelling is preferable. (See -ICIAN, -ITIAN.)

difference. Note the *-ence* ending. (See -ANCE, -ENCE, AFTER R-, 7.)

different. Ends in *-ent.* (See -ANCE, -ENCE, AFTER R-, 7A.)

difficult. Two *-f*'s.

diffidence. Almost always, with only a few exceptions, *-ence* not *-ance,* follows *d-.* (See -ANCE, -ENCE, AFTER D, 1.)

diffident. See *diffidence.*

digestible. If the root forms its noun by the immediate addition of *-ion* (*digestion*), the correct ending is

likely to be *-ible.* (See -IBLE, -ABLE, 2.)

dignitary. Most words with both a primary and secondary accent end in *-ary* rather than *-ery.* (See -ARY, -ERY, 1, 2.)

dilatory. *-Ory,* not *-ary.* (See ARY, -ORY, 2.)

dilemma. One *-l,* two *-m*'s.

dilettante. Note the single *-l* and double *-t* in the middle. The common plural is *dilettantes,* but for a continental flavor you may prefer to use *dilettanti.*

diligence. Because of the "soft" *-g,* *-ence,* not *-ance.* (See -ANCE, -ENCE, AFTER G-, 4.)

dimension. Ends in *-ension.* (See *-ENSION, -ENTION.*)

diner-out. Always hyphenated. (See HYPHENATING, 10A.)

dingey. Variant spelling of *dinghy,* the boat; incorrect for *dingy,* the adjective.

dinginess. Noun form of *dingy*—not to be spelled *dingeyness.*

DINGY, DINGHY

Dingy (pronounced DIN-jee) is an adjective meaning shabby, not bright, etc. It should not be spelled *dingey.*

Dinghy (pronounced DING-ghee, the *-n* nasalized) is a kind of boat. This is the preferable spelling, but *dingy* and *dingey* are also correct for this meaning.

DINNER-

Dinnerware and *dinnertime* are written solid—other compounds are separate (*dinner bell, dinner dance, dinner jacket,* etc.).

---

diphtheria. Note the *-h* after *p-.*

diphthong. Again *-h* after the *p-.*

director. Ends in *-or.* (See -ER, -OR, 5.)

dirigible. Note that the ending is *-ible,*

not -*able*. (See -IBLE, -ABLE, 1.)

dirndl. No -*e*.

DIS-, DISS-

1. If a word starts with *s-*, the addition of the prefix *dis-* will produce a spelling pattern with a double -*s*.

dis-satisfy—dissatisfy
dis-service—disservice
dis-sever—dissever
dis-similar—dissimilar
dis-symmetry—dissymmetry

2. Often this prefix is attached to a Latin root that starts with *s-*. Once again a double -*s* results.

dissect	dissociate
dissemble	dissoluble
disseminate	dissolute
dissent	dissolve
dissertation	dissolution
dissident	dissonance
dissimulate	dissuade
dissipate	

3. However, when *dis-* is added to a word starting with any other letter, only one -*s* will be found.

dis-agree—disagree
dis-appear—disappear
dis-appoint—disappoint
dis-approve—disapprove
dis-connect—disconnect

4. Thus *dissociate,* a combination of *dis-* and the Latin root *sociare,* has a double -*s*; but *disassociate,* a combination of *dis-* plus the word *associate,* has a single -*s* in the first syllable.

See also DYS-.

---

disagree. Only one -*g* in this word and all derived forms; and since it's *agree* plus *dis-*, only one -*s*. (See DIS-, DISS-, 3.)

disagreeable. Always -*able* after -*ee*. (See -ABLE, -IBLE, 4.)

disagreer. Two -*e*'s only, even though it's *disagree* plus -*er*. (See -EER.)

disapate. Frequent misspelling of *dissipate.*

disappear. *Dis-* plus *appear,* hence only one -*s*. (See DIS-, DISS, 3.)

disappearance. Note the -*ance* ending. (See -ANCE, -ENCE, AFTER R, 8.)

disappoint. *Dis-* plus *appoint,* hence one -*s*. (See DIS-, DISS-, 3.)

disapprove. *Dis-* plus *approve,* hence only one -*s*. (See DIS-, DISS-, 3.)

disassociate. *Dis-* plus *associate.* (See DIS-, DISS-, 4.)

disastrous. Even though the noun is *disaster,* there's no -*e* after the *t-* in the adjective.

disbarred, disbarring. The final -*r* of *disbar* is doubled before -*ed* and -*ing*. (See DOUBLING FINAL R-, 2, 3.)

disbelief. The plural of the noun is *disbeliefs.* And -*i* comes before -*e* except after *c-*. (See -IE, -EI, 1; PLURALIZING WORDS IN TERMINAL -F OR -FE, 2.)

disc. See *disk.*

discernible. Note the -*ible* ending. (See -IBLE, -ABLE, 7.)

disciplinary. Most words with both a primary and secondary accent end in -*ary* rather than -*ery*. (See -ARY, -ERY, 1, 2.)

discomfited, discomfiting, discomfiture. Because *discomfit* is *not* accented on the last syllable, final -*t* is *not* doubled before a suffix beginning with a vowel. (See DOUBLING FINAL -T, 3.)

discontinuance. Nouns formed from verbs ending in -*ue* have the -*ance,* rather than -*ence,* suffix. (See -ANCE, -ENCE, AFTER U-, 5.)

discountenance. One of a group of words ending in -*ance,* rather than -*ence,* after *n-*. (See -ANCE, -ENCE, AFTER N-, 3.)

discourageable. The -*e* of *discourage* is retained before -*able* in order to preserve the original "soft" pronunciation of the preceding -*g*. (See -GEABLE.)

discreditable. Note that the ending is

-*able,* not *-ible.* (See -ABLE, -IBLE, 1.)

DISCREET, DISCRETE

Discreet (note the double *-e*) means able to keep a secret, careful about what one says, etc. The noun is *discretion* or *discreetness.*

Discrete means separate or distinct. The noun is *discreteness.*

discretionary. Most words with both a primary and secondary accent end in *-ary* rather than *-ery.* (See -ARY, -ERY, 1, 2.)

discribe. Misspelling of *describe.*

discriminate. Not *descriminate.*

discriminatory. Note that the ending is *-ory,* not *-ary.* (See -ARY, -ORY, 2.)

discription. Misspelling of *description.*

DISCUSS, DISCUS

With the double *-s* it's the verb (to *discuss* his problems); with the single *-s* (pronounced DIS-k's) it's the plate of metal or stone thrown in athletic contests.

disengageable. The *-e* of *disengage* is retained before *-able* in order to preserve the original "soft" (or *j*) pronunciation of the preceding *-g.* (See -GEABLE.)

disfavor, disfavour. The first spelling is American, the second British. (See -OR, -OUR, 1.)

disfunction. Misspelling of *dysfunction.* (See DYS-.)

disguise. Note the *-ise* ending. (See -ISE, 7.)

DISH-

Dishboard, dishcloth, dishpan, dishrag, dishwasher, dishwashing, and *dishwater* are written solid. Most other noun compounds are two words (*dish cover, dish mop, dish towel,* etc.).

dishabille, deshabille. The former spell-

ing is preferable; both are correct.

dishevel. Only one *-s.* Derived forms are preferably spelled with one *-l: disheveled, disheveling.*

dishevelment. One *-s,* one *-l.*

dishonor, dishonour. The first spelling is American, the second British. (See -OR, -OUR, 1.)

disingenuous. Make sure to get in that *-u* before *-ous.* (See -UOUS.)

disippate. Incorrect spelling of *dissipate.*

disk, disc. Both spellings correct, the former commoner and preferable. However, as a term in anatomy (a slipped *disc*) the latter spelling is more frequently seen.

dismayed, dismaying. Since the terminal *-y* of *dismay* follows a vowel, it does *not* change to *-i* before a suffix. (See -Y PLUS A SUFFIX, 9.)

dismissible. When the root ends in *-miss,* the correct ending is *-ible.* (See -IBLE, -ABLE, 4.)

disobedience. Most often, as here, *-ence,* rather than *-ance,* follows *-i.* (See -ANCE, -ENCE, AFTER I-1.)

disobedient. See *disobedience.*

disobeyed, disobeying. Since the terminal *-y* of *disobey* follows a vowel, it does *not* change to *-i* before a suffix. (See -Y PLUS A SUFFIX, 9.)

dispair. Common misspelling of *despair.*

dispatch, despatch. First spelling preferable, both correct.

dispatcher, despatcher. Preferably spelled *dis-,* but *des-* also correct.

dispel. One *-s,* one *-l.* (See -EL, -ELL, 2.)

dispelled, dispelling. Because *dispel* is accented on the last syllable, final *-l* is *doubled* before a suffix starting with a vowel. (See DOUBLING FINAL -L, 1.)

dispensable. Note that the ending is *-able,* not *-ible.* (See -ABLE, -IBLE, 1.)

displayed, displaying. Since the terminal *-y* of *display* follows a vowel, it does *not* change to *-i* before a suffix. (See -Y PLUS A SUFFIX, 9.)

dispossess. Like *possess,* has two sets of double *-s's,* as do all derived forms.

disputatious. One of a few words ending in *-atious,* rather than *-acious.* (See -ACIOUS, -ACEOUS, -ATIOUS, 3.)

DISS-, DIS-. See DIS-, DISS-.

---

dissapate. Common misspelling of *dissipate.*

dissatisfy. *Satisfy* plus *dis-,* hence the double *-s.* (See DIS-, DISS-, 1.)

dissect. The double *-s* occurs because the prefix *dis-* is added to a Latin root that starts with an *-s.* (See DIS-DISS-, 2.)

dissemble. Double *-s.* (See DIS-, DISS-, 2.)

disseminate. Double *-s.* (See DIS-, DISS-, 2.)

dissension. Ends in *-ension.* (See -ENSION, -ENTION.)

dissent. Double *-s.* (See DIS-, DISS-, 2.)

dissertation. Double *-s.* (See DIS-, DISS-, 2.)

disservice. *Service* plus *dis-,* hence the double *-s.* (See DIS-, DISS-, 1.)

dissever. *Sever* plus *dis-,* hence the double *-s.* (See DIS-, DISS-, 1.)

dissidence. Almost always, with only a few exceptions, *-ence,* not *-ance,* follows a *d-;* and note the double *-s.* (See -ANCE, -ENCE, AFTER D-, 1; DIS- DISS-, 2.)

dissident. See *dissidence.*

dissimilar. *Similar* plus *dis-,* hence the double *-s.* (See DIS-, DISS-, 1.)

dissimulate. Double *-s.* (See DIS-, DISS-, 2.)

dissipate. This frequently misspelled and elusive word can be conquered by relying on the mnemonic, *to dissipate, sip scotch.* The double *-s,* single *-p,* and the *-i* preceding the *-p* are all accounted for in this simple phrase. (See DIS-, DISS-, 2.)

dissociate. Double *-s.* (See DIS-, DISS-, 4.)

dissolute. Double *-s.* (See DIS-, DIS-, 2.)

dissolution. Double *-s.* (See DIS-, DISS-, 2.)

dissolve. Double *-s.* (See DIS-, DISS-, 2.)

dissonance. Double *-s,* and ends in *-ance.* (See -ANCE, -ENCE, AFTER N-, 3; DIS-, DISS-, 2.)

dissonant. See *dissonance.*

dissuade. Double *-s.* (See DIS-, DISS-, 2.)

dissymmetry. *Symmetry* plus *dis-,* hence the double *-s.* (See DIS-, DISS-, 1.)

distensible. If the root ends in *-ns,* the likely ending is *-ible,* not *-able.* (See -IBLE, -ABLE, 3.)

distention. Ends in *-ention.* (See -ENSION, -ENTION.)

distill, distil. Double *-l* preferable. Likewise in *distillment, distilment.* (See -IL, -ILL, 4.)

distilled. All other derived forms of *distill* have two *-l's: distilled, distilling, distillery, distiller, distillate, distillation.* (See -IL- -ILL, 4.)

distraught. Note that the pattern is *-aught.* (See -AUGHT, -OUGHT, 1.)

distributor. Ends in *-or.* (See -ER, -OR, 5.)

district attorney. No hyphen. (See HYPHENATING, 5A.)

distrought. Misspelling of *distraught.*

DIVERS, DIVERSE

Divers means various, sundry, or several; *diverse* means different, varied, not similar.

There are *divers* reasons for his refusal.

He carries *divers* drugs in his shop.

These are two very *diverse* reasons.

We've had many *diverse* reactions to what happened.

Divers is pronounced as if it were the plural of the noun *diver; di-*

verse is di-VURSE, dye-VURSE, or DYE-vurse.

---

divice. Misspelling of *device*.

divide. Not *devide*.

divine. Not *devine*.

divise. Misspelling of *devise*.

divisible. The ending is *-ible,* not *-able.* (See -IBLE, -ABLE, 1.)

divisor. Ends in *-or.* (See -ER, -OR, 5.)

divorcee. This is the proper spelling (no accent mark, and two *-e*'s) for a divorced person of either sex, and is preferably pronounced di-vore-SEE, though di-VORE-see is also correct. *Divorcé* (note the accent mark), for the man, and *divorcée,* for the woman, are unnecessary affectations unless distinction has to be shown as to sex. Both these French words are pronounced di-vor-SAY.

doctor. Ends in *-or.* (See -ER, -OR, 5.)

documentary. Ends in *-ary.* (See -ARY, -ERY, 1.)

doesn't. Contraction of *does not,* the apostrophe appearing in place of the missing *-o.* (See APOSTROPHE, USE OF, 1.)

DOG-

The following noun compounds are solid: *dogberry, dogbite, dogface, dogfight, dogfish, doghouse, dogtrot, dogvane, dogwatch, dogwood.*

Dog-ear and *dog's-ear,* noun or verb, are always hyphenated.

Most other noun compounds are two words: *dog Latin, dog biscuit,* etc.

Adjectives are hyphenated: *dogcheap, dog-eared, dog-eyed, dog-tired,* etc., as is also *dog-gone,* whether interjection, adjective, or verb.

---

dogma. For plural see PLURALIZING WORDS IN TERMINAL -A, 5.

doilies. When a word such as *doily* ends in *-y* preceded by a consonant, the plural ends in *-ies.* (See -EYS, -IES, -YS, 3.)

dollar's worth. Note the apostrophe. (See APOSTROPHE, USE OF, 4.)

Dollys. If a proper name ends in *-y,* the plural is formed by the simple addition of *-s.* (See -EYS, -IES, -YS, 5.)

dominance. One of a group of words ending in *-ance* rather than *-ence,* after *n-.* (See -ANCE, -ENCE, AFTER N-, 3.)

dominant. See *dominance.*

dominoes, dominos. The former is the preferable plural; both are correct. (See PLURALIZING WORDS IN TERMINAL -O, 4.)

donkeys. A word such as *donkey,* ending in *-ey,* is pluralized by the simple addition of *-s.* (See -EYS, -IES, -YS, 1.)

donor. Ends in *-or.* (See -ER, -OR, 5.)

don't. The apostrophe shows the omission of the letter *-o.*

DOOR-

Most noun compounds with *door-* are solid: *doorbell, doorjamb, doorknob, doorman, doorstep, doorway,* etc.

The following are two words: *door hinge, door key, door lock, door mat.*

Door-shaped, an adjective, is of course hyphenated.

---

dope. Not *doap.* (See -OPE, -OAP.)

Dorothys. If a proper name ends in *-y,* the plural is formed by the simple addition of *-s.* (See -EYS, -IES, -YS, 5.)

DOUBLE-. See HYPHENATING, 48.

DOUBLE VS. SINGLE CONSONANTS

1. In the following words, the double consonant may look more familiar to some, and is occasionally seen in print, but the single consonant is either exclusively correct or very much preferred.

bias—biased, biases, biasing

chagrin—chagrined, chagrining (only acceptable forms)

combat—combatant, combated, combating, combative (double -*t* incorrect in *combatant* and *combative*)

focus—focused, focuses, focusing

kidnap—kidnaped, kidnaper, kidnaping

program—programed, programer, programing

2. The verb *to canvass* always has a double -*s*, hence *canvassed, canvasser, canvassing*.

See also other DOUBLING categories below.

DOUBLING FINAL -B

When a word of one syllable ends in a single -*b*, preceded by a single vowel (*rub, throb*, etc.), double the -*b* before adding -*ed*, -*er*, -*ing*, or any other suffix that starts with a vowel.

dub—dubbed, dubbing

fib—fibbed, fibber, fibbing

grab—grabbed, grabbing

nab—nabbed, nabbing

rub—rubbed, rubber, rubbing

sob—sobbed, sobbing

throb—throbbed, throbbing

web—webbed, webbing

DOUBLING FINAL CONSO-NANTS—ONE-SYLLABLE WORDS

1. If a one-syllable word ends in a *single* consonant preceded by a *single* vowel (*bit, swim, beg, run*, etc.), double the final consonant before adding a suffix that begins with a vowel (-*ed*, -*er*, -*ing*, etc.).

beg—begged, beggar, begging

grab—grabbed, grabbing

hit—hitter, hitting

run—runner, running

stop—stopped, stopper, stopping

swim—swimmer, swimming

top—topped, topper, topping

2. Words like *quit* or *quiz* belong in this category, the vowel -*u* functioning as a consonant, since it has the sound of *w:*

quit—quitter, quitting

quiz—quizzed, quizzes, quizzing

3. Bus, the shortened form of *omnibus*, preferably contains a single -*s* in the plural—*buses*. (But *busses* is also correct.) The verb *to bus* (i.e., take a bus) follows the original rule and becomes *bussed* and *bussing*.

4. The archaic verb *buss*, to kiss, will of course contain a double -*s* in all forms: *bussed, busses, bussing*.

5. The -*s* of the noun *gas* is *not* doubled in the following: *gases* (plural), *gaseous, gasify*. But the verb to *gas* follows the original rule: *gassed, gasses, gassing*.

DOUBLING FINAL CONSO-NANTS—WORDS OF MORE THAN ONE SYLLABLE

1. As in the case of words of one syllable, a final consonant is doubled when:

A. It is preceded by a *single* vowel; and in addition—

B. The suffix to be added starts with a vowel; and, in further addition—

C. The accent falls on the final syllable in the original word and does not shift when the suffix is added.

This sounds, and indeed is, most complicated, but a couple of examples will make it clear.

Take *control*. Notice that a single final consonant, -*l*, is preceded by a single vowel -*o*. Notice, too, that the accent falls on the final syllable—con-TROL. Now if we add a suffix beginning with a vowel, for instance -*ed*, -*er*, or -*ing*, the accent *remains* on the same syllable—con-TROLled, con-TROL-ler, con-TROL-ling. Hence we double the *-l*.

Or take *allot*. Final *t* is preceded by the single vowel *-o;* the accent falls at the end—al-LOT; adding a suffix beginning with a vowel, *-ed,* keeps the accent on the same syllable; hence, *allotted,* with a double *-t*. Had we added *-ment,* a suffix that starts with a consonant, the *t* is *not* doubled: *allotment.*

2. If the accent does *not* fall on the last syllable, the final consonant is *not* doubled, even though all other conditions are present. For instance, in *travel* or *cover,* the accent falls on the first syllable (TRAV-el, COV-er), and derivative forms are written with a single consonant—*traveled, traveler, traveling; covered, covering.*

3. Also, if the accent shifts when a suffix is added, the final consonant again is *not* doubled, even though all other conditions are present. Con-FER becomes CON-fer-ence—the *-r* is not doubled. Re-FER becomes REF-er-ence; in-FER becomes IN-fer-ence. But oc-CUR becomes oc-CUR-rence, the accent remaining on the *cur;* hence, double *-r.*

DOUBLING FINAL D-

1. If a one-syllable word ends in a *single -d,* preceded by a single vowel (for example, *prod, wad,* etc.), double the *-d* before adding *-ed, -er, -ing, -y,* or any other suffix that starts with a vowel.

bed—bedded, bedding
bid—biddable, bidder, bidding
mud—muddy
prod—prodded, prodding
rid—riddance, ridding
wad—wadded, wadding

2. In words of more than one syllable, the *-d* is doubled *only* if the accent falls on the final syllable of the original word.

embed—embedded
forbid—forbidding
but:
IN-valid—invalided
in-VAL-id—invalidate

DOUBLING FINAL -G

If a word ends in a single *-g,* preceded by a single vowel (*drag, drug, wig,* etc.), double the *-g* before adding *-ed, -er, -ing, -y,* or any other suffix starting with a vowel.

bag—bagged, baggy
beg—beggar, begged, begging
bewig—bewigged
big—bigger, biggest
bug—buggy
drag—dragged, dragging, draggy
hog—hogged, hoggish
hug—huggable, hugged, hugging
humbug—humbugged, humbugger, humbugging
slog—slogged, slogger, slogging
wig—wigged, wiggery

DOUBLING FINAL -L

1. If final *-l* is preceded by a vowel (*control, excel, rebel*), and *the accent is on the last syllable,* double the *-l* before adding a suffix that starts with a vowel (*-ed, -er, -ing,* etc.).

control—controlled, controller, controlling
excel—excelled, excelling
(*Excellent, excellence,* and *excellency* also contain a double *-l,* even though the accent has now shifted back from where it was in *excel.*)
rebel—rebelled, rebelling, rebellious
annul—annulled, annulling
compel—compelled, compelling
dispel—dispelled, dispelling
expel—expelled, expelling
impel—impelled, impelling
patrol—patrolled, patrolling
propel—propelled, propelling
repel—repelled, repelling

2. However, if the accent does

not fall on the last syllable, do *not* double final *-l*.

cancel—canceled, canceling
council—councilor
counsel—counseled, counseling, counselor
enamel—enameled, enameler, enameling
grovel—groveled, groveling
jewel—jeweled, jeweler, jeweling
libel—libeled, libeler, libeling, libelous
marvel—marveled, marveling, marvelous
model—modeled, modeler, modeling
ravel—raveled, raveling
shovel—shoveled, shoveler, shoveling
signal—signaled, signaler, signaling
tranquil—tranquilize, tranquilizer
travel—traveled, traveler, traveling

(*Note:* In most of these words a double *-l* may be used, and generally is, in British spelling; in American spelling the single *-l* is far preferable.)

3. Final *-l* is, of course, *never* doubled when adding a suffix that begins with a *consonant,* regardless of accent.

council—councilman
jewel—jewelry
patrol—patrolman
signal—signalman

4. There are a few important exceptions to Section 2. Although the following words are *not* accented on the last syllable, final *-l* is nevertheless doubled in the derived forms listed.

cancel—cancellation
chancel—chancellery, chancellor
crystal—crystalline, crystallize
metal—metallic, metallurgy
tranquil—tranquility

(but recall the preferable forms, *tranquilize* and *tranquilizer* from Section 2.)

See also -AL, -ALL; -EL, -ELL; -IL, ILL; OL, OLL.

DOUBLING FINAL -M

1. In one-syllable words, if final *-m* is preceded by a single vowel, double the *-m* before adding *-ed, -er, -ing,* or other prefix beginning with a vowel.

ram—rammed, ramming
slim—slimmed, slimming
swim—swimmer, swimming

2. In words of more than one syllable the *-m* is doubled if the accent falls on the last syllable.

bedim—bedimmed

3. When the accent does *not* fall on the last syllable, as, for example in the verbs *diagram* and *program,* theoretically the correct spelling requires a single *-m: diagramed, diagraming; programed, programing.* The single *-m,* however, looks too naked to most people, who prefer to double it in these and similar words; as a result, the double *-m* form is far more popular and equally correct. Note, however, in this connection, that *programmatic* and *diagrammatic,* with the double *-m,* are the only allowable forms. And similarly, from *monogram* and *epigram, monogrammatic* and *epigrammatic,* as well as *epigrammatize,* require a double *-m.* Either *monogramed* or *monogrammed* is correct, the latter being more popular.

DOUBLING FINAL -N

If a one-syllable word ends in a single *-n,* preceded by a single vowel (*pan, thin,* etc.), double the *-n* before adding *-ed, -er, -ing,* or any other prefix starting with a vowel.

pan—panned, panning
plan—planned, planner, planning
run—runner, running
thin—thinned, thinner, thinnest, thinning

DOUBLING FINAL -P

1. If a one-syllable word ends in -*p* preceded by a single vowel (*cup, drop, lap*), double the -*p* before a suffix beginning with a *vowel* (-*er*, -*ing*, -*ed*, -*y*, etc.).

cup—cupping   tip—tipped
drop—dropped   trip—tripped
lap—lapping   stop—stopped
map—mapping   whip—whipped

2. If a word of more than one syllable fulfills all the requirements of Section 1, double the -*p* if the accent falls on the *last syllable*.

equip—equipped, etc.
reship—reshipped, etc.

(Remember that the suffix must start with a vowel if these rules are applicable. *Equip* plus -*ment*, for example, has only one -*p*—*equipment*.)

3. Even though the accent falls on the last syllable, as in *equip*, only one -*p* is used if the accent *shifts back* to a previous syllable after the suffix has been added, as in *equip*—*equipage*, in the latter of which words the accent is now on the first syllable (EK-wi-pij).

4. If, however, the accent does *not* fall on the last syllable, the -*p* is *not* doubled.

develop—developed, developer, developing
envelop—enveloped, enveloping
gallop—galloped, galloping
kidnap—kidnaped, kidnaper, kidnaping
wallop—walloped, walloping
worship—worshiped, worshiper, worshiping

(These derived forms are often spelled with a double -*p*, but the single -*p* is preferable.)

DOUBLING FINAL -R

1. If final -*r* is preceded by a single vowel in a one-syllable word (*blur, fur,* etc.), double the -*r* when adding a suffix beginning with a vowel (-*ed*, -*er*, -*ing*, -*y*).

bar—barred, barring
blur—blurred, blurring, blurry
char—charred, charring
fur—furred, furry
jar—jarred, jarring
mar—marred, marring
slur—slurred, slurring
spar—sparred, sparring
stir—stirred, stirrer, stirring
whir—whirred, whirring

2. In a word of more than one syllable, *accent* determines whether or not the -*r* is doubled. If the accent falls on the *last* syllable, double the -*r*.

concur—concurred, concurrence, concurring
confer—conferred, conferring
defer—deferred, deferring
demur—demurral, demurred, demurring
deter—deterred, deterrence, deterring
disbar—disbarred, disbarring
incur—incurred, incurrence, incurring
infer—inferred, inferring
inter—interred, interring
occur—occurred, occurrence, occurring
prefer—preferred, preferring
recur—recurred, recurrence, recurring
refer—referred, referring

3. Look back for a moment now to Section 2. Notice that the accent not only falls on the last syllable of *demur,* but remains on that syllable (i.e., on -*mur*) in *demurral, demurred,* and *demurring.* A similar process may be observed in *occur, recur, incur,* and *deter*—the accent remains fixed when a suffix is added.

However, something different happens when -*ence* is added to *infer.* We say in-FER, accent on the last syllable, on the -*fer.* But we say IN-fer-ence, the accent shifting back to an earlier syllable. The same phenomenon, a back-shifting of accent, takes place in the following words and in such instances the final -r is *not* doubled.

con-FER   conference (CON-)
de-FER   deference (DEF-)
pre-FER   preference, preferable
           (PREF-)
re-FER   reference (REF-)

4. *Infer,* as we have realized, is accented on the last syllable (*-fer*). In *inference* the accent shifts back to the first syllable (*in-*); in *inferential* it shifts forward to the next syllable (*-ren*); both words have only one -r.

5. In *inferable,* though the accent remains on the *-fer* (in-FER-a-b'e), only one -r is used. This is a glaring exception to the rule, but then it is the rare rule in spelling that has no exception. Spell the same word *inferrible,* a completely acceptable form, and the rule is intact again— accent remains stationary on the last syllable, double final -r.

6. With the forms of *refer* we are on solider ground. In *referred* and *referring,* since there is no accent shift, we double the -r. Similarly in the following:

referrable *or* referrible (re-FER-ab'l)
referral (re-FER-'l)
referrer (re-FER-er)

7. But in the following the accent shifts in either direction off the *fer*— hence one -r.

reference (REF-er-ence)
referable (REF-er-ab'l)
   (same word as *referrable,* but
   pronounced differently)
referee (REF-er-EE)
referendum (REF-er-EN-dum)
referent (REF-er-ent)
referential (REF-e-REN-sh'l)

8. To summarize, then:

A. Single-syllable words ending in -r preceded by a single vowel:

double the -r when adding a suffix that starts with a vowel.

B. In words of more than one syllable, double the -r if the accent falls on the *last* syllable and remains on that syllable in the derived forms. If the accent shifts, use only one -r.

C. If the accent does *not* fall on the last syllable (*suffer,* for example), do *not* double the -r in derived forms.

alter—altered, altering
sever—severed, severing
suffer—suffered, suffering
succor—succored, succoring

DOUBLING FINAL -T

(These rules apply, bear in mind, to words that end in a single -t preceded by a single vowel, when a suffix starting with a vowel is added.)

1. In one-syllable words always double final *-t.*

pat—patted
spot—spotty
twit—twitting

2. In words of more than one syllable, double the *-t* if the accent falls on the last syllable.

a-BUT—abuttal, abutted
ac-QUIT—acquittal, acquitted
ad-MIT—admittance, admitted
al-LOT—allotted, allotting
com-MIT—committal, committed,
   committee
o-MIT—omitted, omitting
per-MIT—permitted, permitting
re-GRET—regrettable, regretting
sub-MIT—submitted, submitting
trans-MIT—transmittal, transmitted,
   transmitting

3. However, if the accent does *not* fall on the last syllable, do not double final *-t.*

BAN-quet—banqueted, banqueter,
   banqueting
BEN-e-fit—benefited, benefiting
COR-set—corseted
COV-et—coveted, coveting,
   covetous

dis-COM-fit—discomfited, discomfiting, discomfiture

in-HIB-it—inhibited, inhibiting, inhibition

MER-it—merited, meriting, meritorious

PROF-it—profitable, profited, profiting

pro-HIB-it—prohibited, prohibiting, prohibition

RIV-et—riveted, riveter, riveting

VIS-it—visited, visiting, visitor

VAL-et—valeted, valeting

4. The verb *combat* may be accented on the last syllable. Preferably, it is pronounced COM-bat; hence the *-t* is preferably *not* doubled.

combatant (only allowable spelling)

combated (though in this and the next word a double *-t* may be used)

combating

5. In the words *ricochet* and *crochet* the final syllable is pronounced *AY*, and the *-t* is preferably not doubled.

6. When a verb is made up of a one-syllable word plus a prefix, the *-t* is doubled, no matter where the accent falls.

befit—befitting
half-wit—half-witted
outfit—outfitted, etc.
outrun—outrunning
outsit—outsitting
outwit—outwitted, etc.
unfit—unfitted, etc.

---

doudy. Misspelling of *dowdy*.
doughnut, donut. See -OUGH. -O.
dour. See -OUR, -OWER, -AUER, 1.
dowdy. Not *doudy*.
dowery. See *dowry*.

DOWN-, -DOWN

Most compounds with *down-* are written solid: *downcast, downcome, downfall, downhearted,* etc.

However, the following are hy-

phenated: *down-beat, down-bow, down-East, down-Easter, down-wind.*

Down-and-out is hyphenated when used as an adjective preceding its noun (*down-and-out* drifters), otherwise written separate (No one is ever completely *down and out*).

When *-down* is used as a noun suffix, it is again written solid: *breakdown, comedown, markdown,* etc.

---

downward, downwards. Use only the first spelling as an *adjective;* use either form as an *adverb*. (See -ARD, -ARDS.)

dowry, dowery. The first spelling is preferable.

draft, draught. *Draft* is the proper spelling for most meanings of the word; *draught* is somewhat commoner for a drink, etc., as a *draught* of ale, or beer on *draught,* but even here the simpler spelling is gaining ground.

drafting, draughting. Both spellings are used for the art or process of making drawings or sketches, with the former becoming more and more popular.

draftsman, draughtsman. Both spellings popular—you have, at the present, a completely free choice.

dragged, dragging, draggy. Double final *-g* of *drag* before adding a suffix starting with a vowel. (See DOUBLING FINAL -G.)

draught. See *draft*.

DRAW-

Most compounds with *draw-* are written solid: *drawback, drawbridge, drawstring,* etc.

Draw poker is two words.

---

drawing room. No hyphen, unless used as an adjective preceding its noun (*drawing-room conversation, drawing-room comedy,* etc.). (See HYPHENATING, 3B.)

dreadnought. Note that the pattern is *-ought*. (See -AUGHT, -OUGHT.)

DRESS-, DRESSING-

Noun compounds with these words usually are written separate (*dress circle, dress shirt, dressing gown, dressing room,* etc.).

Dressmaker and *dressmaking* are solid; *dressing-down* is hyphenated.

---

dried, dries. The *-y* of the verb *dry* changes to *-i* before *-ed* or *-es.* (See -Y PLUS A SUFFIX, 1.)

drier, driest. The *-y* of *dry* changes to *-i* before *-er* and *-est.* (See -IER, -IEST, 2.)

drier, dryer. Either spelling acceptable for one who, or that which, dries.

drily. See *dryly.*

driness. Misspelling of *dryness.*

droop, drupe. See -OOP, -OUP, -UPE, 3G.

dropped, dropping. Final *-p* of *drop* is doubled before a suffix beginning with a vowel. (See DOUBLING FINAL -P, 1.)

DROPPED -E

If a word ends in a single *-e* preceded by one or more consonants (*come, arrive, use, bone,* etc.), drop the *-e* before adding a suffix that starts with a vowel (*-al, -ous, -able, -y, -ing, -ed, er, est,* etc.)

ache—aching
advise—advisable
argue—arguable
   (as used here, *-u* functions as a consonant)
arrive—arrival
austere—austerity
bone—bony
   (*-y,* here, as in many words, functions as a vowel)
come—coming
desire—desirous
face—facing
imagine—imaginable
pore—porous
use—using
waste—wasting

See also -ABLE, -EABLE: RE-TAINED -E.

---

drought, drouth. Either spelling correct, the first preferable. Same holds for the adjectives *droughty, drouthy.*

drowsy. Not *drowzy* or *drousey.*

drunkenness. The adjective *drunken* (as in *a drunken bum*) plus *-ness,* hence two *-n*'s toward the end. No such word, or spelling, as *drunkeness, drunkardness,* or *drunkedness.* (See -NESS AFTER N-.)

drupe, droop. See -OOP, -OUP, -UPE, 3G.

DRY-

Noun compounds with *dry-* are generally separate: *dry cell, dry cleaners, dry cleaning, dry dock,* etc.

Verb and adjective compounds, however, are hyphenated: *dry-clean, dry-dock, dry-farm, dry-eyed,* etc. See also HYPHENATING, 4.

---

dry, drys. A *dry,* colloquially, is one who believes in, or advocates, Prohibition; two or more of them are *drys.* (See *dried, dries;* -EYS, -IES, -YS, 4.)

dryer. See *drier, dryer.*

dryly, drily. The former spelling is preferred. (See -LY, 3.)

dryness. In words of one syllable, such as *dry,* final *-y* is retained before *-ness.* (See -Y PLUS A SUFFIX, 7.)

drys. Correct form for those who support Prohibition.

DUAL, DUEL

Dual refers to two—a *dual* nature, reason, etc.

Duel is a contest between two people—fight a *duel,* a verbal *duel,* etc. The *-l* of the verb is preferably not doubled before a suffix—*dueled, dueler, dueling, duelist.*

---

dually. Note the double *-l,* since the adverbial suffix *-ly* is added to the adjective *dual.* (See -LY, 7.)

dubbed, dubbing. The *-b* of *dub* is

doubled when a suffix is added. (See DOUBLING FINAL -B.)

duel, dueled, dueling. See DUAL, DUEL.

duet. Despite the apparently analogous *quartette* and *quintette, duette* does not exist.

dugout. No hyphen. (See HYPHEN-ATING, 3A.)

dullness. Double -*l* in all derived forms of *dull—duller, dulled, dullness, dulling,* etc. However, *dulness* is an acceptable, but not particularly common, variant of *dullness.*

dully. Only two -*l*'s even though -*ly* has been added to *dull.* (See -LY, 8.)

dulness. See *dullness.*

duly. Though an exception to the general rule, final -*e* of *due* is dropped before the suffix -*ly.* (See -LY, 9; RETAINED -E, 2.)

dumfound, dumbfound. Preferably spelled without the -*b.*

dupe. See -OOP, -OUP, -UPE, 3H.

duplicator. Ends in -*or.* (See -ER, -OR, 5.)

durable. Since -*a* is the principal vowel in another form of the word (*duration*), the correct ending is -*able.* (See -ABLE, -IBLE, 5.)

duteous. Not *dutious,* though *dutiable* is correct.

dwarf. For plural see PLURALIZING WORDS IN TERMINAL -F OR -FE, 4B.

DYE, DIE

To change the color of is to *dye*—the past is *dyed,* the present participle is *dyeing* (note that -*e*), the person who *dyes* is a *dyer.*

Die, to quit life, is *died* in the past, *dying* (no -*e*) in the participle.

---

dying. Participle of *die,* -*ie* changing to -*y* before -*ing.* (See -IE TO -Y.)

dynamo. Pluralize by adding -*s* only: *dynamos.* (See PLURALIZING WORDS IN TERMINAL -O, 2.)

DYS-

Words that start with the prefix *dys-* are for the most part medical terms:

dysentery	dysphoria
dysfunction	dyspnea
dysmenorrhea	dystrophy
dyspepsia	dysuria

If a word has no direct or indirect medical significance, it is more than likely to start with *dis-.*
See also DIS-, DISS-.

---

dysentery. One of the few words with both a primary and secondary accent ending in -*ery,* rather than -*ary.* (See -ARY, -ERY, 2; DYS-.)

E

-EABLE, -ABLE. See -ABLE, -EABLE.

EAR-

Compounds with *ear-* are solid (*earache, eardrum, earphone, earring,* etc.) except for *ear drops* (the medication), and the adjectives *ear-minded* and *ear-shaped,* which are hyphenated.

-EARED

All adjective compounds are hyphenated: *big-eared, flap-eared, long-eared,* etc.

---

earnest. Noun or adjective, spelled *ear-.* The man's name may be *Earnest* or *Ernest,* depending on how the owner of the name wants it.

EARTH-

Adjective compounds are hyphenated: *earth-dwelling, earth-shaking, earth-wide,* etc., except for *earthborn,* and *earthbred,* written solid. Most noun compounds are solid:

earthquake, earthworks, earthworm, etc.

eavesdropper. One who, as it were, stands under the eaves of a house to listen, hence the spelling of the first syllable.

ebullience. Most often *-ence,* rather than *-ance,* follows *i-.* (See -ANCE, -ENCE, AFTER I-, 1.)

ebullient. See *ebullience.*

echo. One of the few words ending in *-o* that are pluralized by the addition of *-es: echoes.* (See PLURALIZING WORDS IN TERMINAL -O, 1.)

echoed, echoing. Correct spelling for the derivative forms of *echo.* (See -O, TERMINAL.)

ecstasy. Note that the ending is *-sy,* not *-cy.* (See -CY, -SY, 4.)

-ECTION, -EXION

For a few words that in America are spelled *-ection* (*connection, deflection, inflection,* etc.) the British often use the ending *-exion* (*connexion, deflexion, inflexion*); since only an Englishman would know intuitively when to use which suffix, it is not a style that an American can safely copy.

However, on either side of the Atlantic, the only correct pattern is *complexion*—the word is derived from Latin *complexio,* not from a verb *complect.* Hence authorities frown on the usage *dark-complected,* preferring *dark-complexioned.*

---

edible. Note that the ending is *-ible,* not *-able.* (See -IBLE, -ABLE, 1.)

Edipus, edipal. See *Oedipus, Oedipal.*

editor. Ends in *-or.* (See -ER, -OR, 5.)

editor in chief. Preferably not hyphenated. Plural is *editors in chief.* (See HYPHENATING, 5B.)

educable. Only the *-able* ending will keep the preceding *-c* "hard." (See -ABLE, -IBLE, 6.)

educator. Ends in *-or.* (See -ER, -OR, 5.)

-EER

A recurrent problem presents itself when we need to add *-er* to words ending in *-ee* (*free, see,* etc.) —how many *-e*'s do we finally have? *Freer* doesn't seem quite right as the comparative of *free,* nor *seer* for *one who sees;* yet who ever heard of *freeer* or *seeer* with their triple *-e*'s? Perhaps the hyphenated *free-er* and *see-er* are the most sensible compromises? No compromises are allowed—if our word ends in *-ee,* we add only *-r,* and try to become accustomed to a pattern that is not pronounced the way it looks.

agree—agreer
  (one who agrees)
decree—decreer
disagree—disagreer
flee—fleer
free—freer, freest
guarantee—guaranteer
  (i.e., one who *guarantees;* but the more common form is *guarantor*)
oversee—overseer
  (pronounced O-ver-see-er)
see—seer
  (pronounced SERE for a prophet, SEE-er for one who sees)
unfree—unfreer, unfreest

---

e'er (poetic). Contraction of *ever,* the apostrophe appearing in place of the missing *-v.* (See APOSTROPHE, USE OF, 1.)

EFFECT, AFFECT. See AFFECT, EFFECT.

EFFECTIVE, AFFECTIVE, AFFECTING

Effective means *producing the required effect* (an *effective* antidote), or *striking and impressive* (an *effective* speech).

Affective refers to the feelings and

is a synonym of *emotional*. It is mostly used in psychological parlance or literature (*affective* results of protracted illness, *affective* changes in the personality, etc.)

Affecting means *emotionally touching, stirring,* or *moving* (an *affecting play or book, appeal for help,* etc.)

---

effervesce. Note the *-esce* ending. (See -ESCE, -ESCENT, -ESCENCE, 1.)

effervescence. Note the *-sc* and the *-ence* ending. (See -ANCE, -ENCE, AFTER C-, 5.)

effervescent. See *effervescence.*

efficient. The combination *-ie,* rather than *-ei,* is always used when the preceding *-c* has the sound of *sh.* (See -IE, EI, 12.)

efflorescent. Note the *-ent* ending. (See -ESCE, -ESCENT, -ESCENCE, 2.)

effluence. Always *-ence,* not *-ance,* after *-fl.* (See -ANCE, -ENCE, AFTER U-, 2.)

effluvium. The plural is either *effluvia* or *effluviums.* (See PLURALIZING WORDS IN TERMINAL -UM, 1.)

-EFY, -IFY. See -IFY, -EFY.

EGG-

Nouns with *egg-* are mostly solid: *eggcup, egghead, eggnogs, eggplant,* etc. *Egg cell* is two words.

Egg-shaped, as an adjective, is hyphenated.

---

egis. See *aegis.*

EGOIST, EGOTIST

Although the two words are often used interchangeably, there is a clear area of distinction worth observing. The *egotist* constantly talks about himself, and always in terms of extreme, often obnoxious, self-approval. He is boastful and conceited, and tries everlastingly to impress others with his accomplishments, abilities, brilliance, or importance. The *egoist* on the other hand, pursues a policy of self-seeking; his own interests, desires, and welfare are the prime considerations that motivate his behavior. In ethics, *egoism* is the doctrine that self-interest is the conscious determining factor in an individual's actions, i.e., whatever one does is, ultimately, self-serving.

-EI, -IE. See -IE, -EI

EIGHT-. See HYPHENATING, 49D, E.

---

eighth. *Eight* plus *-th,* but only one *-t* all the same.

eights. The plural of the number, when written as a word, requires no apostrophe. As a figure, the apostrophe is preferable, but may be omitted: 8's or 8s. (See APOSTROPHE, USE OF, 2, 3.)

EIGHTY-. See HYPHENATING, 49A.

-eign. *-EI,* rather than *-ie,* is the correct spelling in words in which the next letters are *-gn: foreign, reign, sovereign,* etc. (See -IE, -EI, 6, 10.)

either. Note the *-ei* combination; this is an exception to the rule of *-i* before *-e* except after *c-.* (See -IE, -EI, 4.)

-EL, -ELL

1. Words of one syllable will of course end in *-ell: bell, fell, knell, shell,* etc.

2. Verbs of two or more syllables (except for combinations like *retell,* etc.) will end in *-el* no matter where the accent falls: *compel, dispel, excel, expel, impel, propel, rebel, repel; jewel, travel, revel,* etc. (For derived forms of these verbs see DOUBLING FINAL -L.)

3. Note that *lapel* and *parallel* both end in a single *-l*.
See also -AL, -ALL; -IL, -ILL; -OL, -OLL.

elbow grease. Separate words.
elbowroom. Solid word.
-elect. See HYPHENATING, 8.
elector. Ends in -or. (See -ER, -OR, 5.)
electrolysis, electrolytic. Note the *-y* after the *l-*, as in the verb *electrolyze*. (See -IZE, -YZE, 6.)
electrolyze. One of the rare verbs ending in *-yze*. (See -IZE, -YZE, 5.)
elegance. Because of the "hard" *-g*, *-ance*, not *-ence*. (See -ANCE, -ENCE, AFTER G-, 1.)
elementary. Ends in *-ary*. (See -ARY, -ERY, 1.)
elevator. Ends in *-or* for all meanings of the word. (See -ER, -OR, 5.)
elf. The plural is *elves*. (See PLURALIZING WORDS IN TERMINAL -F OR -FE, 1.)
eligible. The ending is *-ible* to keep the preceding *-g* "soft." (See -IBLE, -ABLE, 6.)

-ELL, -EL. See -EL, -ELL.

ellipse. Double *-l*.
ellipsis. Plural is *ellipses*. (See PLURALIZING WORDS IN TERMINAL -IS.)
eloquence. Always *-ence*, not *-ance* after *qu-*. (See -ANCE, -ENCE, AFTER U-, 1.)
elude. See ALLUDE, ELUDE.
embargo. One of the few words ending in *-o* that are pluralized by the addition of *-es* only: *embargoes*. (See PLURALIZING WORDS IN TERMINAL -O, 1.)
embarrassed. One of the ten most frequently misspelled words in the language. The mnemonic *Two robbers* (two *-r*'s) *were embarrassed in Sing Sing* (two *-s*'s) helps most people. Notice also the word *ass*—you are

embarrassed if you make an *ass* of yourself.
embarrassment. Note that this word is a combination of the verb *embarrass* plus the suffix *-ment*, hence no *-e* after the double *s-*. (See -MENT, 1.)
embraceable. The *-e* is retained before *-able* in order to preserve the original "soft" pronunciation of the preceding *-c*. (See -CEABLE.)
embryo. A word ending in *-o* preceded by a vowel is pluralized by the addition of *-s* only: *embryos*. (See PLURALIZING WORDS IN TERMINAL -O, 3.)
emergence. Because of the "soft" *-g*, *-ence*, not *-ance*. (See -ANCE, -ENCE, AFTER G-, 4.)
emergency. See *emergence*.

EMIGRATE, IMMIGRATE

A person *emigrates from* one country or region to settle in another. He is then called an *emigrant*, or, if you wish to be elegant, an *émigré*.

He *immigrates to* the country or region in which he plans to settle—from the point of view of his new home, he is an *immigrant*.

eminence. Somewhat more words end in *-ence* than *-ance* after *n-*, this among others. (See -ANCE, -ENCE, AFTER N-, 1.)
eminent. See *eminence*.
emphatically. Note the *-ally* ending, common to adverbs formed from adjectives ending in *-ic*. (See -LY, -ALLY, 1.)

EMPTY-

Adjective compounds are all hyphenated: *empty-handed*, *empty-headed*, *empty-minded*, etc.

EN-, IN-

A number of English words may start with either the prefix *en-* or *in-* with no change of meaning.

1. In the following, *en-* is by far the more popular, and therefore the preferable, form, although the *in-* spelling is also correct.

encase	enthrone
endorse	entitle
endure	entomb
enfold	entrench
engraft	entrust
engulf	entwine
enmesh	entwist
ensnare	enwrap
enswathe	enwreathe

2. *Enclose* and *inclose* are used with about equal frequency, or perhaps there is a slight edge for *en-*. The same holds for *enclosure* and *inclosure*. Take your choice.

3. In the following, *in-* is the preferable first syllable, although here again the form with *en-* is also correct.

ingrain	insure
inquire	insurance
inquiry	inure

4. Only *en-* may be used for these: *encamp, enforce, engrave, enrich, enshrine, entangle.*

5. But *reinforce* is somewhat preferable to *re-enforce*, with both correct.

6. Only *in-* may be used for these: *incorporate, indoctrinate, infiltrate, invoke.*

enameled, enameler, enameling. Because *enamel* is *not* accented on the last syllable, final *-l* is *not* doubled before a suffix beginning with a vowel. Double *-l* forms are acceptable, but single *-l* forms are far preferable. (See DOUBLING FINAL -L, 2.)

encamp. Never spelled *incamp*. (See EN-, IN-, 4.)

encase. Preferable to *incase*. (See EN-, IN-, 1.)

-ENCE, -ANCE, AFTER C-. See -ANCE, -ENCE, AFTER C-.

-ENCE, -ANCE, AFTER D-. See -ANCE, -ENCE, AFTER D-.

-ENCE, -ANCE, AFTER G-. See -ANCE, -ENCE, AFTER G-.

-ENCE, -ANCE, AFTER I-. See -ANCE, -ENCE, AFTER I-.

-ENCE, -ANCE, AFTER L-. See -ANCE, -ENCE, AFTER L-.

-ENCE, -ANCE, AFTER N-. See -ANCE, -ENCE, AFTER N-.

-ENCE, -ANCE, AFTER R-. See -ANCE, -ENCE, AFTER R-.

-ENCE, -ANCE, AFTER T-. See -ANCE, -ENCE, AFTER T-.

-ENCE, -ANCE, AFTER U-. See -ANCE, -ENCE, AFTER U-.

-ENCE, -ANCE, AFTER V-. See -ANCE, -ENCE, AFTER V-.

-ENCE, -ENSE

1. Where doubt exists, the safer ending is *-ence*, most words of more than one syllable so terminating: *consequence, difference, experience,* etc.

2. The notable exceptions are the American spellings of:

defense license pretense offense (British custom ends these words in *-ence*.)

3. The following words, among others, also end in *-ense*, but rarely present a spelling problem: *condense, sense, dense, intense, recompense, suspense, tense, incense, frankincense, dispense.*

enceinte. Note the *-ei.*

enclose, inclose. Both spellings correct and about equal in popularity. Consider that you have a free choice, as long as you're consistent. (See EN-, IN-, 2.)

enclosure, inclosure. See *enclose, inclose.*

encorporate. Misspelling of *incorporate.*

encourageable. The *-e* of *encourage* is retained before *-able* in order to preserve the original "soft" (or *j*) pronunciation of the *-g.* (See -GEABLE.)

encouragement. The final *-e* of *encourage* is retained before a suffix that starts with a consonant. (See RETAINED -E, 1.)

encyclopedia, encyclopaedia. The latter is quite old-fashioned, almost obsolete.

endeavor, endeavour. The first spelling is American, the second British. (See -OR, -OUR, 1.)

endoctrinate. Misspelling of *indoctrinate.*

endorse. Preferable to *indorse.* (See EN-, IN-, 1.)

endue. Preferable to *indue.* (See EN-, IN-, 1.)

endurance. The suffix *-ance* invariably attaches to a noun formed from a verb ending in *-ure.* (See -ANCE, -ENCE, AFTER R-, 9.)

endure. Preferable to *indure.* (See EN-, IN-, 1.)

enemy. The second vowel is *-e,* not *-a.*

enfiltrate. Misspelling of *infiltrate.*

enfold. Preferable to *infold.* (See EN-, IN-, 1.)

enforce. Never spelled *inforce.* (See EN-, IN-, 4.)

enforceable. The *-e* is retained before *-able* in order to preserve the original "soft" pronunciation of the preceding *-c.* (See -CEABLE.)

engageable. The *-e* of *engage* is retained before *-able* in order to preserve the original "soft" (or *j*) pronunciation of the preceding *-g.* (See -GEABLE.)

engraft. Preferable to *ingraft.* (See EN-, IN-, 1.)

engrain. See *ingrain.*

engrave. Never spelled *ingrave.* (See EN-, IN-, 4.)

engulf. Preferable to *ingulf.* (See EN-, IN-, 1.)

enjoyed, enjoying, enjoyment. Since the terminal *-y* of *enjoy* follows a vowel, it does *not* change to *-i* before a suffix. (See -Y PLUS A SUFFIX, 9.)

enmesh. Preferable to *inmesh.* (See EN-, IN-, 1.)

enquire. See *inquire.*

enquiry. See *inquiry.*

enrageable. The *-e* of *enrage* is retained before *-able* in order to preserve the original "soft" (or *j*) pronunciation of the *-g.* (See -GEABLE.)

enrich. Never spelled *inrich.* (See EN-, IN-, 4.)

enroll, enrol. First spelling, with the double *-l,* preferable. Likewise in *enrollment, enrolment.*

enrolled, enrolling. Double *-l* in both these derived forms. (See -OL, -OLL, 2.)

-ENSE, -ENCE. See -ENCE, -ENSE.

---

enshrine. Never spelled *inshrine.* (See EN-, IN-, 4.)

-ENSION, -ENTION

It is no easy matter to decide whether a noun ends in *-ension* or *-ention.* The best method is reliance on one's visual memory. If that doesn't serve, and both spellings look good enough, it occasionally helps to think of another form of the word; an *-s* in that form indicates *-ension,* and *-t* indicates *-ention.* (Where possible, other forms will be given in parenthesis.) Notice, also, that if the preceding letter is *-h,* the ending is *-ension;* if it is *-v,* the ending is *-ention.*

-ENSION
apprehension (apprehensive)
comprehension (comprehensive)

condescension
declension
dimension
dissension
extension (extensive)
misapprehension
pretension (pretense)
suspension
tension (tense)

-ENTION

abstention
attention (attentive)
circumvention (circumvent)
contention
contravention
convention
detention
distention
intention (intent)
intervention
invention (inventive)
prevention
retention (retentive)

---

ensnare. Preferable to *insnare*. (See EN-, IN-, 1.)

ensurance. See *insurance*.

ensure. See *insure*.

enswathe. Preferable to *inswathe*. (See EN-, IN-, 1.)

-ENT AFTER C-. See -ANCE, -ENCE, AFTER C-.

-ENT AFTER D-. See -ANCE, -ENCE, AFTER D-.

-ENT AFTER G-. See -ANCE, -ENCE, AFTER G-.

-ENT AFTER I-. See -ANCE, -ENCE, AFTER I-.

-ENT AFTER L-. See -ANCE, -ENCE, AFTER L-.

-ENT AFTER N-. See -ANCE, -ENCE, AFTER N-.

-ENT AFTER R-. See -ANCE, -ENCE, AFTER R-.

-ENT AFTER T-. See -ANCE, -ENCE, AFTER T-.

-ENT AFTER U-. See -ANCE, -ENCE, AFTER U-.

-ENT AFTER V-. See -ANCE, -ENCE, AFTER V-.

---

entangle. Never spelled *intangle*. (See EN-, IN-, 4.)

enterprise. Note the *-ise* ending, common to words ending in *-prise*. (See -ISE, 4.)

enthrall, enthral. The form with two *-l's* is preferable; and derived forms *enthralled, enthralling* must have two *-l's*. (See -AL, -ALL, 4.)

enthrallment, enthralment. The first spelling is preferable. (See -AL, -ALL, 4.)

enthrone. Preferable to *inthrone*. (See EN-, IN-, 1.)

-ENTION, -ENSION. See -ENSION, -ENTION.

---

entitle. Preferable to *intitle*. (See EN-, IN-, 1.)

entomb. Preferable to *intomb*. (See EN-, IN-, 1.)

entomology. See ETYMOLOGY, ENTOMOLOGY.

entreat. Preferable to *intreat*. (See EN-, IN-, 1.)

entrench. Preferable to *intrench*. (See EN-, IN-, 1.)

entrepreneur. Note the French ending.

entrust. Preferable to *intrust*. (See EN-, IN-, 1.)

entwine. Preferable to *intwine*. (See EN-, IN-, 1.)

entwist. Preferable to *intwist*. (See EN-, IN-, 1.)

enure. See *inure*.

ENVELOP, ENVELOPE

The first spelling is a verb (clouds *envelop* the earth), the second a noun (an *envelope* of gas). *Envelop* may also be used as a noun, but in practice rarely is.

---

enveloped, enveloping. Single *-p* in these derived forms, since the accent does *not* fall on the last syllable of *envelop*. (See DOUBLING FINAL -P, 4.)

envelopment. Note that this word is a combination of the verb *envelop* plus the suffix *-ment;* hence no *-e* after the *p-*. (See -MENT, 1.)

enviable. *-Able* is the correct suffix after the letter *i-*. (See -ABLE, -IBLE, 3.)

envoke. Misspelling of *invoke*.

enwrap. Preferable to *inwrap*. (See EN-, IN-, 1.)

enwreathe. Preferable to *inwreathe*. (See EN-, IN-, 1.)

eon. See *aeon*.

epaulet, epaulette. The shorter spelling is preferable. (See -ET, -ETTE, 1.)

EPICURE, EPICUREAN

An *epicure* is a connoisseur of good food and drink; an *epicurean* (ep-i-kyoo-REE-'n) gets a kick out of all luxurious living, including the pleasures of the table. As an adjective, *epicurean* may refer to either of the two words.

---

epigrammatic, epigrammatize. Require a double *-m*.

epilogue, epilog. The longer spelling is preferable. (See -OGUE, -OG, 1.)

equator. Ends in *-or*. (See -ER, -OR, 5.)

equilibrium. For plural see PLURAL-IZING WORDS IN TERMINAL -UM, 3.

equipage. Single *-p*. (See DOUBLING FINAL -P, 3.)

equipment. A combination of the verb *equip* plus the suffix *-ment;* hence no *-e* after the *p-*. (See -MENT, 1.)

equipped, equipping. Double *-p*. (See DOUBLING FINAL -P, 2.)

equitable. Note the *-able* ending. (See -ABLE, -IBLE, 7.)

equivalence. Generally *l-* is followed by *-ence*, rather than *-ance*. (See -ANCE, -ENCE, AFTER L-, 1, 3.)

equivalent. See *equivalence*.

-ER, -OR

1. Both suffixes indicate the doer of an action. Since *-er* can be added to almost any verb, it is of course the commoner ending and rarely causes any difficulty (*answerer, banisher, bargainer, gossiper, thunderer,* etc.). However, the following, which do not have complete verbs as the stem, are worth noting.

arbiter	prisoner
idolater	sorcerer
mariner	usurer

2. *Adviser* is the commoner spelling; *advisor,* with the same meaning precisely, is also correct.

3. Whether the simple doer of an action, or one who takes part in theatricals, etc., *actor* is the correct spelling.

4. A *wagerer* is either a *better* or a *bettor,* the latter being the commoner form for those around a poker table, customers of bookies, and frequenters of the pari-mutuel windows at race tracks.

5. The following, all of which end in *-or*, are the words that cause the most perplexity to less-than-perfect spellers.

accelerator	conspirator
administrator	contributor
ambassador	depositor
ancestor	distributor
aviator	educator
bachelor	elevator
commentator	escalator
competitor	exhilarator
conqueror	fabricator

impostor   prevaricator
indicator   protector
inheritor   radiator
inventor   senator
investigator   spectator
investor   supervisor
orator   survivor
predecessor   visitor

-ER, -RE

1. The modernized *-er* ending has almost completely replaced the older *-re* in the following words.

caliber   reconnoiter
center   saber
fiber   saltpeter
luster   scepter
maneuver   sepulcher
meager   somber
meter   specter
philter   theater

To spell these words *centre, metre,* etc., is to make one's writing conspicuous with old-fashioned elegance, though these forms are still current in Great Britain.

2. However, to keep the "hard" sound of *c,* the following end in *-re: acre, chancre* (pronounced SHANG-ker), *euchre* (pronounced YOO-ker), *lucre* (pronounced LOO-ker), *massacre* (pronounced MASS-a-ker), and *nacre* (pronounced NAY-ker).

3. In *acred* (AY-kerd), *chancrous* (SHANG-krus), *chancroid* (SHANG-kroyd), *euchred* (YOO-kerd), *euchring, massacred* (MASS-a-kerd), *massacring,* and *nacred* (NAY-kerd), final *-e* is dropped before the suffix *-ed, -ous,* or *-ing.*

4. In *acreage* (AY-ker-ij) and *nacreous* (NAY-ker-us) the *-e* is retained.

5. The word *ogre* (pronounced O-ger) may be spelled only as indicated. The feminine is *ogress* (O-gress); the adjective is preferably *ogreish* (O-ger-ish), but also *ogrish* (O-grish).

ernest. Misspelling of *earnest.*

erratum. The plural is *errata.* (See PLURALIZING WORDS IN TERMINAL -UM, 1.)

-ERY, -ARY. See -ARY, -ERY.

escalator. Ends in *-or.* (See -ER, -OR, 5.)

-ESCE, -ESCENT, -ESCENCE

1. Note the following verbs, which end in *-esce.* (The *-c* is silent, of course, but cannot be ignored in the spelling.) The suffix generally, though not always, means *becoming* or *growing.*

acquiesce   effloresce
coalesce   evanesce
convalesce   intumesce
deliquesce   obsolesce
effervesce   opalesce
                phosphoresce

2. The adjective forms are spelled correspondingly: *acquiescent, coalescent, convalescent, deliquescent, effervescent, efflorescent, evanescent, intumescent, obsolescent, opalescent, phosphorescent.*

3. Other important *-escent* words:

adolescent   pubescent
crescent   putrescent
excrescent   quiescent
florescent   senescent
fluorescent   turgescent
incandescent   viridescent
iridescent

4. The nouns from Sections 2 and 3 end in *-escence* as expected: *acquiescence, coalescence,* etc.; *adolescence, excrescence,* etc.

5. But *quintessence* is spelled as noted, since the word is *essence* plus the prefix *quint-,* fifth.

Eskimo, Esquimau. The sensible first spelling has quite displaced the flossy *Esquimau.* Plural is *Eskimos* or *Esquimaux.* (See PLURALIZ-

ING WORDS IN TERMINAL -O,
2.)

esophagus, oesophagus. The former is
more modern and far more popular.
Note that the ending is *-gus,* not
-gous. (See -US, -OUS.)

especially. The adverbial ending *-ly*
is added to the adjective *especial,*
hence the double *-l.* (See -LY, 7;
-LY, -ALLY, 4.)

essayed, essaying. Since the terminal *-y*
of *essay* follows a vowel, it does *not*
change to *-i* before a suffix. (See -Y
PLUS A SUFFIX, 9.)

esthetic. See *aesthetic.*

estimable. Since *-a* is the principal vowel in another form of the
word (*estimate*), the correct ending is *-able.* (See -ABLE, -IBLE,
5.)

-ET, -ETTE

1. In some words you have a
choice; the simpler suffix is somewhat preferable, both forms are
correct.

> banneret, bannerette
> (i.e., a small flag)
> coquet, coquette
> (i.e., the verb *to coquet*)
> epaulet, epaulette
> octet, octette
> omelet, omelette
> quartet, quartette
> quintet, quintette
> septet, septette
> sextet, sextette

2. In others *-ette* is preferable, *-et*
also correct.

> baguette, baguet
> cigarette, cigaret
> corvette, corvet
> (i.e., the ship—the Chevrolet
> sports model is spelled only
> *Corvette*).
> kitchenette, kitchenet
> leatherette, leatheret
> pipette, pipet
> toilette, toilet
> (i.e., process of dressing—the

bathroom, of course, is only
toilet).

3. In the following only *-ette* is
correct.

anisette	mignonette
bathinette	novelette
brochette	pirouette
chemisette	roomette
coquette	rosette
(i.e., the person)	roulette
croquette	serviette
(i.e., the food)	silhouette
etiquette	soubrette
farmerette	statuette
gazette	suffragette
grisette	vedette
lorgnette	vignette
luncheonette	wagonette
marionette	

4. And, finally, in these only *-et*
is correct.

amulet	marmoset
banquet	martinet
(i.e., a feast)	minaret
baronet	motet
bassinet	parapet
bayonet	parquet
cadet	(pronounced
castanets	par-KAY)
cellaret	rivulet
clarinet	sestet
coverlet	taboret
croquet	toilet
(i.e., the game)	(i.e., the
epithet	bathroom)
flageolet	tourniquet
floweret	

---

etiquette. Only the *-ette* ending fully
acceptable. (See -ET, -ETTE, 3.)

ETYMOLOGY, ENTOMOLOGY
Though those words look and
sound somewhat alike, there is no
connection in meaning. *Etymology*
is the branch of linguistics that
traces the derivation and development of words. *Entomology* is the
science that deals with insects.

euchre. The ending is *-re* to keep the *-c* "hard." (See -ER, -RE, 2.)

euchred, euchring. See -ER, -RE, 3.

evanesce. Note the *-esce* ending. (See -ESCE, -ESCENT, -ESCENCE, 1.)

evanescence. Note the *-sc* and the *-ence* ending. (See -ANCE, -ENCE, AFTER C-, 5.)

evenness. The suffix *-ness* added to *even,* hence double *-n.* (See -NESS AFTER N-.)

evert. See AVERT, EVERT.

EVERY-

As a pronoun or adverb, compounds with *every-* are solid words. Otherwise, if *every* is clearly an adjective, two separate words are used.

> *solid—pronoun or adverb*
> Is *everybody* happy?
> Has *everyone* left?
> Is *everything* ready?
> We go *everywhere.*
> (always solid)
> *separate—adjective plus noun or pronoun*
> *Every body* (i.e., every corpse) was dug up
> *Every one* of his answers is wrong.
> *Every thing* (i.e., every object) was in place.
> *Every place* was taken.
> (always separate)

See also ANY-; NO-; SOME-.

---

everyday. As an adjective, preferably solid. Otherwise two words. (See HYPHENATING, 3A.)

every time. Always two words.

everywhere, everywheres. The *-s* form is in poor repute and should be avoided.

evesdropper. Misspelling of *eavesdropper.*

evidence. Almost always, with only a few exceptions, *-ence,* not *-ance,* follows a *d-.* (See -ANCE, -ENCE, AFTER D-, 1.)

evilly. Note the double *-l,* since the adverbial suffix *-ly* is added to the adjective *evil.* (See -LY, 7.)

evincible. The ending is *-ible* to keep the preceding *-c* "soft." (See -IBLE, -ABLE, 5.)

eviscerate. The *-c* is silent.

evocation. Note that the *-k* of *evoke* has changed to *-c* before the vowel *-a.* (See -K TO -C.)

evolutionary. Ends in *-ary.* (See -ARY, -ORY, 1.)

ex-. Hyphen follows this prefix when it means former, as in *ex-husband, ex-president,* etc. (See HYPHENATING, 37.)

exaggerate. Note the double *-g.*

excede. Misspelling of *exceed.*

exceed. One of the only three words ending in *-ceed.* (See -CEED, -SEDE, -CEDE, 1.)

excel. Ends in one *-l,* not two. (See -EL, -ELL, 2.)

excelled, excelling. Because *excel* is accented on the last syllable, final *-l* is doubled before a suffix starting with a vowel. (See DOUBLING FINAL -L, 1.)

excellence. Generally *-l* is followed by *-ence,* rather than *-ance.* And note the double *-l.* (See -ANCE, -ENCE, AFTER L-, 1, 3.)

excellent. See *excellence.*

EXCEPT, ACCEPT. See ACCEPT, EXCEPT.

---

exchequer. This highly British form is still retained in American spelling.

excise. One of five verbs ending in *-cise,* rather than *-cize.* (See -ISE, 6.)

excitable. Note that the ending is *-able,* not *-ible.* (See -ABLE, -IBLE, 2.)

excrescent. Note the *-sc.* (See -ESCE, -ESCENT, -ESCENCE, 3.)

excusable. Again, *-able,* not *-ible.* (See -ABLE, -IBLE, 2.)

executor. Ends in *-or.* (See -ER, -OR, 5.)

exemplary. Ends in *-ary.* (See -ARY, -ERY, 1.)

exercise. One of five words ending in *-cise,* rather than *-cize.* (See -ISE, 6.)

exhaustible. If the root forms its noun by the immediate addition of *-ion* (*exhaustion*), the correct ending is likely to be *-ible.* (See -IBLE, -ABLE, 2.)

exhibitor. Ends in *-or.*

exhilarate, exhilaration. Note the single *l-,* followed by *-a,* as in the related word *hilarious.*

exhilarator. See ACCELERATOR, EXHILARATOR.

exhort, exhortation. The *-h* is silent.

exigence, exigency. The "soft" *g-* must be followed by *-e,* not *-a.* (See -ANCE -ENCE, AFTER G-, 4.)

-EXION, -ECTION. See -ECTION, -EXION.

---

existence. Ends in *-ence.* (See -ANCE, -ENCE, AFTER T-, 3.)

existent. Ends in *-ent.* (See -ANCE, -ENCE, AFTER T-, 4.)

exorcise. Not to be confused with *exercise,* entirely unrelated in meaning. (See -ISE, 6.)

expansible. If the root forms its noun by the immediate addition of *-ion* (*expansion*), the correct ending is likely to be *-ible.* (See -IBLE, -ABLE, 2.)

expectant. Ends in *-ant,* not *-ent.* (See -ANCE, -ENCE, AFTER T-, 2.)

expedience. Most often, as here, *-ence,* rather than *-ance,* follows *i-.* (See -ANCE, -ENCE, AFTER I-, 1.)

expedient. See *expedience.*

expedition. Ends in *-ition.* (See -ICIOUS, -ITIOUS, 4.)

expeditious. Ends in *-itious,* not *-icious.* (See -ICIOUS, -ITIOUS, 3.)

expel. One *-l.* (See -EL, -ELL, 2.)

expeled, expelling. Double *-l* in these derived forms of *expel.* (See DOUBLING FINAL, -L, 1.)

expendable. Note that the ending is *-able,* not *-ible.* (See -ABLE, -IBLE, 1.)

expense. Not *expence.*

experience. Most often, as here, *-ence,* rather than *-ance,* follows *-i.* (See -ANCE, -ENCE, AFTER I-, 1.)

experimentally. Note that *-ly* is added to the adjective *experimental,* hence the *-ally* ending. (See -LY, -ALLY, 3.)

explanatory. The ending is *-ory.* (See -ARY, -ORY, 2.)

explicable. Only the *-able* ending will keep the preceding *-c* "hard." (See -ABLE, -IBLE, 6.)

expose, exposé. Use the accent (and pronounce it EX-po-ZAY) when the word is a noun meaning public disclosure of something discreditable; otherwise, as a verb, just plain *expose.*

expressible. If the root forms its noun by the immediate addition of *-ion* (*expression*), the correct ending is likely to be *-ible.* (See -IBLE, -ABLE, 2.)

extacy, extasy. Misspellings of *ecstasy.*

extension. Ends in *-ension.* (See -ENSION, -ENTION.)

extol. Ends in a single *-l.* (See -OL, -OLL, 4.)

extravagance, extravagant. Since the *g-* is hard, *-a,* not *-e,* follows it. (See -ANCE, -ENCE, AFTER G-, 1.)

exuberance. Ends in *-ance,* since the verb is *exuberate.* (See -ANCE, -ENCE, AFTER R-, 10.)

exuberant. Note the *-ant* ending. (See -ANCE, -ENCE, AFTER R-, 10A.)

EYE-

Noun compounds with *eye-* are written solid (*eyeglasses, eyelid, eyesore,* etc.), except for *eye opener* and *eye shadow,* which are separate.

Eye-minded, an adjective, has a hyphen.

-EYED

1. Compounds with *-eyed,* since they are adjectives, are hyphenated: *cross-eyed, gray-eyed, one-eyed, open-eyed,* etc.

2. Except for *cockeyed* and *wall-eyed,* written solid.

---

eyeing, eying. Either spelling is correct.

-EYS, -IES, -YS

1. Nouns that end in *-ey* are generally pluralized by the simple addition of *-s:*

> alley—alleys
> attorney—attorneys
> donkey—donkeys
> key—keys
> monkey—monkeys
> valley—valleys
> whiskey—whiskeys

2. *Money* may be pluralized either as *moneys* or, variantly, as *monies;* and the British spelling *storey* (of a building) is *storeys* in the plural, while American *story* is *stories.*

3. Nouns that end in *-y* preceded by a consonant are pluralized by changing *-y* to *-i* and adding *-es:*

> beauty—beauties
> dairy—dairies
> delivery—deliveries
> diary—diaries
> doily—doilies
> fly—flies
> lady—ladies
> sally—sallies
> sky—skies
> soliloquy—soliloquies
> spy—spies
> story—stories
> whisky—whiskies

4. But the plural of *guy* is *guys;* of *dry* (i.e., a Prohibitionist), *drys.*

5. If a proper name ends in *-y,* the plural is formed by adding *-s.*

> Dolly—Dollys
> Dorothy—Dorothys
> Harry—Harrys
> Jerry—Jerrys
> McCarthy—McCarthys
> Mary—Marys
> Sally—Sallys
> Timothy—Timothys

F

fabricator. Ends in *-or.* (See -ER, -OR, 5.)

FACE-

Noun compounds with *face-* are generally separate (*face card, face lifting, face powder*).

Face-about (i.e., an *about-face*) is hyphenated.

-FACED

Except for *catfaced, shamefaced, sheepfaced,* and *wheyfaced,* adjective compounds are hyphenated: *angel-faced, grim-faced, pasty-faced,* etc.

---

facing. The *-e* of *face* is dropped before a suffix beginning with a vowel. (See DROPPED -E.)

factitious. Ends in *-itious,* not *-icious.* (See -ICIOUS, -ITIOUS, 3.)

factor. Ends in *-or.* (See -ER, -OR, 5.)

Fahrenheit. Ends in *-eit;* always capitalized. (See -IE, -EI, 7.)

---

faint. See FEINT, FAINT.

fainthearted. Solid word. (See -HEARTED.)

fair. See FARE, FAIR.

FAIR-

Noun compounds are mostly separate: *fair ball, fair play, fair sex,* etc.

However, *fairgrounds* and *fairway* are solid.

Adjective compounds are hyphenated: *fair-haired, fair-minded, fair-weather* (friends), etc.

FAKER, FAKIR

A *faker* is one who fakes, or pretends; a *fakir* (pronounced fa-KEER or FAY-ker) is a member of a Moslem or Hindu sect in Asia. *Fakeer* is a less common spelling of *fakir*.

fallible. Note that the ending is *-ible*, not *-able*. (See -IBLE, -ABLE, 1.)

FAR-

Adjective compounds with *far-* are regularly hyphenated: *far-flung, far-famed, far-advanced,* etc., when preceding their nouns.
Farfetched, however, is solid.

FARE, FAIR

As a noun, *fare* is (a) payment for transportation, (b) a passenger, (c) the food one eats. As a verb, *fare* means happen, result, get along, or eat.
Fair is an adjective (*fair* weather, *fair* offer, etc.), or a noun denoting an exhibition, etc. (to hold a *fair*).

farfetched. Solid word. (See FAR-.)

FARM-

Noun compounds are solid: *farmhouse, farmstead, farmyard,* etc.

farmerette. Ends in *-ette.* (See -ET, -ETTE, 3.)

fascinate. Note the *-sc.*

fascism. Spelled *-sc,* even though the most popular pronunciation is FASH-izm.

FAST-

Adjective compounds are hyphenated (*fast-flowing, fast-moving,* etc.) when preceding their noun.

FAT-

Adjective compounds are hyphenated (*fat-bellied, fat-cheeked, fat-witted,* etc.) except for *fatheaded,* which is written solid, as is also the noun *fathead.*

father-in-law. Always hyphenated; plural is *fathers-in-law.* (See HYPHENATING, 6A.)

fatuous. Note the *-u* before *-ous.* (See -UOUS.)

faught. Misspelling of *fought.*

favor, favour. The first spelling is American, the second British. (See -OR, -OUR, 1.)

feasible. Note that the ending is *-ible,* not *-able.* (See -IBLE, -ABLE, 1.)

FEATHER-

Most compounds with *feather-,* noun or adjective, are solid: *feather-bedding, featherbrained, featherweight,* etc.
Exceptions are *feather-covered,* which is hyphenated; and noun combinations in which feather is used literally—*feather bed, feather pillow,* etc., as well as the slang *feather merchant*—which are written as separate words.

-FEATHERED

Adjective compounds are hyphenated: *fine-feathered, soft-feathered,* etc.

-FEATURED

Adjective compounds are hyphenated: *coarse-featured, fair-featured,* etc.

February. Pronounced as spelled—not *Febuary.*

FEEBLE-

Adjective compounds mostly hyphenated (*feeble-bodied, feeble-minded, feeble-witted,* etc.), except for *feeblebrained* and *feeblehearted,* which are written solid.

feedback. Solid word.

feed bag. Two words.

feign. When sounded as *-ay,* the spelling *-ei* is always correct. (See -IE, -EI, 6.)

FEINT, FAINT

Feint, noun or verb, refers to pretense, usually to catch someone off guard. *Faint,* noun, verb, or adjective, is the spelling for any other meanings.

-FEIT

-EI, rather than *-ie,* is the correct pattern in any word containing *-feit: counterfeit, forfeit, surfeit,* etc.

fellow feeling. No hyphen. (See HYPHENATING, 3B.)

fellow traveler. No hyphen. (See HYPHENATING, 3B.)

fenagle. See *finagle.*

ferocious. Ends in *-cious,* not *-tious.* (See -OCIOUS.)

-FES, -FS, -VES. See PLURALIZING WORDS IN TERMINAL -F OR -FE.

fetal, foetal. First spelling preferable.

fetish, fetich. First spelling preferable.

fetus, foetus. First spelling preferable.

feud. Not *fued.*

feudal. Not *fuedal.*

fiancé, fiancée. With one *-e,* a man; with two *-e*'s, a woman. Pronounced the same, no matter how spelled: fee-ahn-SAY.

fibbed, fibber, fibbing. Note that the *-b* of *fib* is doubled when a suffix is added. (See DOUBLING FINAL -B.)

fiber, fibre. The latter spelling is now old-fashioned, though current in Great Britain. (See -ER, -RE.)

fickle. Note the *-le* ending. (See -ICKLE, -ICKEL.)

fiction. Ends in *-ition.* (See -ICIOUS, -ITIOUS, 4.)

fictitious. Ends in *-itious,* not *-icious.* (See -ICIOUS, -ITIOUS, 3.)

fidget. Not *fidgit.*

field. *-I* before *-e* except after *c-.* (See -IE, -EI, 1.)

fiend. *-I* before *-e* except after *c-.* (See -IE, -EI, 1.)

fiery. *-Ie,* not *-ei.* (See -IE, -EI, 8.)

fife. The plural is *fifes.* (See PLURALIZING WORDS IN TERMINAL -F OR -FE, 2.)

FIFTY-. See HYPHENATING, 49A.

figurehead. Solid word.

figure of speech. No hyphens.

FIGURES. See HYPHENATING, 49.

Filipino. One *-l,* one *-p,* even though *Philippines* is spelled with two *-p*'s. Plural is *Filipinos.* (See PLURALIZING WORDS IN TERMINAL -O, 2.)

finagle, fenagle. The first spelling is far preferable.

finale. One *-l.*

finally. *Final* plus the adverbial ending, *-ly;* hence double *-l.* (See -LY, -ALLY, 4.)

financier. This *-ie* combination, despite the immediately preceding *-c,* is the only common exception to the rule. (See -IE, -EI, 3.)

FINE-

Adjective compounds are hyphenated (*fine-cut, fine-drawn, fine-feathered, fine-spoken,* etc.), except for *finespun,* which is written solid. *Fine arts* is written separate.

FINENESS, FINESSE

Fineness is the noun form of the adjective *fine; finesse* (pronounced fi-NESS) means skill, adroitness, subtlety, etc.

FIRE-

Certain noun compounds are separate:

fire alarm	fire insurance
fire boat	fire irons
fire brigade	fire sale
fire company	fire screen
fire department	fire ship
fire drill	fire station
fire engine	fire tower
fire escape	fire wall
fire extinguisher	

Certain others are solid:

firearm	firelight
fireball	fireman
firebird	fireplace
firebrand	fireplug
firebreak	firepower
firebrick	fireside
firebug	firestone
firecracker	firetrap
firedamp	firewarden
firedog	firewater
firefly	firewood
fireguard	fireworks
firehouse	

Fire-eater is hyphenated.

Adjectives are hyphenated: *fire-breathing, fire-scarred,* etc., but *fireproof* is solid.

FIRST-. See HYPHENATING, 51.

---

first-aid. Hyphenated if used as an adjective (*first-aid* course), separate if a noun (administered *first aid*). (See HYPHENATING, 2.)

first lieutenant. No hyphen. (See HYPHENATING, 5A.)

FIVE-. See HYPHENATING, 49D, E.

---

five cents' worth. Note the apostrophe. (See APOSTROPHE, USE OF, 4.)

fives. The plural of the number, when written as a word, requires no apostrophe. As a figure, the apostrophe is preferable, but may be omitted:

5's or *5s.* (See APOSTROPHE, USE OF 2, 3.)

flagellate. Double *-l* after the *-e* in this word and all derived forms.

flageolet. The first *-e* is necessary to keep the *-g* "soft." (See -ET, -ETTE, 4.)

flagitious. Ends in *-itious,* not *-icious.* (See -ICIOUS, -ITIOUS, 3.)

flagrance. Ends in *-ance.*

flagrant. Ends in *-ant.*

FLAIR, FLARE

Flair, a noun, is a natural talent, etc. (a *flair* for painting).

Flare, noun or verb, is the spelling for all other meanings.

---

flambeau. The plural is either *flambeaux* or *flambeaus.* (See PLURALIZING WORDS IN TERMINAL -EAU, 2.)

flamingos, flamingoes. The former is the preferable plural; both are correct. (See PLURALIZING WORDS IN TERMINAL -O, 5.)

flammable. Since *-a* is the principal vowel in another form of the word (*inflammation*), the correct ending is *-able.* (See -ABLE, -IBLE, 5.)

flare. See FLAIR, FLARE.

FLAT-

Adjective compounds preceding their nouns are hyphenated: *flat-bottomed, flat-chested, flat-footed,* etc.

Noun compounds are largely written solid: *flatboat, flatcar, flatiron, flattop, flatware,* etc.

A few are separate: *flat knot, flat silver, flat tire.*

---

flatulence. Generally *l-* is followed by *-ence,* rather than *-ance.* (See -ANCE, -ENCE, AFTER L-, 1, 3.)

flavor, flavour. The first spelling is American, the second British. (See -OR, -OUR, 1.)

FLEA, FLEE
> The first is the insect, the second the verb to run away, etc.

fleer. Two *-e*'s only, even though it's *flee* plus *-er;* pronounced FLEE-er. There is also a verb *to fleer,* pronounced in one syllable. (See -EER.)

FLEW, FLUE
> *Flew* is the past tense of the verb *fly; flue,* a noun, has a number of different meanings (the most common is a chimney *flue*), one of which is a fishing net, in which instance it may also be spelled *flew.*

flexible. Note the *-ible* ending. (See -IBLE, -ABLE, 7.)
flier, flyer. Both correct for all meanings, but *flier* is preferable.
flies. Not *flys.* (See -EYS, -IES, -YS, 3.)
flimsy. Not *flimsey.*
flippancy. Ends in *-ancy.*
flippant. Ends in *-ant.*
flirtatious. One of a few words ending in *-atious,* rather than *-acious.* (See -ACIOUS, -ACEOUS, -ATIOUS, 3.)

FLOOD-
> *Flood control* and *flood tide* are written separate; *floodgate* and *floodlight* are written solid.
> Adjective compounds are, of course, hyphenated: *flood-ravaged,* etc.

FLOOR-
> Most noun compounds are written separate: *floor leader, floor plan, floor show,* etc.
> *Floorcloth* and *floorwalker* are solid.

flour. See -OUR, -OWER, -AUER, 1.
flower. See -OUR, -OWER, -AUER, 2.

floweret. Ends in *-et.* (See -ET, -ETTE, 4.)
flue. See FLEW, FLUE.
fluky, flukey. First spelling preferable.
flunky, flunkey. Preferable spelling omits the *-e.* Plural *flunkies* preferable to *flunkeys.*
fluorescent. Note the *-sc.* (See -ESCE, -ESCENT, -ESCENCE, 3.)

FLY-
> Most noun compounds are solid: *flycatcher, flyleaf, flyspeck,* etc.
> Adjective compounds are generally hyphenated (*fly-bitten, fly-by-night, fly-covered,* etc.), but *flyblown* is solid.

flyer. See *flier.*
flys. Misspelling of *flies.*
focus. For plural see PLURALIZING WORDS IN TERMINAL -US, 2.
focused, focuses, focusing. Single *-s* preferable in all derived forms of *focus.* (See DOUBLE VS. SINGLE CONSONANTS.)
foetus. See *fetus.*
folio. Plural is *folios.* (See PLURALIZING WORDS IN TERMINAL -O, 3.)
folioed, folioing. These are the correctly spelled derivative forms of the verb *folio,* even if the succession of vowels looks strange. (See -O, TERMINAL.)
follow-through. Hyphenated when a noun.
follow-up. Hyphenated when a noun or adjective.
foolproof. Solid word. (See -PROOF.)
foolscap, fool's cap. The solid word is a kind of paper; the two-word term, with an apostrophe, refers to the hat with bells once worn by court jesters.

FOOT-
> Most nouns are written solid: *footbridge, footgear, footlights,* etc.
> *Foot brake, foot doctor, foot rule,* and *foot soldier* are written separate.

Foot-pound and *foot-ton* are hyphenated nouns.

Adjectives, as usual, are hyphenated: *foot-loose, foot-licking, foot-weary,* etc.; but *footsore* is solid.

-FOOTED

Most adjective compounds are hyphenated: *flat-footed, four-footed, sure-footed,* etc.

But the following are solid: *barefooted, clubfooted, splayfooted.*

FOR-, FORE-. See FORE-, FOR-.

---

forbade. See FORE-, FOR-, 4.

forbear (verb). See FORE-, FOR-, 3, 4.

forbear (noun). See *forebear.*

forbearance. Note the *-ance* ending. (See -ANCE, -ENCE, AFTER R-, 8; FORE-, FOR-, 4.)

forbid, forbidden. See FORE-, FOR-, 4.

forbiddance. One of the few words in which *-ance,* not *-ence,* follows a *d-.* (See -ANCE, -ENCE, AFTER D-, 3.)

forbore. See FORE-, FOR-, 4.

forcible. The ending is *-ible* to keep the preceding *-c* "soft." (See -IBLE, -ABLE, 5.)

FORE-, FOR-

Whether to use the prefix *fore-* or *for-* on a word is a recurrent cause of confusion to many spellers. But consider:

1. With but one exception, *fore-* as the initial syllable of a word indicates *before, early,* or *earlier* (whether in time or place, order or rank), *front, front part of, previous,* or something closely associated to one of these ideas. Here, for example, is as complete a list as you'll ever need of words starting with *fore-,* in all of which the prefix contains one of the ideas mentioned.

forearm
 (noun or verb)
forebear
 (i.e., an ancestor)
 forebode,
  foreboding
forecast
forecastle
forefather
forefinger
forefoot
forefront
foregoing
 (i.e., previous)
foregone
foreground
forehead
forejudge
foreknow
foreknowledge
forelady
foreleg
forelock
foreman

foremost
forename
forenoon
foreordain
forepart
forepaw
forerunner
foresail
foresee
foreshadow
foreshorten
foreshow
foresight,
 foresighted
foreskin
forestall
foretaste
foretell
forethought
foretoken
foretold
forewarn
forewoman
foreword

2. The one exception is *foreclose* (and its various derivatives, *foreclosure, foreclosed,* etc.), in which the prefix has none of the meanings indicated.

3. Merely as a matter of interest, *forebear* (i.e., an ancestor) may also be spelled *forbear,* but should not be confused with the verb *to forbear,* not permissible in any other pattern.

4. All other words in which the prefix has no relationship to the idea of *before* or *early* are spelled *for-.* The following are those most often misspelled.

forbade
forbear
 (i.e., the verb)
forbearance
forbid, forbidden
forbore
forfeit, forfeiture
forfend (archaic)
forgather
forgave
forget

forgive
forgiveness
forgiving
forgo
forgone
forgot, forgotten
forlorn
forsake, forsaken
forsooth (*archaic*)
forswear
forward

5. Three of the words in Section 4 may variantly be spelled *fore-* (*forefend, foregather, forego*), but it would be better to avoid confusion by ignoring these alternative forms.

---

forearm. See FORE-, FOR-, 1.

forebear (noun). Preferably so spelled, though *forbear* is also acceptable. (See FORE-, FOR-, 1, 3.)

forebode, foreboding. See FORE-, FOR-, 1.

forecast. See FORE-, FOR-, 1.

forecastle. See FORE-, FOR-, 1.

foreclose, foreclosure. The only words in which the prefix *fore-* has no meaning of *before, earlier, previous,* etc. (See FORE-, FOR-, 2.)

forefather. See FORE-, FOR-, 1.

forefinger. See FORE-, FOR-, 1.

forefoot. See FORE-, FOR-, 1.

forefront. See FORE-, FOR-, 1.

foregather. See *forgather*.

forego. See *forgo*.

foregoing. See FORE-, FOR-, 1.

foregone. See FORE-, FOR-, 1.

foreground. See FORE-, FOR-, 1.

forehead. See FORE-, FOR-, 1.

foreign, foreigner. Note the *-ei* combination. (See -IE, -EI, 10.)

foreignness. *Foreign* plus *-ness,* hence the double *-n.* (See -NESS AFTER N-.)

forejudge. See FORE-, FOR-, 1.

foreknow. See FORE-, FOR-, 1.

foreknowledge. See FORE-, FOR-, 1.

forelady. See FORE-, FOR-, 1.

foreleg. See FORE-, FOR-, 1.

forelock. See FORE-, FOR-, 1.

foreman. See FORE-, FOR-, 1.

foremost. See FORE-, FOR-, 1.

forename. See FORE-, FOR-, 1.

forenoon. See FORE-, FOR-, 1.

foreordain. See FORE-, FOR-, 1.

forepart. See FORE-, FOR-, 1.

forepaw. See FORE-, FOR-, 1.

forerunner. See FORE-, FOR-, 1.

foresail. See FORE-, FOR-, 1.

foresee. See FORE-, FOR-, 1.

foreshadow. See FORE-, FOR-, 1.

foreshorten. See FORE-, FOR-, 1.

foreshow. See FORE-, FOR-, 1.

foresight, foresighted. See FORE-, FOR-, 1.

foreskin. See FORE-, FOR-, 1.

forestall. See FORE-, FOR-, 1.

foretaste. See FORE-, FOR-, 1.

foretell. See FORE-, FOR-, 1.

forethought. See FORE-, FOR-, 1.

foretoken. See FORE-, FOR-, 1.

foretold. See FORE-, FOR-, 1.

forewarn. See FORE-, FOR-, 1.

forewoman. See FORE-, FOR-, 1.

foreword. See FORE-, FOR-, 1.

FOREWORD, FORWARD

Often confused, especially in spelling, but two entirely different and unrelated words. The noun *foreword* (i.e., a *fore word,* or word beforehand) is a preface or introduction to a book or other piece of writing. *Forward* is an adjective or adverb built on the meaning of *ahead, front,* etc., or a verb meaning to send ahead, advance, etc.

---

forfeit, forfeiture. Note the *-ei* combination. (See -IE, -EI, 9.)

forfend (archaic). Preferably so spelled, though *forefend* is also acceptable. (See FORE-, FOR-, 4, 5.)

forgather. Preferably so spelled, though *foregather* is also correct. (See FORE-, FOR-, 4, 5.)

forgave. See FORE-, FOR-, 4.

forget. See FORE-, FOR-, 4.

forgive. See FORE-, FOR-, 4.

forgiveness. *Forgive* plus *-ness,* only one *-n.*

forgiving. See FORE-, FOR-, 4.

forgo. Preferably so spelled, though *forego* is also correct. (See FORE-, FOR-, 4, 5.)

forgone. See FORE-, FOR-, 4.

forgot, forgotten. See FORE-, FOR-, 4.

forlorn. See FORE-, FOR-, 4.

formidable. Note the -able ending. (See -ABLE, -IBLE, 7.)

formula. For plural see PLURALIZ-
ING WORDS IN TERMINAL -A,
3.

forsake, forsaken. See FORE-, FOR-,
4.

forsooth (archaic). See FORE-, FOR-,
4.

forswear. See FORE-, FOR-, 4.

forty. The word has no -*u*, although
fourteen does.

FORTY-. See HYPHENATING, 49A.

---

forward. See FOREWORD, FOR-
WARD.

---

forward, forwards. Use only the first
spelling as an *adjective;* use either
form as an *adverb.* (See -ARD,
ARDS.)

fought. Not *faught.* (See -AUGHT,
-OUGHT, 1.)

foul. See FOWL, FOUL.

FOUR-. See HYPHENATING, 49D,
E.

---

fours. The plural of the number, when
written as a word, requires no apostrophe. As a figure, the apostrophe
is preferable, but may be omitted:
4's or *4s.* (See APOSTROPHE,
USE OF 2, 3.)

fourteen. This word has a -*u*, though
forty doesn't.

fourty. Misspelling of *forty.*

FOWL, FOUL

The noun *fowl* includes all edible
birds, domestic or wild, or the flesh
of such birds prepared as food. The
verb *fowl* means to hunt, catch, or
trap wild birds for eating.

Foul is the spelling for all other
meanings, whether noun, adjective,
or verb.

FRACTIONS. See HYPHENATING,
50.

---

fragmentary. The ending is -*ary.* (See
-ARY, -ORY, 1.)

fragrance. Ends in -*ance.*

fragrant. Ends in -*ant.*

franchise. Note the -*ise* ending. (See
-ISE, 8.)

frankincense. Built on the word *incense,* hence the -*c.*

fraudulence. Generally *l-* is followed
by -*ence* rather than -*ance.* (See
-ANCE, -ENCE, AFTER L-, 1, 3.)

fraught. The pattern is -*aught.* (See
-AUGHT, -OUGHT, 1.)

FREE-

Adjectives with *free-* as a prefix
are usually hyphenated: *free-lance,
free-living, free-moving, free-soil,
free-spoken, free-swimming, free-
trade,* etc.

However, the following adjectives
are written solid:

freeborn	freethinking
freehand	freewheeling
freehanded	freewill
freehearted	

The verb *free-lance* is hyphenated;
the verb *freeboot* is solid; the noun
free lance is two words.

The following nouns are solid
words, most others are written
separate:

freeboard	freestone
freebooter	freethinking
freehold	freethinker
freeman	freeway
freemason	freewheeling
freemasonry	

Free-for-all, noun or adjective, is,
of course, hyphenated.

-FREE

Adjectives with -*free* as a suffix
are generally hyphenated: *anxiety-
free, duty-free,* etc.

But *carefree* is solid.

---

freeable. Note that both -*e's* are retained before -*able.* (See -ABLE,
-EABLE, 3; -ABLE, -IBLE, 4.)

freer, freest. Two -*e*'s only, even though it's *free* plus -*er* or -*est*. (See -EER.)

freeze. See FRIEZE, FREEZE.

freight. When sounded as -*ay*, the spelling -*ei* is always correct. (See -IE, -EI, 6.)

freind, frend. Misspellings of *friend*.

fricassee. You'll be hard put to it to find anyone who can spell this demon correctly. Think that the concoction can be served in a *casserole* —and note the -*cass* in both words.

friend. A surprisingly often misspelled word—note the -*ie* combination. Likewise, *friendly, friendliness, friendship, befriend,* etc. (See -IE, EI, 13.)

FRIEZE, FREEZE

Both words are pronounced identically, but are unrelated in meaning. *Frieze* is a noun identifying a type of decoration or fabric; *freeze,* noun or verb, refers to extremely low temperatures, and has a number of allied meanings.

---

frolicked, frolicking. The -*k* must be inserted in these derived forms of *frolic* in order to preserve the original pronunciation of final -*c*. (See -C, -CK, 1.)

frolicsome. No -*k* necessary here.

frontier. Ends in -*ier*. (See -IE, -EI, 1.)

frontispiece. The -*i* after the *t*- is tricky.

frontward, frontwards. Use only the first spelling as an *adjective;* use either form as an *adverb.* (See -ARD, -ARDS.)

frought. Misspelling of *fraught*.

frowzy, frowsy, frouzy, frousy. All these spellings correct, but by far the preferable one is *frowzy*.

frozenness. *Frozen* plus -*ness,* hence the double -*n*. (See -NESS AFTER N-.)

fued, fuedal. Misspellings of *feud, feudal*.

-FUL

Only one -*l* when this particle is a suffix: *powerful, skillful, willful, helpful, spoonful, handful,* etc.

-FUL, PLURALIZING WORDS ENDING IN. See PLURALIZING WORDS IN TERMINAL -FUL.

---

fulfill, fulfil. *Fulfill* is preferable. Likewise, *fulfillment* is better than *fulfilment*. Note, however, that the first syllable is *ful-*, not *full-*. (See -IL, -ILL, 3.)

fulfilled, fulfilling. Double -*l* only in the second syllable. Note that the first syllable is *ful-*, not *full-*. (See -IL, -ILL, 3.)

FULL-

Full- as a prefix to an adjective is generally hyphenated: *full-blooded, full-blown, full-bodied, full-fledged, full-grown,* etc.

Nouns combined with *full-* are usually written as two words: *full dress, full house, full stop,* etc.

Fullback is the only common word of any currency spelled solid.

---

fullness, fulness. Both correct, *fullness* preferable.

fully. Only two -*l*'s even though the word is *full* plus -*ly*.

fulsome. One -*l* only.

funereal. Ends in -*eal*, not -*ial*.

FUNGOUS, FUNGUS

Fungous is an adjective only; *fungus* is usually, and preferably, the noun, but sometimes used as a variant spelling for the adjective.

---

fungus. For plural see PLURALIZING WORDS IN TERMINAL -US, 14.

furbelow. Ends in -*ow*.

furlough. But this one ends in -*ough*.

furred, furry. Note the double -*r* in

these derived forms of *fur*. (See DOUBLING FINAL -R, 1.)

fury. Not *furey.*

fuselage. Second vowel is *-e,* not *-i* or *-a.*

G

(Rules for double *-g:* See DOUBLING FINAL *-G.*)

gage. See *gauge.*

gaiety, gayety. The former is the much-preferred spelling.

gaily, gayly. The former spelling is preferable. (See -LY, 4.)

GAIT, GATE

Gait is a manner of walking; *gate,* with a score of related meanings, refers directly or otherwise to a means of entrance or exit.

---

gallant. Ends in *-ant.*

galloped, galloping. Single *-p* in all derived forms of *gallop,* since the accent does *not* fall on the last syllable. (See DOUBLING FINAL -P, 4.)

GAMBLE, GAMBOL

To *gamble* is to wager, take risks, etc.; to *gambol* is to jump and skip around in play, the way a lamb or goat does. Both words are also nouns.

The derived forms of *gambol* are preferably spelled with one *-l: gamboled, gamboling.*

-GANCE, -GENCE. See -ANCE, -ENCE, AFTER G-.

---

gangrene. Often mispronounced as well as misspelled. No relation, in meaning or spelling, to the color *green.* Pronounce in two syllables only. Adjective is *gangrenous.*

-GANT, -GENT. See -ANCE, -ENCE, AFTER G-.

---

gantlet. See *gauntlet.*

gaol. See *jail.*

garrulous. Two *-r*'s, followed by *-u.*

gases, gaseous, gasify. One *-s;* final *-s* of the *noun gas* is *not* doubled when a suffix is added. (See DOUBLING FINAL CONSONANTS— ONE-SYLLABLE WORDS, 5.)

gasoline, gasolene. The first spelling preferable and much more common.

gassed, gasses, gassing, When *gas* is used as a *verb,* the *-s* is doubled before *-ed* or *-ing.* (See DOUBLING FINAL CONSONANTS— ONE-SYLLABLE WORDS, 5.)

gate. See GAIT, GATE.

gauge, gage. In the sense of measurement, the former is the preferable spelling. But meaning a pledge, *gage* is the correct form.

gauntlet, gantlet. The longer spelling preferable for the meaning of glove, and in the phrase "take up the *gauntlet*"; the shorter for the name of the military punishment, and therefore in the phrase "run the *gantlet.*"

gayer, gayest. Comparative and superlative of *gay.* (See -IER, -IEST, 6.)

gayety. See *gaiety.*

gayly. Correct, but *gaily* is far preferable.

gazette. Ends in *-ette.* (See -ET, -ETTE, 3.)

gazetteer. Two *-t*'s.

-GEABLE

The letter *-g* is regularly "hard" (as in *game, regard,* etc.) before an *-a;* for this reason, the final *-e* of words ending in *-ge* (*change, manage,* etc.) is retained before *-able,* thus assuring the preservation of the original "soft," or *j,* sound.

acknowledge—acknowledgeable

abridge—abridgeable
bridge—bridgeable
change—changeable
damage—damageable
discourage—discourageable
disengage—disengageable
encourage—encourageable
engage—engageable
enrage—enrageable
exchange—exchangeable
interchange—interchangeable
knowledge—knowledgeable
manage—manageable
marriage—marriageable
mortgage—mortgageable
salvage—salvageable
wage—wageable
See also -ABLE, -EABLE; -CEABLE.

---

genealogy. Note that the ending is *-alogy*, not *-ology*. Hence the spelling of *genealogist, genealogical,* etc.

generator. Ends in *-or.*

genius. Not *genious.* For plural see PLURALIZING WORDS IN TERMINAL -US, 3.

gentle, genteel. *Genteel* is today used only with the meaning of pretentiously well bred, polite, refined, etc., though formerly it had other meanings.

genus. For plural see PLURALIZING WORDS IN TERMINAL -US, 4.

gewgaw. Not *geegaw.*

ghetto. Note the *-h.*

gigolo. One *-g* in the middle; plural is *gigolos.* (See PLURALIZING WORDS IN TERMINAL -O, 2.)

GILD, GUILD

Gild is the verb meaning to cover with gold or gold coloring.

A *guild* is any association for mutual benefit, especially the kinds that flourished in the Middle Ages. It may also be spelled *gild,* but rarely is.

---

gilder. See *guilder.*
gipsy. See *gypsy.*

giraffe. One *-r,* two *-f*'s; the plural is *giraffes.* (See PLURALIZING WORDS IN TERMINAL -F OR -FE, 2.)

gladiator. Ends in *-or.* (See -ER, -OR, 5.)

gladiolus. For plural see PLURALIZING WORDS IN TERMINAL -US, 5.

glamor. See *glamour.*

glamorous, glamourous. The first spelling is preferable. (See -OR, -OUR.)

glamour, glamor. The first spelling is very much preferable. (See -OR, -OUR, 2.)

glassful. The plural is *glassfuls.* (See PLURALIZING WORDS IN TERMINAL -FUL.)

glazier. Note the *-z.*

glower. See -OUR, -OWER, -AUER, 2.

gneiss. When sounded *eye,* the combination *-ei* is used, except when the following letter is an *-r.* (See -IE, -EI, 7.)

GO-

Words with this prefix are usually hyphenated: *go-between, go-by, go-cart, go-getter,* etc. See HYPHENATING, 10A.

---

go-between. Plural is *go-betweens.*

GOD-, god-

Adjective compounds usually hyphenated: *God-giving, God-fearing, God-loving,* etc.

However, *Godforsaken* (need not be capitalized) and *goddamned* (also spelled *goddamn* and *goddam*) are solid. The adjective *godlike* is, of course, also solid, as are almost all compounds with *-like.*

All *godparents* and *godchildren* are written solid: *godfather, godmother, godson,* etc.

---

goddess. Double *-d.*

GOLD-, GOLDEN-

Adjective compounds preceding their nouns are hyphenated: *gold-colored, gold-star, golden-haired,* etc.

Noun compounds in which *gold* is used more or less literally are usually separate words: *gold certificate, gold digger, gold dust, gold rush,* etc.

Otherwise solid, as *goldbug, goldfinch, goldfish,* etc. But *gold star* is separate, and *goldsmith* solid.

The slang verb *goldbrick* and its derivative noun, *goldbricker,* are solid.

GOOD-. See HYPHENATING, 45.

---

good-by, good-bye. Equally correct, the former more common. The modern trend is to write these words solid, especially in informal writing (*goodby, goodbye*). To pluralize, merely add an *-s: good-bys, good-byes.*

good-for-nothing. Always hyphenated. (See HYPHENATING, 10A.)

GORILLA, GUERRILLA

The first is the animal, the second a member of a band of irregular soldiers. Pronounced identically.

---

gourmand, gormand. The first spelling is preferable—but the verb is *gormandize* only.

gourmet. Not *gormet.*

government. Note the *-n* after *r-.*

governor-elect. See HYPHENATING, 8.

grabbed, grabber, grabbing. The *-b* of *grab* is doubled before a suffix starting with a vowel. (See DOUBLING FINAL -B.)

gram, gramme. The latter is British, the former American.

grammar. Ends in *-ar—poor grammar mars one's speech.*

GRAND-

In noun compounds showing family relationships always solid— *grandmother, grandchild, grandson,* etc.

Otherwise separate: *grand duke, grand larceny,* etc.

---

grandeur. Ends in *-eur.*

grandiloquence. Always *-ence,* not *-ance,* after *-qu.* (See -ANCE, -ENCE, AFTER U-, 1.)

grantor. Ends in *-or.* (See -ER, -OR, 5.)

grateful. Misspelled *greatful* by students writing compositions. Comes from the same Latin root as *gratitude.*

gray. This is the preferred American spelling, though the British, on the other hand, prefer *grey.*

GRAY-

Adjective compounds are hyphenated: *gray-bearded, gray-blue, gray-colored, gray-haired,* etc.
See also HYPHENATING, 47.

---

grayed, graying, grayly, grayness. Since the terminal *-y* of *gray* follows a vowel, it does *not* change to *-i* before a suffix. (See -Y PLUS A SUFFIX, 9.)

grayer, grayest. Comparative and superlative of *gray.* (See -IER, -IEST, 6.)

GREAT- See HYPHENATING, 35.

---

greatful. Misspelling of *grateful.*

GREEN-

Adjective compounds are hyphenated: *green-blue, green-colored, green-eyed, green-haired,* etc.

Some noun compounds are **separate** words:

green glass   green soap
green light   green tea
green pepper   green thumb
  Others are solid:
greengage   greenroom
greengrocer   (in the theater)
greengrocery   greenwood
greenhouse

greenness. *Green* plus *-ness,* hence the double *-n.* (See -NESS AFTER N-.)

grewsome. See *gruesome.*

grey. See *gray.*

grief. *-I* before *-e* except after *c-;* the plural is *griefs.* (See -IE, -EI, 1; PLURALIZING WORDS IN TERMINAL -F OR -FE, 2.)

grievance. Ends in *-ance;* and the vowel combination is *-ie,* not *-ei.* (See -ANCE, -ENCE, AFTER V-; -IE, -EI, 1.)

grieve. See *grief.*

grievous. See *grief.*

grip, grippe. With the double *-p* it's the disease, always preceded by *the* (or, to be elegant, the French *la*). *Grip* also is an allowable, but not common, spelling for the ailment.

grisette. Ends in *-ette.* (See -ET, -ETTE, 3.)

grope. Not *groap.* (See -OPE, -OAP.)

grottoes, grottos. The former is the preferable plural; both are correct. (See PLURALIZING WORDS IN TERMINAL -O, 4.)

groveled, groveling. Because *grovel* is *not* accented on the last syllable, final *-l* is *not* doubled before a suffix beginning with a vowel. Double *-l* forms are acceptable, but single *-l* forms are far preferable. (See DOUBLING FINAL -L, 2.)

gruesome, grewsome. The first spelling is preferable and far commoner.

guarantee, guaranty. To make life simple for yourself, spell any use of the noun or verb with the *-ee* ending, since *guarantee* is correct for all meanings, *guaranty* for only some.

guaranteer. Two *-e*'s only, even though it's *guarantee* plus *-er.* The commoner form is *guarantor.* (See -EER.)

guarantor. Ends in *-or.* (See -ER, -OR, 5.)

guaranty. See *guarantee.*

guerilla. See GORILLA, GUERRILLA.

guidance. One of the few words in which *-ance,* not *-ence,* follows a *d-.* (See -ANCE, -ENCE, AFTER D-, 3.)

guild. See GILD, GUILD.

guilder, gilder. The Dutch unit of currency may be spelled either way, but the first is preferable.

guillotine. Double *-l.*

guise. Note the *-ise* ending. (See -ISE, 7.)

guitar. One *-t.*

gulf. The plural is *gulfs.* (See PLURALIZING WORDS IN TERMINAL -F OR -FE, 2.)

gullible. Note the *-ible* ending. (See -IBLE, -ABLE, 7.)

gunwale, gunnel. Both spellings correct, the former preferable—but pronounced as if spelled *gunnel.*

guttural. It's that second *-u* that most people get hung up on.

gymnasium. The Anglicized plural *gymnasiums* is commoner than the Latin-derived *gymnasia.* (See PLURALIZING WORDS IN TERMINAL -UM, 2.)

gypsy, gipsy, gypsey. All spellings correct, but the first is by far preferable. Plural is *gypsies.*

H

HAIL, HALE

The distinction between these words can be easily understood.

Hail, verb. To call to, name, salute, cheer, come from, come or send down upon, etc.: They *hailed* him as leader, *hailed* a taxi, *hail* from Louisiana, *hailed* epithets upon us; it was *hailing* all night.

Hail, the noun, has similar meanings: He heard a *hail;* received their *hails* in silence; he's now within *hail*, or within *hailing* distance; a *hail* of abuse, arrows, or bullets; the *hail* came down all night; quite a *hailstorm;* as big as *hailstones.*

Hale, adjective. Healthy, strong, etc. (Also, less commonly, spelled *hail*.): He's *hale* and hearty for an old man.

Hale, verb. To pull, drag, force to come or go: He was *haled* before the judge as soon as he was apprehended.

Hale is *never* a noun.

---

hailstone. See HAIL, HALE.
hailstorm. See HAIL, HALE.

HAIR-
Hyphenated in adjective compounds (*hair-curling, hair-raising, hair-trigger*, etc.), but solid in *hairsplitting.*

Solid in certain noun compounds.

hairband	hairline
hairbrush	hairpin
haircut	hairsplitter
hairdresser	hairsplitting
hairdressing	hairspring

Separate in most other noun compounds: *hair dye, hair net, hair ribbon, hair tonic,* etc.

Hair-do is hyphenated; *hairbreadth* or *hairsbreadth*, whether noun or adjective, is solid, unless spelled *hair's-breadth*, in which case it is hyphenated.

---

hairbrained. Misspelling of *harebrained.*
hairbreadth, hairsbreadth, hair's-breadth. Noun or adjective, all these spellings are correct.

-HAIRED
Adjectives with this suffix are hyphenated: *black-haired, straight-haired, wire-haired*, etc.

HAIRY-
Adjectives with this prefix are hyphenated: *hairy-armed, hairy-faced*, etc.

---

hale. See HAIL, HALE.
half. The plural is *halves.* (See PLURALIZING WORDS IN TERMINAL -F OR -FE, 1.)

HALF-. See HYPHENATING, 6B, 28.

---

hallelujah, halleluiah, alleluia. All these spellings correct, the first preferable.
hallmark. Solid word.
hallucination. Two *-l*'s here and in all related forms.
hallway. Solid word.
halos, haloes. The former is the preferable plural; both are correct. (See PLURALIZING WORDS IN TERMINAL -O, 5.)

HAND-
Most noun compuonds are solid: *handbag, handbook, handout, handwriting*, etc.

The following nouns, among others, are separate:

hand baggage	hand luggage
hand bell	hand organ
hand glass	hand screw
hand grenade	

Verbs are hyphenated: *hand-mix, hand-sew, hand-wash*, etc.

Adjectives are hyphenated: *hand-knit, hand-picked, hand-to-hand, hand-to-mouth*, etc.

Except *handmade*, which is solid. *Hand-me-down* is hyphenated whether noun or adjective.

-HANDED

Compounds are generally hyphenated: *big-handed, empty-handed, left-handed,* etc.

But the following, which, for the most part, have figurative rather than literal meanings, are solid:

backhanded	ironhanded
barehanded	largehanded
evenhanded	openhanded
forehanded	overhanded
freehanded	shorthanded
heavyhanded	underhanded
highhanded	weakhanded

handful. The plural is *handfuls.* (See PLURALIZING WORDS IN TERMINAL -FUL.)

handkerchief. Note the *-ie* combination; the plural is *handkerchiefs.* (See -IE, -EI, 11; PLURALIZING WORDS IN TERMINAL -F OR -FE, 2.)

hanger, hangar. Only when a shed, etc., for aircraft is meant is the second spelling used.

hanger-on. Hyphenated; the plural is *hangers-on.* (See HYPHENATING, 10A.)

hangman. Solid word.

hang-out. Hyphenated.

hangover. Solid word. But one is *hung over,* in two words.

haphazard. Solid word.

happily. The *-y* of *happy* changes to *-i* before *-ly.* (See -LY, 2.)

happiness. The *-y* of *happy* changes to *-i* before *-ness.* (See -Y PLUS A SUFFIX, 6.)

harangue. Note *-ue* at the end.

harass. Unlike *embarrass,* only one *-r. Harassment* is so spelled: no *-e* after the double *s-.*

harbor, harbour. The first spelling is American, the second British. (See -OR, -OUR, 1.)

HARD-

Adjectives are almost always hyphenated: *hard-bitten, hard-boiled,* *hard-bound, hard-earned, hard-shell, hard-won,* etc.

But the following adjectives are written solid:

hardfisted	hardheaded
hardhanded	hardhearted

Nouns are usually separate (*hard cash, hard labor,* etc.), except:

hardhead	hardtop
hardpan	hardware
hardtack	hardwood

hardiness. The *-y* of *hardy* changes to *-i* before *-ness.* (See -Y PLUS A SUFFIX, 6.)

harebrained. Not *hairbrained.*

harpsichord. The pattern is *-si,* not *-is.*

harried. Two *-r*'s, from the verb to *harry.*

Harrys. If a proper name ends in *-y,* the plural is formed by the simple addition of *-s.* (See -EYS, -IES, -YS, 5.)

hasn't. Contraction of *has not,* the apostrophe appearing in place of the missing *-o.* (See APOSTROPHE, USE OF, 1.)

HAT-

These nouns are solid:

hatband	hatmaking
hatbox	hatpin
hatbrim	hatrack
hatbrush	hatstand
hatmaker	

Most others are separate: *hat hook, hat shop, hat tree,* etc.

Hat-shaped, the adjective, is hyphenated; so is *hat-in-hand* preceding its noun.

hatful. The plural is *hatfuls.* (See PLURALIZING WORDS IN TERMINAL -FUL.)

haven't. The apostrophe denotes the omission of *-o.* (See APOSTROPHE, USE OF, 1.)

hay! Misspelling of *hey!*

HAY-

Most common noun compounds are solid: *hayfield, hayloft, hayrack,* etc.

These nouns are written separate: *hay baler, hay cutter, hay fever, hay hook, hay loader, hay press, hay wagon.*

Adjectives are hyphenated: *hay-colored, hay-fed,* etc.

hayday. Misspelling of *heyday.*

hazard, hazardous. Only one *z-,* followed by a single *-a* in these words.

haziness. The *-y* of *hazy* changes to *-i* before *-ness.* (See -Y PLUS A SUFFIX, 6.)

HEAD-. See HYPHENATING, 33.

-HEADED

Most adjectives built on the suffix *-headed* are hyphenated: *bald-headed, gray-headed,* etc.

The following, however, are written solid:

addleheaded	lightheaded
bareheaded	muddleheaded
blockheaded	pigheaded
bullheaded	pinheaded
clearheaded	redheaded
coolheaded	softheaded
fatheaded	thickheaded
hardheaded	thunderheaded
hotheaded	woodenheaded
levelheaded	wrongheaded

HEAL, HEEL

To *heal* is to cure, get well, etc.

To *heel* is to lean or slant, as a ship, etc.

Heel, as a noun, designates the back of the foot, or, as a verb, to follow at the heels of, etc.

HEAR, HERE

Hear is a verb; *here* an adverb.

I *hear* you.

Let's stop *here.*

HEARD, HERD

Heard is the past tense and past participle of the verb *to hear*—never spelled *heared.*

Herd is a group of animals; as a verb, it means to form into a group— *herd* the passengers to the rear of the bus.

HEART-

Adjective compounds with *heart-* are usually hyphenated: *heart-free, heart-hardened, heart-rending, heart-stricken, heart-warming, heart-to-heart,* etc.

But the following are written solid:

heartbreaking	heartsick
heartbroken	heartsore
heartfelt	

Noun compounds are generally solid: *heartache, heartbeat, heart-break, heartstrings, heartthrob,* etc.

Heartsease is solid unless written with the apostrophe, in which case it is hyphenated—*heart's-ease.*

-HEARTED

Adjectives with *-hearted* as a suffix are written solid: *brokenhearted, coldhearted, hardhearted, heavy-hearted, softhearted,* etc. *Heavy-hearted* (with the hyphen) is also correct.

heaviness. The *-y* of *heavy* changes to *-i* before *-ness.* (See -Y PLUS A SUFFIX, 6.)

HEAVY-

Adjective compounds with *heavy-* are solid: *heavy-bosomed, heavy-set,* etc.

Heavyhanded, heavyhearted and *heavyweight* are exceptions, though *heavy-hearted* is also correct.

he'd. Contraction of *he had* or *he would,* the apostrophe appearing in place of the missing letters. (See APOSTROPHE, USE OF, 1.)

heel. See HEAL, HEEL.

heifer. Note the *-ei* combination. (See -IE, -EI, 14.)

height. *-Ei* is correct for the sound *eye,* except when the next letter is *-r.* (See -IE, -EI, 7, 8.)

heinous. When sounded as *ay* the spelling *-ei* is always correct. (See -IE, -EI, 6.)

he'll. Contraction of *he will,* the apostrophe appearing in place of the missing letters. (See APOSTROPHE, USE OF, 1.)

helloed, helloing. These are the correctly spelled derivative forms of the verb *hello,* even if the successive vowels look strange. (See -O, TERMINAL.)

hemorrhage. The familiar *-rrh* pattern found in many medical terms.

hemorrhoid. Again, *-rrh,* as in *hemorrhage.*

herbaceous. Ending is *-aceous,* not *-acious.* (See -ACIOUS, -ACEOUS, -ATIOUS, 2.)

herd. See HEARD, HERD.

here. See HEAR, HERE.

hereafter. Don't slip up on the *-e* following the first *r-.*

hereditary. The ending is *-ary.* (See -ARY, -ORY, 1.)

hereinafter. As in *hereafter,* watch that *-e* after the first *r-.*

heresy. Note that the ending is *-sy,* not *-cy.* (See -CY, -SY, 4.)

heretofore. See *hereafter.*

hereupon. See *hereafter.*

herewith. See *hereafter.*

hero. Plural is *heroes.* (See PLURALIZING WORDS IN TERMINAL -O, 1.)

heroine. If you leave off the final *-e* you have a powerful narcotic, not the feminine of *hero.*

hesitance. *-Ance* is found somewhat more often than *-ence* after *t-.* (See -ANCE, -ENCE, AFTER T-, 1.)

hesitant. *-Ant* slightly more common

than *-ent* after *t-.* (See -ANCE, -ENCE, AFTER T-, 2.)

heterogeneous, heterogeneity. The *-e* after the *g-* is the letter that causes trouble to poor spellers.

hew. See HUE, HEW.

hey! The interjection should not be spelled *hay!,* though it often is.

heyday. A solid word—and note the first syllable is *hey-,* not *hay-.*

hiccup, hiccough. Either spelling, the first preferable—pronounced HIK-up no matter how you spell it.

hiddenness. *Hidden* plus *-ness,* hence the double *-n.* (See -NESS AFTER N-.)

hideous. Ends in *-eous,* not *-ious.*

hierarchy. Note the *-ie* combination. (See -IE, -EI, 8.)

hieroglyphic. Again, *-ie.* (See -IE, -EI, 8.)

HIGH-

Most adjective compounds with this prefix are hyphenated: *high-brow, high-class, high-colored, high-flown, high-priced, high-strung,* etc.

These adjectives are solid:

highborn	highhanded
highbred	highhearted

Nouns are, for the most part, separate words: *high comedy, high fidelity, high hand, high hat, high light,* etc.

But the following are solid:

highball	highland
highbinder	highlander
highboy	highroad
highchair	highway
highflier	highwayman
highjacker	

(*preferably* hijacker)

These nouns are hyphenated: *high-brow, high-muck-a-muck.*

High-brow, noun or adjective, may also be written solid: *highbrow.*

The verbs *high-hat* and *high-pressure* are hyphenated; *highball, highjack* (preferably spelled *hijack*), *highlight* are solid.

higher-up (noun). Hyphenated.

highfalutin, highfaluting. The first form is preferable.

high-hat. Hyphenate when a verb or adjective, write separate (*high hat*) when a noun.

highjack, highjacker. See *hijack, hijacker.*

high jinks, hijinks, hi-jinks. The first spelling is the only technically correct one, but in informal use the other two are much more common.

high-pressure, high pressure. Hyphenated as an adjective or verb, separate as a noun.

hijack, hijacker. These are the preferable spellings, though *highjack, highjacker* are also correct.

hijinks, hi-jinks. See *high jinks.*

hindrance. Ends in *-ance.*

hipocracy, hipocrasy. Misspellings of *hypocrisy.*

hipocrite. Misspelling of *hypocrite.*

hippopotamus. After the *t-* is *-a*, not *-o*, and the ending is *-us*, not *-ous.* (See PLURALIZING WORDS IN TERMINAL -US, 6.)

hitchhike, hitchhiker. Both solid words.

hoarse, horse. A person's voice sounds *hoarse;* the four-legged animal is spelled *horse.*

hobos, hoboes. The former is the preferable plural; both are correct. (See PLURALIZING WORDS IN TERMINAL -O, 5.)

hoed. Note the single *-e.* (See -OE, TERMINAL, 4.)

hoeing. Note the retained *-e* of *hoe* before *-ing.* (See -OE, TERMINAL, 4.)

hogged, hoggish. Double the *-g* of *hog* before a suffix starting with a vowel. (See DOUBLING FINAL -G.)

holdout. No hyphen. (See HYPHENATING, 10B.)

holdover. No hyphen. (See HYPHENATING, 10B.)

holdup. No hyphen. (See HYPHENATING, 10B.)

holey, holy. The former means full of holes, the latter means pious, sacred, etc. The noun from *holy* is *holiness.* (See -Y, -EY, 3; -Y PLUS A SUFFIX, 6.)

holiday. Originally a *holy day*, hence one *-l.*

holocaust. One *-l.*

holy. See *holey, holy.*

HOME-

Adjective compounds are usually hyphenated: *home-baked, home-grown*, etc.

However, *homemade, homesick*, and *homespun* are solid.

Among noun compounds, *home-brew* and *home-coming* are hyphenated.

The following are written solid:

homeland	homeroom
homemaker	homestead
homemaking	homestretch
homeowner	homework

Others are separate words: *home economics, home rule, home run, home town*, etc.

---

homeward, homewards. Use only the first spelling as an *adjective;* use either form as an *adverb.* (See -ARD, -ARDS.)

homey, homy. Though both correct, the former spelling is preferable. (See -Y, -EY, 2.)

homogencity. This is a noun form of *homogeneous.*

homogeneous, homogenous. The first word, with *-e* following *n-* (and pronounced ho-mo-JEE-nee-us), is the word in common use meaning uniform or similar in composition—*homogeneous* grouping, classes, etc. *Homogenous* (ho-MOJ-e-nus) is a technical term in biology meaning similar in structure because of common ancestry; more often it is simply a misspelling of *homogeneous.*

honor, honour. The first spelling is American, the second British. (See -OR, -OUR, 1.)

honorary. The ending is -*ary.* (See -ARY, -ORY, 1.)

hoof. For plural see PLURALIZING WORDS IN TERMINAL -F OR -FE, 4C.

hookup. No hyphen. (See HYPHENATING, 3A.)

hoop. See -OOP, -OUP, -UPE, 1.

hoping. Not *hopeing.* (See DROPPED -E.)

horrible. The ending is -*ible.* (See -IBLE, -ABLE, 1.)

horribly. The -*e* of *horrible* has been changed to -*y.* (See -LY, 5.)

hors d'oeuvres. No hyphen—and the *oeu-* after *d'-* makes this a real demon.

horse. See *hoarse.*

HORSE-

Adjectives are, of course, hyphenated (*horse-drawn, horse-faced, horse-loving,* etc.).

Most standard noun compounds are written solid (*horsecar, horseflesh, horseman,* etc.), except for the following, which are separate:

horse chestnut	horse race
horse latitudes	horse racing
horse mackerel	horse sense
horse opera	

horseshoeing. Note that the terminal -*e* of *horseshoe* is retained before -*ing.* (See -OE, TERMINAL, 2.)

horseshoer. One who fits horses with shoes; note the single -*e* before the -*r.* (See -OE, TERMINAL, 2.)

hosiery. No -*z.*

hospitable. Since -*a* is the principal vowel in another form of the word (*hospitality*), the correct ending is -*able.* (See -ABLE, -IBLE, 5.)

hospitably. The -*e* of *hospitable* changes to -*y.* (See -LY, 5.)

HOT-

Adjective compounds are, of course, hyphenated: *hot-blooded, hot-eyed, hot-tempered,* etc. Exceptions are *hotheaded* and *hothearted.*

Noun compounds are usually written separate: *hot air, hot cake, hot cross bun, hot dog,* etc. Exceptions are *hotbed, hotbox, hothead, hothouse.*

Hotfoot, verb or adverb, is solid; but *hot-foot,* a noun, is hyphenated (give someone a *hot-foot,* i.e., secretly insert a match above the sole of his shoe and light it—an adolescent prank causing much amusement among its devotees).

hour's delay. Note the apostrophe. (See APOSTROPHE, USE OF, 4.)

HOUSE-

For the most part, compounds are solid: *houseboat, housebroken, housedress, household, housemaid, housewarming, housewife,* etc.

The following are separate: *house organ, house painter, house party, house physician.*

HUE, HEW

Hue is a shade of color—also, in the phrase *hue and cry,* a call or shout.

Hew is a verb meaning to shape, cut, chisel, etc. The past participle is *hewn.*

Rough-*hewn* timbers.

Let's *hew* to the straight and narrow.

Huguenot. The second -*u* keeps the -*g* "hard."

hullabaloo. First a double -*l,* then a single one.

hulloed, hulloing. These are the correctly spelled derivative forms of the verb *hullo,* even if the successive vowels look strange. (See -O, TERMINAL.)

humbugged, humbugging. Double final -*g* of *humbug* before -*ed, -er, -ing.* (See DOUBLING FINAL -G.)

humor, humour. The first spelling is

American, the second British. (See
-OR, -OUR, 1.)

humpbacked. No hyphen. (See HY-
PHENATING, 25.)

hunchbacked. No hyphen. (See HY-
PHENATING, 25.)

hurly-burly. Hyphenated.

hurrah. The derived forms are *hur-
rahed, hurrahing.*

Hygeia. See *hygiene.*

hygiene. *-I* before *-e* except after *c-*.
But the Greek goddess of health is,
contradictorily, *Hygeia, -e* before *-i.*
(See -IE, -EI, 1.)

HYPHENATING

(Rules for dividing words at the end
of a line: See SYLLABICATING.)

adjective compounds, 2
adjective compounds with prepositions, 11
adjectives made up of verb forms
and prepositions, 11
adjectives of two or more words, 2
adverbs with participles, 13
age, 49B, 49C
ante-, 21
anti-, 20
back-, 24
-backed, 25
by-, 46
co-, 14
colors, 47
compass points, 41
counter-, 36
cross-, 32
double-, 48
-elect, 8
ex-, 37
figures, 49
first-, 51
fractions, 50
good-, 45
great-, 35
half-, 28
half-, in relationships, 6B
head-, 33
hyphenate, when to, 1
hyphenate, when not to, 3
ill-, 29
in-laws, 6
left-, 26
letters, 52
-like, 40
mid-, 23
neo-, 39
no hyphens, 3
non-, 18
noun compounds, 1, 9
noun compounds with prepositions,
1, 10
nouns, combined, 1, 9
nouns, proper, with prefix, 12
numbers, 49
off-, 31
post-, 22
pre-, 17
prepositions in compounds, 10, 11
pro-, 34
proper nouns with prefix, 12
pseudo-, 42
quasi-, 44
rank, 5, 7, 8
re-, 16
relationships, 6
right-, 27
second-, 51
self-, 38
semi-, 43
separate words, 3B
solid words, 3A
step-, in relationships, 6B
symbols, 52
third-, 51
titles, 5, 7, 8
triple-, 48
un-, 19
unco-, 15
verb compounds with prepositions,
11
verbs, 4
vice- in titles, 7
well-, 30

1. when to hyphenate.

Two or more individual words
combined into a simple, unified
meaning or idea are generally hyphenated. For example: *cat's-paw,
chicken-hearted, court-martial, cross-
examination, first-rate, hand-to-*

mouth, jack-in-the-pulpit, Johnny-come-lately, letter-perfect, make-believe (noun or adj.), *make-up* (noun), *middle-aged, mother-in-law, ne'er-do-well, off-color, pick-me-up, rake-off, runner-up, soldier-states-man, stay-at-home,* etc. (*Stomach-ache* is hyphenated because of the repetition of *-ch; bellyache* and *headache* are written solid.)

As detailed in the following sections, certain words combined with prefixes, suffixes, or prepositions are hyphenated, some are not.

2. adjectives of two or more words.

Phrases that are treated as individual and separate words ordinarily become hyphenated compounds when used as adjectives, especially preceding the modified noun. Consider:

He is finally *up to date* on his work.

An *up-to-date* revision.

For an old man, he's really *up-to-date* in his views.

He administered immediate *first aid.*

He took a short *first-aid* course.

This table is *upside down.*

He has an *upside-down* view of life.

Let's *make believe.*

It's a *make-believe* world.

This stock has *no par value.*

A *no-par-value* issue of stock.

Other, and typical examples: *able-bodied, brand-new, God-fearing, law-abiding, lion-hearted, long-lived, low-spirited, middle-aged,* etc. Examples of phrases hyphenated especially preceding a noun are *hard-working* parents, *long-overdue* bills, *much-needed* love, *never-to-be-forgotten* night, *seldom-used* gadgets, *soft-spoken* answer, etc.

3. when not to hyphenate.

The current trend is to eliminate hyphens wherever practical and to write instead either a solid word or two or more separate words. For example:

A. solid words

bellboy	postgraduate
bellyache	roommate
boxcar	selfsame
bygone	subnormal
byword	teamwork
cabinetmaker	today
carryall	tomorrow
churchgoer	tonight
clubhouse	toothache
coeducation	transship
dressmaker	washcloth
dugout	washday
everyday	washout
goodby	washrag
hookup	washroom
horsepower	waterproof
lookout	weekday
network	weekend
newsstand	whereabouts
pocketbook	workroom
pocketknife	workshop

B. separate words

bird cage	ice cream
box seat	ill health
drawing room	letter carrier
fellow feeling	living room
fellow traveler	mail car
fire escape	pen name

A good rule to follow is this: *If you are in doubt about using a hyphen, omit it if the compound word looks proper without it.*

4. verbs.

Compound nouns written as separate words are hyphenated when used as verbs.

dry cleaning or *dry cleaners,* but to *dry-clean* a garment.

a boat in *dry dock,* but to *dry-dock* a boat.

a *high hat,* but to *high-hat* your poorer friends.

a *wet nurse,* but to *wet-nurse* a child.

5. titles.

A. Titles denoting a single office or rank are written as two separate words.

> assistant professor
> associate professor
> attorney general
> brigadier general
> deputy mayor
> district attorney
> first lieutenant
> first mate
> full professor
> judge advocate
> lieutenant commander
> lieutenant colonel
> lieutenant general
> lieutenant governor
> maid of honor
> major general
> notary public
> poet laureate
> postmaster general
> second lieutenant
> second mate
> sergeant major

B. The following may be written either hyphenated or as three separate words, the separate words now preferable.

attorney at law *or* attorney-at-law
commander in chief *or* commander-in-chief
editor in chief *or* editor-in-chief

6. relationships.

A. Various in-laws are hyphenated: *mother-in-law, father-in-law, brother-in-law, sister-in-law, son-in-law, daughter-in-law, cousin-in-law,* and so on.

B. Written separate are *half brother* and *half sister;* written solid are combinations with *step-: stepmother, stepfather, stepson, stepdaughter,* etc.

7. vice- in titles.

As a prefix to a title or rank, *vice-* is regularly followed by a hyphen.

vice-admiral   vice-consul
vice-chancellor   vice-president

However, *vice president* may also be written as two separate words, and, in fact, today usually is, especially when capitalized to mean the executive officer of the U.S. (*Vice President* Johnson, the *Vice President* entered; etc.)

Vicegerent and *viceroy* are of course solid words, since *vice-* is not a prefix to *-gerent* or *-roy.*

8. -elect.

This suffix is always separated from the title by a hyphen: *president-elect, governor-elect,* etc.

9. nouns, combined.

When two nouns combine to refer to one person or thing, the compound is hyphenated: *author-editor, owner-operator, scissors-knife, soldier-statesman, student-delegate,* etc.

10. noun compounds with prepositions.

A. Noun compounds containing prepositions are generally hyphenated.

diner-out	pick-me-up
finder-out	rake-off
go-between	runner-up
good-for-nothing	sergeant-at-arms
hanger-on	show-off
jack-in-the-box	shut-in
jack-in-the-pulpit	sit-in
looker-in	stand-in
looker-on	stay-at-home
man-of-war	stay-out
mother-in-law, etc.	step-up
(see Section 6)	will-o'-the-wisp
mother-of-pearl	work-up
passer-by	

B. But *holdout, holdover, holdup, pickup, washout,* and *workout* are now preferably spelled solid. And *attorney at law, commander in chief,* and *editor in chief* are now preferably spelled as separated words (see *section 5B*).

11. adjectives made up of verb forms and prepositions.

Such compounds are hyphenated when followed by a noun: *built-in, built-up, hand-to-mouth, lying-in, stepped-up, uncalled-for, unheard-of, unhoped-for, unlooked-for, washed-out,* etc., as in *built-in* baby-sitter, *lying-in* hospital, *stepped-up* production, etc.

12. proper nouns with prefix.

When a prefix precedes a proper noun, i.e., a noun starting with a capital, the compound is hyphenated: *Afro-American, Italo-American, post-Hellenic, pro-England, quasi-Freudian, un-American,* etc.

13. adverbs with participles.

A phrase containing an *-ly* adverb, like *happily married,* sounds so much as if the two words are a single idea that one is tempted to hyphenate them before a noun, as in *happily-married man.* This usage, however, is neither popular nor sanctioned. Keep the words separate: *a happily married man, a poorly made car, a frequently used gadget, a surprisingly young woman, a heavily laden horse, a conveniently situated house,* etc.

14. co-.

A. Words in which the prefix *co-* precedes the letter *-o* are best hyphenated to avoid mispronunciation. However, they may also, generally, be written solid, or with a dieresis over the second *-o* (ö). Examples are:

co-operate	co-ordinate
co-operation	co-ordinated
co-operative	co-ordinates

B. Otherwise, words should be written solid: *coaction, coed (co-ed* also acceptable), *coeducation, co-equal, coextend, coinsurance,* etc.

15. unco-.

Hence, the best spellings are *uncooperative* and *unco-ordinated,* though these words are also occasionally seen with two hyphens (*un-co-operative, un-co-ordinated*), or with the dieresis on the second *o* (ö) re-placing the hyphen (*uncoöperative, uncoördinated*).

16. re-.

A. To avoid awkward appearance and mispronunciation, the prefix *re-* is separated from a root beginning with *e-* by a hyphen.

re-echo	re-entrance
re-educate	re-entry
re-enforce	re-examine
re-enter	re-export

B. Before other vowels, no hyphen is necessary: *react, reincarnation, reinforce, reinsure, reopen, reorder, reorganize, reunite, reunion, reused,* etc. As an exception, *re-use* is generally spelled with a hyphen, but need not be. (*Reuse,* unhyphenated, might tempt to mispronunciation.)

C. However, a hyphen is necessary if without it a word might have a meaning other than the one intended. Thus, *recollect* is generally understood as a synonym of *remember.* If *collect again* is meant, the word is written *re-collect.* Similar examples:

re-act (act again)
re-call (call again)
re-cover (cover again)
re-dress (dress again)
re-form (form again)
re-mark (mark again)
re-turn (turn again)

17. pre-.

A. As in the case of *re-,* the prefix *pre-* is separated by a hyphen from a root beginning with the vowel *-e,* to avoid awkward appearance and mispronunciation.

pre-elect	pre-establish
pre-eminent	pre-exist
pre-empt	pre-existent

B. These words may also be spelled with a dieresis over the second *-e* (*preëlect,* etc.), but the hyphenated form is preferable.

C. Before other letters, no hyphen is necessary: *prearrange, preoccupy,* etc., unless the root word starts with a capital letter (*pre-Raphaelite, pre-Cambrian, pre-Renaissance,* etc.).

18. non-.

After the prefix *non-,* the hyphen is commonly and preferably omitted, unless the root word starts with a capital letter (*non-English, non-Chinese, non-American,* etc.).

The proper forms are *noninterference, nonnaval, nonproductive,* etc.

19. un-.

Un-, too, is written solid with its root (*unaggressive, unnegotiable, unseasonable,* etc.), but hyphenated before a capital letter (*un-American, un-Freudian,* etc.).

20. anti-.

The same holds true for *anti-;* use a hyphen only before a capital letter, as in *anti-English, anti-American, anti-Semitic,* etc., or when the root starts with an *i-,* as in *anti-immigration* or *anti-integration.* Even in words like *antilabor, antislavery, antiwar,* etc., the solid word is correct.

21. ante-.

And again for *ante-;* solid except before a capital (*anteroom, antenuptial; ante-Norman, ante-Victorian*). The Latin phrase *ante bellum* is two separate words, *ante-mortem* is hyphenated.

22. post-.

Similarly for *post-;* hyphenated before a capital (*post-Biblical, post-Victorian,* etc.), solid otherwise (*postnuptial, postseasonal,* etc.). The Latin phrase *post bellum* is two separate words, *post-mortem* is hyphenated.

23. mid-.

Hyphenated before a capital letter (*mid-October, mid-Victorian,* etc.), and in some less-than-common compounds (*mid-career, mid-century, mid-ocean, mid-position,* etc.).

Generally solid otherwise, the modern tendency omitting the hyphen wherever possible: *midchannel, midday, midland, midmorning, midnight, midpoint, midterm, midway, midweek, Midwest, midwinter,* etc.

24. back-.

A. The prefix *back-* generally merges so completely into the meaning of its root word, that a hyphen is rarely used. For example:

backbiting	backstroke
backdoor (*adj.*)	backswept
backfire	backswing
backhanded	backtrack (*verb*)
backlash	backup
backslapper	backwash

B. However, a hyphen *is* used in the following:

back-formation	back-scratcher
back-paddle	back-seat
(*verb*)	(driver)

C. And in the following, the words are separate:

back end	back stairs (*noun*)
back page	back street
back rest	back talk
back seat	back yard

25. -backed.

As a suffix, *-backed* is generally connected to its root by a hyphen (*broad-backed, low-backed, strong-backed,* etc.), except in the following, which are written solid:

barebacked	hunchbacked
humpbacked	

26. left-.

Compounds with this prefix are generally hyphenated:

left-hand (*adj.*)　　left-wing (*adj.*)
left-handed

But *leftover,* noun or adjective, is solid.

27. right-.

As a prefix, generally hyphenated:

right-angled	right-minded
right-hand (*adj.*)	right-wing (*adj.*)
right-handed (*adj.*)	

28. half-.

As a prefix, generally hyphenated:

half-baked	half-staff
half-blooded	half-truth
half-breed	half-wit
half-caste	half-witted
half-mast	

But the following are solid: *half-back, halfhearted, halfway.*

29. ill-.

A. Adjectives with the word *ill* as a prefix are all hyphenated (*ill-advised, ill-disposed, ill-gotten, ill-timed,* etc.), except for *ill at ease,* written as three separate words.

B. Nouns are mainly separate words (*ill fame, ill nature, ill will,* etc.), except that *ill-humor, ill-treatment,* and *ill-usage* are preferably hyphenated. They are also correct, however, as separate words: *ill humor, ill treatment, ill usage.*

C. *Ill-wisher* is always hyphenated.

D. The verbs *ill-treat* and *ill-use* are hyphenated.

30. well-.

Hyphenated if prefixed to an adjective preceding its noun:

well-balanced personality
well-groomed lawns
well-informed citizens
well-known author
He is *well balanced.*
They are *well groomed.*
She was *well informed.*
He is *well known.*

The noun *well-being* is hyphenated, the adjective *wellborn* is solid.

31. off-.

A few compounds with *off-* are hyphenated, notably:

off-chance	off-stage
off-color	off-white

Others are solid: *offbeat, offset, offshore,* etc.

32. cross-.

A. A few compounds are hyphenated, notably:

cross-country	cross-legged
cross-examine	cross-linked
cross-eye	cross-purpose
cross-eyed	cross-question
cross-fertilized	cross-refer
cross-grained	cross-town (*adj.*)
cross-index	

B. Others are written solid: *crossroad, crosswalk,* etc.; or as separate words: *cross reference, cross section, cross street.*

33. head-.

Two compounds with *head-* are hyphenated (*head-hunter, head-on*); others are solid (*headrest, headlong, headway,* etc.); where *head* is clearly a separate adjective, two words are used (*head counselor, head wind,* etc.).

34. pro-.

When this is prefixed to a word to mean *in favor of,* a hyphen is used: *pro-American, pro-government, pro-integration, pro-Negro, pro-war,* etc.

35. great-.

To denote ancestry, *great-* is followed by a hyphen: *great-aunt, great-grandchild, great-grandfather.* Otherwise, noun componds are written solid (*greatcoat*) or as separate words (*great Dane*), depending on the sense.

Adjective compounds are hyphenated (*great-minded, great-souled,* etc.), but *greathearted* is solid.

36. counter-.

This prefix is invariably spelled solid with the root (*countercharge, counterirritant, countermeasures,* etc.).

37. ex-.

Meaning *former, ex-* is always hyphenated to its root: *ex-husband, ex-president, ex-wife,* etc.

38. self-.

As a prefix, invariably connected to its root with a hyphen: *self-assured, self-centered, self-respect, self-serving,* etc.

39. neo-.

No hyphen when this prefix attaches to a common noun or its adjective, in which case it is spelled with a lower-case *n-*: *neoclassical, neoimpressionism*, etc.; hyphen and capital *N-* before a proper noun or its adjective: *Neo-Catholic, Neo-Freudian*, etc.

40. -like.

When this suffix attaches to a word ending in a single or double *-l*, a hyphen is used to avoid a confusing succession of *-l*'s: *ball-like, cell-like, girl-like*, etc. But *childlike, ghostlike, knifelike, scissorslike*, etc., are written solid.

41. compass points.

Written solid: *northeast, southwest*, etc. Hyphenated: *north-northwest, south-southwest*, etc.

42. pseudo-.

Written solid with technical and scientific nouns (*pseudomorphism, pseudopodia*, etc.), and in the common word *pseudonym*. Solid also with all adjectives (*pseudoenthusiastic, pseudofeminine, pseudointellectual, pseudopsychological*, etc.), unless the first letter of the adjective is an *o-*, in which case the compound is hyphenated (*pseudo-oriented, pseudo-orthodox*, etc.) to avoid the awkward combination of two *-o's*.

Hyphenated also before any adjective beginning with a capital letter (*pseudo-American, pseudo-Freudian*, etc.).

Separated and considered an adjective in its own right before any nontechnical noun: *pseudo brother, pseudo Freudians, pseudo satire*, etc.

43. semi-.

Generally written solid: *semiautomatic, semicircle, semidetached, semiofficial*, etc., except, of course, before a proper noun, as *semi-Chinese, semi-Freudian*, etc.

44. quasi-.

Hyphenated before adjectives and adverbs, as *quasi-efficiently, quasi-intellectual, quasi-judicial*, etc.; treated as a separate word rather than a prefix before nouns: *quasi intellectualism, quasi wisdom*, etc.

45. good-.

The following combinations with *good-* are hyphenated:

good-humored   good-sized
good-looking   good-tempered
good-natured

46. by-.

A. This prefix is joined to a word by a hyphen in: *by-election, by-line, by-pass, by-product, by-talk, by-work*.

B. In the following, it is solid: *bygone, bylaw, byname, bypath, byplay, byroad, bystander, bystreet, byway, byword*.

47. colors.

A serviceable rule to follow is that a two-word shade of color is written separate as a *noun*, hyphenated as an *adjective*. Thus, as nouns: *greenish blue, indigo blue, moss green, jade green, ruby red*, etc. But as adjectives: *greenish-blue vase, indigo-blue fabric, moss-green stone, jade-green ornament, ruby-red lips*, etc.

48. double, triple.

A. When *double* is used as a *prefix* (as in *double-jointed, double-park*, etc.), the compound is hyphenated. However, if *double* is clearly an adjective modifying a noun, as in *double play, double boiler, double standard*, etc., no hyphen is necessary. The following are especially worth noting.

> *hyphenated*
> double-cross (*verb*)
> double-dealer
> double-entendre
> double-header
> *separate*
> double cross (*noun*)
> double up (*verb*)

B. The same principles apply to *triple*.

49. numbers, figures.

A. Numbers from twenty-one through ninety-nine use a hyphen:

twenty-one	sixty-eight
thirty-two	seventy-nine
forty-five	eighty-four
fifty-seven	ninety-six

B. In order to show age, a hyphen is used between a number and *year-old:*

a one-year-old boy
a nineteen-year-old girl
a fifty-nine-year-old man
a six-year-old

C. *Teen-age,* as an adjective, and *teen-ager* are hyphenated.

D. After numbers, whether written as figures or words, the hyphen is generally used.

one-sided	two-way
one-time	three-cornered
one-track	three-sided
one-way	four-wheel
two-by-four	five-finger
two-edged	six-footer
two-faced	seven-footer
two-fisted	eight-sided
two-handed	nine-sided
two-sided	ten-sided

E. However, the following are written solid:

oneself	foursome
twofold	fivefold
twopenny	sixfold
twopence	sevenfold
twosome	eightfold
threefold	eightball
threepenny	ninefold
threepence	ninepins
threesome	tenfold
fourfold	tenpins
fourpenny	tenpenny

50. fractions.

Fractions are hyphenated (*one-half, two-thirds, three-quarters,* etc.), but if a hyphen occurs in either the numerator or the denominator, no hyphen is used between the two (*three one-hundredths, eighty-two five-thousandths,* etc.).

51. first-, second-, third-, etc.

When these adjectives show rank or degree of excellence, they are separated from their root by a hyphen, as in *first-rate, first-class, second-string, third-rate, third-degree,* etc.

52. letters, symbols.

These are usually connected by hyphens to the next word, as *X-ray* (also *ex-ray*), *U-boat, V-shaped, $-sign,* etc. Exceptions are *T square* and *U bolt.*

hypocrisy. This is the only correct spelling; *hipocrisy, hypocricy, hypocracy,* and *hypocrasy* are common errors.

hypocrite. Not *hipocrite.*

hypothesis. Plural is *hypotheses.* (See PLURALIZING WORDS IN TERMINAL -IS.)

I

-IANCE, -IENCE. See -ANCE, -ENCE, AFTER I-.

-IANT, -IENT. See -ANCE, -ENCE, AFTER I-.

-IBLE, -ABLE

(For words ending in *-able* see -ABLE, -IBLE.)

1. If the root is *not* a full word in its own right, the proper suffix is likely to be *-ible,* not *-able.* (There are, of course, exceptions; these will be found under -ABLE, -IBLE.)

Note, for example, that dropping *-ible* in the following does not leave a real word.

*aud*ible	*divis*ible
*combust*ible	*ed*ible
*compat*ible	*feas*ible
*cred*ible	*horr*ible
*dirig*ible	*indel*ible

_plaus_ible _suscep_tible
_poss_ible _terr_ible
_ris_ible _vis_ible

2. If the root plus the _immediate_ addition of -ion produces the noun form, again the ending is likely to be -ible.

accessible (accession)
affectible (affection)
collectible (collection)
compressible (compression)
connectible (connection)
contractible (contraction)
convertible (conversion *)
corrodible (corrosion **)
corruptible (corruption)
destructible (destruction)
digestible (digestion)
exhaustible (exhaustion)
expansible (expansion)
expressible (expression)
impressible (impression)
perfectible (perfection)
repressible (repression)
reversible (reversion)
suggestible (suggestion)
suppressible (suppression)

(Important exceptions to this principle: _correctable, detectable, predictable,_ all of which have immediate -ion forms—_correction, detection, prediction._)

3. If the root ends in -ns, the ending is probably -ible. (Important exceptions: _dispensable_ and _indispensable._)

comprehensible ostensible
defensible reprehensible
distensible responsible
expansible sensible

4. Similarly, if the root ends in -miss.

admissible permissible
dismissible transmissible

---

* -_T_ changes to -_s_, which does not change the principle.
** -_D_ changes to -_s_, which again does not affect the principle.

5. Or if the root ends in "soft" -_c_ (pronounced like _s._)

coercible irascible
convincible miscible
evincible producible
forcible reducible
inducible seducible
invincible

(Exceptions are those words, like _noticeable,_ in which the -_e_ is retained before -_able_ in order to preserve the "soft" -_c_ pronunciation. For a full list see -CEABLE.)

6. Or "soft" -_g_ (pronounced as in _gem._)

eligible legible
incorrigible negligible
intelligible tangible

(Exceptions are those words, like _chargeable,_ in which the -_e_ is retained before -_able_ in order to preserve the "soft" -_g_ pronunciation. For a full list, see -GEABLE.)

7. Certain -_ible_ words do not fit into any useful categories. These you must become so familiar with visually that only the correct suffix looks right.

collapsible flexible
contemptible gullible
discernible resistible

See also -ABLE, -EABLE; -ABLE, -IBLE; -CEABLE; -GEABLE.

ICE-

Adjectives are generally hyphenated (_ice-capped, ice-clad, ice-cooled, ice-free,_ etc.); however, _ice-bound_ is solid.

Ice cream is hyphenated as an adjective (_ice-cream_ cone), separate as a noun (chocolate _ice cream_).

Noun compounds are mostly separate (_ice age, ice bag, ice water,_ etc.), except the following, which are solid:

iceberg icebreaker
iceblink icecap
iceboat icehouse
icebox iceman

-ICIAN, -ITIAN

Professional and occupational titles almost always end in *-ician;* typical examples are *electrician, magician, mathematician, musician, physician, politician,* etc.

However, *dietitian* is the preferred spelling, though *dietician* is also correct.

See also -ISSION; -ITION.

-ICIOUS, -ITIOUS

1. The following nontechnical words end in *-icious.*

auspicious	malicious
avaricious	meretricious
capricious	officious
delicious	pernicious
inauspicious	suspicious
injudicious	vicious
judicious	

2. Notice that many of the adjectives in Section 1 have noun forms containing *-c: auspices, avarice, caprice, malice, suspicion, vice.*

3. The following end in *-itious.*

adscititious	flagitious
adventitious	nutritious
ambitious	propitious
expeditious	seditious
factitious	superstitious
fictitious	supposititious

4. Notice that most of the adjectives in Section 3 have noun forms ending in *-ition: ambition, expedition, fiction, nutrition, sedition, superstition, supposition.* See also -ACIOUS, -ACEOUS, -ATIOUS; -OCIOUS.

ICKLE, -ICKEL

For this sound, most common words are spelled *-ickle,* with the important exception of *nickel,* the only correct pattern for both the coin and the metal.

fickle	stickle
pickle	strickle
prickle	tickle
sickle	trickle

I'd. Contraction of *I had* or *I would,* the apostrophe appearing in place of the missing letters. (See APOSTROPHE, USE OF, 1.)

ideally. Note the double *-l,* since the adverbial suffix *-ly* is added to the adjective *ideal.* (See -LY, 7.)

ideology. *-O* follows *e-,* even though *idea* exhibits a differing pattern.

idiosyncrasy. The ending is *-sy,* not *-cy.* (See -CY, -SY, 4.)

IDLE, IDOL, IDYL

Idle is an adjective or verb referring, among other things, to lack of work, movement, etc.; *idol* is a noun designating a person, thing, etc., that is worshiped; and *idyl* is a kind of poem or prose work.

He is now *idle.*

He *idled* away the day.

He makes an *idol* out of his wife.

He writes *idyls* as a hobby.

idolater. Ends in *-er.* (See -ER, -OR, 1.)

idyl, idyll. The one *-l* spelling is preferable. See IDLE, IDOL, IDYL.

idyllic. Two *-l*'s.

-IE, -EI

WHEN SOUNDED *EE,* AS IN *GRIEF.*

1. The general pattern is *-i* before *-e* except after *c-.*

achieve	grievous
brief	niece
field	siege
grief	thief
grieve	

2. Immediately following the letter *c-,* then, *-ei* is used.

ceiling	perceive
conceit	preconceive
conceive	receipt
deceit	receive
deceive	

3. The notable exception to the previous rule is *financier,* in which

-ie is used despite the immediately preceding *-c.*

4. Certain other words are spelled *-ei,* though *there is no immediately preceding -c.*

either	seizure
inveigle	sheik
leisure	weir
neither	weird
seize	

A. Also certain terms from chemistry, as: *caffeine, codeine, protein.*

5. Likewise, certain proper names: *Goldstein, Keith, Neil, O'Neil, Reid.*

WHEN SOUNDED *AY,* AS IN *NEIGH.*

6. With such a sound, the pattern *-ei* is always correct.

chow mein	reign
feign	rein
freight	skein
heinous	sleigh
inveigh	veil
inveigle	vein
neigh	weigh
neighbor	weight

WHEN SOUNDED *EYE,* AS IN *HEIGHT.*

7. Again the pattern *-ei* is used.

Fahrenheit	seismic
gneiss	seismograph
height	sleight (of hand)
leitmotif	stein

8. But *-ie* before the letter *-r: fiery, hierarchy, hieroglyphic.*

WITH THE SOUND OF SHORT *-I,* AS IN *HIT.*

9. *-Ei* is used in words ending in *-feit: counterfeit, forfeit, surfeit.*

10. And in the combination *-eign: foreign, foreigner, sovereign, sovereignty.*

11. Otherwise, *-ie* is used.

handkerchief	quotient
mischief	sieve
patient	transient

12. *-Ie* also after *c-* that is pronounced *sh.*

ancient	omniscient
conscience	prescient
deficient	proficient
efficient	sufficient

WHEN PRONOUNCED *E,* AS IN *LED.*

13. The important word to bear in mind is *friend* and its derivative forms, all with the *-ie* pattern.

befriend	friendship
friend	unfriendly
friendly	

14. Contrarily, *heifer* and *nonpareil* (pronounced non-pa-RELL) have the *-ei* pattern.

-IE TO -Y

In verbs ending in *-ie,* substitute *-y* before adding *-ing.*

belie—belying	tie—tying
die—dying	vie—vying
lie—lying	

-ied. See -Y PLUS A SUFFIX, 1.
-iegn. See *-eign.*

-IER, -IEST

1. If an adjective ends in *-y* preceded by a consonant (*lively, stingy, happy*), the comparative and superlative are formed by changing *-y* to *-i* before adding *-er* or *-est: livelier, liveliest; stingier, stingiest; happier, happiest.*

2. In the adjective *dry,* the same principle is observed—*drier, driest.*

3. When *dry* is a *verb, -y* again changes to *-i* before *-es* or *-ed: dries, dried.*

4. In the adjectives *shy* and *sly* again the *-y* is changed to *-i;* but spellings that retain the *-y* are also correct. Thus:

shy—shier *or* shyer; shiest *or* shyest
sly—slier *or* slyer; sliest *or* slyest

5. However, for *wry,* the comparative and superlative are spelled only *wrier* and *wriest*.

6. But in *coy, gay,* and *gray,* words in which the *-y* is preceded by a *vowel,* the *-y* is retained.

coy—coyer, coyest
gay—gayer, gayest
gray—grayer, grayest

See also -Y PLUS A SUFFIX, 3.

-ies. See -Y PLUS A SUFFIX, 1.

-IES, -YS, -EYS. See -EYS, -IES, -YS.

-IEST, -IER. See -IER, -IEST.

-IFY, -EFY

1. The overwhelmingly common ending on verbs is *-ify: classify, nullify, qualify, ratify, testify,* etc.

2. The very few verbs ending in *-efy,* and almost universally misspelled, are:

liquefy   stupefy
putrefy   torrefy
rarefy

(Also *defy,* never misspelled.)

3. Hence, the noun forms of these five verbs also contain an *-e* before the *-f:*

liquefaction   stupefaction
putrefaction   torrefaction
rarefaction

4. However, adjective forms end in *-id: liquid, putrid, stupid, torrid.*

5. And though *rarefy* is spelled as noted, *purify* follows the common pattern, notwithstanding that in both instances the adjective ends in *-e* (*rare, pure*), and the noun in *-ity* (*rarity, purity*).

ignominious. The third *-i* (preceding the *-ous*) is often ignored by poor spellers.

ignorance, ignorant. Note the *-ance* and *-ant* endings. (See -ANCE, -ENCE, AFTER R-, 10, 10A.)

-IL, -ILL

1. Words of one syllable end in a double *-l: chill, drill, fill, hill, mill,* etc. (*Nil* is one of the very few exceptions.)

2. Compounds of the verb *fill* end in a double *-l: overfill, refill,* etc.

3. *Fulfill* is the preferable spelling, though *fulfil* is also correct. (Note the single *-l* terminating the *first* syllable in either form.) Derived forms have the double *-l* (*fulfilled, fulfilling, fulfillment*), except that *fulfilment* is also correct.

4. Likewise, *instill* and *distill* (double *-l*) are preferred; *instil* and *distil* also correct. In the derived forms keep the double *-l: instilled, instilling, instillation; distilled, distilling, distiller, distillery, distillate, distillation. Instillment, distillment* are preferred, *instilment, distilment* also correct.

5. *Until* has one *-l,* the shortened form *till* has two.

See also -AL, -ALL; DOUBLING FINAL -L; -EL; -ELL; -OL, -OLL.

I'll. Contraction of *I will* or *I shall,* the apostrophe appearing in place of the missing letters. (See APOSTROPHE, USE OF, 1.)

ILL-. See HYPHENATING, 29.

illegible. The ending is *-ible* to keep the preceding *-g* "soft." (See -IBLE, -ABLE, 6.)

illegitimate. Note the *-e* after the double *l-.*

illiteracy, illiterate. Note the *-e* after the *t-.*

illusion. See ALLUSION, ILLUSION.

illustrator. Ends in *-or.* (See -ER, -OR, 5.)

I'm. Contraction of *I am,* the apostrophe appearing in place of the missing *-a.* (See APOSTROPHE, USE OF, 1.)

imaginable. The -*e* of *imagine* is dropped before a suffix beginning with a vowel. (See DROPPED -E.)

imaginary. Ends in -*ary.* (See -ARY, -ERY, 1.)

imbroglio. The -*g* is silent.

imitable. Since -*a* is the principal vowel in another form of the word (*imitate*), the correct ending is -*able.* (See -ABLE, -IBLE, 5.)

imitator. Ends in -*or.* (See -ER, -OR, 5.)

immaculate. Double -*m,* one -*c.*

immalleable. Ends in -*able.* (See -ABLE, -IBLE, 7.)

immanent. See IMMINENT, IMMANENT.

immeasurable. Double -*m.*

immediate. Double -*m.*

immense. Double -*m.*

immensely. *Immense* plus -*ly;* make sure to get that -e in before the adverbial ending.

IMMINENT, IMMANENT

Anything *imminent* is likely to happen soon: his *imminent* departure; war is *imminent;* prepared for an *imminent* snowstorm.

Immanent, the far less common word, means inherent, indwelling, subjective, or remaining or operating within: *immanent* qualities of serpents; such reactions are *immanent* to man.

Note that both words have a double -*m.*

immovable. Note that the ending is -*able,* not -*ible. Immoveable* not correct. (See -ABLE, -IBLE, 2.)

impalpable. Ends in -*able.* (See -ABLE, -IBLE, 7.)

IMPASSABLE, IMPASSIBLE

An *impassable* road is one that cannot be passed, traveled over, etc.

Impassible, from the same root as *impassive,* means incapable of feeling, pain, suffering or other emotional reactions.

impeccable. Double -*c,* as in *peccadillo,* which is from the same Latin root.

impel. Ends in one -*l,* not two. (See -EL, -ELL, 2.)

impelled, impelling. Because *impel* is accented on the last syllable, final -*l* is *doubled* before a suffix starting with a vowel. (See DOUBLING FINAL -L, 1.)

impellent. Ends in -*ent.*

impenetrable. Since -*a* is the principal vowel in another form of the word (*penetrate*), the correct form is -*able.* (See -ABLE, -IBLE, 5.)

impenitence, impenitent. End in -*ence* and -*ent.* (See -ANCE, -ENCE, AFTER T-, 3, 4.)

imperishable. The ending is -*able,* not -*ible.* (See -ABLE, -IBLE, 1.)

impermanence, impermanent. Two of the many words ending in -*ence* or -*ent* after *n-.* (See -ANCE, -ENCE, AFTER N-, 1.)

impertinence, impertinent. Again, -*ence* or -*ent* after *n-.* (See -ANCE, -ENCE, AFTER N-, 1.)

imperturbable. Ends in -*able.* (See -ABLE, -IBLE, 1.)

impetuous. Note the -*u* before -*ous.* (See -UOUS.)

impetus. Not *impetous.* (See -US, -OUS.)

implacable. Only the -*able* ending will keep the preceding -*c* "hard." (See -ABLE, -IBLE, 6.)

implausible. The ending is -*ible,* not -*able.* (See -IBLE, -ABLE, 1.)

importable. -*Able.* (See -ABLE, -IBLE, 1.)

importance, important. End in -*ance* or -*ant.* (See -ANCE, -ENCE, AFTER T-, 1.)

impossible. The ending is -*ible.* (See -IBLE, -ABLE, 1.)

impostor. Ends in -*or.* (See -ER, -OR, 5.)

impotence, impotency, impotent. Note

that -*e*, not -*a*, follows the *t*-. (See -ANCE, -ENCE, AFTER T-, 5.)

impracticable. Only the -*able* ending will keep the preceding -*c* "hard." (See -ABLE, -IBLE, 6.)

impregnable. Since -*a* is the principal vowel in another form of the word (*pregnant*), the correct ending is -*able*. (See -ABLE, -IBLE, 5.)

impresario. One -*s;* plural is *impresarios.* (See PLURALIZING WORDS IN TERMINAL -O, 3.)

impressible. If the root forms its noun by the immediate addition of -*ion* (*impression*), the correct ending is likely to be -*ible.* (See -IBLE, -ABLE, 2.)

impressionable. Ends in -*able.* (See -ABLE, -IBLE, 1.)

improbable. This word ends -*able.* (See -ABLE, -IBLE, 7.)

impromptu. Watch that second -*p*.

improvidence, improvident. Almost always, with only a few exceptions, -*ence* or -*ent* follows a *d*-. (See -ANCE, -ENCE, AFTER D-, 1.)

improvise. Note the -*ise* ending, common to all words ending in -*vise.* (See -ISE, 2.)

imprudence, imprudent. Almost always, with only a few exceptions, -*ence* or -*ent* follows a *d*-. (See -ANCE, -ENCE, AFTER D-, 1.)

impudence, impudent. Usually -*ence* or -*ent* follows a *d*-. (See -ANCE, -ENCE, AFTER D-, 1.)

IN-, EN-. See EN-, IN-.

---

inaccessible. Ends in -*ible* (See -IBLE, -ABLE, 2.)

inadmissible. When the root ends in -*miss*, the correct ending is -*ible.* (See -IBLE, -ABLE, 4.)

inadvertence, inadvertent. Frequently misspelled -*ance* and -*ant.* (See -ANCE, -ENCE, AFTER T-, 3, 4.)

inapplicable. Only the -*able* ending will keep the preceding -*c* "hard." (See -ABLE, -IBLE, 6.)

inasmuch as. Note that the first part is solid, followed by the word *as*.

inaudible. The ending is -*ible*, not -*able*. (See -IBLE, -ABLE, 1.)

inaugurate. The vowel after *g*- is -*u*.

inauspicious. Ends in -*icious*, not -*itious.* (See -ICIOUS, -ITIOUS, 1.)

incandescent. Note the -*sc*. (See -ESCE, -ESCENT, -ESCENCE, 3.)

incapable. Since -*a* is the principal vowel in another form of the word (*incapacity*), the correct form is -*able*. (See -ABLE, -IBLE, 5.)

incase. See *encase.*

incaution. Ends in -*tion.* (See -AUTIOUS.)

incautious. Ends in -*tious.* (See -AUTIOUS.)

incense. Though the noun (What *incense* are you burning?) and the verb (Don't *incense* your parents.) are utterly different in meaning, the spelling is the same for both; note the -*c*.

incestuous. -*U* before -*ous.* (See -UOUS.)

incidence. Almost always, with only a few exceptions, -*ence*, not -*ance*, follows a *d*-. (See -ANCE, -ENCE, AFTER D-, 1.)

incidentally. -*Ly* is added to the adjective *incidental*, hence the -*ally* ending. Not *incidently.* (See -LY, -ALLY, 3).

incipience, incipient. Most often, as here, -*ence* or -*ent* follows *i*-. (See -ANCE, -ENCE, AFTER I-, 1.)

incise. One of five verbs ending in -*cise* rather than -*cize.* (See -ISE, 6.)

incisor. Ends in -*or.* (See -ER, -OR, 5.)

inclose. See *enclose.*

inclosure. See *enclosure.*

incoherence, incoherent. End in -*ence* and -*ent.* (See -ANCE, -ENCE, AFTER R-, 4, 4A.)

incompatible. The ending is -*ible*, not -*able*. (See -IBLE, -ABLE, 1.)

incompetence, incompetent. The ending is *-ence* or *-ent.* (See -ANCE, -ENCE, AFTER T-, 3, 4.)

incomprehensible. If the root ends in *-ns,* the likely ending is *-ible,* not *-able.* (See -IBLE, -ABLE, 3.)

incongruence. With very few exceptions *-ence,* rather than *-ance,* follows *u-.* (See -ANCE, -ENCE, AFTER U-, 3.)

incongruous. *-U* before *-ous.* (See -UOUS.)

inconsequence. Always *-ence,* not *-ance* after *qu-.* (See -ANCE, -ENCE, AFTER U-, 1.)

inconsistency, inconsistent. *-E,* not *-a,* after the *t-.*

inconspicuous. *-U* before *-ous.* (See -UOUS.)

incontinence, incontinent. Somewhat more words end in *-ence* or *-ent* after *n-,* rather than in *-ance, -ant.* (See -ANCE, -ENCE, AFTER N-, 1.)

inconvenience, inconvenient. Most often, as here, *-ence* or *-ent,* rather than *-ance* or *-ant,* follows *i-.* (See -ANCE, -ENCE, AFTER I-, 1.)

incorrigible. The ending is *-ible* to keep the preceding *-g* "soft." (See -IBLE, -ABLE, 6.)

incorruptible. If the root forms its noun by the immediate addition of *-ion* (*corruption*), the correct ending is likely to be *-ible.* (See -IBLE, -ABLE, 2.)

incredible. The ending is *-ible,* not *-able.* (See -IBLE, -ABLE, 1.)

incubator. Ends in *-or.* (See -ER, -OR, 5.)

incubus. Not *incubous.* (See -US, -OUS.)

incurable. Ends in *-able.* (See -ABLE, -IBLE, 2.)

incurred, incurrence, incurring. The final *-r* of *incur* is doubled before *-ed, -ence,* and *-ing,* since the accent falls on the last syllable (*cur*) and remains there in the derived forms. (See DOUBLING FINAL -R, 2, 3.)

incurrence. Note the double *-r* and the *-ence* ending (See -ANCE, -ENCE, AFTER R-, 3.)

indefatigable. No *-u,* even though it comes from *fatigue;* the *-able* ending keeps the *-g* "hard." (See -ABLE, -IBLE, 6.)

indefensible. If the root ends in *-ns,* the likely ending is *-ible,* not *-able.* (See -IBLE, -ABLE, 3.)

indefinable. Ends in *-able.* (See -ABLE, -IBLE, 2.)

indefinitely. See *definitely.*

indelible. *-Ible,* not *-able.* (See -IBLE, -ABLE, 1.)

independence, independent. Almost always, with only a few exceptions, *-ence* or *-ent,* not *-ance* or *-ant,* follows a *d-.* (See -ANCE, -ENCE, AFTER D-, 1.)

indescribable. *-Able,* not *-ible.* (See -ABLE, -IBLE, 2.)

indispensable. Misspelling of *indispensable.*

indestructible. If the root forms its noun by the immediate addition of *-ion* (*destruction*), the correct ending is likely to be *-ible.* (See -IBLE, -ABLE, 2.)

indicator. Ends in *-or.* (See -ER, -OR, 5.)

INDICT, INDITE

These verbs are pronounced the same but are spelled differently and have different meanings.

He was *indicted* (i.e., accused) by the grand jury.

They *indited* a complaint to the president of the company (i.e., put into writing).

The nouns are *indictment* and *inditement.*

indifference, indifferent. Ends in *-ence* or *-ent.* (See -ANCE, -ENCE, AFTER R-, 7, 7A.)

indigence. Because of the "soft" *-g,* *-ence,* not *-ance.* (See -ANCE, -ENCE, AFTER G-, 4.)

indigenous. *-E,* not *-i,* after the *g-*.

indigestible. If the root forms its noun by the immediate addition of *-ion* (*indigestion*), the correct ending is likely to be *-ible.* (See -IBLE, -ABLE, 2.)

indiscreet, indiscrete. See DISCREET, DISCRETE.

indispensable. Remember the ending by thinking that only an *able* man is *indispensable.* Not also the *-i* following *d-,* from the original verb *to dispense.* (See -ABLE, -IBLE, 1.)

indisputable. Ends in *-able.* (See -ABLE, -IBLE, 2.)

indistinguishable. This word ends in *-able.* (See -ABLE, -IBLE, 1.)

indite. See INDICT, INDITE.

indivisible. *-IBLE,* not *-able.* (See -IBLE, -ABLE, 1.)

indolence, indolent. Generally, but not always, *l-* is followed by *-ence* or *-ent,* rather than *-ance* or *-ant.* (See -ANCE, -ENCE, AFTER L-, 1, 3.)

indomitable. Ends in *-able.* (See -ABLE, -IBLE, 7.)

indorse. See *endorse.*

indubitable. Ends in *-able.*

inducible. The ending is *-ible* to keep the preceding *-c* "soft." (See -IBLE, -ABLE, 5.)

indue. See *endue.*

indure. See *endure.*

inedible. Ends in *-ible.* (See -IBLE, -ABLE, 1.)

ineffable. Note the *-able* ending. (See -ABLE, -IBLE, 7.)

ineligible. The ending is *-ible* to keep the preceding *-g* "soft." (See -IBLE, -ABLE, 6.)

inequitable. Note the *-able* ending. (See -ABLE, -IBLE, 7.)

ineradicable. Ends in *-able.* (See -ABLE, -IBLE, 6.)

inerasable. Again, *-able.* (See -ABLE, -IBLE, 2.)

-iness. See -Y PLUS A SUFFIX, 6.

inestimable. Since *-a* is the principal vowel in another form of the word (*estimate*), the correct form is *-able* (See -ABLE, -IBLE, 5.)

inevitable. Ends in *-able.* (See -ABLE, -IBLE, 7.)

inexcusable. This word ends in *-able.* (See -ABLE, -IBLE, 2.)

inexhaustible. If the root forms its noun by the immediate addition of *-ion* (*exhaustion*), the correct ending is likely to be *-ible.* (See -IBLE, -ABLE, 2.)

inexorable. Ends in *-able.* (See -ABLE, -IBLE, 7.)

inexpedience, inexpedient. Most often, as here, *-ence* or *-ent,* rather than *-ance* or *-ant,* follows *i-*. (See -ANCE, -ENCE, AFTER I-, 1.)

inexperience. The ending is *-ence.* (See -ANCE, -ENCE, AFTER I-, 1.)

inexplicable. Only the *-able* ending will keep the preceding *-c* "hard." (See -ABLE, -IBLE, 6.)

inexpressible. If the root forms its noun by the immediate addition of *-ion* (*expression*), the correct ending is likely to be *-ible.* (See -IBLE, -ABLE, 2.)

inextinguishable. *-Able.* (See -ABLE, -IBLE, 1.)

inextricable. *-Able,* to keep the preceding *-c* "hard." (See -ABLE, -IBLE, 6.)

infallible. The ending is *-ible,* not *-able.* (See -IBLE, -ABLE, 1.)

inferable. An exception to the rule; though the accent remains on what was the last syllable of *infer* (in-FER-a-ble), only one *-r* is used. (See DOUBLING FINAL -R, 5.)

inference. Only one *-r,* since the accent has shifted back to the first syllable; and note the *-ence* ending. (See -ANCE, -ENCE, AFTER R-, 1; DOUBLING FINAL -R, 3.)

inferential. Only one *-r.* (See DOUBLING FINAL -R, 4.)

inferred, inferring. The final *-r* of *infer* is doubled before *-ed* and *-ing,* since the accent falls on the last syllable (*fer*) and remains there in the derived forms. (See DOU-BLING FINAL -R, 2, 3.)

inferrible. A substitute, and equally satisfactory, spelling for *inferable*.

infirmary. Ends in *-ary*.

inflammable. Since *-a* is the principal vowel in another form of the word (*inflammation*), the correct ending is *-able*. (See -ABLE, -IBLE, 5.)

inflammatory. As in *inflammation*, *-a* after *mm-*.

inflection, inflexion. The latter is British. (See -ECTION, -EXION.)

inflexible. Ends in *-ible*. (See -IBLE, -ABLE, 7.)

influence. Always *-ence*, not *-ance*, after *fl-*. (See -ANCE, -ENCE, AFTER U-, 2.)

infold. See *enfold*.

inforce. Misspelling of *enforce*.

INGENIOUS, INGENUOUS

The first word, pronounced in-JEEN-yus, means clever, inventive, etc.; the second, pronounced in-JEN-yoo-us, means possessing child-like frankness, openness, innocence, naïveté, etc.

---

ingraft. See *engraft*.

ingrain. Preferable to *engrain*. (See EN-, IN-, 3.)

ingrave. Incorrect spelling of *engrave*.

in-group (noun). Hyphenated.

ingulf. See *engulf*.

inhabitant, inhabitance. End in *-ant* and *-ance*. (See -ANCE, -ENCE, AFTER T-, 1, 2.)

inherent, inherence. End in *-ent* and *-ence*. (See -ANCE, -ENCE, AFTER R-, 4, 4A.)

inheritance. *-Ance* is found somewhat more often than *-ence* after *t-*. (See -ANCE, -ENCE, AFTER T-, 1.)

inheritor. Ends in *-or*. (See -ER, -OR, 5.)

inhibited, inhibiting. Because *inhibit* is *not* accented on the last syllable, final *-t* is *not* doubled before a suffix

beginning with a vowel. (See DOU-BLING FINAL -T, 3.)

inhospitable. Since *-a* is the principal vowel in another form of the word (*hospitality*), the correct form is *-able*. (See -ABLE, -IBLE, 5.)

inimitable. Since *-a* is the principal vowel in another form of the word (*imitate*), the correct form is *-able*. (See -ABLE, -IBLE, 5.)

injudicious. Ends in *-icious*, not *-itious*. (See -ICIOUS, -ITIOUS, 1.)

in-laws. See HYPHENATING, 6.

inmesh. See *enmesh*.

innkeeper. No hyphen.

innocence, innocent. *-Ence* or *-ent*, rather than *-ance* or *-ant*, to keep the preceding *-c* "soft." (See -ANCE, -ENCE, AFTER C-, 1.)

innoculate. Misspelling of *inoculate*.

innocuous. Two *-n's*, one *-c*, as in *innocent*, which comes from the same Latin root. (See -UOUS.)

innuendo. Double *-n* after *i-*; the plural is *innuendoes*. (See PLURALIZING WORDS IN TERMINAL -O, 1.)

innumerable. Double *-n*, ends in *-able*. (See -ABLE, -IBLE, 5.)

inoculate. Like its synonym *inject*, has only one *-n*, one *-c*, though most people are fond of using two of either or both.

inoperable. Ends in *-able—operate*, the parent form, also has an *-a* after the *r-*. (See -ABLE, -IBLE, 5.)

inquire, inquiry. Preferable to *enquire, enquiry*. (See EN-, IN-, 3.)

insatiable. *-Able* is the correct suffix after the letter *i-*. (See -ABLE, -IBLE, 3.)

inscrutable. Ends in *-able*. (See -ABLE, -IBLE, 7.)

insensible. If the root ends in *-ns*, the likely ending is *-ible*, not *-able*. (See -IBLE, -ABLE, 3.)

inseparable. Ends in *-able; separate*, the parent word, also has *-a* after the *r-*. (See -ABLE, -IBLE, 5.)

insignificance, insignificant. *-Ance* or *-ant*, rather than *-ence* or *-ent*, to keep the -c "hard." (See -ANCE, -ENCE, AFTER C-, 3.)

insipience. Most often, as here, -ence, rather than -ance, follows i-. (See -ANCE, -ENCE, AFTER I-, 1.)

insistence, insistent. Note the -ence and -ent endings. (See -ANCE, -ENCE, AFTER T-, 3, 4.)

insnare. See ensnare.

insolence, insolent. Generally, but not always, l- is followed by -ence or -ent, rather than -ance or -ant. (See -ANCE, -ENCE, AFTER L-, 1, 3.)

insolvent, insolvency. Note that -e, not -a, follows the v-.

insouciance, insouciant. -Ance and -ant. (See -ANCE, -ENCE, AFTER I-, 4.)

inspector. Ends in -or. (See -ER, -OR, 5.)

install. Double -l at the end. (See -AL, -ALL, 1.)

installation. Double -l. (See -AL, -ALL, 2.)

installment, instalment. The first spelling (two -l's) is preferable. (See -AL, -ALL, 2.)

instead. Not insted.

instigator. Ends in -or. (See -ER, -OR, 5.)

instill, instil. Double -l preferable. The same with instillment, instilment. (See -IL, -ILL, 4.)

instilled, instilling. These forms must have two -l's. (See -IL, -ILL, 4.)

insufferable. Ends in -able. (See -ABLE, -IBLE, 1.)

insuperable. This word has the -able ending. (See -ABLE, -IBLE, 7.)

insurable. Ends in -able. (See -ABLE, -IBLE, 2.)

insurance. Preferable to ensurance. The suffix -ance invariably attaches to a noun formed from a verb ending in -ure. (See -ANCE, -ENCE, AFTER R-, 9; EN-, IN-, 3.)

insure. Preferable to ensure.

insurmountable. Ends in -able, not -ible. (See -ABLE, -IBLE, 1.)

inswathe. See enswathe.

intangible. The ending is -ible, to keep the preceding -g "soft." (See -IBLE, -ABLE, 6.)

intangle. Misspelling of entangle.

intelligence, intelligent. Because of the "soft" -g, -ence or -ent, not -ance or -ant. (See -ANCE, -ENCE, AFTER G-, 4.)

intelligentsia. Final -t of intelligent retained in this word.

intelligible. The ending is -ible, to keep the preceding -g "soft." (See -IBLE, -ABLE, 6.)

intemperance. Ends in -ance. (See -ANCE, -ENCE, AFTER R-, 6.)

intemperant. This word obsolete; the adjective is intemperate.

intention. Ends in -ention. (See -ENSION, -ENTION.)

INTER-
 Never a hyphen in compounds with this prefix (interchange, interrelationship, etc.) unless the root starts with a capital letter (inter-American, etc.).

---

intercede. -Cede is the common ending for such verbs, but there are exceptions. (See -CEED, -SEDE, -CEDE, 3.)

interesting. The first -e is not always pronounced, but must be spelled.

interference. Ends in -ence. (See -ANCE, -ENCE, AFTER R-, 4.)

interlocutor. Ends in -or. (See -ER, -OR, 5.)

interlope. Not interloap. (See -OPE, -OAP.)

intermittent, intermittence, intermittency. -E not -a, after the tt-. (See -ANCE, -ENCE, AFTER T-, 3, 4.)

interred, interring. The final -r of inter is doubled before -ed and -ing, since the accent falls on the last syllable (ter) and remains there in the derived forms. (See DOUBLING FINAL -R, 2, 3.)

intervention. Ends in -ention. (See -ENSION, -ENTION.)

inthrone. See *enthrone.*

intitle. See *entitle.*

intolerable. The parent word, *tolerate,* also has an -*a* after the *r*-. (See -ABLE, IBLE, 5.)

intolerance, intolerant. End in -*ance* and -*ant.* (See -ANCE, -ENCE, AFTER R-, 10.)

intomb. See *entomb.*

intractable. Ends in -*able.* (See -ABLE, -IBLE, 7.)

intransigeance, intransigeant. The -*e* before the suffix keeps the -*g* "soft." (See -ANCE, -ENCE, AFTER G-, 3.)

intransigence, intransigent. Equally correct spellings of *intransigeance, intransigeant,* and probably more popular.

intreat. See *entreat.*

intrench. See *entrench.*

intresting. Misspelling of *interesting.*

intrust. See *entrust.*

intumesce, intumescent. Note the -*sc.* (See -ESCE, -ESCENT, -ESCENCE, 1, 2.)

intwine. See *entwine.*

intwist. See *entwist.*

inure. Preferable to *enure.* (See EN-, IN-, 3.)

invalided. Final -*d* of the verb *invalid* not doubled before a suffix. (See DOUBLING FINAL -D, 2.)

inveigh. When sounded as *ay,* the spelling -*ei* is always correct. (See -*IE,* -*EI,* 6.)

inveigle. As in *inveigh,* -*ei.* (See -IE, EI, 4, 6.)

invention. The ending is -*ention.* (See -ENSION, -ENTION.)

inventor. Ends in -*or.* (See -ER, -OR, 5.)

investigator. The ending is -*or.* (See -ER, -OR, 5.)

investor. Ends in -*or.* (See -ER, -OR, 5.)

invincible. The ending is -*ible* to keep the preceding -*c* "soft." (See -IBLE, -ABLE, 5.)

inviolable. Since the verb *violate* has

an -*a* after the *l*-, this adjective ends in -*able.*

invisible. Ends in -*ible.* (See -IBLE, -ABLE, 1.)

invocation. The -*k* of *invoke* has changed to -*c* before the vowel -*a.* (See -K to -C.)

involuntary. Ends in -*ary.* (See -ARY, -ERY, 1.)

invulnerable. Ends in -*able.* (See -ABLE, -IBLE, 7.)

inwrap. See *enwrap.*

inwreathe. See *enwreathe.*

ipecac. Not *ipicac.*

Iraq, Iraqi. These are the only English words in which a *q*- is not followed by -*u.* *Iraq* may also be spelled *Irak,* but rarely is.

irascible. The ending is -*ible* to keep the preceding -*c* "soft." (See -IBLE, -ABLE, 5.)

iridescence, iridescent. One of the most frequently misspelled words in the language. The *iri-* at the beginning can be remembered if the *iris* of the eye is kept in mind—both words come from the same root, the Greek goddess of the rainbow. See -ANCE, -ENCE, AFTER C-, 5; -ESCE, -ESCENT, -ESCENCE, 3.)

ironclad. Solid word.

irreconcilable. -*Able.* (See -ABLE, -IBLE, 2.)

irredeemable. Ends in -*able.* (See -ABLE, -IBLE, 1.)

irredescent. Misspelling of *iridescent.*

irreducible. The ending is -*ible* to keep the preceding -*c* "soft." (See -IBLE, -ABLE, 5.)

irrefutable. -*Able.* (See ABLE, -IBLE, 2.)

irrelevance, irrelevant. Generally after *v*- the correct suffix is -*ance* or -*ant,* not -*ence* or -*ent.* (See -ANCE, -ENCE, AFTER V-, 1.)

irreparable. Since -*a* is the principal vowel in another form of the word (*reparation*), the correct ending is -*able.* (See -ABLE, -IBLE, 5.)

irrepressible. If the root forms its noun

by the immediate addition of *-ion*
(*repression*), the correct ending is
likely to be *-ible*. (See -IBLE,
-ABLE, 2.)

irreproachable. *-Able.* (See -ABLE,
-IBLE, 1.)

irresistible. Not only the *-ible* ending,
but also the second vowel, makes
this a spelling demon of the first
order. Think of *resist,* then add the
prefix *ir-* to one end, the suffix *-ible*
to the other. (See -IBLE, -ABLE,
7.)

irresponsible. If the root ends in *-ns,*
the likely ending is *-ible,* not *-able.*
(See -IBLE, -ABLE, 3.)

irrevelance. Misspelling of *irrelevance.*

irreverence, irreverent. End in *-ence,*
-ent. (See -ANCE, -ENCE, AFTER
R-, 4, 4A.)

irreversible. The root *revers-* forms its
noun by the immediate addition of
-ion (*reversion*); this is a sign for
the *-ible* ending. (See -IBLE,
-ABLE, 2.)

irrevocable. Only the *-able* ending will
keep the preceding *-c* "hard." (See
-ABLE, -IBLE, 6.)

irridescent. Misspelling of *iridescent.*

irrisistible. Misspelling of *irresistible.*

irritable. Since *-a* is the principal vowel
in another form of the word (*irri-
tate*), the correct ending is *-able.*
(See -ABLE, -IBLE, 5.)

-ISE

Of a substantial number of words
ending in *-ise,* the following may be
troublesome and should be noted.

1. Those built on the base *-wise:*
contrariwise   otherwise
likewise   sidewise

2. Those ending in *-vise:*
advise   revise
devise   supervise
improvise

3. Those built on the word "*rise*"
as a base:
arise   sunrise
moonrise   uprise

4. Those ending in *-prise:*
apprise   reprise
comprise   surprise
enterprise

(However, the actual word *prize*
and combinations built on it, such
as *overprize* or *underprize,* are exceptions.)

5. Three special words ending in
-mise: compromise, demise, surmise.
All others end in *-mize: academize,
astronomize, economize, euphemize,
macadamize,* etc.

6. Five special words ending in
-cise:
circumcise   exorcize
excise   incise
exercise
All others end in *-cize: criticize,
italicize, ostracize,* etc.

7. The word *guise* and a related form, *disguise.*

8. Five words that do not fit into
any special group:
advertise   franchise (including re-
chastise   lated forms: *enfran-
despise   chise, disenfranchise,*
etc.)
merchandise
See also -IZE, -YZE.

---

isle. See AISLE, ISLE.

isn't. Contraction of *is not,* the apostrophe appearing in place of the
missing *-o.* (See APOSTROPHE,
USE OF, 1.)

-ISSION

Nouns formed from verbs built on
the root *-mit* (*admit, permit, sub-
mit,* etc.) end in *-ission: admission,
emission, permission, submission,
transmission,* etc. See also -ICIAN,
-ITIAN; -ITION.

---

isthmus. The *-th* is silent in pronunciation.

it'd. Contraction of *it would,* the apostrophe appearing in place of the
missing letters. (See APOS-
TROPHE, USE OF, 1.)

-ITIAN, -ICIAN. See -ICIAN, -ITIAN.

-ITION
The common ending for abstract nouns is *-ition: acquisition, addition, prohibition,* etc., through a list of many hundreds.
See also -ICIAN, -ITIAN; -ISSION.

-ITIOUS, -ICIOUS. See -ICIOUS, -ITIOUS.

it'll. Contraction of *it will,* the apostrophe appearing in place of the missing letters. (See APOSTROPHE, USE OF, 1.)

ITS, IT'S
Its shows possession:
The cat licked *its* paws.
Has the baby had *its* bath?
It's is a contraction of *it is.*
It's raining hard.
It's going to be a long, cold winter.

I've. Contraction of *I have.* (See APOSTROPHE, USE OF, 1.)

-IZE, -YZE
1. Most verbs that seem to offer a choice will end in *-ize.*

appetize	harmonize
civilize	modernize
generalize	revolutionize

2. Only two common words end in *-yze:*

analyze   paralyze

3. Hence the derived forms are spelled similarly: *-y* follows *l-.*

analyst	paralyzed
analysis	paralysis
analytic	paralytic

4. *Psychoanalyze,* a word built on *analyze,* also has derived forms that contain a *-y:*

psychoanalysis   psychoanalytic
psychoanalyst

5. A few technical terms end in *-yze,* notably:

catalyze	electrolyze
dialyze	

6. Hence the derived forms also contain a *-y:*

catalyst	dialytic
catalytic	electrolysis
catalysis	electrolytic
dialysis	

See also -ISE

J

jack-in-the-box. Always hyphenated. The plural is *jacks-in-the-box.*

jail, gaol. The second is the British spelling.

janitor. Ends in *-or.* (See -ER, -OR, 5.)

jarred, jarring. Note the double *-r* in these derived forms of *jar.* (See DOUBLING FINAL -R, 1.)

jealousy. The ending is *-sy,* not *-cy.* (See -CY, -SY, 4.)

Jerrys. If a proper name ends in *-y,* the plural is formed by the simple additon of *-s.* (See -EYS, -IES, -YS, 5.)

jeweled, jeweler, jeweling. Because jewel is *not* accented on the last syllable, final *-l* is *not* doubled before a suffix beginning with a vowel. Double *-l* forms are acceptable, but single *-l* forms are far preferable. (See DOUBLING FINAL -L, 2.)

jubilance. One of a comparatively few words in which *-ance,* rather than *-ence,* follows *l-.* (See -ANCE, -ENCE, AFTER I-, 3.)

judge advocate. No hyphen; plural is *judge advocates.* (See HYPHENATING, 5A.)

judgment. When a word ends in *-dge,* the *-e* is preferably dropped before *-ment.* (See -DGMENT, -DGEMENT.)

judicious. Ends in *-icious,* not *-itious.* (See -ICIOUS, ITIOUS, 1.)

jujitsu. This is the common spelling, but the following forms are also correct: *jujutsu, jiujitsu, jiujutsu.*

jurisprudence. Almost always, with only a few exceptions, *-ence,* not *-ance,* follows a *d-.* (See -ANCE, -ENCE, AFTER D-, 1.)

juror. Ends in *-or.* (See -ER, -OR, 5.)

justifiable. *-Able* is the correct suffix after the letter *i-.* (See -ABLE, -IBLE, 3.)

K

-K TO -C

A verb ending in *-oke* has noun forms or adjective forms in which the *-k* changes to *-c* before the vowel *-a.* For example:

convoke—convocation, convocator, convocable.

evoke—evocation, evocative, evocable.

invoke—invocation, invocatory, invocable.

provoke—provocation, provocative.

revoke—revocation, revocable, irrevocable, revocatory. (The spelling *revokable* is technically correct but seldom used.)

kahki. Misspelling of *khaki.*

kaleidoscope. *-Ei,* not *-ie,* in the second syllable. (See -IE, -EI, 7.)

karakul, caracul, karakule. All these spellings correct, the first preferable.

karat. See CARAT, KARAT, CARET, CARROT.

keenness. Keen plus *-ness,* hence the double *-n.* (See -NESS AFTER N-.)

Keith. Proper names are more likely to be spelled *-ei* than *-ie.* (See -IE, -EI, 5.)

kerb. See *curb.*

KETCHUP, CATCHUP, CATSUP

All three spellings are correct, all three refer to the selfsame special sauce. The word comes from Malay, which in turn derived it from Chinese, and in our effort to approximate the sounds of these languages we find ourselves with a bewildering variety of choice. However, the first spelling is now the commonest, as is also the pronunciation KETCH-up for all forms. *Catchup* and *catsup,* however, may also be pronounced as spelled.

keyed, keying. Since the terminal *-y* of *key* follows a vowel, it does *not* change to *-i* before a suffix. (See -Y PLUS A SUFFIX, 9.)

keys. A word ending in *-ey* is pluralized by the simple addition of *-s.* (See -EYS, -IES, -YS, 1.)

khaki. Note that the *-h* follows the first *k-.*

Khrushchev. This much-misspelled name is in most newspapers and magazines as shown. Note three *-h*'s, especially the one after *K-.*

kidnaped, kidnaper, kidnaping. Single *-p* preferable in all derived forms of *kidnap,* since the accent does not *fall* on the last syllable. However, double *-p* also correct. (See DOUBLE VS. SINGLE CONSONANTS; DOUBLING FINAL -P, 4.)

kimono. The ending is *-o,* not *-a.* Plural is *kimonos.* (See PLURALIZING WORDS IN TERMINAL -O, 2.)

kitchenette, kitchenet. The longer spelling is preferable. (See -ET, -ETTE, 2.)

kitty-cornered. See *cater-cornered.*

KN-, N-

1. The ubiquitous silent *k-* before *-n* rarely bothers most people, but a few words are occasionally con-

fusing even to the most sophisticated, and worth a little pondering.

> knack, *not* nack
> knapsack, *not* napsack
> knoll, *not* noll
> knuckle, *not* nuckle

2. However, *knob* may also be spelled *nob,* and *knickknack* may also be spelled *nicknack*—in both cases the *kn-* forms are preferable.

knack. May not be spelled without the initial *k-.* (See KN-, N-, 1.)

knapsack. The initial *k-* is necessary. (See KN-, N-, 1.)

KNEE-
> Hyphenated in adjective compounds: *knee-deep, knee-high,* etc.
>
> Solid in the following noun compounds: *kneecap, kneehole, kneepad, kneepiece.*
>
> Otherwise separate: *knee action, knee breeches,* etc.

-KNEED
> Always hyphenated: *bare-kneed, weak-kneed,* etc.

knickknack. Yes, those two *-k*'s do come together in the middle, and the solid word is preferable to *knickknack.* Or spell it *nicknack* if you like, though this is less common. (See KN-, N-, 2.)

knife. The plural is *knives.* (See PLURALIZING WORDS IN TERMINAL -F OR -FE, 1.)

knight-errant. Plural is *knights-errant.*

knob, nob. The former spelling is preferable. (See KN-, N-, 2.)

knoll. May not be spelled without the initial *k-.* (See KN- N-, 1.)

knowledgeable. The final *-e* of *knowledge* is retained before *-able* in order to preserve the original "soft" (or *j*) pronunciaiton of the preceding *-g.* (See -GEABLE.)

knuckle. Not *nuckle.* (See KN- N-, 1.)

Krushchev. See *Khrushchev.*

L

(Rules for double *-l:* See DOUBLING FINAL -L.)

labor, labour. The first spelling is American, the second British. (See -OR, -OUR, 1.)

laceable. The *-e* of *lace* is retained before *-able* in order to preserve the original "soft" pronunciation of the preceding *-c.* (See -CEABLE.)

lachrymal, lachrymose. These forms, with the *-h,* are preferable to *lacrymal, lacrymose.*

ladies. Plural of *lady.* When a word ends in *-y* preceded by a consonant, the plural ends in *-ies.* (See -EYS, -IES, -YS, 3.)

laid. The past tense of *lay,* never spelled *layed.* Likewise any combinations—*mislaid, outlaid, waylaid,* etc. (See -AYED, -AID.)

lama. See LLAMA, LAMA.

lamasery. One of the few words with both a primary and secondary accent ending in *-ery* rather than *-ary.* (See -ARY, -ERY, 2.)

lambaste. Much preferable to *lambast.*

lamentable. Ends in *-able.* (See -ABLE, -IBLE, 1.)

-LANCE, -LENCE. See -ANCE, -ENCE, AFTER L-.

LAND-
> Adjectives preceding their nouns are generally hyphenated: *land-grant* (college), *land-office* (business), *land-poor, land-sheltered,* etc.
>
> But *landlocked* and *landowning* are solid:
>
> The following noun compounds are solid:

landfall	landmark
landholder	landowner
landlady	landslide
landlord	landslip
landlubber	landsman

> *Land-grabber* is hyphenated.
>
> Other noun compounds are writ-

ten separate: *land power, land wind,*
etc.

---

languor, languorous. Watch that *-u*
after the *g-*.

-LANT, -LENT. See -ANCE, -ENCE,
AFTER L-.

---

lapel. Ends in one *-l*, not two. (See
-EL, -ELL, 2.)

lapped, lapping. Final *-p* of a one-
syllable word like *lap* is doubled
before a suffix beginning with a
vowel. (See DOUBLING FINAL
-P, 1.)

larva. Plural is *larvae*. (See PLURAL-
IZING WORDS IN TERMINAL
-A, 1.)

lascivious. Note the *-c*.

lasso. Plural is *lassos* or *lassoes*. (See
PLURALIZING WORDS IN
TERMINAL -O, 2.)

LATER, LATTER

The distinction can best be seen
by comparing the following sentences.

It's *later* than you think.

Dinner will be served *later* than
usual.

Men and women are probably
equally capable—but the *latter*
rarely earn as much money as the
former.

John Swensen and George Goldstein are both tall—the *latter* is the
tallest man I've ever seen.

LATHE, LATH

A *lathe* (*-th* as in *the*) is a
machine for shaping things; a *lath*
(*-th* as in *thing*) is a strip of wood
or metal used in building.

Both words can also be used as
verbs.

---

latter. See LATER, LATTER.

laudable. Ends in *-able*. (See -ABLE,
-IBLE, 1.)

laughable. The ending is *-able*. (See
-ABLE, -IBLE, 1.)

lavender. Ends in *-er*, not *-ar*.

LAW-

Lawbreaking and *lawmaking* are
solid adjectives; *law-abiding* is hyphenated.

Most noun comounds are solid:
*lawbook, lawbreaker, lawmaker,
lawsuit,* etc.

Law merchant (the rules of trade
or commerce) is written separate.

---

laziness. The *-y* of *lazy* changes to *-i*
before *-ness*. (See -Y PLUS A SUF-
FIX, 6.)

LEAD, LED

Pronounced LEED, *lead* is the
present tense of the verb; the metal
lead is pronounced LED.

Led is the past tense of *lead*.

---

leaf. The plural is *leaves*. (See PLU-
RALIZING WORDS IN TERMI-
NAL -F OR -FE, 1.)

leak, leek. The vegetable is a *leek;*
for all other meanings, use *leak*.

leatherette, leatheret. The longer spelling is preferable. (See -ET, -ETTE,
2.)

leather-lunged. See *-lunged*.

led. See LEAD, LED.

leek. See *leak, leek*.

leeward. Often pronounced LOO-erd,
but spelled as shown.

LEFT-. See HYPHENATING, 26.

---

legible. The ending is *-ible* to keep
the preceding *-g* "soft." (See -IBLE,
-ABLE, 6.)

legislator. Ends in *-or*. (See -ER, -OR,
5.)

legitimate. The letter after the *t-* is *-i*.

leisure. Note the *-ei* combination—this
is an exception to the rule "*-i* before
-e except after *c-*." (See -IE, -EI, 4.)

leisurely. This spelling is for both the adjective and adverb. (See -LY, 6.)

leitmotif. First syllable spelled *-ei*, not *-ie*. (See -IE, -EI, 7.)

lenience, lenient. End in *-ence, -ent*. (See -ANCE, -ENCE, AFTER I-, 1.)

leopard. Not *lepard*.

LETTER-

Most noun compounds are written separate: *letter box, letter carrier, letter of credit, letters patent, letter writer*, etc.

Solid are *lettergram* and *letterhead*.

The adjective *letter-perfect* is hyphenated.

LETTERS. See HYPHENATING, 52.

---

libeled, libeler, libeling, libelous. Because *libel* is *not* accented on the last syllable, final *-l* is *not* doubled before a suffix beginning with a vowel. Double *-l* forms are acceptable, but single *-l* forms are far preferable. (See DOUBLING FINAL -L, 2.)

library. Ends in *-ary*. (See -ARY, -ERY, 1.)

libretto. Note the double *-t*. The common plural is *librettos*, but people in musical circles prefer *libretti* when referring to the words or text of an opera, oratorio, etc.

license. This American spelling is preferable to the British *licence*. (See -ENCE, -ENSE, 2.)

lie. The participle is spelled *lying*.

lieutenant. *-Ieu* in the first syllable, ends in *-ant*.

lieutenant colonel. No hyphen. (See HYPHENATING, 5A.)

life. The plural is *lives*. (See PLURALIZING WORDS IN TERMINAL -F OR -FE, 1.)

LIFE-

Most adjective compounds are hyphenated: *life-giving, life-prolonging, life-size*, etc.

But *lifelong, lifesaving,* and *lifetime* are solid.

Most noun compounds are written separate (*life belt, life insurance*, etc.). The following, however, are solid:

lifeblood	lifesaving
lifeboat	lifetime
lifeguard	lifework
lifesaver	

Life-giver is hyphenated.

LIGHT-

Most adjective compounds are hyphenated: *light-armed, light-fingered, light-footed*, etc.

Solid adjectives are:

lightface	lighthearted
lightheaded	lightweight

These noun compounds are solid:

lightface	lightship
lighthead	lightweight
lighthouse	lightwood

Hyphenated are: *light-horseman, light-o'-love*, and *light-year*.

Others are separate (*light infantry, light opera*, etc.).

LIGHTNING, LIGHTENING

Lightning is the noun designating the celestial phenomenon associated with thunder. The verb, not often used, is to *lighten*.

Lightening comes from the verb *lighten* (i.e., grow or make less heavy); it is the spelling, also, for the sense of decreased pressure felt by a pregnant woman sometime before labor sets in.

I'm interested in *lightening* your burdens (cares, worries, etc.).

My troubles are *lightening*.

Flashes of *lightning* pierced the sky.

It's *lightning* out.

---

likable. *Likeable* also correct, but the preferable spelling omits the unnecessary -e. (See -ABLE, -EABLE, 2.)

-LIKE. See HYPHENATING, 40.

likelihood. Note that the *-y* of *likely* has changed to *-i*.

likewise. Note the *-ise* ending, common to all words built on the base *-wise.* (See -ISE, 1.)

lily. The flower has only one *-l* before the *-y,* though the girls' names may be spelled either *Lily* or *Lilly, Lilian* or *Lillian.*

linage In this spelling, pronounced *LY-nij,* the word means the number of lines on a page. A variant form, *lineage,* is also acceptable. (See -AGE AFTER FINAL -E, 1.)

lineage In this spelling, the word is pronounced *LIN-ee-ij,* and means *ancestry.* (See -AGE AFTER FINAL -E, 2.)

linen. One *-n* in the middle.

lingerie. Ends in *-rie,* even though most people pronounce the last syllable *-ray.*

liquefy. One of only five nontechnical verbs in English that end in *-efy.* The noun, correspondingly, is spelled *liquefaction,* again with an *-e* preceding the *-f.* (See -IFY, -EFY, 2.)

litigant. "Hard" *-g,* hence *-ant.* (See -ANCE, -ENCE, AFTER G-, 2.)

livelihood. Note the *-i* before *-hood.*

living room. No hyphen. (See HYPHENATING, 3B.)

LLAMA, LAMA

Double *l-,* the South American animal; single *l-,* the Buddhist priest.

LOAD, LODE

Lode designates a deposit or vein of metallic ore. For all other meanings, noun or verb, use *load.*

loadstar. See *lodestar.*

loadstone, lodestone. The first is the preferable spelling.

loaf. The plural is *loaves.* (See PLURALIZING WORDS IN TERMINAL -F OR -FE, 1.)

LOATH, LOTH, LOATHE

Loath (*-th* as in *thing;* also, less frequently, spelled *loth*) is the adjective meaning *reluctant*—he's *loath* to go.

Loathe (*-th* as in *the*) is the verb to hate intensely—we *loathe* him.

loathsome. Though built on the verb *loathe,* no *-e* after the *th-.*

locus. For plural see PLURALIZING WORDS IN TERMINAL -US, 7.

lode. See LOAD, LODE.

lodestar, loadstar. The first is the preferable spelling.

lodestone. See *loadstone.*

lodgment. When a word ends in *-dge,* the *-e* is preferably dropped before *-ment.* (See -DGMENT, -DGEMENT.)

loneliness. Often misspelled *lonliness.*

lonely. Note particularly that final *-e* of *lone* is retained before the adverbial suffix *-ly.* (See -LY, 10.)

lonesome. Again, keep the *-e* of *lone* before *-some.*

LONG-

Adjective compounds preceding nouns are mostly hyphenated (*long-awaited, long-drawn, long-forgotten, long-haired, long-range,* etc.).

However, the following are solid: *longfelt, longhair* (slang), *longshore, longspun.*

Long-headed is preferably hyphenated, but may also be solid.

Noun compounds generally written separate (*long division, long dozen,* etc.), except the following, which are solid:

longboat	longhead
longbow	longhair (*slang*)
longcloth	longhorn
longhand	longshoreman

lonliness. Misspelling of *loneliness.*
lonly. Misspelling of *lonely.*
lonsome. Misspelling of *lonesome.*

looker-on. Always hyphenated. Plural is *lookers-on.* (See HYPHENATING, 10A.)

look-in. Hyphenated.

lookout. No hyphen. (See HYPHENATING. 3A.)

look-see. Hyphenated.

loop. See -OOP, -OUP, -UPE, 1.

LOOSE-

Adjectives are hyphenated: *loosejointed, loose-leaf, loose-tongued,* etc. But *loosemouthed* is solid.

LOOSE, LOSE

Loose is an adjective (a *loose* button), or a verb meaning *loosen,* i.e., make or become *loose* (*loose* your hold on the wheel).

Lose is a verb, the past tense of which is *lost.* (Did you *lose* your way?)

looward. Misspelling of *leeward.*

lorgnette. Ends in *-ette.* (See -ET, -ETTE, 3.)

lose. See LOOSE, LOSE.

loth. See LOATH, LOTH, LOATHE.

LOUD-

Adjectives are hyphenated (*loudlaughing, loud-spoken,* etc.), except *loudmouthed,* which is solid.

The noun *loudmouth* (*slang*) is solid; *loud-speaker* is hyphenated.

lour. See -OUR, -OWER, -AUER, 1.

lovable. *Loveable* also correct, but preferable spelling omits the unnecessary *-e.* (See -ABLE, -EABLE, 2.)

LOVE-

Adjectives are hyphenated (*lovecrossed, love-mad,* etc.), except *lovelorn* and *lovesick,* written solid.

Lovebird is solid, *love-making* hyphenated, other nouns separate (*love affair, love seat,* etc.).

LOW-

Adjectives are hyphenated (*lownecked. low-spirited,* etc.), except the following, written solid: *lowborn, lowbred, lowland.*

The following nouns are hyphenated: *low-brow, low-down, low-life. Lowboy, lowland,* and *lowlands* are solid.

Others are separate: *low comedy, low relief,* etc.

lower. See -OUR, -OWER, -AUER, 2.

loyally. The adverbial ending, *-ly,* is added to the adjective *loyal,* hence the double *-l.* (See -LY, 7; -LY, -ALLY, 4.)

lucre. The ending is *-re* to keep the *-c* "hard." (See -ER, -RE, 2.)

luncheon. Ends in *-eon.*

luncheonette. Ends in *-ette.* (See -ET, -ETTE, 3.)

-lunged. So spelled in compounds like *leather-lunged, weak-lunged,* etc., even though it looks like the past of *lunge* and therefore tempts to mispronunciation.

luscious. To a person of imagination, the spelling has almost as much glamour as the meaning. Note the *-sci* combination that is so often pronounced *sh* (*conscience, omniscience,* etc.).

luster, lustre. The latter spelling is now old-fashioned, though still current in Great Britain. (See -ER, -RE.)

luxuriance, luxuriant. Very occasionally, as here, *-ance* or *-ant,* not *-ence* or *-ent,* follows *i-.* (See -ANCE, -ENCE, AFTER I-, 4.)

-LY

1. To form an adverb, add *-ly* to the adjective.

accidental—accidentally
rapid—rapidly
slow—slowly

2. If the adjective ends in a *-y* that has the sound of long *-e* (*happy,* *merry*, etc.), change *-y* to *-i* before adding *-ly*.

busy—busily
dizzy—dizzily
happy—happily
merry—merrily
weighty—weightily

3. However, if the *-y* ending an adjective does *not* have the sound of long *-e* found in the words of Section 2 (*coy, dry, gay,* for example), the *-y* is usually not changed.

coy—coyly   sly—slyly
dry—dryly   spry—spryly
shy—shyly   wry—wryly

(But the variant spellings *drily, shily,* and *slily* are also correct, though less preferable.)

4. An exception is *gaily,* preferred to *gayly,* though the latter is also acceptable.

5. If an adjective ends in *-ble* (*miserable, terrible,* etc.), the adverb is formed by changing final *-e* to *-y.*

horrible—horribly
hospitable—hospitably
irresistible—irresistibly
miserable—miserably
terrible—terribly
visible—visibly

6. If the adjective already ends in *-ly*, as a few do, the adverbial form is the same word, unchanged. Examples are: *bodily, brotherly, fatherly, leisurely, lonely,* etc.

7. If the adjective ends in a single *-l,* the addition of the adverbial suffix will result in an *-lly* ending.

beautiful—beautifully
cool—coolly
dual—dually
especial—especially
evil—evilly
ideal—ideally
loyal—loyally
oral—orally
principal—principally
real—really
royal—royally
special—specially

total—totally
truthful—truthfully

8. But if the adjective ends in double *-l,* only *-y* is added to form the adverb.

dull—dully
full—fully
ill—illy

9. In the following exceptional words, final *-e* of the adjective is dropped before *-ly* is added.

due—duly
one—only
true—truly
whole—wholly

10. Note that final *-e* is retained in other adjectives. The following are especially prone to misspelling.

bare—barely
lone—lonely
scarce—scarcely
sincere—sincerely

See also -LY, -ALLY.

-LY, -ALLY

1. If an adjective ends in *-ic,* the adverb is generally formed by adding *-ally:*

academic—academically
aristocratic—aristocratically
artistic—artistically
automatic—automatically
emphatic—emphatically
prophetic—prophetically
scholastic—scholastically

2. The important exception is:
public—publicly

3. In other instances, an adverb is formed by adding *-ly* to the *adjective* only. Note, therefore, the following chart.

NOUN
accident
coincidence
experiment
incident
ornament

ADJECTIVE
accidental
coincidental

experimental
incidental
ornamental

ADVERB
accidentally
coincidentally
experimentally
incidentally
ornamentally

It is thus clear why *accidently, incidently,* and *coincidently,* though tempting, are totally incorrect.

4. If an adjective ends in *-al,* the addition of *-ly* will produce an *-ally* ending.

confidential—confidentially
especial—especially
loyal—loyally
principal—principally
real—really
royal—royally
special—specially

See also -LY.

---

lying. Participle of *lie, -ie* changing to *-y* before *-ing.* (See -IE TO -Y.)
lying-in. Hyphenated when used as an adjective preceding the noun. (See HYPHENATING, 11.)

M

(Rules for double *-m:* See DOUBLING FINAL -M.)

macabre, macaber. Unlike other *-er, -re* choices, *macabre* is preferable—and note the single *-c.*
macaroni. Has one *-c.*
macaroon. Spelled with one-*c.*
madam. The plural is usually the French *mesdames* (may-DAM); but for the female head of a brothel, *madams.*
madam, madame. The first spelling (pronounced MAD-'m) can be used for most meanings of the word, in-

cluding the head of a brothel; the second (pronounced ma-DAM) is the French title equivalent to *Mrs.,* and is used today for a married woman of most foreign countries other than Britain or British Commonwealth countries.
magneto. The plural is *magnetos.* (See PLURALIZING WORDS IN TERMINAL -O.)
magnificence, magnificent. *-Ence* or *-ent,* rather than *-ance* or *-ant,* to keep the preceding *-c* "soft." (See -ANCE, -ENCE, AFTER C-, 1.)
magniloquence, magniloquent. Always *-ence* or *-ent* after *qu-.* (See -ANCE, -ENCE, AFTER U-, 1.)
Mahomet. See *Mohammed.*
maid of honor. No hyphens; plural is *maids of honor.* (See HYPHENATING, 5A.)

MAIL-

Most nouns are solid: *mailbox, mailboat, mailman, mailplane,* etc.

Mail car and *mail order* are separate; and *mail boat* and *mail plane* may be written in two words, though the solid spellings are preferable.

The adjective *mail-order* (*mail-order operations,* etc.) is hyphenated; *mailclad* is solid.

---

mailable. Ends in *-able.* (See -ABLE, -IBLE, 1.)
maintenance. The verb is *maintain,* but notice the change of vowels from *-ai* to *-e* after the *t-;* and the ending is *-ance.* (See -ANCE, -ENCE, AFTER N-, 3.)
major-domo. Hyphenated.
major general. No hyphen. (See HYPHENATING, 5A.)
make-believe. Hyphenated as a noun or adjective, not when *make* is a verb (a *make-believe* world; indulging in *make-believe;* Let's *make believe.*). (See HYPHENATING, 1, 2.)
make-up. Hyphenated as a noun or

adjective, not as a verb. She put on more *make-up* from her *make-up* kit; let's *make up*. (See HYPHEN-ATING, 1.)

malefactor. Letter after the *l-* is *-e*.

maleficence. *-Ence,* rather than *-ance,* to keep the preceding *-c* "soft." (See -ANCE, -ENCE, AFTER C-, 1.)

maleficent. Not *maleficient.* Pronounced *ma-LEF-i-s'nt.*

malevolence, malevolent. Generally *-l* is followed by *-ence* or *-ent.* (See -ANCE, -ENCE, AFTER L-, 1, 3.)

malicious. Ends in *-icious,* not *-itious.* (See -ICIOUS, -ITIOUS, 1.)

malleable. Note the *-able* ending. (See -ABLE, -IBLE, 7.)

mama, mamma. Meaning *mother,* may be spelled either way.

mammalogy. Note that the ending is *-alogy, not -ology.* (See -ALOGY, -OLOGY.)

MAN-

Adjective compounds are hyphenated: *man-eating, man-hating, man-stopping.*

Most nouns are solid (*manhole, manhunt, manpower,* etc.), as are also the verb *manhandle* and the adjective *manlike.*

Man hunt may, however, also be written as two words.

Also separate are such phrases as *man about town, man and boy, man of God, man on horseback,* etc.

Hyphenated are *man-child, man-hater, man-hour,* and *man-of-war.*

-MAN

Most compounds are solid: *footman, gunman, mailman, selectman,* etc.

Separate are *hatchet man, minute man* (also *minuteman*), *miracle man, pivot man, plain-clothes man, railway man, red man, sandwich man, squaw man,* and *yes man.*

manageable. The *-e* of *manage* is retained before *-able* in order to

preserve the original "soft" (or *j*) pronunciation of the preceding *-g.* (See -GEABLE.)

maneuver, maneuvre, manoeuvre. The first spelling far preferable to the others. (See -ER, -RE.)

mangoes, mangos. The former is the preferable plural; both are correct. (See PLURALIZING WORDS IN TERMINAL -O, 4.)

manifesto. Plural is *manifestoes.* (See PLURALIZING WORDS IN TERMINAL -O, 1.)

manoeuvre. See *maneuver.*

man-of-war. Plural is *men-of-war.*

MANTEL, MANTLE

The facing around, or shelf above, a fireplace may be spelled either way, but *mantel* is preferable.

For all other meanings, noun or verb, *mantle* is the only spelling.

mantelpiece. One word.

manufacture. Note that the second vowel is a *-u,* not an *-a.*

mapped, mapping. Final *-p* of *map* is doubled before a suffix beginning with a vowel. (See DOUBLING FINAL -P, 1.)

marangue, maringue. Misspelling of *meringue.*

mariner. Ends in *-er.* (See -ER, -OR, 1.)

marionette. Ends in *-ette.* (See -ET, -ETTE, 3.)

MARITAL, MARTIAL

Marital refers to *marriage, martial* to *war;* and while the two may on occasion be the same, the words must be distinguished if you wish to avoid unintended jokes.

marmoset. Ends in *-et.* (See -ET, -ETTE, 4.)

MARQUEE, MARQUIS

A *marquee* is a rooflike structure over a theater, hotel, etc.; a *marquis* (pronounced MAR-kwis or mar-KEE) is a European nobleman.

marred, marring. Note the double -r in these derived forms of *mar*. (See DOUBLING FINAL -R, 1.)

marriageable. The -e of *marriage* is retained before -*able* in order to preserve the original "soft" (or *j*) pronunciation of the preceding -*g*. (See -GEABLE.)

married, marries. The -*y* of *marry* changes to -*i* before -*ed* or -*es*. (See -Y PLUS A SUFFIX, 1.)

MARTEN, MARTIN

The first spelling designates the fur-bearing mammal, the second a bird of the swallow family.

martial. See MARITAL, MARTIAL.

martin. See MARTEN, MARTIN.

martinet. Ends in -*et*. (See -ET, -ETTE, 4.)

marveled, marveling. Because *marvel* is *not* accented on the last syllable, final -*l* is *not* doubled before a suffix beginning with a vowel. Double -*l* forms are acceptable, but single -*l* forms are far preferable. (See DOUBLING FINAL -L, 2.)

marvelous, marvellous. The single -*l* spelling is preferable.

Marys. If a proper name ends in -*y*, the plural is formed by the simple addition of -*s*. (See -EYS, -IES, -YS, 5.)

masquerade. Not *maskerade*.

massacre. The ending is -*re* to keep the -*c* "hard." (See -ER, -RE, 2.)

massacred, massacring. See -ER, -RE, 3.

masseur. Not *massuer*. Feminine is *masseuse*.

MASTER-

Most compounds are two words: *master hand*, *master key*, *master stroke*, etc.

Solid are *mastermind* (noun or verb), *masterpiece*, and *masterwork*.

MATERIAL, MATERIEL, MATÉRIEL

The last two spellings—the final one, with the accent, preserves the French flavor—mean military supplies or, less frequently, the equipment required for any work or profession; the first one is used for all other meanings and is both a noun and an adjective.

mathematics. Not *mathamatics*.

matinee, matinée. The preferable spelling omits the accent.

matrix. For plural, see PLURALIZING WORDS IN TERMINAL -X, 1.

maximum. The Anglicized plural *maximums* is commoner than the Latin-derived *maxima*. (See PLURALIZING WORDS IN TERMINAL -UM, 2.)

maybe, may be. If you mean perhaps, use one word; *may be* requires a subject. *Maybe* I'll be there; it *may be* that it will rain; we *may be* short-changed, etc.

mayonnaise. Double -*n*.

mayn't. Contraction of *may not*. (See APOSTROPHE, USE OF, 1.)

McCarthys. If a proper name ends in -*y*, the plural is formed by the simple addition of -*s*. (See -EYS, -IES, -YS, 5.)

meager, meagre. The latter spelling is current in Great Britain. (See -ER, -RE.)

mealy-mouthed, mealymouthed. Preferably hyphenated, but need not be.

meanness. *Mean* plus -*ness*, hence the double -*n*. (See -NESS AFTER N-.)

measly. Not *measley*.

medallion. Unlike *battalion*, this word has a double -*l*.

medieval, mediaeval. The latter spelling is old-fashioned.

medium. Plural is *media* or *mediums*, but only *mediums* for those who conduct séances. (See PLURALIZ-

ING WORDS IN TERMINAL -UM, 1.)

meerschaum. Note the *-sch.*

mellifluence. Always *-ence,* not *-ance,* after *fl-.* (See -ANCE, -ENCE, AFTER U-, 2.)

mellifluous. Note the *-u* before *-ous.* (See -UOUS.)

melon. Not *mellon.*

mementos, mementoes. The former is the preferable plural; both are correct. (See PLURALIZING WORDS IN TERMINAL -O, 5.)

memorable. Note the *-able* ending. (See -ABLE, -IBLE, 7.)

memorandum. The plural is either *memoranda* or *memorandums.* (See PLURALIZING WORDS IN TERMINAL -UM, 1.)

menstruate. Note the *-u.*

-MENT

1. The suffix *-ment* is added directly to a verb to form a noun.

develop—development
embarrass—embarrassment
envelop—envelopment
equip—equipment

Note that in the words above there is no reason for an *-e* preceding *-ment,* for the verb does not end in *-e.*

entangle—entanglement
manage—management
place—placement

Note, in the words above, that since the verb ends in *-e* the noun contains an *-e* preceding the suffix.

2. An important, and often misspelled, exception is *argue,* from which the final *-e* is dropped before *-ment: argue—argument.*

3. In verbs ending in *-dge* (*judge, lodge,* etc.), the preferable spelling drops final *-e* before the suffix— *judgment, lodgment,* etc.

See also -DGMENT.

---

merangue. Misspelling of *meringue.*

mercenary. Ends in *-ary.* (See -ARY, -ERY, 1.)

merchandise. Note the *-ise* ending. (See -ISE, 8.)

merciful. The *-y* of mercy changes to *-i* before *-ful.* (See -Y PLUS A SUFFIX, 8A.)

meretricious. Ends in *-icious,* not *-itious.* (See -ICIOUS, -ITIOUS, 1.)

meridian. Adjective or noun, ends in *-an.*

meridional. As a noun, means an inhabitant of Southern Europe, especially the South of France; as an adjective, means (a) southern, (b) pertaining to inhabitants of Southern Europe, or (c) pertaining to a meridian. Note that this word, unlike *meridian,* has *-ion* after the *d-.*

meringue. Pronounced me-RANG, but ends in *-ingue.*

merited, meriting, meritorious. Because *merit* is *not* accented on the last syllable, final *-t* is *not* doubled before a suffix beginning with a vowel. (See DOUBLING FINAL -T, 3.)

merry-go-round. Hyphenated.

merrymaker, marrymaking. Both words solid.

mesdames. See *madam.*

Messieurs. This is the complete word that is abbreviated Messrs. or MM. in the salutation of letters.

Messrs. See *Messieurs.*

METAL-

Adjective compounds preceding nouns are hyphenated: *metal-bearing, metal-lined,* etc.

Noun compounds are solid: *metalware, metalworker,* etc.

METAL, METTLE

It is the second spelling that means character, spirit, etc.—on one's *mettle,* test one's *mettle,* etc.

---

metaled, metaling. These derived forms of the verb *metal* preferably have only one -*l*. (See DOUBLING FINAL -L, 2.)

metalist, metallist. Single -*l* is preferable.

metalize, metallize. Single -*l* preferable.

metallic. Single -*t*, double -*l*. (See DOUBLING FINAL -L, 4.)

metalline. Double -*l* in this one.

metalloid. Has double -*l*.

metallurgy. Spell with double -*l*. (See DOUBLING FINAL -L, 4.)

meter, metre. The latter spelling is more current in Great Britain than here. (See -ER, -RE.)

mettle. See METAL, METTLE.

mezzanine. Two -*z*'s.

mezzo-soprano. Two -*z*'s, and hyphenated.

microorganism, microörganism, micro-organism. All these spellings correct, but the first is the best.

MID-. See HYPHENATING, 23.

MIDDLE-
Adjective compounds are hyphenated (*middle-aged, middle-class, middle-sized,* etc.), except for *middleweight,* written solid.

Noun compounds mostly separate (*middle age, middle class, Middle East,* etc.), except for *middleman* and *middleweight,* written solid.

---

midwife. The plural is *midwives.* (See PLURALIZING WORDS IN TERMINAL -F OR -FE, 1.)

mignonette. Ends in -*ette*. (See -ET, -ETTE, 3.)

mileage. Final -*e* of *mile* is retained before the suffix -*age*. (See -AGE AFTER FINAL -E, 2.)

MILESTONE, MILLSTONE
A *milestone* is a stone or other marker showing the distance of a mile from a designated place; or, figuratively, a turning point in a life, career, history, etc.

A *millstone* is one of two large

stones for grinding, or, figuratively, a heavy burden, as a *millstone* around one's neck.

MILK-
Adjective compounds preceding nouns hyphenated: *milk-and-water, milk-fed,* etc.; but *milkwhite* is solid.

Most noun compounds are two words (*milk bottle, milk shake, milk sugar,* etc.), except the following, which are solid:

   milkmaid   milksop
   milkman   milkweed
   milkshed

MILL-
Most noun compounds solid (*milldam, millpond,* etc.), except *mill wheel,* written separate.

---

millennial. Double -*l*, double -*n*.

millennium. Has double -*l*, double -*n*.

millinery. One of the few words with both a primary and secondary accent ending in -*ery* rather than -*ary*. (See -ARY, -ERY, 2.)

millionaire. Only one -*n*.

millstone. See MILESTONE, MILLSTONE.

minaret. Ends in -*et*. (See -ET, -ETTE, 4.)

mimicked, mimicker, mimicking. The -*k* must be inserted in the derived forms of *mimic* in order to preserve the original pronunciation of final -*c*. (See -C, -CK, 1.)

MINER, MINOR
A *miner* works in a mine; a *minor* is under legal age, which in most places is 21.

---

mineralogy. Note that the ending is -*alogy*, not -*ology*. (See -ALOGY, -OLOGY.)

minimum. The Anglicized plural *minimums* is commoner than the Latin-derived *minima*. (See PLURALIZ-

ING WORDS IN TERMINAL
-UM, 2.)

minor. See MINER, MINOR.

minuet. Ends in -*et*. (See -ET, -ETTE,
4.)

minutia. Plural is *minutiae*. (See PLU-
RALIZING WORDS IN TERMI-
NAL -A, 1.)

mirror. Ends in -*or*. (See -ER, -OR, 5.)

MIS-, MISS-

1. The prefix *mis-* gives a negative
force to a word: *apprehension—
misapprehension; conduct—miscon-
duct; place—misplace; understand—
misunderstand;* etc.

2. If *mis-* is prefixed to a word
that *starts with an s-,* a double -*s*
will occur. Note the following carefully, most of which are commonly
misspelled:

say—missay
shape—misshapen
speak—misspeak
spell—misspell
spend—misspend
state—misstate
step—misstep

See also DIS-, DISS-.

---

misalliance. Ending is -*ance*. (See
-ANCE, -ENCE, AFTER I-, 3.)

misapprehension. Ends in -*ension*.
(See -ENSION, -ENTION.)

miscellaneous. The -*c*, double -*l*, and
-*eous* ending are all pitfalls.

mischief. Note the -*ie* combination.
(See -IE, -EI, 11.)

misguidance. One of the few words
in which -*ance*, not -*ence*, follows
d-. (See -ANCE, -ENCE, AFTER
D-, 3.)

mishap. One -*s*.

mislaid. Not *mislayed*.

MISS-, MIS-. See MIS-, MISS-.

---

missay. A combination of *say* with
the negative prefix *mis-,* hence the
double -*s*. (See MIS-, MISS, 2.)

misshapen. A combination of *shape*
with the negative prefix *mis-,* hence
double -*s*. (See MIS-, MISS-, 2.)

-MISSION. See -ISSION.

---

misspeak. A combination of *speak* with
the negative prefix *mis-,* hence the
the double -*s*. (See MIS-, MISS-, 2.)

misspell. A combination of *spell* with
the negative prefix *mis-,* hence the
double -*s*. (See MIS-, MISS-, 2.)

misspend. A combination of *spend*
with the negative prefix *mis-,* hence
the double -*s*. (See MIS-, MISS-,
2.)

misstate. A combination of *state* with
the negative prefix *mis-,*˙hence the
double -*s*. (See MIS-, MISS-, 2.)

misstep. A combination of *step* with
the negative prefix *mis-,* hence the
double -*s*. (See MIS-, MISS-, 2.)

misterious, mistery, mistify. Misspellings of *mysterious, mystery, mystify.*

MM. See *Messieurs.*

mnemonic. The first *m-* is silent.

MOAT, MOTE

A *moat* is a ditch around a for-
tress, castle, etc.; a *mote* is a speck
of dust.

---

moccasin. Two -*c*'s, one -*s*.

modeled, modeler, modeling. Because
model is *not* accented on the last
syllable, final -*l* is *not* doubled
before a suffix beginning with a
vowel. Double -*l* forms are acceptable, but single -*l* forms are far
preferable. (See DOUBLING
FINAL -L, 2.)

moderator. Ends in -*or*. (See -ER,
-OR, 5.)

modernness. *Modern* plus -*ness*, hence
the double -*n*. (See -NESS AFTER
N-.)

Mohammed, Mahomet, Muhammad.
The first is the commonest, and preferable, spelling.

Mohammedan, Muhammadan, Mu-

hammedan. All these spellings correct, but the first is preferable.

molatto. Misspelling of *mulatto*.

mold, mould. The shorter, modern spelling is preferable. (See -O, -OU, 1.)

molder, moulder. The shorter, modern spelling is preferable. (See -O, -OU, 1.)

moldy, mouldy. *Moldy* is preferable. (See -O, -OU, 1.)

molt, moult. The first spelling is preferable. (See -O, -OU, 1.)

momentary. The ending is *-ary*. (See -ARY, -ORY, 1.)

monastery. One of the few words with both a primary and secondary accent ending with *-ery*, rather than *-ary*. (See -ARY, -ERY, 2.)

monetary. The ending is *-ary*, not *-ery*. (See -ARY, -ERY, 1.)

MONEY-

Adjective compounds preceding nouns are hyphenated (*money-mad, money-making*, etc.), except *moneysaving*, which is solid.

Noun compounds are solid (*moneybag, moneylender*, etc.), except *money-maker*, hyphenated, and *money order*, separate.

moneys, monies. The first is the preferable plural of *money*, at least by rule, but the second is more commonly seen. (See -EYS, -IES, -YS, 2.)

monitor. Ends in *-or*. (See -ER, -OR, 5.)

monkeys. A word such as *monkey*, ending in *-ey*, is pluralized by the simple addition of *-s*. (See -EYS, -IES, -YS, 1.)

monogramed, monogrammed. Both correct, the latter more popular.

monogrammatic. Requires a double *-m*.

monologue, monolog. The longer spelling is preferable. (See -OGUE, -OG, 1.)

Monsieur. The plural is *Messieurs*.

Monsignor. The plural for the Italian form of address is *Monsignori;* otherwise *Monsignors*.

mooed, mooing. These derived forms of *moo* are correctly spelled, although the three successive vowels may look strange at first. (See -OO, TERMINAL.)

MOON-

Adjective compounds are hyphenated (*moon-eyed, moon-faced, moon-stricken*, etc.), except *moonlighted, moonlit*, and *moonstruck*, which are solid.

Most noun compounds are solid (*moonlight, moonlighting, moonrise*, etc.), except *moon blindness*, which is solid, and *moon-gazing*, which is hyphenated.

moonrise. Note the *-ise* ending, common to all words built on *rise* as a base. (See -ISE, 3.)

MORAL, MORALE

As a noun, a *moral* is a maxim or saying, or a lesson taught by a story, etc.

Morale, on the other hand, is discipline, confidence, enthusiasm, etc.—he attempted to lift the *morale* of the workers.

mordant. The adjective that means biting, caustic, etc., ends in *-ant;* the noun is *mordancy*.

moreover. Solid word; do not omit the the *-e* after *mor-*.

morocco. One *-r*, two *-c*'s. Capitalized if the name of the country in Africa.

mortgage. Note the silent *-t*.

mortgageable. The *-e* of *mortgage* is retained before *-able*. (See -GEABLE.)

MORTGAGOR, MORTGAGEE

The *mortgagor* borrows money on his property from the *mortgagee*. When you buy a house with money borrowed from a bank, you are the *mortgagor,* the bank is the *mortgagee. Mortgagor* may also be spelled *mortgager,* and in either form is pronounced MORE-ga-jer; *Mortgagee* is pronounced more-ga-JEE.

mosquito. Plural is *mosquitoes.* (See PLURALIZING WORDS IN TERMINAL -O, 1.)

mote. See MOAT, MOTE.

motet. Ends in *-et.* (See -ET, -ETTE, 4.)

moth-eaten. Hyphenated.

MOTHER-

Most noun compounds are written separate (*mother country, mother superior, mother tongue,* etc.), except *motherland,* which is solid, and the hyphenated *mother-in-law* and *mother-of-pearl.* See also HYPHENATING, 6A, 10A.

mother-in-law. Plural is *mothers-in-law.* (See HYPHENATING, 6A.)

MOTOR-

Compounds generally two words (*motor corps, motor traffic,* etc.), except *motorbike, motorboat, motorbus, motorcade, motorcar, motorcycle, motordrome, motorman,* and *motorway,* which are solid.

motto. Plural is *mottoes.* (See PLURALIZING WORDS IN TERMINAL -O, 1.)

mould. See *mold.*

moulder. See *molder.*

mouldy. See *moldy.*

moult. See *molt.*

moustache. See *mustache.*

-MOUTHED

The following common adjective compounds, among others, are solid:

bigmouthed	foulmouthed
closemouthed	loosemouthed
evilmouthed	loudmouthed

Bloody-mouthed, broad-mouthed, open-mouthed, and *square-mouthed* are the common hyphenated compounds.

Mealy-mouthed may be hyphenated or written solid.

movable, moveable. First spelling is preferable; ends in *-able.* (See -ABLE, -EABLE, 2; -ABLE, -IBLE, 2.)

MUCH-

Invariably hyphenated in adjective compounds that precede their nouns: *much-admired* work, *much-loved* paintings, etc. But note that we do not hyphenate when the adjective is in the predicate: He was *much loved* by his contemporaries.

MUCOUS, MUCUS

The *-ous* ending is for the adjective, *-us* for the noun; *mucous* membrane, *mucous* secretions, *mucous* in texture, etc.; brings up *mucus,* with the texture of *mucus,* etc.

Muhammad. See *Mohammed.*

Muhammadan, Muhammedan. See *Mohammedan.*

mulatto. Note the single *-l,* double *-t.* Plural is *mulattoes.* (See PLURALIZING WORDS IN TERMINAL -O, 1.)

munificence. Ending is *-ence,* rather than *-ance,* to keep the preceding *-c* "soft." (See -ANCE, -ENCE, AFTER C-, 1.)

murmured, murmuring. Final *-r* of *murmur* is *not* doubled before a suffix. (See DOUBLING FINAL -R, 8C.)

muscle. Some people leave out the *-c,* or double the *-s.* If you keep the adjective *muscular* in mind, you can avoid both errors.

mussel. The edible bivalve.

mussle. Misspelling of *muscle* or *mussel.*

mustache, mustachio, moustache. All

correct, but the first spelling is the commonest.

mysterious, mystery, mystify. Note that the first vowel is -*y*, not -*i*.

N

(Rules for double -*n:* See DOUBLING FINAL -N.)

N-, KN-. See KN-, N-.

nabbed, nabbing. Note that the -*b* of *nab* is doubled when a suffix is added. (See DOUBLING FINAL -B.)

nack. Misspelling of *knack*.

nacre. The ending is -*re* to keep the -*c* "hard." (See -ER, -RE, 2.)

nacred, nacreous. See -ER, -RE, 3, 4.

naive, naïve. The spelling without the the dieresis (··) is commoner.

naivete, naiveté, naïveté, naivety. All these spellings acceptable, with the first, which is the simplest, probably somewhat commoner than any of the others.

-NANCE, -NENCE. See -ANCE, -ENCE, AFTER N-.

-NANT, -NENT. See -ANCE, -ENCE, AFTER N-.

naphtha. Often misspelled *naptha*, since it's commonly pronounced that way.

napsack. Misspelling of *knapsack*.

naptha. Misspelling of *naphtha*.

naught, nought. Either spelling is acceptable, the former somewhat preferable. The word is commonly used with the meaning of *zero*, and may also occur in a phrase such as *I'll give you naught*, or *I care naught for your feelings*, if an archaic flavor is aimed at. (See AUGHT, OUGHT.)

nausea. Not *nausha*.

nauseous. Not *naushous*.

nautilus. Not *nautilous*. (See -US, -OUS.)

NAVAL, NAVEL

Naval refers to a navy—*naval* officer, *naval* maneuvers, etc.

Navel is a more elegant term for belly button, or for any similar depression, as in *navel* orange.

navigable. Only the -*able* ending will keep the preceding -*g* "hard." (See -ABLE, -IBLE, 6.)

navigator. Ends in -*or*. (See -ER, -OR, 5.)

nearsighted. Solid word.

nebula. Plural is *nebulae* or, less commonly, *nebulas*. (See PLURALIZING WORDS IN TERMINAL -A.)

necessary. Double -*s*, ends in -*ary*. (See -ARY, -ERY, 1.)

necessity. Double -*s*.

NECK-

Noun compounds are solid (*necklace, necktie, neckwear*, etc.).

Adjective compounds preceding nouns are hyphenated—*neck-breaking, neck-high*, etc.

-NECKED

Adjective compounds are hyphenated (*bull-necked, thin-necked*, etc.), except the solidly written *barenecked*.

ne'er (poetic). Contraction of *never*, the apostrophe appearing in place of the missing -*v*. (See APOSTROPHE, USE OF, 1.)

negligence, negligent. -*E*, not -*a*, follows "soft" *g*-. (See -ANCE, -ENCE, AFTER G-, 4.)

negligible. -*Ible*, not -*able*, follows "soft" *g*-. (See -IBLE, -ABLE, 6.)

Negro. Plural is *Negroes*. (See PLURALIZING WORDS IN TERMINAL -O, 1.)

neighbor, neighbour. The first spelling is American, the second British; note the *-ei* combination. (See -IE, -EI. 6; -OR, -OUR, 1.)

Neil. Proper names are more likely to be spelled *-ei* than *-ie*. (See -IE, -EI, 5.)

neither. Note the *-ei* combination; this is an exception to the rule of *-i* before *-e* except after *c-*. (See -IE, -EI, 4.)

nemonic. Misspelling of *mnemonic*.

NEO-. See HYPHENATING, 39.

nescience. Most often, as here, *-ence*, rather than *-ance*, follows *i-*. (See -ANCE, -ENCE, AFTER I-, 1.)

-NESS AFTER N-

The suffix *-ness* is attached directly to an adjective ending in *-n* (*barren*, etc.). This may not look right until you get used to it, but is nonetheless the only correct form.

barrenness	greenness
brazenness	hiddenness
brokenness	keenness
cleanness	modernness
commonness	stubbornness
drunkenness	suddenness
evenness	sullenness
foreignness	vainness
frozenness	wantonness

-NESS AFTER -Y. See -Y PLUS A SUFFIX, 6, 7.

network. No hyphen. (See HYPHENATING, 3A.)

NEU-

For words that sound as if they start with *neu-*, see *PNEU-*.

NEVER-

Adjective compounds preceding nouns are hyphenated: *never-dying, never-ending,* etc.

NEW-

Adjective compounds are hyphenated: *new-built, new-fashioned, new-model, new-mown,* etc.

But *newfangled* is solid.

newsstand. No hyphen, double *-s*. (See HYPHENATING, 3A.)

-NGE

1. If a verb ends in *-nge* (*cringe, derange, twinge,* etc.), the present participle is formed regularly by dropping final *-e* and adding *-ing*— *cringing, deranging, twinging.* Such spellings do not tempt into mispronunciation, as there are no similar words with which they might be confused.

2. However *singe, swinge,* and *tinge* must retain final *-e* in the participle, for there is no other means of distinguishing them from the participles of *sing, swing,* and *ting.* Note, then, the following:
singe (burn lightly)—singeing
swinge (whip)—swingeing
tinge (color)—tingeing
(*tinging* also acceptable, but unnecessarily confusing)

3. A *singer* may be a vocalist or someone who (or that which) *singes,* but there is nothing we can do about that problem—*singeer* is out of the question, for obvious reasons.

nickel, nickle. *Nickel* is the only correct form, *nickle* appealing to people of logical minds who think of analogous words like *pickle, sickle, tickle,* etc. Incidentally, whether the word refers to the metal or the coin, the spelling is the same.

nickel's worth. Note the apostrophe. (See APOSTROPHE, USE OF, 4.)

nickle. Misspelling of *nickel*.

nicknack. See knickknack.

niece. *-I* before *-e* except after *c-*. (See -IE, -EI, 1.)

NIGHT-

Noun compounds are largely solid (*nightcap, nightdress, nighttime,* etc.), except for the following:

night blindness	night light
night clothes	night owl
night club	night school
night crawler	night stick
night latch	night watch
night letter	

Adjectives are hyphenated: *night-feeding, night-riding,* etc.

night, nite. The second spelling unacceptable though much used in signs, advertisements, and friendly letters.

nil. One *-l.* (See -IL, -ILL, 1.)

NINE-. See HYPHENATING, 49D, E.

nines. The plural of the number, when written as a word, requires no apostrophe. As a figure, the apostrophe is preferable but may be omitted: *9's* or *9s.* (See APOSTROPHE, USE OF, 2, 3.)

NINETY-. See HYPHENATING, 49A.

ninth. Though an exception to the general rule, final *-e* of *nine* is dropped before the suffix *-th.* (See RETAINED -E, 2.)

nite. Misspelling of *night.*

no. Plural is *noes.* (See PLURALIZING WORDS IN TERMINAL -O, 1.)

NO-

1. As a pronoun or adverb, *no-* in compounds makes solid words, with one exception. If *no* is clearly an adjective, two separate words are used.

SOLID—PRONOUN OR ADVERB

Nobody but nobody undersells Gimbels.

Nothing happened today.

We went *nowhere* all summer.

(always solid)

2. The exception is *no one,* generally spelled as two words (to avoid *noone,* which tempts to mispronunciation), occasionally hyphenated *no-one.* (This is rare, however, and not recommended, even though technically correct.)

3. SEPARATE — ADJECTIVE PLUS NOUN

No body (i.e., no corpse) was found in the wreckage.

No one thing caused his defeat— it was a combination of circumstances.

There's *no place* like home.

(always separate)

nob. See *knob.*

nobody, no body. See NO-.

noll. Misspelling of *knoll.*

NON-. See HYPHENATING, 18.

noncompliance. Ending is *-ance.* (See -ANCE, -ENCE, AFTER I-, 3.)

non-co-operation. Hyphenated as shown.

nonpareil. Note the *-ei* combination. (See -IE, -EI, 14.)

no one. Two words. (See NO-, 2.)

no place. Always two words.

notary public. No hyphen; plural is *notaries public.* (See HYPHENATING, 5A.)

nothing, no thing. See NO-.

noticeable. The *-e* of *notice* is retained before *-able* in order to preserve the original "soft" pronunciation of the preceding *-c.* (See -CEABLE.)

nought. See *naught.*

NOUN COMPOUNDS. See HYPHENATING, 1, 9, 10, 12.

novelette. Ends in *-ette.* (See -ET, -ETTE, 3.)

nowhere. Always a solid word. (See NO-.)

nowhere, nowheres. Good style avoids the final *-s* here and in words like *somewhere, anywhere,* etc.

nuckle. Misspelling of *knuckle.*

nucleus. Not *nucleous.* For plural see PLURALIZING WORDS IN TERMINAL -US, 15.)

nuisance. Ends in *-ance.*

null. Not *nul,* even though a similar word is spelled *nil.*

NUMBERS HYPHENATED. See HYPHENATING, 49.

---

numerator. Ends in *-or.* (See -ER, -OR, 5.)

numskull. Not *numbskull.*

nusance. Misspelling of *nuisance.*

nutrition. Ends in *-ition.* (See -ICIOUS, -ITIOUS, 4.)

nutritious. Ends in *-itious,* not *-icious.* (See -ICIOUS, -ITIOUS, 3.)

O

-O, -OU

1. Certain words in which the sound *-o* was once spelled *-ou* have been modernized in American spelling and are now almost always seen with the single vowel. For example:

mold has replaced *mould*
molder has replaced *moulder*
moldy has replaced *mouldy*
molt has replaced *moult*
smolder has replaced *smoulder.*

2. However, the following, though pronounced *-o,* must be spelled *-ou.*

boulder   poultice   poultry

-O, -OUGH. See -OUGH, -O.

-O, TERMINAL

When a verb ends in *-o,* the usual suffixes, such as *-ed* and *-ing,* are

added directly, even though a number of vowels then appear in succession. For example:

echo—echoed, echoing
folio—folioed, folioing
hello—helloed, helloing
hullo—hulloed, hulloing
radio—radioed, radioing

See also -OO, TERMINAL; PLURALIZING WORDS IN TERMINAL -O.

---

oaf. The plural is *oafs.* (See PLURALIZING WORDS IN TERMINAL -F OR -FE, 2.)

-OAP, -OPE. See -OPE, -OAP.

---

oasis. Plural is *oases.* (See PLURALIZING WORDS IN TERMINAL -IS.)

obbligato, obligato. Either spelling, the first preferable. Only one *-t.*

obedience, obedient. Most often, as here, *-ence* or *-ent,* rather than *-ance* or *-ant,* follows *i-.* (See -ANCE, -ENCE, AFTER I-, 1.)

obeisance, obeisant. One *-s.*

objector. Ends in *-or.* (See -ER, -OR, 5.)

obligato. Correct, but *obbligato* is preferable.

oboist. The *-e* of *oboe* is dropped before *-ist.*

observance, observant. Generally after *v-* the correct suffix is *-ance* or *-ant,* not *-ence* or *-ent.* (See -ANCE, -ENCE, AFTER V-, 1.)

obsess, obsession. Unlike *possess, possession,* single *-s* and then double *-s.*

obsolesce, obsolescence, obsolescent. Note the *-sc.* (See -ESCE, -ESCENT, -ESCENCE, 1, 2.)

occasional. As in *treasure, measure, leisure,* etc., a single *-s* is used for the *zh* sound. Common error is to double the *-s* unnecessarily.

occurred, occurring. The final *-r* of *occur* is doubled before *-ed* and *-ing* since the accent falls on the last syllable (*cur*) and remains there in the derived forms. (See DOUBLING FINAL -R, 2, 3.)

occurrence. Note the double -*r* and the -*ence* ending. (See -ANCE, -ENCE, AFTER R-, 3.)

ocher, ochre. The former spelling is preferable. (See -ER, -RE.)

-OCIOUS

The standard ending is -*ocious* rather than -*otious: atrocious, ferocious, precocious.* Note that each of these adjectives has a corresponding noun form in -*ocity: atrocity, ferocity, precocity.*

See also -ACIOUS, -ACEOUS, -ATIOUS; -ICIOUS, -ITIOUS.

---

o'clock. Contraction of *of the clock,* the apostrophe appearing in place of the missing letters. (See APOSTROPHE, USE OF, 1.)

octet, octette. The shorter spelling is preferable. (See -ET, -ETTE, 1.)

octopus. For plural see PLURALIZING WORDS IN TERMINAL -US, 8.

odor, odour. The first spelling is American, the second British. (See -OR, -OUR, 1.)

Odyssey. Double -*s.* If any extended journey is signified, the *o-* need not be capitalized.

-OE, TERMINAL

Words that end in -*oe* cause justifiable confusion when a suffix must be added. Consider these:

1. shoe—*shoer* has only one -*e,* and *shoeing* retains the terminal -*e* before -*ing.*
2. horseshoe—*horseshoer* and *horseshoeing,* as above.
3. canoe—in *canoer* and *canoed,* note the single -*e* at the end; in *canoeing,* note the retained -*e* before -*ing.*
4. hoe—past is *hoed* (one -*e*), participle is *hoeing* (with terminal -*e* retained).

5. toe—past is *toed,* participle is *toeing.*
6. woe—in *woeful* and *woebegone* note that terminal -*e* is retained. However, the variant *wobegone* is also acceptable, though not common.
7. tiptoe—past is *tiptoed,* participle is *tiptoeing,* the person is a *tiptoer.*

Oedipus, Oedipal. Pronounced ED-i-pus or ED-i-p'l, but the strange, Greek-flavored *oe-* is generally retained in the spelling. Many writers in the psychoanalytic field now favor *Edipus* and *Edipal,* but these forms are not yet completely sanctioned.

o'er (poetic). Contraction of *over* (See APOSTROPHE, USE OF, 1.)

-OES, -OS. See PLURALIZING WORDS IN TERMINAL -O.

---

oesophagus. See *esophagus.*

OFF-. See HYPHENATING, 31.

---

offense. This American spelling is preferable to the British *offence.* (See -ENCE, -ENSE, 2.)

officious. Ends in -*icious,* not -*itious.* (See -ICIOUS, -ITIOUS, 1.)

oftentimes, ofttimes. Written as solid words.

-OG, -OGUE. See -OGUE, -OG.

---

ogre, ogreish, ogress. See -ER, -RE, 5.

-OGUE, -OG

1. The ending -*ogue* has been shortened to -*og* in a number of words, notably: *analogue* or *analog; catalogue* or *catalog; Decalogue* or *Decalog; demagogue* or *demagog; dialogue* or *dialog; epilogue* or *epilog; monologue* or *monolog; pedagogue* or *pedagog; prologue* or

prolog; synagogue or *synagog; travelogue* or *travelog.* Though both spellings are technically correct, the *-ogue* form is far preferable in all the words above, with the possible exceptions of *catalogue, catalog* and *travelogue, travelog.*

2. The following, however, may be spelled only with the longer ending: *apologue* and *mystagogue,* as well as, of course, *brogue, rogue* and *vogue.*

OIL-

The following noun compounds are written solid: *oilcan, oilcloth, oilcup, oilpaper, oilskin, oilskins, oilstone.*

Others are separate: *oil field, oil painting,* etc.

-OKE. See -K TO -C.

-OL, -OLL

1. Words of one syllable end in double *-l: roll, toll, troll,* etc.

2. *Enroll* is preferably spelled with two *-l's,* also correct with one —*enrol.* Likewise *enrollment, enrolment.* However *enrolled, enrolling* with two *-l's* only.

3. Compounds of *roll*—*reroll, unroll,* etc.—with double *-l* in all forms.

4. Certain other verbs end in a single *-l,* notably: *control, extol, patrol.* (For rule on doubling *-l* in derived forms of these verbs, see DOUBLING FINAL -L, 1, 3.)

See also -AL, -ALL; -EL, -ELL; -IL, -ILL.

OLD-

Adjective compounds are hyphenated: *old-fashioned, old-line, old-maidish, old-time, old-world,* etc.

Noun compounds are two words: *Old Fashioned* (the drink), *old hat* (slang), *old maid, Old World,* etc.

However, *old-timer* is hyphenated.

-OLD. See HYPHENATING, 49B.

old fogy, old fogey. Either spelling. The adjective is either *old-fogyish* or *old-fogeyish.*

-OLL, -OL. See -OL, -OLL.

-OLOGY, -ALOGY. See -ALOGY, -OLOGY.

omelet, omelette. The shorter spelling is preferable. (See -ET, -ETTE, 1.)

ominous. Note that there is no *-i* following the *n-.*

omitted, omitting. Because *omit* is accented on the last syllable, the final *-t* is doubled before a suffix beginning with a vowel. (See DOUBLING FINAL -T, 2.)

omnibus. Plural is *omnibuses.* (See -US, -OUS.)

omnipotence, omnipotent. Note the *-e* after the *t-.* (See -ANCE, -ENCE, AFTER T-, 5.)

omniscience, omniscient. Note the *-ie* combination. (See -ANCE, -ENCE, AFTER I-, 1; -IE, -EI, 12.)

omnivorous. Not *omniverous*—from Latin *vor-,* to devour, found also in *carnivorous* and *herbivorous.*

ONE-. See HYPHENATING, 49D, E.

O'Neill. Proper names are more likely to be spelled *-ei* than *-ie.* (See -IE, -EI, 5.)

ones. The plural of the number, when written as a word, has no apostrophe. As a figure, the apostrophe is preferable, but may be omitted: *1's* or *1s.* (See APOSTROPHE, USE OF, 2, 3.)

only. The *-e* of *one* has been dropped before the adverbial suffix *-ly.* (See -LY, 9.)

onslaught. Note that the pattern is *-aught.* (See -AUGHT, -OUGHT, 1.)

onto, on to. Either spelling when used

as a preposition—he got *onto* (or *on to*) the bus.

-OO, TERMINAL

When a suffix such as *-ed, -er,* or *-ing* must be added to a verb ending in *-oo,* the long stretch of three successive vowels causes natural doubt in the minds of some spellers. However, the following derived forms are correctly spelled, and one has only to become visually adjusted to them.

coo—cooed, cooing
moo—mooed, mooing
shoo—shooed, shooing
taboo—tabooed
tattoo—tattooed, tattooer,
 tattooing

See also -O, TERMINAL.

---

opalesce, opalescence, opalescent. Note the *-sc.* (See -ANCE, -ENCE, AFTER C-, 5; -ESCE, -ESCENT, -ESCENCE, 1.)

-OOP, -OUP, -UPE

1. In words of this kind the *-oop* ending is commonest, for instance *coop, droop, hoop, loop, poop, scoop, sloop, swoop, whoop,* etc.

2. Rarely misspelled are the two common words ending in *-oup*— *group* and *soup.*

3. The following may cause some confusion.

A. *croup*—the respiratory ailment; also an animal's rump. There is no word spelled *croop.*

B. *roup*—a poultry disease; also, less frequently, hoarseness in a human.

C. *recoup*—to get back. No word spelled *recoop.*

D. *stoop, stoup*—two acceptable spellings for the same word. *Stoup* is preferable only for a kind of drinking cup (now an archaic word) or a basin of holy water; for all other meanings *stoop* is by far the preferable form.

E. *troop, troupe. Troop* refers to any group of people working together as a unit; *troupe* to a company of actors, singers, musicians, circus performers, etc. Hence, a *trouper* is one member of a *troupe,* or, by extension, any experienced actor, while a *trooper* is a mounted police officer or a member of the state police.

F. *cantaloupe, cantaloup.* Either spelling acceptable for this word, but no other, even though the word rhymes with *antelope.*

G. *droop, drupe. Drupe* is a botanical term for a kind of fleshy fruit; *droop,* noun or verb, is the common word meaning *hanging down,* etc. The adjective, then is spelled *droopy.*

H. *dupe.* About the only common one-syllable word ending in *-upe.*

I. *coupé.* A kind of car; this word should be written with the accent and is preferably pronounced koo-PAY, but many people call it a *koop.*

-OPE, -OAP

A fault of the illiterate speller is to use *-oap* for the very common *-ope* ending. *Soap* is the only common word ending in *-oap;* all others are *-ope:*

antelope   kaleidoscope
dope   misanthrope
grope   mope
hope   scope
interlope   slope

Cantaloupe, despite its similarity in sound, is correct as indicated; or, alternatively, may drop final *-e: cantaloup.*

OPEN-

Adjective compounds are hyphenated: *open-air, open-minded, openmouthed,* etc.

Except *openhanded* and *openhearted,* written solid.

Noun compounds are written separate: *open air, open letter, open secret,* etc.

Except *openwork,* written solid.

---

operator. Ends in *-or.* (See -ER, -OR, 5.)

opponent. Ends in *-ent.*

opposite. Two *-p*'s one *-s.*

oppress, oppressed, oppressing, oppression. Double *-p,* double *-s* in all forms.

cppressor. Ends in *-or.* (See -ER, -OR, 5.)

optimism. You might be amazed at how many people write it *optomism.* Note that all forms, including *optimist, optimal, optimum,* etc., have an *-i* before the *-m,* as do *pessimism, pessimist,* etc.

optometrist. Not *optomitrist.*

optomism. Misspelling of *optimism.*

opulence, opulent. Generally, but not always, *l-* is followed by *-ence,* or *-ent,* rather than *-ance* or *-ant.* (See -ANCE, -ENCE, AFTER L-, 1, 3.)

-OR, -ER. See -ER, -OR.

-OR, -OUR

1. American spelling prefers *-or* as an ending in words such as the following, though British custom favors *-our.*

armor	humor
behavior	labor
candor	neighbor
clamor	odor
clangor	parlor
color	rigor
demeanor	rumor
disfavor	savor
dishonor	splendor
endeavor	tumor
favor	valor
flavor	vapor
harbor	vigor
honor	

2. But *glamour* is far preferable to *glamor,* even though the derived forms are *glamorous* and *glamorize.*

ORAL, AURAL

Oral refers to speech or the mouth, or means *spoken*—an *oral* exam, *oral* expression, *oral* opening, etc.

Aural refers to the ear or the sense of hearing—*aural* acuity, etc.

---

orally. Note the double *-l,* since the adverbial suffix *-ly* is added to the adjective *oral.* (See -LY, 7.)

orator. Ends in *-or.* (See -ER, -OR, 5.)

ordinance. One of a group of words ending in *-ance* rather than *-ence,* after *n-.* (See -ANCE, -ENCE, AFTER N-, 3.)

ORDINANCE, ORDNANCE

With the *-i* the word means a decree or local law; without the *-i* it means cannon, artillery, or other military supplies.

---

ornamentally. Note that *-ly* is added to the adjective *ornamental,* hence the *-ally* ending. (See -LY, -ALLY, 3.)

-ORY, -ARY. See -ARY, -ORY.

-OS, -OES. See PLURALIZING WORDS IN TERMINAL -O.

---

oscillate. The verb and all its derived forms have a double *-l;* and note the *-sc* combination.

ostensible. If the root ends in *-ns,* the likely ending is *-ible,* not *-able.* (See -IBLE, -ABLE, 3.)

ostentatious. One of a few words ending in *-atious* rather than *-acious.* (See -ACIOUS, -ACEOUS, -ATIOUS 3.)

otherwise. Note the *-ise* ending, common to all words built on the base *-wise.* (See -ISE, 1.)

-OU, -O. See -O, -OU.

-OUGH, -O

Some words ending in *-ough* have been simplified by dropping the last three letters, but the shorter spellings are considered easygoing to the point of being casual, and should be used, if at all, only in the most informal writing. For example:

borough, boro
though, tho
thorough, thoro
through, thru

(But superhighways are officially called *thruways*.)

doughnut, donut
thoroughfare, thorofare

(But traffic signs, i.e., *no thorofare*, often use the shorter form to save space.)

ought. See AUGHT, OUGHT.

-OUGHT, -AUGHT. See -AUGHT, -OUGHT.

-OUP, -OOP, -UPE. See -OOP, -OUP, -UPE.

-OUR, -OR. See -OR, -OUR.

-OUR, -OWER, -AUER

The words considered here all rhyme, more or less, with *sour*. Consider the following.

1. -OUR: *scour; lour* (i.e., the verb meaning to scowl or threaten, often found in the participle *louring*, and more frequently spelled *lower*, *lowering*, with no change in pronunciation); *dour* (i.e., gloomy, stern, forbidding, etc., and pronounced variously to rhyme with *sour*, *poor*, or *fore*—take your choice); *flour* (for making bread, and not to be confused with *flower*, i.e., a blossom).

2. -OWER: *bower; cower; glower;*

flower (i.e., the blossom, not to be confused with *flour*, above); *deflower* (i.e., to rob of virginity, or remove blossoms from); *lower*, the preferable spelling of *lour*, in Section 1, above; *shower* (of rain, etc.); *power*.

3. -AUER: Two foods of German origin, *sauerkraut* and *sauerbraten*, are so spelled, not *sourkraut* or *sourbraten*.

ours. This word is never written with an apostrophe.

-OUS, -US. See -US, -OUS.

OUT-

Invariably compounds with *out-* are written solid, whether nouns, verbs, or adjectives: *outbreak*, *outcome*, etc.; *outbid*, *outdistance*, etc.; *outbound*, *outdated*, etc.

Adjective compounds of three or more words preceding their nouns are hyphenated: *out-and-out*, *out-of-date*, *out-of-door*, *out-of-doors*, *out-of-print*, *out-of-the-way*, etc.

The *out-group*, as contrasted with the *in-group*, is hyphenated.

Out- preceding a capital letter is also hyphenated: *out-Herod* Herod, *out-Machiavelli*, etc.

outlaid. Not *outlayed*.

OVER-

Compounds are invariably solid, whether nouns, verbs, or adjectives.

The only exceptions of any consequence are the adjectives *over-all* and *over-the-counter* (stocks), which are hyphenated. But *overall* may also be written solid.

overseer. Two *-e*'s only, even though it's *oversee* plus *-er*. (See -EER.)

overwrought. Note that the pattern is *-ought*. (See -AUGHT, -OUGHT, 1.)

-OWER, -OUR, -AUER. See -OUR, -OWER, -AUER.

P

(Rules for double -*p*: See DOUBLING FINAL -P.)

pageant, pageantry. The -*e* keeps the *g*- "soft," i.e., with a *j* sound.

paid. Not *payed*, except in *payed out* rope, cable, etc., or in the sense of coating with tar or pitch. (See -AYED, -AID, 2.)

PAIL, PALE

Pail, a noun, designates only the container—*pale,* whether noun, verb, or adjective, is the spelling for all other meanings, including the phrase *beyond the pale.*

pailful. The plural is *pailfuls.* (See PLURALIZING WORDS IN TERMINAL -FUL.)

PAIN, PANE

Pain, noun or verb, refers to suffering, punishment, hurt, or care (take *pains*); *pane,* as a noun, is a flat side or face, a sheet of glass for a window or door, etc.

PAIR, PARE, PEAR

A *pair* is two; *pare* is a verb meaning to cut, shave, or trim (*pare* an apple); *pear* is the fruit. *Pair* is also a verb, as in *pairing* up for the work.

pajamas, pyjamas. The first spelling is preferable.

palatable. Ends in -*able.* (See -ABLE, -IBLE, 2.)

PALATE, PALETTE, PALLET

The *palate* is the roof of the mouth, hence, also, the sense of taste, etc.

A painter's *palette* is the board on which he mixes his paints. It may also be spelled *pallet,* but this pattern is infrequent.

Pallet is the correct spelling for all other meanings.

pale. See PAIL, PALE.
palette. See PALATE, PALETTE, PALLET.
pallet. See PALATE, PALETTE, PALLET.
palpable. Ends in -*able.* (See -ABLE, -IBLE, 7.)
palsy. Not *palsey.*
pane. See PAIN, PANE.
panicked, panicking, panicky. The -*k* must be inserted in the derived forms of *panic* in order to preserve the original pronunciation of final -*c.* (See -C, -CK, 1.)
panned, panning. Note that the -*n* of *pan* is doubled when a suffix beginning with a vowel is added. (See DOUBLING FINAL -N.)

PAPER-

Of the common noun compounds these are solid: *paperback, paperboy, papermaking, paperweight.*

Most others are written separate: *paper cutter, paper hanger,* etc.

Adjective compounds are invariably hyphenated: *paper-covered, paper-thin,* etc.

-PAPER

Noun compounds with this word as suffix are mostly written separate (*carbon paper, wax paper,* etc.), except *curlpaper, flypaper, sandpaper,* and *wallpaper.*

paragoric. Misspelling of *paregoric.*
paraffin. One -*r,* two -*f*'s, though the word sounds as if it ought to be the other way around.

parallel. Where the double *-l* comes confuses many people. Look for the word *all* in the middle.

paralyze. This and *analyze* are the only two common verbs ending in *-yze.* (See -IZE, -YZE, 2.)

paralyzed, paralysis, paralytic. Note the *y-* after the *-l,* as in the verb *paralyze.* (See -IZE, -YZE, 3.)

parapet. Ends in *-et.* (See -ET, -ETTE, 4.)

parapeted. Only one *-t.*

pare. See PAIR, PARE, PEAR.

paregoric. Not *paragoric.*

parenthesis. Plural is *parentheses.* (See PLURALIZING WORDS IN TERMINAL -IS.)

parliament. The *-i* is generally silent.

parlor, parlour. The first spelling is American, the second British. (See -OR, -OUR, 1.)

parrafin. Misspelling of *paraffin.*

participance, participant. End in *-ance, -ant.*

PASS-

Noun compounds invariably solid (*passbook, passkey, passport, password,* etc.).

PASSABLE, PASSIBLE

With *-able,* the word means either (a) good enough, as a *passable* accomplishment; (b) able to be passed, as a *passable* student or law, or (c) admitting passageway or travel, as *passable* roads.

Passible means able to feel, suffer, or react emotionally—humans are *passible* creatures.

See also IMPASSABLE, IMPASSIBLE.

---

passageway. Solid word.

PASSED, PAST

Passed is the past tense of the verb *pass*—we *passed* your house today, *passed* time pleasantly, etc.

Past is a noun, adjective, adverb

or preposition—let's forget the *past;* the *past* tense; let's go *past;* he went *past* your house today.

---

passer-by. Hyphenated; plural is *passers-by.*

passible. See PASSABLE, PASSIBLE.

passtime. Misspelling of *pastime.*

past. See PASSED, PAST.

pasteurize. Named after the Frenchman Louis Pasteur, hence the Gallic *-eur* as a middle syllable.

pastime. One *-s,* illogically enough.

patience, patient. *-Ie* is the correct pattern, and the endings are *-ence, -ent.* (See -ANCE, -ENCE, 1; -IE, -EI, 11.)

patio. Plural is *patios.* (See PLURALIZING WORDS IN TERMINAL -O, 3.)

patrol. Ends in a single *-l.* (See -OL, -OLL, 4.)

patrolled, patrolling. Because *patrol* is accented on the last syllable, final *-l* is doubled before a suffix starting with a vowel. (See DOUBLING FINAL -L, 1.)

payed. See *paid.*

payer, paying. The *-y* of *pay* is retained before *-er, -ing.* (See -Y PLUS A SUFFIX, 9.)

PEA-

The noun compounds *pea bean, pea green, pea jacket,* and *pea soup* are two words.

These are solid: *peacock, peahen, peanut, peashooter.*

Adjectives are hyphenated: *pea-green, pea-shaped,* etc.

---

peaceable. The *-e* of *peace* is retained before *-able* in order to preserve the original "soft" pronunciation of the preceding *-c.* (See -CEABLE.)

PEAL, PEEL

Peal, noun or verb, refers to a loud sound, as of bells or thunder; *peel* is the skin of fruit, etc. As a verb, *peel* means to take the surface or outermost layer from something.

pear. See PAIR, PARE, PEAR.

peavish. Misspelling of *peevish.*

peccadilloes, peccadillos. The former is the preferable plural; both are correct. Note the double *-c,* double *-l.* (See PLURALIZING WORDS IN TERMINAL -O, 4.)

pedagogue, pedagog. The longer spelling is preferable. (See -OGUE, -OG, 1.)

peddler, pedlar. The first is much the commoner spelling.

peel. See PEAL, PEEL.

peevish. Not *peavish.*

pell-mell, pellmell. Hyphenated or solid, the former preferable.

PEN-
    Penknife and *penman* are solid, *pen name* separate.

penetrable. Since *-a* is the corresponding vowel in another form of the word (*penetrate*), the correct ending is *-able.* (See -ABLE, -IBLE, 5.)

penitence, penitent. End in *-ence, -ent.* (See -ANCE, -ENCE, AFTER T-, 3, 4.)

pen name. No hyphen. (See HYPHENATING, 3B.)

PENNY-
    Penny ante and *penny dreadful* are separate; *pennyroyal, pennyweight,* and *pennyworth* are solid.
    Penny-wise is hyphenated.

penny's worth. Note the apostrophe. (See APOSTROPHE, USE OF, 4.)

PER-, PRE-
    Because of careless or faulty pronunciation some speakers are not clear whether certain words begin with *per-* or *pre-*. Errors are made mainly in the following, and can be avoided by saying the first syllable

of each word distinctly, and as spelled.

PER (pronounced PURR)

perceive	perspiration
perception	perspire
perfume	perturb
perhaps	perverse
persist	

PRE (pronounced PREE)

precarious	prerogative
precaution	prescribe
precede	prescription
precise	preserve
precision	preside
preclude	presume
precocious	presumption
predict	presumptuous
predominant	pretend
prefer	pretentious
preliminary	prevail
premonitory	prevaricate
prepare	prevent
preponderant	prevention
preposterous	

perambulator. Ends in *-or.* (See -ER, -OR, 5.)

percaution. Misspelling of *precaution.*

perceive. *-E* before *-i* after *c-.* (See -IE, -EI, 2.)

per cent. The preferable way to write this is as two separate words without punctuation (unless, of course, you prefer the symbol %), as *ten per cent of his money.* Also acceptable as *per centum* or *per cent.* (with the period).

perceptible. Ends in *-ible,* since the noun is formed by the immediate addition of *-ion* to the root (*perception*). (See -IBLE, -ABLE, 2.)

perception. The first syllable is *per-,* not *pre-.* (See PER-, PRE-.)

percipience. Most often, as here, *-ence,* rather than *-ance,* follows *i-.* (See -ANCE, -ENCE, AFTER I-, 1.)

percise. Misspelling of *precise.*

percolator. Ends in *-or.* (See -ER, -OR, 5.)

perclude. Misspelling of *preclude.*

perdominant. Misspelling of *predominant.*

peremptory. Note that the ending is *-ory,* not *-ary.* (See -ARY, -ORY, 2.)

perfectible. If the root forms its noun by the immediate addition of *-ion* (*perfection*), the correct ending is likely to be *-ible.* (See -IBLE, -ABLE, 2.)

perfer. Misspelling of *prefer.*

perfessor. Misspelling of *professor.*

performable. Ends in *-able.* (See -ABLE, -IBLE, 1.)

performance. Ends in *-ance.*

perhaps. The first syllable is *per-,* not *pre-.* (See PER-, PRE-.)

perishable. The ending is *-able.* (See -ABLE, -IBLE, 1.)

perliminary. Misspelling of *preliminary.*

permanence, permanent. The endings are *-ence, -ent.* (See -ANCE, -ENCE, AFTER N-, 1.)

permissible. When the root ends in *-miss,* the correct ending is *-ible.* (See -IBLE, -ABLE, 4.)

permitted, permitting. Because *permit* is accented on the last syllable, the final *-t* is doubled before a suffix beginning with a vowel. (See DOUBLING FINAL -T, 2.)

pernicious. Ends in *-icious,* not *-itious.* (See -ICIOUS, -ITIOUS, 1.)

pernickety, persnickety. Either spelling.

perogative. Misspelling of *prerogative.*

perpare. Misspelling of *prepare.*

perpetrator. Ends in *-or.* (See -ER, -OR, 5.)

perponderant. Misspelling of *preponderant.*

perposterous. Misspelling of *preposterous.*

perscribe, perscription. Misspellings of *prescribe, prescription.*

perserve. Misspelling of *preserve.*

perservere. Misspelling of *persevere.*

perseverance. Unlike most nouns from verbs ending in *-ere,* this one has an *-ance* suffix. (See -ANCE, -ENCE, AFTER R-, 5.)

persevere. No *-r* before the *-v.*

persistence, persistent. Note the *-ence* and *-ent* endings. (See -ANCE, -ENCE, AFTER T-, 3, 4.)

persnickety. See *pernickety.*

personable. The ending is *-able.* (See -ABLE, -IBLE, 1.)

PERSONAL, PERSONNEL

The first spelling is the adjective referring to a person; the latter a collective noun meaning the staff of any organization.

---

perspire, perspiration. Note that the first syllable is *per-,* not *pre-.* (See PER-, PRE-.)

persuit. Misspelling of *pursuit.*

persume, persumption, persumptuous. Misspellings of *presume, presumption, presumptuous.*

pertend. Misspelling of *pretend.*

pertinence, pertinent. The endings are *-ence, -ent.* (See -ANCE, -ENCE, AFTER N-, 1.)

peruke. Not *peruque.*

pervail. Misspelling of *prevail.*

pervaricate. Misspelling of *prevaricate.*

pervent, pervention. Misspelling of *prevent, prevention.*

pervertible. Ends in *-ible.* (See -IBLE, -ABLE, 2.)

pessimism, pessimist. The vowel before the *-m* is *-i.*

pestilence. Generally, though not always, *l-* is followed by *-ence* rather than *-ance.* (See -ANCE, -ENCE, AFTER L-, 1, 3.)

petulance. One of a comparatively few words in which *-ance,* rather than *-ence,* follows *l-.* The adjective would, of course, be spelled similarly —*petulant.* (See -ANCE, -ENCE, AFTER L-, 3.)

Phebe. See *Phoebe.*

Phenicia. See *Phoenicia.*

phenix. See *phoenix.*

phenomenon. Note that the vowel after *m-* is *-e.* Plural is *phenomena* or *phenomenons*. (See PLURALIZING WORDS IN TERMINAL -ON.)

Philippines. One -*l*, double -*p*. The native is a *Filipino*—one -*p*.

philter, philtre. The first spelling is preferable. (See -ER, -RE.)

Phoebe, Phebe. The first spelling is preferable.

Phoenicia, Phenicia. *Phoe-* preferable.

phoenix, phenix. The first spelling is preferable.

phony, phoney. Either spelling for this slang word.

phosphorescence, phosphorescent. Note the -*sc* and the -*ence* or -*ent* ending. (See -ANCE, -ENCE, AFTER C-, 5; -ESCE, -ESCENT, -ESCENCE.)

phosphorus, phosphorous. The first spelling is a noun, the second an adjective. (See -US, -OUS.)

phraseology. The -*e* of *phrase* is retained both in the spelling and the pronunciation of *phraseology*.

phthisic. Popular trick word offered in spelling bees, since its pronunciation is so unlike what you'd expect—TIZ-ik.

phthisis. Another trick word, pronounced THY-sis. Both this and *phthisic* mean tuberculosis of the lungs.

physicked, physicking. The -*k* must be inserted in the derived forms of *physic* in order to preserve the original pronunciation of final -*c*. (See -C, -CK, 1.)

piano. Plural is *pianos*. (See PLURALIZING WORDS IN TERMINAL -O, 2.)

piazza. Double -*z*.

piccalilli. Double -*c*, single -*l*, then double -*l*.

piccolo. Double -*c*, one -*l*. Plural is *piccolos*. (See PLURALIZING WORDS IN TERMINAL -O, 2.)

PICK-

Noun compounds are solid: *pickax, picklock, pickpocket, pickup.*

Pick-me-up, however, is hyphenated.

pickax, pickaxe. Either spelling, the first commoner.

pickle. Note the -*le* ending. (See -ICKLE, -ICKEL.)

picnicked, picnicker, picnicking. The -*k* must be inserted in the derived forms of *picnic* in order to preserve the original "hard" pronunciation of final -*c*. (See -C, -CK, 1.)

pidgeon. Misspelling of *pigeon*.

pidgin. The correct spelling in *pidgin* English; *pigeon* is also acceptable, but rarely used.

piece. -*I* before -*e*, except after *c*-. (See -IE, -EI, 1.)

PIG-

Most noun compounds are solid (*pigpen, pigskin, pigsty, pigtail,* etc.).

Pig iron and *pig Latin* are written separate.

Adjective compounds are hyphenated (*pig-eating, pig-faced,* etc.), except *pigheaded,* which is solid.

pigeon. No -*d*.

PIGEON-

The nouns *pigeon breast, pigeon hawk,* and *pigeon house* are written separate; *pigeonhole* is solid.

The adjective *pigeon-toed* is hyphenated.

Pigmy. See *Pygmy*.

PIN-

Noun or verb compounds mostly solid (*pinfeather, pinhead, pinhole, pinpoint, pinprick,* etc.), except *pin-up,* hyphenated as a noun or adjective.

pinochle. This is the preferred spelling, though the rarely used *pinocle, pinuchle,* and *pinuckle* are also correct.

PIPE-

Nouns are mostly separate (*pipe dream, pipe line, pipe organ, pipe of peace,* etc.), except *pipefish, pipestem,* and *pipestone,* written solid.

Adjectives are hyphenated (*pipe-cleaning, pipe-drilling,* etc.).

pipette, pipet. The longer spelling is preferable. (See -ET, -ETTE, 2.)

pirouette. Ends in *-ette.* (See -ET, -ETTE, 3.)

pistachio. Plural is *pistachios.* (See PLURALIZING WORDS IN TERMINAL -O, 3.)

piteous. Ends in *-eous,* not *-ious.*

pitiful. The *-y* of *pity* changes to *-i* before *-ful.* (See -Y PLUS A SUFFIX, 8A.)

pittance. *-Ance* is found somewhat more often than *-ence* after *t-*. (See -ANCE, -ENCE, AFTER T-, 1.)

pityful. Misspelling of *pitiful.*

pizza. This is the popular Italian pie, pronounced PEET-sa.

pizzicato. Two *-z*'s; plural is *pizzicati.*

placable. Only the *-able* ending will keep the preceding *-c* "hard." (See -ABLE, -IBLE, 6.)

plagiarism. Not *plajiarism.*

plaguy, plaguey. The first spelling is preferable.

plain-clothes man. The hyphen is between the first two words; the third is separate. (See -MAN.)

planned, planner, planning. Note that the *-n* of *plan* is doubled when a suffix beginning with a vowel is added. (See DOUBLING FINAL -N.)

plateau. The plural is either *plateaus* or *plateaux.* (See PLURALIZING WORDS IN TERMINAL -EAU, 3.)

platypus. Not *platypous.* (See -US, -OUS.)

plausible. The ending is *-ible.* (See -IBLE, -ABLE, 1.)

PLAY-

Noun compounds are mostly solid (*playbill, playboy, playground, plaything,* etc.).

These are written separate: *play acting, play actor, play doctor, play on words.*

The noun *play-off* is hyphenated.

played, player, playing. Since the terminal *-y* of *play* follows a vowel, it does not change to *-i* before a suffix. (See -Y PLUS A SUFFIX, 9.)

playwright, playwriter. The latter is the less common term.

pleasant. Ends in *-ant.*

pleasurable. Drop final *-e* of *pleasure* before adding *-able.* (See -ABLE, -EABLE, 1; -ABLE, -IBLE, 2.)

plebeian. Note the second *-e;* not *plebian.*

plebiscite. The vowel after the *b-* is *-i,* not *-e.*

pledgor, pledgeor. The first spelling is preferable, even though the *-g* is pronounced as a *-j.*

plenitude. Not *plentitude.*

plenteous. Ends in *-eous,* not *-ious.*

plentiful. The *-y* of *plenty* changes to *-i* before *-ful.* (See -Y PLUS A SUFFIX, 8A.)

plentitude. Misspelling of *plenitude.*

pleurisy. Ends in *-isy.*

pliancy, pliant. Not *pliency* or *plient.*

plow, plough. Both spellings are current, the former more popular today.

PLURALIZING WORDS IN TERMINAL -A

1. Certain technical words of Latin origin ending in *-a* are pluralized by adding *-e,* as *nebula—nebulae.* (The final syllable is then pronounced to rhyme with *see.*)

     alga—algae
     larva—larvae
     minutia—minutiae
     nebula—nebulae or, less
        commonly, nebulas

vertebra—vertebrae or, less commonly, vertebras

2. When *antenna* refers to the feeler of an insect or other creature, it is usually *antennae* in the plural, although *antennas* is also acceptable; for a radio or television aerial *antennas* is the only plural.

3. When *formula* is used technically, *formulae* is the common plural; nontechnically, *formulas* is preferable.

4. *Alumna,* a female graduate, is *alumnae* in the plural; a male graduate, *alumnus* is pluralized to *alumni* (pronounced a-LUM-nigh).

5. *Dogma,* from the Greek, is commonly pluralized *dogmas,* but the more learned *dogmata* is also acceptable.

6. *Stigma,* also from the Greek, is commonly pluralized *stigmas,* although *stigmata* may also be used; but as a medical, zoological, or botanical term, the plural *stigmata* is generally preferred.

PLURALIZING WORDS IN TERMINAL -EAU

1. Such words are derived from French, in which language they are regularly pluralized by the addition of *-x.* In English this exotic plural form is retained for words that are still distinctively Gallic.

> bandeau—bandeaux
> bateau—bateaux
> château—châteaux
> rondeau—rondeaux
> tableau—tableaux

2. For words still retaining a certain Gallic flavor but that have gained increased currency in everyday usage, both the French plural and an Anglicized form are found, the *-x* ending slightly more popular.

chapeau—chapeaux or chapeaus
flambeau—flambeaux or flambeaus
trousseau—trousseaux or trousseaus

3. And for those words that have lost a good deal of their French flavor, the plural in *-s* is commoner than that in *-x.*

> beau—beaus or beaux
> bureau—bureaus or bureaux
> plateau—plateaus or plateaux
> portmanteau—portmanteaus or portmanteaux

PLURALIZING WORDS IN TERMINAL -F OR -FE

1. Certain nouns so terminating, and familiar to most spellers, change *-f* or *-fe* to *-ves* for the plural. Often the *-f* in such words follows *l-* or a long vowel.

calf—calves	knife—knives
elf—elves	leaf—leaves
half—halves	life—lives
self—selves	loaf—loaves
shelf—shelves	midwife—
werewolf—	midwives
werewolves	sheaf—sheaves
wolf—wolves	thief—thieves
housewife—	wife—wives
housewives	

2. The following, among others, merely add *-s* to form the plural.

belief—beliefs	mischief—
brief—briefs	mischiefs
chef—chefs	oaf—oafs
chief—chiefs	reef—reefs
disbelief—	reproof—
disbeliefs	reproofs
fife—fifes	safe—safes
giraffe—giraffes	serf—serfs
grief—griefs	spoof—spoofs
gulf—gulfs	waif—waifs
handkerchief—	
handkerchiefs	

3. Words ending in *-ff* also merely add *-s: bluffs, cliffs, cuffs,* etc.

4. In the following, usage is divided or depends on meaning.

A. beef—*beeves* is the preferable plural for *steers, cows, oxen,* etc., though *beefs* may also be so used; only *beefs* as the plural of *beef,* slang for complaint.

B. dwarf—*dwarfs* is the correct form, though the now obsolete *dwarves* is sometimes seen.

C. hoof—*hoofs* is correct, *hooves* now rare, except in poetry, or among people addicted to elegant expression.

D. roof—*roofs* is correct, no authority whatever for *rooves*.

E. scarf—both *scarfs* and *scarves* correct, the former preferable in America, the latter commoner in England, though still much seen in this country.

F. staff—*staffs* by far the commoner plural, though *staves* is also correct for sticks, poles, rods, etc.

G. turf—*turfs* is correct, *turves* archaic.

H. wharf—*wharves* is preferable, *wharfs* also correct.

PLURALIZING WORDS IN TERMINAL -FUL

For words like *cupful, spoonful,* etc., -*s* follows the terminal -*l,* since it is the total quantity that is being indicated. There is no acceptable word *cupsful* or *spoonsful,* and *two cups full* or *five spoons full* would be written only if there are two separate cups or five separate spoons, each one full.

The proper pattern, then, is as follows: *bucketfuls, bushelfuls, capfuls, cupfuls, glassfuls, handfuls, hatfuls, pailfuls, pocketfuls, shovelfuls, spoonfuls, tablespoonfuls, teaspoonfuls,* etc.

PLURALIZING WORDS IN TERMINAL -IS

Certain words with terminal -*is* are pluralized by changing -*is* to -*es.*
  amanuensis—amanuenses
  analysis—analyses
  antithesis—antitheses
  axis—axes
  basis—bases
  crisis—crises

ellipsis—ellipses
hypothesis—hypotheses
oasis—oases
parenthesis—parentheses
synopsis—synopses
thesis—theses

PLURALIZING WORDS IN TERMINAL -O

1. When in doubt, simply add -*s,* as most words ending in -*o* are thus pluralized. To the following, however, -*es* must be added.
  echo—echoes
  embargo—embargoes
  hero—heroes
  innuendo—innuendoes
  manifesto—manifestoes
  mosquito—mosquitoes
  motto—mottoes
  mulatto—mulattoes
  Negro—Negroes
  no—noes
  potato—potatoes
  tomato—tomatoes
  torpedo—torpedoes
  veto—vetoes

2. You will notice that the preceding words all end in -*o* preceded by a *consonant,* and some spellers are under the misapprehension that most such words are pluralized by the addition of -*es.* The fact is, as the following list shows, that far more consonant -*o* words simply add -*s.* (The most efficient method for avoiding confusion is to become thoroughly familiar with the fourteen -*es* words in Section 1, and pluralize all others by affixing -*s* only.)

  albino—albinos
  alto—altos
  armadillo—armadillos
  auto—autos
  banjo—banjos
  basso—bassos
  bolero—boleros
  bronco—broncos
  burro—burros

casino—casinos
cello—cellos*
concerto—concertos*
contralto—contraltos*
dynamo—dynamos
Eskimo—Eskimos
Filipino—Filipinos
kimono—kimonos
libretto—librettos*
piano—pianos
proviso—provisos
salvo—salvos
silo—silos
solo—solos
sombrero—sombreros
soprano—sopranos*
tobacco—tobaccos
torso—torsos
tyro—tyros
violoncello—violoncellos
virtuoso—virtuosos

3. The one rule you can rely on is that if -o is preceded by a vowel (as in *radio*), only -s may be added (-y is considered a vowel if it has the sound of -i).

cameo—cameos
embryo—embryos
folio—folios
impresario—impresarios
patio—patios
pistachio—pistachios
portfolio—portfolios
radio—radios
ratio—ratios
rodeo—rodeos
Romeo—Romeos
seraglio—seraglios
studio—studios

4. The following may be spelled either way, -oes being preferable.

buffaloes, buffalos
cargoes, cargos
desperadoes, desperados

---

* *cello, concerto, contralto, libretto,* and *soprano* may also be pluralized in Italian style as *celli, concerti, contralti, libretti,* and *soprani. Concerti* and *libretti* are particularly favored in musical circles.

dominoes, dominos
grottoes, grottos
mangoes, mangos
peccadilloes, peccadillos
porticoes, porticos
tornadoes, tornados
viragoes, viragos
volcanoes, volcanos

5. While in the following, -os is preferable.

flamingos, flamingoes
halos, haloes
hobos, hoboes
lassos, lassoes
mementos, mementoes
stilettos, stilettoes
zeros, zeroes

PLURALIZING WORDS IN TERMINAL -ON

Words of Greek origin ending in -on are generally pluralized by substituting the suffix -a. However, the Anglicized plural formed by adding -s is also acceptable.

automaton—automata or automatons
criterion—criteria or criterions
phenomenon—phenomena or phenomenons

PLURALIZING WORDS IN TERMINAL -UM

1. Words of Latin origin ending in -um (*memorandum, datum,* etc.) are generally pluralized by substituting the suffix -a. However, for many of these, the Anglicized plural (formed by adding -s) is also correct, though less common.

addendum—addenda
agendum—agenda
arcanum—arcana or arcanums
bacterium—bacteria
candelabrum—candelabra or candelabrums (but *candelabra* itself is now often used as a singular, the plural of which is *candelabras*)

curriculum—curricula or curriculums
datum—data
desideratum—desiderata
effluvium—effluvia or effluviums
erratum—errata
medium—media or mediums (only *mediums* for those who conduct séances)
memorandum—memoranda or memorandums
referendum—referenda or referendums
spectrum—spectra or spectrums
stratum—strata or stratums
ultimatum—ultimata or ultimatums
2. In the following the Anglicized plural is commoner.
gymnasium—gymnasiums or gymnasia
maximum—maximums or maxima
minimum—minimums or minima
stadium—stadiums or stadia
symposium—symposiums or symposia
3. For *equilibrium* the plural form *equilibriums* is commoner in everyday usage, *equilibria* in reference to the forces studied in physics.

PLURALIZING WORDS IN TERMINAL -US

Usage and rules are not particularly uniform for this group; it will therefore be more efficient to consider words individually.

1. *cumulus.* A technical term in meteorology—pluralize it with the Latin ending, *cumuli,* the last syllable rhyming with *sigh.*

2. *focus.* As a technical term in mathematics, medicine, etc., *foci* (pronounced FOE-sigh) is commoner; otherwise *focuses.*

3. *genius.* With the meaning of a Roman deity, a guardian spirit, etc., the plural is *genii* (pronounced JEE-nee-eye); otherwise *geniuses.*

4. *genus.* Mostly used as a technical term, so the Latin plural, *genera,* is correct, although an alternative plural, *genuses* is just barely acceptable and rarely used.

5. *gladiolus.* The Anglicized plural, *gladioluses,* has a slight edge on the Latin *gladioli* (GLAD-ee-OH-lye).

6. *hippopotamus.* The common plural *hippopotamuses* preferable to the learned *hippopotami.*

7. *locus.* Mostly a technical term, so the Latin plural, *loci* (LOW-sigh) is correct.

8. *octopus.* As in *hippopotamus,* above, the common plural, *octopuses,* is best, but you can, if you're so inclined, exhibit erudition by using *octopodes* (ok-TOP-o-deez) or *octopi* (OK-to-pie).

9. *radius.* Largely a technical term, so *radii* (RAY-dee-eye) is common; but *radiuses* is also acceptable.

10. *stimulus.* Use the Latin plural, *stimuli* (STIM-yoo-lye).

11. *terminus.* Use either the common *terminuses* or the erudite *termini* (TUR-mi-nye).

12. *alumnus.* The plural is *alumni* (a-LUM-nye). An *alumnus* is a male graduate, not to be confused with *alumna,* a female graduate.

13. *syllabus.* Again a technical term, so *syllabi* (SIL-a-BYE) is common; but *syllabuses* is also acceptable.

14. *fungus.* Again a technical term, so *fungi* (FUN-jye) preferable; *funguses* is also acceptable.

15. *nucleus. Nuclei* (NOO-klee-eye) preferable, *nucleuses* acceptable.

PLURALIZING WORDS IN TERMINAL -X

A number of words of Latin origin with the terminal letter -*x* may be pluralized either with the original Latin ending or by the simple addition of -*es.*

1. apex—apexes or apices
2. appendix—appendixes or appendices
3. matrix—matrices or matrixes
4. vertex—vertexes or vertices
5. vortex—vortexes or vortices

PLURALIZING WORDS IN TERMINAL -Y. See -EYS, -IES, -YS.

PLURALS, TO MAKE POSSESSIVE. See POSSESSIVES, 2, 5.

PNEU-

These common words, in which initial *p-* is silent, start with *pneu-:*
pneumatic   pneumonia
pneumococcus   pneumothorax

POCKET-

The following compound nouns are solid: *pocketbook* (i.e., for money), *pocketknife.*

Others are written separate: *pocket book* (i.e., a small book), *pocket flask, pocket veto,* etc.

The adjectives *pocket-size* and *pocket-sized* are hyphenated.

pocketful. The plural is *pocketfuls.* (See PLURALIZING WORDS IN TERMINAL -FUL.)

poet laureate. Plural is *poets laureate.* No hyphen.

-POINT

The following noun compounds with *-point* are solid: *counterpoint, crosspoint, standpoint,* and *viewpoint.*

Most others are separate: *decimal point, strong point, turning point,* etc.

point-blank. Hyphenated.

pokiness. The *-y* of *poky* changes to *-i* before *-ness.* (See -Y PLUS A SUFFIX, 6.)

poky, pokey. The first spelling is preferable.

politicked, politicking. The *-k* must be inserted in these derived forms of *politic* in order to preserve the original "hard" pronunciation of final *-c.* (See -C, -CK, 1.)

pommel, pummel. Whether noun or verb, *pommel* is the preferable spelling, but both are correct. The derived forms of the verb are preferably *pommeled* and *pommeling* (or *pummeled* and *pummeling*), though double *-l* is also correct. (See DOUBLING FINAL -L, 2.)

Pompeian. Note the *-e* before *-ian.*

Pompeii. The ancient city ends in two *-i*'s.

Pompey. The Roman general ends in *-ey.*

ponderable. Ends in *-able.* (See -ABLE, -IBLE, 1.)

poniard. The *-i* follows the *n-.* Pronounced PON-yerd, but not spelled that way.

poop. See -OOP, -OUP, -UPE, 1.

POOR-

Poorhouse is a solid word; other nouns are separate: *poor farm, poor laws, poor whites,* etc.

The adjective, *poor-spirited* is hyphenated.

porcelain. Not *porcelin.*

PORE, POUR

As a verb, *pore,* usually followed by *over,* means to read carefully, study intently, etc.—He's *poring* over the newest statistics; he *pored* over his books; etc.

Pour, as a verb, means to flow, rain hard, discharge, serve, etc.—The water *pours* out; he *poured* the sugar into the bowl; it's *pouring* out; Mrs. Jones will *pour;* etc.

porous. The *-e* of *pore* is dropped before a suffix beginning with a vowel. (See DROPPED -E.)

porridge. Note the *-d.*

portable. Ends in *-able*. (See -ABLE, -IBLE, 7.)

portentous. No *-i* or *-u* before *-ous*.

portfolio. Plural is *portfolios*. (See PLURALIZING WORDS IN TERMINAL -O, 3.)

porticoes, porticos. The former is the preferable plural; both are correct. (See PLURALIZING WORDS IN TERMINAL -O, 4.)

portmanteau. The plural is either *portmanteaus* or *portmanteaux*. (See PLURALIZING WORDS IN TERMINAL -EAU, 3.)

possess. This verb, as well as its derived forms—*possession, possessive, possessor,* etc.—has two sets of double *-s*'s.

POSSESSIVES

1. Generally, to make a noun possessive, add *-'s*.

> boy—boy's
> children—children's
> girl—girl's
> Mary—Mary's
> men—men's
> Tom—Tom's
> wife—wife's
> women—women's

2. If a plural noun ends in *-s*, merely add the apostrophe.

> books—books'
> boys—boys'
> girls—girls'
> secretaries—secretaries'
> wives—wives'
> workers—workers'

3. To a proper noun (i.e., a name) ending in *-s*, such as *Jones*, the rule is to add *'s*, and pronounce the word with an extra syllable.

> Burns—Burns's
> Dickens—Dickens's
> Gross—Gross's
> Jesus—Jesus's
> Jones—Jones's
> Keats—Keats's
> Lewis—Lewis's
> Moses—Moses's
> Ross—Ross's
> Wells—Wells's

4. It is also correct, however, to affix only the apostrophe to such names, i.e., *Burns', Dickens', Gross', Jesus', Jones', Keats', Lewis', Moses', Ross', Wells',* in which case no syllable is added in pronunciation. In a long name ending in *-s* this is certainly the less awkward procedure: *Euripides', Socrates', Sophocles', Ulysses',* etc.

5. It may occasionally be necessary to make the *plural* of a proper noun possessive. To do this, add only an apostrophe.

> the Browns—the Browns'
> the Grosses—the Grosses'
> the Joneses—the Joneses'
> the Lewises—the Lewises'
> the Rosses—the Rosses'
> the Smiths—the Smiths'

6. Frequently a standard name that shows possession is nevertheless, by house rules, written without the apostrophe, as *All Souls Church, Johns Hopkins University, Teachers College,* etc.

7. A hyphenated or compound word always receives the apostrophe at the end: *attorney general's, editor in chief's, letter carrier's, mother-in-law's, someone else's,* etc.

8. Personal and relative pronouns in the possessive case are never written with an apostrophe: *its,* not *it's; ours,* not *our's; theirs,* not *their's; whose,* not *who's,* unless you mean *who is.* On the other hand, other pronouns do have an apostrophe to indicate possession: *anyone's, no one's, one's, someone's,* etc.

See also APOSTROPHE, USE OF.

---

possessor. Ends in *-or*. (See -ER, -OR, 5.)

possible. Ends in *-ible*. (See -IBLE, -ABLE, 1.)

POST-. See HYPHENATING, 22.

postmaster general. No hyphen. Plural is *postmasters general.* (See HYPHENATING, 5A.)

potable. Note the *-able* ending. (See -ABLE, -IBLE, 7.)

potato. Plural is *potatoes.* (See PLURALIZING WORDS IN TERMINAL -O, 1.)

potency. *-Ency,* not *-ancy,* is the suffix. (See -ANCE, -ENCE, AFTER T-, 5.)

potent. *-Ent* ending. (See -ANCE, -ENCE, AFTER T-, 5.)

poultice. Though the first syllable is pronounced POLE, the vowel sound must be spelled *-ou.* (See -O, -OU, 2.)

poultry. Pronounced POLE-tree, but spelled *-ou.* (See -O, -OU, 2.)

pour. See PORE, POUR.

power. See -OUR, -OWER, -AUER, 2.

powwow. One word, despite the two medial *-w*'s.

practicable. Only the *-able* ending will keep the preceding *-c* "hard." (See -ABLE, -IBLE, 6.)

PRACTICE, PRACTISE

Practice is the only spelling for the noun; it is also the preferred spelling for the verb, though *practise* (as a verb) is common enough and also correct.

The adjective may be spelled either *practiced* or *practised,* the form with the *-c* again preferable.

---

practitioner. Ends in *-er.* (See -ER, -OR.)

prair, praier. Misspellings of *prayer.*

prairie. Not *prairy.*

PRAY, PREY

Pray is a verb only—*pray* to God, let us *pray,* I *pray* you to come, etc.

Prey, as a verb, is followed by *on* or *upon,* and means to plunder, live on by eating, weigh heavily on, etc.—They *preyed* on the poor; lions *prey* on small mammals; it *preyed* on his mind, etc.

Prey is also a noun—bird of *prey;* fell *prey* to temptation; catch their *prey* at night; etc.

---

prayed, prayer, praying. Since the terminal *-y* of *pray* follows a vowel, it does *not* change to *-i* before a suffix. (See -Y PLUS A SUFFIX, 9.)

prayer. Pronounced PRAIR when it means an entreaty to God or a humble request or appeal; pronounced PRAY-er when it designates one who *prays.* But the spelling is the same no matter which it means.

PRE-. See HYPHENATING, 17.

PRE-, PER-. See PER-, PRE-.

---

precarious. *Pre-,* not *per-.* (See PER-, PRE-.)

precaution. Ends in *-tion.* (See -AUTIOUS.)

precautious. Ends in *-tious.* (See -AUTIOUS.)

precede. *-Cede* is the common ending for such verbs, but there are exceptions. (See -CEED, -SEDE, -CEDE, 3.)

precedence. Almost always, with only a few exceptions, *-ence,* not *-ance,* follows a *d-.* (See -ANCE, -ENCE, AFTER D-, 1.)

precedent. See *precedence.*

preceed. Misspelling of *precede.*

preceive, preception. Misspellings of *perceive, perception.*

precipitance. *-Ance* is found somewhat more often than *-ence* after *t-.* (See -ANCE, -ENCE, AFTER T-, 1.)

precipitant. *-Ant* slightly more common than *-ent* after *t-.* (See -ANCE, -ENCE, AFTER T-, 2.)

precise. The first syllable is *pre-,* not *per-.* (See PER-, PRE-.)

precision. *Pre-,* not *per-.* (See PER-, PRE-.)

preclude. Not *perclude.* (See PER-, PRE-.)

precocious. Ends in *-cious,* not *-tious.* (See -OCIOUS.)

preconceive. *-E* before *-i* after *c-.* (See -IE, -EI, 2.)

precursor. Ends in *-or.* (See -ER, -OR, 5.)

predecessor. Ends in *-or.* (See -ER, -OR, 5.)

predict. Not *perdict.* (See PER-, PRE-.)

predictable. The ending is *-able,* not *-ible.* (See -ABLE, -IBLE, 1.)

predominance, predominant. End in *-ance, -ant,* not *-ence, -ent.* (See -ANCE, -ENCE, AFTER N-, 3.)

pre-eminence, pre-eminent. End in *-ence, -ent;* a hyphen is used when *pre-* precedes an *-e.* (See -ANCE, -ENCE, AFTER N-, 1; HYPHEN-ATING, 17A.)

prefer. Not *perfer.* (See PER-, PRE-.)

preferable. Only one *-r,* since the accent is on the first syllable. (See DOUBLING FINAL -R, 3.)

preference. Only one *-r,* since the accent is on the first syllable; ends in *-ence.* (See -ANCE, -ENCE, AFTER R-, 1; DOUBLING FINAL -R, 3.)

preferred, preferring. The final *-r* of *prefer* is doubled before *-ed* and *-ing,* since the accent falls on the last syllable (*fer*) and remains there in the derived forms. (See DOUBLING FINAL -R, 2, 3.)

pregnable. Since *-a* is the corresponding vowel in another form of the word (*pregnant*), the correct ending is *-able.* (See -ABLE, -IBLE, 5.)

prejudice. No *-d* before the *-j.*

preliminary. Not *perliminary.* (See PER-, PRE-.)

preponderance, preponderant. The final *-r* is followed by *-a,* as in the verb *preponderate.* (See -ANCE, -ENCE, AFTER R-, 10.)

PREPOSITIONS IN COMPOUNDS. See HYPHENATING, 10, 11.

prepossessing. Two sets of double *-s's,* as in all other derivatives of *possess.*

preposterous. Not *perposterous.* (See PER-, PRE-.)

prescience. Most often, as here, *-ence,* rather than *-ance,* follows *i-.* (See -ANCE, -ENCE, AFTER I-, 1.)

prescient. The combination *-ie,* rather than *-ei,* is always used when the preceding *-c* has the sound of *-sh.* (See -IE, -EI, 12.)

prescribe, prescription. The first syllable is *pre-,* not *per-.* (See PER-, PRE-.)

presentable. Ends in *-able.* (See -ABLE, -IBLE, 1.)

prespire, prespiration. Misspellings of *perspire, perspiration.*

presumable. The ending is *-able.* (See -ABLE, -IBLE, 2.)

presumption. Don't omit the second *-p.*

presumptuous. Note the *-u* before *-ous.* (See -UOUS.)

pretense. This American spelling is preferable to the British *pretence.* (See -ENCE, -ENSE, 2.)

pretension. Ends in *-ension.* (See -ENSION, -ENTION.)

pretentious. Ends in *-ious.*

prevalence, prevalent. Generally, though not always, *l-* is followed by *-ence* or *-ent,* rather than *-ance* or *-ant.* (See -ANCE, -ENCE, AFTER L-, 1, 3.)

prevaricator. Ends in *-or.* (See -ER, -OR, 5.)

preventable. Ends in *-able.* (See -ABLE, -IBLE, 1.)

prevention. Ends in *-ention.* (See -ENSION, -ENTION.)

prey. See PRAY, PREY.

preyed, preyer, preying. Since the terminal *-y* of *prey* follows a vowel, it does *not* change to *-i* before a suffix. (See -Y PLUS A SUFFIX, 9.)

prickle. Note the *-le* ending. (See -ICKLE, -ICKEL.)

primitive. Not *primative.*

PRINCIPAL, PRINCIPLE

Spell it *principle* only when you mean *rule* (note the *-le* ending in both words), theory, law, doctrine, etc. For all other meanings spell it *principal*.

Principle

The *principles* of Marxism.

The *principles* by which he lives.

A man of *principles*.

A highly *principled* character.

Principal

(This spelling will always involve, in some way, the idea of *main*; note the *-a* in both words.)

The *principal* seaport of the country (main seaport).

Five-per-cent interest on his *principal* (main sum of money).

One of the *principals* in the negotiations (main people).

The *principal* of the school (main teacher).

---

principally. The adverbial ending *-ly* is added to the adjective *principal*, hence the double *-l*. (See -LY, 7; -LY, -ALLY, 4.)

principle. See PRINCIPAL, PRINCIPLE.

printable. Ends in *-able*. (See -ABLE, -IBLE, 1.)

prisoner. Ends in *-er*. (See -ER, -OR, 1.)

privilege. No *-d* in this word—avoid *priviledge*.

PRO-. See HYPHENATING, 34.

---

probable. Ends in *-able*. (See -ABLE, -IBLE, 7.)

proboscis. Watch the *-sc*.

procede. Misspelling of *proceed*.

procedure. Note the single *-e* following *c-*, despite the contradictory spelling of *proceed*.

proceed. One of the only three words ending in *-ceed*. (See -CEED, -SEDE, -CEDE, 1.)

proctor. Ends in *-or*. (See -ER, -OR, 5.)

procurable. Ends in *-able*. (See -ABLE, -IBLE, 1.)

procurance. The suffix *-ance*, rather than *-ence*, invariably attaches to a noun formed from a verb ending in *-ure*. (See -ANCE, -ENCE, AFTER R-, 9.)

prodigy. See PROTÉGÉ, PRODIGY.

producible. The ending is *-ible* to keep the preceding *c-* "soft." (See -IBLE, -ABLE, 5.)

professional. One *-f*, two *-s*'s, as in the verb *profess*.

professor. One *-f*, two *-s*'s, as in the verb *profess*.

proficient. The combination *-ie*, rather than *-ei*, is always used when the preceding *-c* has the sound of *-sh*. (See -IE, -EI, 12.)

profitable. The ending is *-able*. (See -ABLE, -IBLE, 1.)

profited, profiting. Because *profit* is *not* accented on the *last* syllable, final *-t* is not doubled before a suffix beginning with a vowel. (See DOUBLING FINAL -T, 3.)

program, programme. The second spelling is somewhat old-fashioned and gradually fading from use.

programed, programing. The single *-m* spelling is theoretically correct, but *programmed* and *programming* are more popular and fully acceptable. (See DOUBLE VS. SINGLE CONSONANTS.)

programmatic. Only the double *-m* spelling is permitted here.

prohibited, prohibiting. Because *prohibit* is *not* accented on the *last* syllable, final *-t* is *not* doubled before a suffix beginning with a vowel. (See DOUBLING FINAL -T, 3.)

prologue, prolog. The longer form is preferable. (See -OGUE, -OG, 1.)

prominence, prominent. End in *-ence*, *-ent*. (See -ANCE, -ENCE, AFTER N-, 1.)

prompt. Note the second *-p*.

pronounceable. The *-e* of *pronounce* is retained before *-able* in order to preserve the original "soft" pronunciation of the preceding *-c*. (See -CEABLE.)

pronunciation. Even though the verb is *pronounce,* the noun drops the *-o* in the second syllable.

proof. The plural is *proofs.* (See PLURALIZING WORDS IN TERMINAL -F OR -FE, 2.)

-PROOF
     Most often this suffix is attached to a root without a hyphen: *heatproof, stainproof, waterproof, windproof,* etc.

propagator. Ends in *-or.* (See -ER, -OR, 5.)

propel. Ends in one *-l.* (See -EL, -ELL, 2.)

PROPELLANT, PROPELLENT
     The noun may be spelled with either ending, the *-ant* preferable.
     The adjective is spelled only *-ent.*

propelled, propelling. Because *propel* is accented on the last syllable, final *-l* is doubled before a suffix starting with a vowel. (See DOUBLING FINAL -L, 1.)

propeller. Ends in *-er.* (See -ER, -OR, 1.)

PROPHECY, PHOPHESY
     Prophecy, the *noun,* ends in *-cy,* and is pronounced PROF-e-see; *prophesy,* the *verb,* is spelled *-sy,* and is pronounced PROF-e-sigh. Derived forms of the verb must contain an *-s: prophesies, prophesied, prophesying,* etc. (There is no acceptable word *prophesize* or *prophecize;* either is a misusage for *prophesy.*) The plural of the noun is *prophecies.*
     His *prophecy* astounded us. (noun)

Can you *prophesy* who will win the election? (verb)

His *prophecies* are incredible. (noun)

He *prophesied* that the world would end within a hundred years. (verb)

prophetically. Note the *-ally* ending, common to adverbs formed from adjectives ending in *-ic.* (See -LY, -ALLY, 1.)

propitiatory. Note that the ending is *-ory.* (See -ARY, -ORY, 2.)

propitious. Ends in *-itious,* not *-icious.* (See -ICIOUS, -ITIOUS, 3.)

proprietary. Here the ending is *-ary.* (See -ARY, -ORY, 1.)

proprietor. Ends in *-or.* (See -ER, -OR, 5.)

prosecutor. Ends in *-or.* (See -ER, -OR, 5.)

PROSTATE, PROSTRATE
     The *prostate* (no *-r* after the *t-*) is a gland in the male reproductive system. *Prostrate* is the adjective or verb in patterns like *He lay prostrate at her feet; he prostrated himself at her feet.*

protector. Ends in *-or.* (See -ER, -OR, 5.)

PROTÉGÉ, PRODIGY
     A *protégé* (pronounced PRO-te-ZHAY and acceptably spelled without the accent marks if you prefer to avoid them) is a person under the protection or sponsorship of another. To emphasize that this person is a female, you may spell it with two final *-e*'s: *protégée.*
     A *prodigy* is any person or thing so unusual as to inspire wonder and, often, admiration — a musical *prodigy,* a child *prodigy,* etc.

protein. *-Ei,* rather than *-ie.* (See -IE, -EI, 4.)

protractor. Ends in -*or*.

protuberance, protuberant. Not *protruberance* or *protruberant,* despite the verb *protrude.* And note that the endings are -*ance,* -*ant.* (See -ANCE, -ENCE, AFTER R-, 10, 10A.)

provable. Drop final -*e* of *prove* before adding -*able.* (See -ABLE, -EABLE. 1.)

providence, provident. Almost always, with only a few exceptions, -*ence* or -*ent,* not -*ance* or -*ant,* follows -*d.* (See -ANCE, -ENCE, AFTER D-, 1.)

proviso. Plural is *provisos.* (See PLURALIZING WORDS IN TERMINAL -O, 2.)

provocation. Note that the -*k* of *provoke* has changed to -*c* before the vowel -*a.* (See -K to -C.)

prudence, prudent. Almost always, with only a few exceptions, -*ence* or -*ent,* not -*ance* or -*ant,* follows *d-.* (See -ANCE, -ENCE, AFTER D-, 1.)

prurience, prurient. Most often, as here, -*ence* or -*ent,* rather than -*ance* or -*ant,* follows *i-.* (See -ANCE, -ENCE, AFTER I-, 1.)

PS-, S-

In the following words initial -*p* is silent but must, of course, appear in the spelling: *psalm, pseudo, pseudonym, pshaw, psittacosis, psoriasis, psyche, psychiatrist, psychic, psychoanalysis, psychology, psychopath, psychosis, psychotic,* and other words starting with *psycho-.*

PSEUDO-. See HYPHENATING, 42.

---

psychoanalyze. One of the few verbs ending in -*yze;* hence -*y* follows *l-* in all derived forms: *psychoanalysis, psychoanalytic,* etc. (See -IZE, -YZE, 4.)

PT-, T-

In the following words initial -*p* is silent but must, of course, appear in the spelling: *ptarmigan, pterodactyl,* and other biological terms beginning with *ptero-;* *Ptolemy, ptomaine* (also spelled *ptomain*), *ptosis.*

---

pubescence, pubescent. Note the -*sc.* (See -ESCE, -ESCENT, -ESCENCE, 3.)

publicly. The only common adverb ending in -*icly;* most others end in -*ically,* as *fanatically, fantastically, sarcastically, sardonically,* etc. (See -LY, -ALLY, 2.)

pulchritude. That -*h* is the letter some poor spellers ignore.

pumice. One -*m.*

pummel. See *pommel.*

punishable. Ends in -*able.* (See -ABLE, -IBLE, 1.)

purchasable. Ends in -*able.* (See -ABLE, -IBLE, 1.)

purlieu. Note the -*ieu* ending.

pursuance. Nouns formed from verbs ending in -*ue* have -*ance,* rather than -*ence,* as a suffix. (See -ANCE, -ENCE, AFTER U-, 5.)

pursue. Not *persue.*

pursuit. Not *persuit.*

purveyor. Ends in -*or.* (See -ER, -OR, 5.)

putrefy. One of only five nontechnical verbs in English that end in -*efy;* the noun, correspondingly, is spelled *putrefaction,* again with an -*e* preceding the -*f.* (See -IFY, -EFY, 2.)

putrescence, putrescent. Note the -*sc.* (See -ESCE, -ESCENT, -ESCENCE, 3.)

Pygmy, Pigmy. Either spelling is correct, the first preferable. Capitalize the *p-* if referring to the African groups; otherwise use a small letter.

pyjamas. See *pajamas.*

pyorrhea. Note the -*rrh* combination found in so many medical terms—*diarrhea, leucorrhea, catarrh,* etc.

Q

(Q- is regularly followed by -u, except in Iraq and Iraqi.)

QUARTER-

The following noun compounds are written solid: *quarterback, quartermaster, quartersaw, quarterstaff.*

The following are written separate: *quarter grain, quarter note, quarter round, quarter step, quarter tone.*

(It will be noted that *quarter-* in separately written compounds has its literal meaning of *one-fourth;* in solid compounds it is used figuratively.)

The *quarter-deck* of a ship is preferably hyphenated, but is also correct written solid *(quarterdeck). Quarter-hour* is also preferably hyphenated, but may be written separate *(quarter hour).*

---

quartermaster general. No hyphen; plural is *quartermasters general.*

quartet, quartette. The former is the modernized spelling and is increasingly popular.

QUASI-. See HYPHENATING, 44.

---

quay. Though pronounced *key,* spelled only as shown.

querulous. The letter after *r-* is *-u,* not *-a.*

questionnaire. Double *-n,* unlike *millionaire,* with its single *-n.*

QUEUE, CUE

A *queue* is a plait of hair or a line of people; it is also a verb *(queue up for tickets)* meaning form a, or wait in, line.

As a noun, *queue* may also be spelled *cue;* while correct, this pattern is fairly rare. As a verb, *cue* means, among other things, to braid (the hair); this spelling may not substitute for the verb *queue up,* to wait in line, etc.

Cue as a noun has a number of meanings—an actor's or musician's signal, a hint, a rod used in pool or billiards, etc. As a verb, in addition to the meaning in the preceding paragraph, it signifies to give a signal.

QUICK-

Most adjectives are hyphenated: *quick-acting, quick-fire, quick-flowing, quick-frozen, quick-tempered, quick-witted,* etc. Except for *quickborn* and *quickhearted,* written solid.

The following nouns are solid: *quicklime, quicksand, quicksilver, quickstep.*

These are separate: *quick assets, quick bread, quick fire, quick grass, quick time.*

The verb *quick-freeze* is hyphenated.

---

quiescence, quiescent. Note the *-sc* and the *-ence, -ent* endings. (See -ANCE, -ENCE, AFTER C-, 5; -ESCE, -ESCENT, -ESCENCE.)

quintessence. The word *essence* plus the Latin prefix *quint-,* fifth; there is no *-sc.*

quintet, quintette. The shorter spelling is preferable. (See -ET -ETTE, 1.)

quitter, quitting. Note the double *-t.* (See DOUBLING FINAL CONSONANTS — ONE-SYLLABLE WORDS, 2.)

quiver. One *v.*

quiz. One *-z* in this form, but compare *quizzed,* etc.

quizzed, quizzer, quizzes, quizzing. Note the double *-z.* (See DOUBLING FINAL CONSONANTS— ONE-SYLLABLE WORDS, 2.)

quizzical. Again, two *-z*'s.

quotient. The correct pattern is *-ie.* (See -IE, -EI, 11.)

R

(Rules for double -*r*. See DOUBLING
FINAL -R.)

R-, RH-. See RH-, R-.

---

raccoon, racoon. Double -*c* preferable.

racket, racquet. The second form is
the British spelling of the implement
used in tennis, badminton, etc.

radiance. Very occasionally, as here,
-*ance*, not -*ence*, follows *i*-. (See
-ANCE, -ENCE, AFTER I-, 4.)

radiant. See *radiance*.

radiator. Ends in -*or*. (See -ER, -OR,
5.)

radio. Plural is *radios*. (See PLURAL-
IZING WORDS IN TERMINAL
-O, 3.)

radioed, radioing. These are the correctly spelled derivative forms of
the verb *radio*, even if the successive vowels look strange. (See -O,
TERMINAL.)

radish. One -*d*.

radius. For plural see PLURALIZING
WORDS IN TERMINAL -US, 9.

ragamuffin. One -*g*.

RAIN-

Adjective compounds are hyphenated (*rain-bearing, rain-swept*, etc.),
except *rainbound, rainproof*, and
raintight, which are solid.

The following noun compounds
are solid: *rainband, rainbow, rain-
coat, raindrop, rainfall, rainspout,
rainstorm*.

These are two words: *rain check,
rain gauge, rain pipe, rain water*.

The verb *rainproof* is solid.

---

raith. Misspelling of *wraith*.

rajah, raja. Both spellings correct, the
first preferable.

rake-off. Note the hyphen. (See HY-
PHENATING, 1.)

ramekin, ramequin. Both spellings correct, the first preferable.

rammed, ramming. Double the -*m* of
the verb *ram* before adding a suffix
that starts with a vowel. (See DOU-
BLING FINAL -M, 1.)

-RANCE, -RENCE. See -ANCE,
-ENCE, AFTER R-.

---

rancor, rancour. The first spelling is
American, the second British. However you decide to spell the noun,
the adjective is *rancorous*. (See -OR,
-OUR.)

rangy. Not *rangey*.

RANK, TITLE, ETC. See HYPHEN-
ATING, 5, 7, 8.

-RANT, -RENT. See -ANCE, -ENCE,
AFTER R-.

RAP, WRAP

To *rap* someone (or something) is
to hit him (or it) quickly and
sharply. The word is also a noun.

She *rapped* his knuckles.

He received a *rap* on his knuckles.

To *wrap* is to cover, clothe, con-
ceal, etc. A *wrap* is a garment,
blanket, cover, etc.

He *wrapped* himself in a com-
forter.

She put on her *wrap* and left.

---

rapsody. Misspelling of *rhapsody*.

rarefy. One of only five nontechnical
verbs in English that end in -*efy;*
the noun is spelled *rarefaction*, again
with an -*e* preceding the -*f*. (See
-IFY, -EFY, 2.)

rarity. Though the adjective is *rare,*
the noun is spelled as shown.

ratio. Plural is *ratios*. (See PLURAL-
IZING WORDS IN TERMINAL
-O, 3.)

raveled, raveling. Because *ravel* is *not*
accented on the last syllable, final
-*l* is *not* doubled before a suffix
beginning with a vowel. Double -*l*
forms are acceptable, but single -*l*

forms are far preferable. (See DOU-BLING FINAL -L, 2.)

RE-. See HYPHENATING, 16.

-RE, -ER. See -ER, -RE.

READ, RED
The past tense of the verb *read* is pronounced RED, but spelled *read. Red* is used for the color only.

---

readiness. The *-y* of *ready* changes to *-i* before *-ness.* (See -Y PLUS A SUFFIX, 6.)

REAL, REEL
Real is the adjective meaning actual, true, factual, etc. (As a noun, it is also a Spanish coin of former times.)

As a verb or noun with other meanings, *reel* is the correct spelling.

---

really. The adverbial ending *-ly* is added to the adjective *real,* hence the double *-l.* (See -LY, -ALLY, 4.)

realtor. Ends in *-or.* (See -ER, -OR, 5.)

reappearance. Note the *-ance* ending. (See -ANCE, -ENCE, AFTER R-, 8.)

reassurance. The suffix *-ance* invariably attaches to a noun formed from a verb ending in *-ure.* (See -ANCE, -ENCE, AFTER R-, 9.)

rebel. Ends in one *-l,* not two. (See -EL, -ELL, 2.)

rebelled, rebelling, rebellious. Because the verb *rebel* is accented on the last syllable, final *-l* is *doubled* before a suffix starting with a vowel. (See DOUBLING FINAL -L, 1.)

recede. *-Cede* is the common ending for such verbs, but there are exceptions. (See -CEED, -SEDE, -CEDE, 3.)

receed. Misspelling of *recede.*

receipt. *-E* before *-i* after *c-.* (See -IE, -EI, 2.)

receive. *-E* before *-i* after *c-.* (See -IE, -EI, 2.)

recipient, recipience, recipiency. *-E,* not *-a,* follows the second *i-.* (See -ANCE, -ENCE, AFTER I-, 1.)

recommend. The verb *commend* plus the prefix *re-,* hence one *-c,* two *-m*'s.

reconnaissance. Note the double *-n* and double *-s.* A variant spelling, rarely used, is *reconnoissance.*

reconnoiter, reconnoitre. The first spelling is preferable, but note the one *-c,* double *-n,* in both. (See -ER, -RE.)

recoop, recoup. See -OOP, -OUP, -UPE, 3C.

recrudesce, recrudescence, recrudescent. Note the *-sc.* (See -ESCE, -ESCENT, -ESCENCE.)

rector. Ends in *-or.* (See -ER, -OR, 5.)

recurred, recurrence, recurring. The final *-r* of *recur* is doubled before *-ed, -ence, -ent,* and *-ing,* since the accent falls on the last syllable (*cur*) and remains there in the derived forms. (See DOUBLING FINAL -R, 2, 3.)

recurrence, recurrent. Note the double *-r* and the *-ence, -ent* endings. (See -ANCE, -ENCE, AFTER R-, 3.)

red. See READ, RED.

RED-
Adjective compounds are hyphenated (*red-blooded, red-handed, red-letter,* etc.), except *redheaded,* which is solid.

Noun compounds are largely two words (*red flag, red fox, red light,* etc.), but the following are solid:

redbaiter	redpoll
redbaiting	redroot
redbird	redskin
redbreast	redstart
redbug	redtop
redcap	redware
redcoat	redwing
redfin	redwood
redhead	

The verb *redbait* is also solid.

REDDISH-

Adjective compounds preceding nouns are hyphenated: *reddish-brown*, *reddish-yellow*, etc.

redolence, redolent. Generally, but not always, *l-* is followed by *-ence* or *-ent*, rather than *-ance* or *-ant*. (See -ANCE, -ENCE, AFTER L-, 1, 3.)

reducible. The ending is *-ible* to keep the preceding *-c* "soft." (See -IBLE, -ABLE, 5.)

reef. The plural is *reefs*. (See PLURALIZING WORDS IN TERMINAL -F OR -FE, 2.)

reel. See REAL, REEL.

re-enforce. See *reinforce*.

referable. Pronounced REF-er-a-b'l, hence one *-r*. Also spelled *referrable*, and then accented on the second syllable. (See DOUBLING FINAL -R, 7.)

referee. Not accented on the *-fer*, hence only one *-r*. (See DOUBLING FINAL -R, 7.)

reference. Note the single *-r* and the *-ence* ending. (See -ANCE, -ENCE, AFTER R-, 1; DOUBLING FINAL -R, 7.)

referendum. One *-r;* the plural is either *referenda* or *referendums*. (DOUBLING FINAL -R, 7; PLURALIZING WORDS IN TERMINAL -UM, 1.)

referent, referential. *Not* accented on the *fer*, hence again only one *-r*. (See DOUBLING FINAL -R, 7.)

referrable, referrible. Variant, and equally acceptable, spelling of *referable*, pronounced re-FER-a-b'l, hence the double *-r*. (See DOUBLING FINAL -R, 6.)

referral. Double *-r*, since the accent remains on the last syllable of the source word, *refer*. (See DOUBLING FINAL -R, 6.)

referred, referring. The final *-r* of *refer* is doubled before *-ed* and *-ing*, since the accent falls on the last syllable (*fer*) and remains there in the derived forms. (See DOUBLING FINAL -R, 2, 3.)

referrer. Double *-r*, as in *referrable*, and *referral*. (See DOUBLING FINAL -R, 6.)

reflector. Ends in *-or*. (See -ER, -OR, 5.)

refluence. Always *-ence*, not *-ance*, after *fl-*. (See -ANCE, -ENCE, AFTER U-, 2.)

refrigerator. Ends in *-or*. (See -ER, -OR, 5.)

registrar. Ends in *-ar*.

regrettable, regretted, regretting. Because *regret* is accented on the last syllable, the final *-t* is doubled before a suffix beginning with a vowel. (See DOUBLING FINAL -T, 2.)

Reid. Proper names are more likely to be spelled *-ei* than *-ie* (See -IE, -EI, 5.)

reign. When sounded as *ay*, the spelling *-ei* is always correct. (See -IE, -EI, 6.)

rein. When sounded as *ay*, the spelling *-ei* is correct. (See -IE, -EI, 6.)

reinforce. Somewhat preferable to *re-enforce*, both correct. (See -EN-, IN-, 5.)

reinsurance. The suffix *-ance* invariably attaches to a noun formed from a verb ending in *-ure*. (See -ANCE, -ENCE, AFTER R-, 9.)

relaid, relayed. The former is the past tense of the verb that means *to lay again;* the latter of the verb meaning *to send*. (See -AYED, -AID, 4.)

relevance, relevant. Generally after *v-* the correct suffix is *-ance* or *-ant*, not *-ence* or *-ent*. (See -ANCE, -ENCE, AFTER V-.)

reliable. *-Able* is the correct suffix after the letter *i-*. (See -ABLE, -IBLE, 3.)

reliance, reliant. End in *-ance, -ant*. (See -ANCE, -ENCE, AFTER I-, 2.)

relied, relies. The *-y* of *rely* changes

to -*i* before -*ed* or -*es*. (See -Y PLUS A SUFFIX, 1.)

relief. -*I* before -*e* except after *c*-. (See -IE, -EI, 1.)

religion, religious. No -*d* in either word.

reluctance, reluctant. -*Ance* or -*ant* is found somewhat more often than -*ence* or -*ent* after *t*-. (See -ANCE, -ENCE, AFTER T-, 1.)

remarkable. The ending is -*able*. (See -ABLE, -IBLE, 1.)

remembrance. Ends in -*ance*.

reminisce, reminiscence, reminiscent. Note the -*sc*.

remittance. -*Ance* is found somewhat more often than -*ence* after *t*-. (See -ANCE, -ENCE, AFTER T-, 1.)

remonstrance. Ending is -*ance*, not -*ence*.

rendezvous. This French import is spelled as shown—no hyphen.

renege. Often pronounced re-NIG, but spelled only as shown.

reparable. Since -*a* is the corresponding vowel in another form of the word (*reparation*), the correct ending is -*able*. (See -ABLE, -IBLE, 5.)

repel. Ends in one -*l*, not two. (See -EL, -ELL, 2.)

repelled, repelling. Because *repel* is accented on the last syllable, final -*l* is doubled before a suffix starting with a vowel. (See DOUBLING FINAL -L, 1.)

repellent, repellence, repellency. Double -*l* because *repel* is accented on the last syllable; and note that the endings are -*ent*, -*ence*, -*ency*, not -*ant*, etc. (See DOUBLING FINAL -L, 1.)

repentance, repentant. -*Ance* or -*ant* is found somewhat more often than -*ence* or -*ent* after *t*-. (See -ANCE, -ENCE, AFTER T-, 1.)

repetition, repetitious. From the verb *repeat*, hence *p*- followed by -*e*, not -*i*.

replaceable. The final -*e* of *replace* is retained before -*able* in order to preserve the original "soft" pronunciation of the preceding -*c*. (See -CEABLE.)

repository. Note that the ending is -*ory*, not -*ary*. (See -ARY, -ORY, 2.)

repossess. This verb and all its forms contain two sets of double -*s*'s as in the source word, *possess*.

reprehensible. If the root ends in -*ns*, the likely ending is -*ible*, not -*able*. (See -IBLE, -ABLE, 3.)

repressible. If the root forms its noun by the immediate addition of -*ion* (*repression*), the correct ending is likely to be -*ible*. (See -IBLE, -ABLE, 2.)

reprise. Note the -*ise* ending, common to words ending in -*prise*. (See -ISE, 4.)

reproof. The plural is *reproofs*. (See PLURALIZING WORDS IN TERMINAL -F OR -FE, 2.)

repugnance, repugnant. Endings are -*ance*, -*ant*. (See -ANCE, -ENCE, AFTER N-, 3.)

reshipment. The suffix starts with a consonant—*ment*, hence single -*p*.

reshipped, reshipper, reshipping. Final -*p* of *reship* is doubled before a suffix starting with a vowel. (See DOUBLING FINAL -P, 2.)

residence, resident. Almost always, with only a few exceptions, -*ence* or -*ent*, not -*ance* or -*ant*, follows a *d*-. (See -ANCE, -ENCE, AFTER D-, 1.)

residuum. As in *vacuum*, two -*u*'s.

resilience, resilient. Most often, as here, -*ence* or -*ent*, rather than -*ance*, or -*ant*, follows *i*-. (See -ANCE, -ENCE, AFTER I-, 1.)

resistance, resistant. -*Ance* or -*ant* is found somewhat oftener than -*ence* or -*ent* after *t*-. (See -ANCE, -ENCE, AFTER T-, 1.)

resistible. Contradictorily, however, this word and its negative, *irresistible*, end, not in -*able*, but in -*ible*. (See -IBLE, -ABLE, 7.)

resonance. One of a group of words ending in *-ance,* rather than *-ence,* after *n-*. (See -ANCE, -ENCE, AFTER N-, 3.)

resonant. See *resonance.*

respectable. Not *respectible.* (See -ABLE, -IBLE, 1.)

RESPECTFULLY, RESPECTIVELY

The first adverb indicates respect—he spoke *respectfully* to his parents.

The second means *in the order mentioned*—the months of January, February, and April have 31, 28, and 30 days *respectively.*

responsible. If the root ends in *-ns,* the likely ending is *-ible,* not *-able.* (See -IBLE, -ABLE, 3.)

restaurant. The *-au* is a stumbling block for some spellers.

resurrect. Double *-r* in the middle.

resuscitate. Note the *-sc.*

RETAINED -E

1. The final *-e* following a consonant (*waste, use,* etc.) is generally retained when a suffix starting with a consonant (*-ly, -ful, -ment,* etc.) is added.

> encourage—encouragement
> sure—sureness
> use—useful
> waste—wasteful

2. However, there are important, and frequently misspelled, exceptions—words in which the *-e* is *dropped* before a suffix that starts with a consonant.

> argue—argument
> awe—awful
> due—duly
> nine—ninth
> true—truly
> whole—wholly

See also DROPPED -E.

retention. Ends in *-ention.* (See -ENSION, -ENTION.)

reticence. *-Ence,* rather than *-ance,* to keep the preceding *-c* "soft." (See -ANCE, -ENCE, AFTER C-, 1.)

reticent. See *reticence.*

retrievable. *-I* before *-e* except after *c-;* and the ending is *-able.* (See -ABLE, -IBLE, 2; -IE, -EI, 1.)

re-use. Hyphenate or not as you please; most people do, since *reuse* tempts to mispronunciation. But *reused* is solid. (See HYPHENATING, 16B.)

reveille. Pronounced REV-e-lee, but retains its French spelling.

revelance, revelant. Misspellings of *relevance, relevant.*

reveled, reveler, reveling. Single *-l* preferable in these derived forms of *revel,* since the verb is *not* accented on the final syllable. (See DOUBLING FINAL -L, 2.)

reverence, reverent. Note the *-ence, -ent* endings. (See -ANCE, -ENCE, AFTER R-, 4, 4A.)

reverie, revery. Either spelling, the first preferable.

reversible. If the root forms its noun by the immediate addition of *-ion* (*reversion*), the correct ending is likely to be *-ible.* (See -IBLE, -ABLE, 2.)

revise. Note the *-ise* ending, common to all words ending in *-vise.* (See -ISE, 2.)

revocable. Only the *-able* ending will keep the preceding *-c* "hard." *Revokable* is a correct but rarely used alternative. (See -ABLE, -IBLE, 6.)

revocation. Note that the *-k* of *revoke* has changed to *-c* before the vowel *-a.* (See -K to -C.)

revolutionary. Ends in *-ary.* (See -ARY, -ERY, 1.)

RH-, R-

Certain common words start with *rh-;* you should become familiar with the following:

rhapsody	rheostat
Rhenish	rhesus

rhetoric
rheum
rheumatic
rheumatism
Rhine
rhinestone
rhinitis

rhinoceros
rhododendron
rhombus
rhubarb
rhyme
rhythm

rhapture. Misspelling of *rapture.*

rhinoceros. Note the *-os,* not *-us,* at the end. The plural is formed by simply adding *-es,* not *-i.*

RHYME, RIME

Both spellings are correct for verse, poetry, etc., but the former has almost completely replaced the latter. Oddly enough, *rime* is historically more accurate, but nonetheless far less popular.

A totally different word, spelled *rime* only, means an icy coating on grass.

rhythm. Not *rythm.*
rhythmic. Not *rythmic.*
riddance. One of the few words in which *-ance,* not *-ence,* follows a *d-.* (See -ANCE, -ENCE, AFTER D-, 3.)
ridiculous. The second letter is *-i,* not *-e;* think of the noun *ridicule.*
riffraff. Note the two sets of double *-f's.*

RIGHT-. See HYPHENATING, 27.

righteous. Ends in *-eous.*
rigor, rigour. The first spelling is American, the second British. Either way, the adjective is *rigorous.* (See -OR, -OUR, 1.)
rime. See RHYME, RIME.

RING, WRING

To ring is to surround, or to make, or cause to make, a bell-like sound; *to wring* is to twist, extort, etc.

risible. The ending is *-ible.* (See -IBLE, -ABLE, 1.)

risqué. Usually spelled with the French accent, but need not be.
riveted, riveter, riveting. Because *rivet* is *not* accented on the last syllable, final *-t* is *not* doubled before a suffix beginning with a vowel. (See DOUBLING FINAL -T, 3.)
rivulet. Ends in *-et.* (See -ET, -ETTE, 4.)

ROAD-

The following are solid compounds: *roadbed, roadblock, roadfellow, roadhouse, roadside, roadstead, roadway.*

The following are written separate: *road agent, road hog, road metal, road runner, road tar.*

Adjectives are hyphenated: *roadgrading, road-weary,* etc.

-ROAD

Most noun compounds with this suffix are written separate (*back road, main road,* etc.).

However, the following are solid: *byroad, crossroad, highroad, railroad.*

ROCK-

Adjective compounds are hyphenated: *rock-covered, rock-drilling, rock-rubbed,* etc.

rococo. No double *-c's.*
rodeo. Plural is *rodeos.* (See PLURALIZING WORDS IN TERMINAL -O, 3.)
rogue. Like *intrigue, vague,* etc., ends in *-gue.* (See -OGUE, -OG, 2.)

ROLE, RÔLE, ROLL

The part or function played by someone is a *role,* the preferred spelling, though the somewhat old-fashioned *rôle* is also seen occasionally.

For all other meanings *roll,* whether noun or verb, is the correct spelling.

Romeo. Plural is *Romeos.* (See PLU-RALIZING WORDS IN TER-MINAL -O, 3.)

rondeau. The plural is *rondeaux.* (See PLURALIZING WORDS IN TERMINAL -EAU, 1.)

roof. For plural see PLURALIZING WORDS IN TERMINAL -F OR -FE, 4D.

ROOF-

Noun compounds are generally two words: *roof beam, roof line,* etc.; *roofman* is solid.

Adjectives are hyphenated: *roof-shaped,* etc.

-ROOM

Most compounds with this suffix are solid: *ballroom, bathroom, bedroom, workroom,* etc.

The following are written separate: *baggage room, breakfast room, dining room, drawing room, dressing room, engine room, guest room, living room, music room, reading room, reception room, shipping room, sitting room, smoking room, waiting room, writing room.*

roomette. Ends in *-ette.* (See -ET, -ETTE, 3.)

roommate. No hyphen. (See HY-PHENATING, 3A.)

roop, roup. See -OOP, -OUP, -UPE, 3B.

rosette. Ends in *-ette.* (See -ET, -ETTE, 3.)

ROUGH-

Most adjective compounds, particularly if they precede the noun, are hyphenated: *rough-and-ready, rough-and-tumble, rough-cut, rough-looking, rough-mannered,* etc.

The following adjectives, however, are solid: *roughhearted, rough-shod.*

The verbs *rough-dry* and *rough-*

hew are hyphenated; *roughcast* and *roughhouse* are solid.

The nouns *roughhouse, roughneck, roughrider* are solid.

roulette. Ends in *-ette.* (See -ET, -ETTE, 3.)

ROUND-

Adjectives are hyphenated (*round-shouldered, round-table, round-trip,* etc.), except for *roundabout,* written solid.

Nouns are largely written separate (*round dance, round table, round trip,* etc.), except for the following, which are solid: *round-house, roundsman, roundup, round-worm.*

roup, roop. See -OOP, -OUP, -UPE, 3B.

rowdy. Not *roudy* or *rowdey.* Plural is *rowdies.* Other derived forms: *rowdily, rowdiness, rowdyish.*

royally. Note the double *-l,* since the adverbial suffix *-ly* is added to the adjective *royal.* (See -LY, 7.)

rubbed. The final consonant of *rub* is doubled before *-ed* or any other suffix that starts with a vowel. (See DOUBLING FINAL -B.)

rudiment. One *-d.*

ruminant. Ends in *-ant.*

rumor, rumour. The first spelling is American, the second British. (See -OR, -OUR, 1.)

RUN-

The following noun compounds are solid: *runabout, runaway, run-back, runround, runway.*

These nouns are hyphenated: *run-around, run-down, run-in, run-off.*

These adjectives are hyphenated: *run-down, run-in, run-on, run-of-the-mill, run-of-the-mine.*

runner, running. Note that the *-n* of *run* is doubled when a suffix beginning with a vowel is added. (See DOUBLING FINAL -N.)

runner-up. Hyphenated. (See HY-PHENATING, 10A.)

rythm. Misspelling of *rhythm.*

S

S-, PS-. See PS-, S-.

Sabbath. Two -*b*'s.

sabbatical. From the same root as *Sabbath,* so again two -*b*'s.

saber, sabre. *Saber* preferable, though *sabre* is current in Great Britain. (See -ER, -RE.)

saccharin, saccharine. The chemical used as a sugar substitute is preferably spelled without the terminal -*e,* but may also be spelled with it. The adjective, however, ends in -*ine,* no matter what meaning it has. Note, in addition, the -*cch* combination.

sacrifice. Not *sacrafice.*

sacrilege. Similar in construction to *privilege.*

sacrilegious. Note that the two vowels after the *r-* are in *reverse* order to those of *religious;* in a way, the meanings of the two words are also opposed. May be pronounced either sak-ri-LEE-jus or sak-re-LIJ-us, but spelled only as shown.

safe. The plural is *safes.* (See PLU-RALIZING WORDS IN TER-MINAL -F OR -FE, 2.)

SAFE-

The following noun compounds are written solid: *safeblower, safeblowing, safebreaker, safecracking, safeguard, safekeeping.*

The following words are hyphenated: *safe-conduct* (noun or verb), *safe-cracker, safe-deposit* (adjective).

The baseball term *safe hit* is written as two words.

SAFETY-

All compounds are written as two words: *safety belt, safety match, safety zone,* etc.

---

said. Not *sayed.* (See -AYED, -AID, 2.)

sailor. Ends in -*or.* (See -ER, -OR, 5.)

salaam. Noun or verb, this word has that rare combination, a double -*a.*

salable. *Saleable* also correct, but preferable spelling omits the unnecessary -*e.* (See -ABLE, -EABLE, 2.)

salience, salient. Most often, as here, -*ence* or -*ent,* rather than -*ance* or -*ant,* follows *i-.* (See -ANCE, -ENCE, AFTER I-, 1.)

sallies. The noun *sally* ends in -*y* preceded by a consonant, hence the plural ends in -*ies.* (See -EYS, IES, -YS, 3.)

Sallys. If a proper name ends in -*y,* the plural is formed by the simple addition of -*s.* (See -EYS, -IES, -YS, 5.)

salm. Misspelling of *psalm.*

SALON, SALOON

At one time, and still so theoretically today, the words were interchangeable. In practice, however, *saloon* is now used mainly for the pre-Prohibition type of drinking establishment with swinging half-doors at the entrance, cuspidors on the floor, and an all-male clientele. (These vanished bits of Americana have been replaced by bars or cocktail lounges, and are no longer lacking in female adornment.)

A *salon* is a reception room of any kind, a place for the exhibition of works of art, a service shop (*beauty salon*), etc.

---

saltpeter, saltpetre. The latter spelling is current in Great Britain. (See -ER, -RE.)

salutary. Note that the ending is -*ary*, not -*ory*. (See -ARY, -ORY, 1.)

salvageable. The -*e* of *salvage* is retained before -*able* in order to preserve the original "soft" (or -*j*) pronunciation of the preceding -*g*. (See -GEABLE.)

salvo. The plural is *salvos*. (See PLURALIZING WORDS IN TERMINAL -O, 2.)

sanatorium. See -ARY, -ORY, 3D.

sanatory. See -ARY, -ORY, 3C.

sanctuary. Most words with both a primary and secondary accent end in -*ary* rather than -*ery*. (See -ARY, -ERY, 1, 2.)

SAND-

The following common noun compounds are written as two words: *sand bar, sand dollar, sand flat, sand flea, sand fly, sand lily, sand pail, sand trap.*

Most others are solid: *sandbox, sandglass, sandhog, sandman, sandpaper*, etc.

Compound adjectives are hyphenated: *sand-blind, sand-blown, sand-lot*, etc.

The verb *sandblast*, like the noun, is solid.

---

sanitarium. See -ARY, -ORY, 3D.

sanitary. See -ARY, -ORY, 3C.

sanitory. See -ARY, -ORY, 3C.

saphire. Misspelling of *sapphire*.

Sapho. Misspelling of *Sappho*.

sapience, sapient. Most often, as here, -*ence* or -*ent*, rather than -*ance* or -*ant*, follows *i*-. (See -ANCE, -ENCE, AFTER I-, 1.)

sapphire. Double -*p*.

Sappho. Double -*p* here and in all derived forms.

sarcophagus. Not *sarcophagous*. (See -US, -OUS.)

sargent. Misspelling of *sergeant*.

satellite. One -*t*, two -*l*'s.

satiric, satirical. See SATYRIC, SATIRIC.

satirize. See SATYRIC, SATIRIC.

satisfiable. -*Able* is the correct suffix after the letter *i*-. (See -ABLE, -IBLE, 3.)

satyr. Note the -*y*.

SATYRIC, SATIRIC

With the -*ty* the word refers to *satyrs;* the longer form, *satyrical,* is also used.

Satiric, or the longer *satirical,* refers to *satire.* The verb is *satirize;* the writer of *satires* is a *satirist.*

---

sauerbraten. See -OUR, -OWER, -AUER, 3.

sauerkraut. See -OUR, -OWER, -AUER, 3.

saught. Misspelling of *sought*.

savior, Saviour. The second spelling, and note the capital *S*, is for Jesus Christ only.

savor, savour. The first spelling is American, the second British. (See -OR, -OUR, 1.)

says. Pronounced SEZ, but spelled only as shown.

scarcely. The -*e* of *scarce* is retained before the adverbial suffix -*ly*. (See -LY, 10.)

scarf. For plural see PLURALIZING WORDS IN TERMINAL -F OR -FE, 4E.

scent. See CENT, SCENT.

scepter, sceptre. The latter spelling is British. (See -ER, -RE.)

sceptical. See *skeptical*.

schism. Pronounced *sizm*, but spelled only as shown.

scholastically. Note the -*ally* ending, common to adverbs formed from adjectives ending in -*ic*. (See -LY, -ALLY, 1.)

SCHOOL-

Noun compounds are largely two words (*school age, school board, school year*, etc.), except the following, written solid: *schoolbag, schoolbook, schoolboy, schoolfellow, school-*

girl, schoolhouse, schoolma'am, schoolman, schoolmarm, schoolmaster, schoolmate, schoolmistress, schoolroom, schoolteacher, schoolwork, schoolyard.

science. Ending is *-ence.* (See -ANCE, -ENCE, AFTER I-, 1.)

scimitar, scimiter. Either spelling, the first preferable. Note, also, the *-c* following *s-.*

scintilla. Double *-l.*

scintillate. Double *-l* in this verb and all its derived forms.

scion, cion. Both spellings correct, but the latter rarely used.

scissors. Ends in *-ors.*

scithe. Misspelling of *scythe.*

scoop. See -OOP, -OUP, -UPE, 1.

scour. See -OUR, -OWER, -AUER, 1.

scurrilous. Double *-r.*

scythe. Note the *-y.*

SEA-

Adjectives are mostly hyphenated (*sea-blue, sea-born, sea-borne,* etc.), except the following, which are solid: *seaboard, seagirt, seagoing, seasick, seaside, seaworthy. Seaborne* may be solid, but is preferably hyphenated.

Noun compounds are mostly two words (*sea breeze, sea food, sea gull, sea lion, sea wall,* etc.), except the following, which are solid:

seaboard	seaport
seacoast	seaquake
seafarer	seascape
seafaring	seashore
seaflower	seasickness
seafowl	seaside
seaman	seaware
seamanship	seaway
seamark	seaweed
seaplane	

SEAM, SEEM

A *seam* is a fold, wrinkle, etc. It is also a verb with corresponding meanings.

Seem is the verb meaning to appear—he *seems* tired.

séance, seance. Preferably spelled with the accent mark.

seasonable. Ends in *-able.* (See -ABLE, -IBLE, 1.)

sebaceous. Ending is *-aceous,* not *-acious.* (See -ACIOUS, -ACEOUS, -ATIOUS, 2.)

secede. *-Cede* is the common ending for such verbs, but there are exceptions. (See -CEED, -SEDE, -CEDE, 3.)

seceed. Misspelling of *secede.*

SECOND-. See HYPHENATING, 51.

secondary. Most words with both a primary and secondary accent end in *-ary* rather than *-ery.* (See -ARY, -ERY, 1, 2.)

second lieutenant. No hyphen. (See HYPHENATING, 5A.)

secretary. Most words with both a primary and secondary accent end in *-ary* rather than *-ery.* (See -ARY, -ERY, 1, 2.)

secretary-general. Hyphenated. The plural is *secretaries-general.*

sector. Ends in *-or.* (See -ER, -OR, 5.)

securable. Ends in *-able.* (See -ABLE, -IBLE, 2.)

-SEDE, -CEDE, -CEED. See -CEED, -SEDE, -CEDE.

sedentary. Most words with both a primary and secondary accent end in *-ary* rather than *-ery.* (See -ARY, -ERY, 1, 2.)

sedition. Ends in *-ition.* (See -ICIOUS, -ITIOUS, 4.)

seditious. Ends in *-itious,* not *-icious.* (See -ICIOUS, -ITIOUS, 3.)

seducible. The ending is *-ible,* to keep the preceding *-c* "soft." (See -IBLE, -ABLE, 5.)

seeable. Always *-able* after *-ee.* (See -ABLE, -IBLE, 4.)

seem. See SEAM, SEEM.

seer. Only two -*e*'s, whether meaning a prophet or one who sees. (See -EER.)

seige. Misspelling of *siege*.

seismograph, seismic. When sounded *eye*, the combination -*ei* is used, except when the following letter is an -*r*. (See -IE, -EI, 7.)

seive. Misspelling of *sieve*.

seize. One of the exceptions to the rule of -*ie*, -*ei*. Note the -*ei* combination here and also in the noun *seizure*, although *siege* is spelled -*ie*. (See -IE, -EI, 4.)

seizure. Note the -*ei* combination; this is an exception to the rule of -*i* before -*e* except after *c*-. (See -IE, -EI, 4.)

self. The plural is *selves*. (See PLURALIZING WORDS IN TERMINAL -F OR -FE, 1.)

SELF-. See HYPHENATING, 38.

---

self-reliance. Ending is -*ance*. (See -ANCE, -ENCE, AFTER I-, 3.)

selfsame. No hyphen. (See HYPHENATING, 3A.)

SEMI-. See HYPHENATING, 43.

---

senator. Ends in -*or*. (See -ER, -OR, 5.)

senescence, senescent. Note the -*sc*. (See -ESCE, -ESCENT, -ESCENCE, 3.)

seneschal. Note the -*sch* combination.

sensative. Misspelling of *sensitive*.

sensible. If the root ends in -*ns*, the likely ending is -*ible*, not -*able*. (See -IBLE, -ABLE, 3.)

sensitive. The letter before -*t* is -*i*, not -*a*.

sentence. Ends in -*ence*, not -*ance*. (See -ANCE, -ENCE, AFTER T-, 3.)

separable. Since -*a* is the corresponding vowel in another form of the word (*separate*), the correct ending is -*able*. (See -ABLE, -IBLE, 5.)

separate. Whether noun or verb, the word has the idea of *parting* in it, hence -*par*, not -*per*. But compare *desperate*.

seperate. Incorrect though popular spelling of *separate*.

septet, septette. The shorter spelling is preferable. (See -ET, -ETTE, 1.)

sepulcher, sepulchre. The latter spelling is British. (See -ER, -RE.)

sequence. Always -*ence*, not -*ance*, after *qu*-. (See -ANCE, -ENCE, AFTER U-, 1.)

seraglio. Plural is *seraglios*. (See PLURALIZING WORDS IN TERMINAL -O, 3.)

seraph. Plural is either the Anglicized *seraphs* or the biblical *seraphim*.

serf. The plural is *serfs*. (See PLURALIZING WORDS IN TERMINAL -F OR -FE, 2.)

sergeant. Commonly misspelled *sargent*. Note the first -*e*, and the -*e* following *g*- before -*ant*, which serves to keep the *g*- "soft."

sergeant-at-arms. Hyphenated; the plural is *sergeants-at-arms*. (See HYPHENATING, 10A.)

sergeant major. No hyphen; plural is *sergeants major*. (See HYPHENATING, 5A.)

series. -*I* before -*e* except after *c*-. (See -IE, -EI, 1.)

serviceable. The terminal -*e* of *service* is retained before -*able* in order to preserve the original "soft" pronunciation of the preceding -*c*. (See -CEABLE.)

serviette. Ends in -*ette*. (See -ET, -ETTE, 3.)

sesame. Pronounced SES-a-mee, single -*s* after the first *e*-.

sestet. Ends in -*et*, not -*ette*. (See -ET, -ETTE, 4.)

setaceous. Ending is -*aceous*, not -*acious*. (See -ACIOUS, -ACEOUS, -ATIOUS, 2.)

seudo. Misspelling of *pseudo*.

SEVEN-. See HYPHENATING, 49D, E.

sevens. The plural of the number, when written as a word, requires no apostrophe. As a figure, the apostrophe is preferable but may be omitted: *7's* or *7s.* (See APOSTROPHE, USE OF, 2, 3.)

SEVENTY-. See HYPHENATING, 49A.

severance. Note the *-ance* ending. (See -ANCE, -ENCE, AFTER R-, 6.)

SEW, SOW

To use a needle and thread is *to sew.*

To spread, disseminate, inculcate, etc., is *to sow.*

He *sewed* a button on.

He *sowed* the field, *sowed* discontent among the members, *sowed* his wild oats, *sowed* revolutionary ideas among the citizens, etc.

sextet, sextette. The shorter spelling is preferable. (See -ET, -ETTE, 1.)

sez. Misspelling of *says.*

shamefaced. Solid word. (See -FACED.)

-SHAPED

Adjective compounds are invariably hyphenated: *bell-shaped, oval-shaped, wedge-shaped,* etc.

sharlatan. Misspelling of *charlatan.*

SHARP-

Adjective compounds are hyphenated: *sharp-eyed, sharp-tongued, sharp-witted,* etc.

The noun *sharpshooter* is written solid.

shassis, shassy, chassy. All common misspellings of *chassis.*

shaw. Misspelling of *pshaw.*

sheaf. The plural is *sheaves.* (See PLURALIZING WORDS IN TERMINAL -F OR -FE, 1.)

SHEAR, SHEER

Shear is the verb meaning to cut, shave, clip, etc.

The noun *shear* has corresponding meanings, and *shears* means *scissors.*

Sheer is an adjective with a variety of meanings: thin, pure, steep, etc.; as an adverb, *sheer* has corresponding meanings.

The verb *sheer* means to curve, turn, deviate, swerve, etc. The noun *sheer* has corresponding meanings.

SHEEP-

Most noun compounds are written separate: *sheep barn, sheep farming,* etc.

However, the following are solid: *sheepcote, sheepfold, sheepherder, sheepkeeper, sheepman, sheeppen, sheepshank, sheepshead, sheepshearer, sheepshearing, sheepshed, sheepskin, sheepstealing, sheepwalk.*

And *sheep-dip* is hyphenated.

Adjectives are mostly hyphenated (*sheep-owning, sheep-witted,* etc.), except *sheepfaced, sheepheaded,* and *sheephearted,* which are solid.

sheer. See SHEAR, SHEER.

sheik. Note the *-ei* combination; this is an exception to the rule of *-i* before *-e* except after *c-.* (See -IE, -EI, 4.)

shelf. The plural is *shelves.* (See PLURALIZING WORDS IN TERMINAL -F OR -FE, 1.)

SHELL-

The following common nouns are written solid: *shellback, shellbark, shellfire, shellfish.*

Other nouns are written as two words: *shell game, shell jacket, shell shock,* etc.

The adjectives *shellproof* and *shellshocked* are solid.

she'll. Contraction of *she will.* (See APOSTROPHE, USE OF, 1.)

shellacked, shellacker, shellacking. The -*k* must be inserted in the derived forms of *shellac* in order to preserve the original pronunciation of final -*c.* (See -C, -CK, 1.)

-SHELLED

Adjective compounds are hyphenated: *hard-shelled, soft-shelled,* etc.

sheriff. The law officer who, for our purposes, controls the *riff*raff, hence -*riff.* Tariff has the same -*riff* ending.

shew. This variant spelling for the noun or verb *show* is almost never found in print in this country, though it has some popularity in England.

shibboleth. Double -*b.*

shiek. Misspelling of *sheik.*

shier, shiest. Preferable to *shyer, shyest.* (See -IER, -IEST, 4.)

shily. See *shyly.*

SHIP-

Most common noun compounds are solid: *shipbuilder, shipowner, shipwreck,* etc.

The nouns *ship biscuit, ship canal, ship chandler,* and *ship money* are written separate.

The adjective *ship-rigged* is hyphenated; *shipshape,* adjective or adverb, is solid.

SHOCK-

Noun compounds are mostly separate: *shock absorber, shock therapy, shock troops,* etc.

The adjective *shockheaded* is solid.

SHOE-

The following noun compounds are solid: *shoebill, shoeblack, shoebrush, shoehorn, shoelace, shoemaker, shoemaking, shoeshine, shoeshop, shoesmith, shoestring.*

Others are separate words: *shoe box, shoe leather, shoe store,* etc.

shoed. See *shooed.*

shoeing. Participle of the verb *shoe;* note that the terminal -*e* is retained. (See -OE, TERMINAL, 1.)

shoer. Correct spelling for one who shoes horses; note the single -*e.* (See -OE, TERMINAL, 1.)

shooed. Correct past tense of the verb *shoo,* i.e., to drive away by crying, "Shoo!," and not to be confused with the past tense of *shoe,* which is *shod,* not *shoed.* (See -OO, TERMINAL.)

shooing. Participle of the verb *to shoo,* not to be confused with *shoeing.*

SHOP-

Most compounds, noun or adjective, are solid: *shopkeeper, shoplifting, shopworn,* etc.

Shop steward is two words.

-SHOP

Compounds with this suffix are invariably solid: *bakeshop, pawnshop, workshop,* etc.

SHORT-

Most adjective compounds are hyphenated: *short-haired, short-handed, short-winded,* etc.

Shorthand and *shortsighted* are solid; *shortheaded* may be solid but is preferably hyphenated (*short-headed*).

The following noun compounds are solid: *shortbread, shortcake, shortcoming, shortstop.*

Most others are two words: *short circuit, short story, short wave,* etc.

The verb *shortchange* is solid; *short-circuit* is hyphenated.

shoulder. Note the -*ou.*

shouldn't. Contraction of *should not.* (See APOSTROPHE, USE OF, 1.)

shoveled, shoveler, shoveling. Because

shovel is *not* accented on the last syllable, final *-l* is *not* doubled before a suffix beginning with a vowel. Double *-l* forms are acceptable, but single *-l* forms are far preferable. (See DOUBLING FINAL -L, 2.)

shovelful. The plural is *shovelfuls.* (See PLURALIZING WORDS IN TERMINAL -FUL.)

SHOW-

These noun compounds are separate: *show bill, show card, show business, show place, show window.*

These are solid: *showboat, showcase, showdown, showman, showpiece, showroom.*

Show-off, as a noun, is hyphenated. As a verb, of course, it is separate: *to show off.*

shower. See -OUR, -OWER, -AUER, 2.

shugar, shure. Misspellings of *sugar, sure.*

SHUT-

The nouns *shutdown, shutoff,* and *shutout* are solid. *Shut-eye* and *shut-in,* noun or adjective, are hyphenated.

shyer. See *shier.*

shyly, shily. The former spelling is preferred.

shyness. In words of one syllable, such as *shy,* final *-y* is retained before *-ness.* (See -Y PLUS A SUFFIX, 7.)

sibilance. One of a comparatively few words in which *-ance,* rather than *-ence,* follows *l-.* (See -ANCE, -ENCE, AFTER L-, 3.)

sibilant. See *sibilance.*

sibilate. Unlike *oscillate, vacillate,* and similar verbs, *sibilate* has only one *-l.* Likewise, the noun *sibilation.*

sibyl. The word for sorceress, prophetess, fortuneteller, etc., has an *-i* in the first syllable, *-y* in the second.

(The girl's name is spelled either *Sibyl* or *Sybil.*) The adjectives are either *sibylic* or *sibyllic,* but only *sibylline* (two *-l's*).

SICK-

Compounds are generally two words (*sick bay, sick call, sick headache,* etc.); but the following are solid: *sickbed, sickroom.*

-SICK

Adjective compounds with this suffix are solid: *airsick, lovesick, seasick,* etc., as are also the nouns formed from them: *airsickness, lovesickness,* etc.

sickle. Note the *-le* ending. (See -ICKLE, -ICKEL.)

SIDE-

Noun compounds generally are two words (*side arms, side dish, side light, side step,* etc.); but the following are solid: *sideboard, sideburns, sidecar, sidepiece, sideslip, sidewalk, sidewinder.*

Side-kick and *side-wheeler* are hyphenated.

Verbs are mostly solid: *sideline* (sports), *sideslip, sideswipe, sidetrack.* But *side-step* is hyphenated.

The adjective *side-splitting* is hyphenated.

-SIDE

Compounds are solid: *bedside, fireside, roadside,* etc.

-SIDED

Adjective compounds mostly hyphenated (*double-sided, one-sided, slab-sided,* etc.), except *ironsided* and *lopsided,* which are solid.

sideward, sidewards. Use only the first spelling as an *adjective;* use either form as an *adverb.* (See -ARD, ARDS.)

sidewise. Note the *-ise* ending, common to all words built on the base *-wise*. (See -ISE, 1.)

siege. *-I* before *-e* except after *c-;* contradictorily, *seize* is spelled *-ei.* (See -IE, -EI, 1.)

siesmic. Misspelling of *seismic.*

sieve. Note the *-ie* combination. (See -IE, -EI, 11.)

sieze, siezure. Misspelling of *seize, seizure.*

signaled, signaler, signaling. Because *signal* is *not* accented on the last syllable, final *-l* is *not* doubled before a suffix beginning with a vowel. Double *-l* forms are acceptable, but single *-l* forms are far preferable. (See DOUBLING FINAL -L, 2.)

significance, significant. *-Ance* and *-ant,* rather than *-ence* and *-ent,* in order to keep the *-c* "hard." (See -ANCE, -ENCE, AFTER C-, 3.)

silhouette. Ends in *-ette.* (See -ET, -ETTE, 3.)

sillable. Misspelling of *syllable.*

silliness. The *-y* of *silly* changes to *-i* before *-ness.* (See -Y PLUS A SUFFIX, 6.)

silo. Plural is *silos.* (See PLURALIZING WORDS IN TERMINAL -O, 2.)

SILVER-

Noun compounds mostly two words (*silver foil, silver wedding,* etc.), except the following, written solid: *silverfish, silversmith, silverware.*

Adjectives are hyphenated: *silver-haired, silver-plated,* etc.

---

simitar. Misspelling of *scimitar.*

SIMPLE-

Adjective compounds are hyphenated: *simple-hearted, simple-minded, simple-witted,* etc.; *simple-hearted* may also be spelled solid.

---

simplified, simplifies. The *-y* of *simplify* changes to *-i* before *-ed* or *-es.* (See -Y PLUS A SUFFIX, 1.)

sincerely. Note particularly that final *-e* of *sincere* is retained preceding the adverbial suffix *-ly.* (See -LY, 10.)

sinecure. Not *sinacure.*

singeing. Note the *-e* preceding *-ing* when we refer to surface burning. (See -NGE, 2.)

SINGLE-

Adjective compounds are hyphenated: *single-breasted, single-minded,* etc. *Single-handed* and *single-hearted* are preferably hyphenated, but may also be written solid: *singlehanded, singlehearted.*

Noun compounds are mostly two words: *single file, single standard,* etc.

As noun or verb, *single-foot* is hyphenated.

---

sinuous. Note the *-uous* ending.

siphon, syphon. Either spelling, the first preferable.

sirocco. One *-r,* two *-c*'s.

sirup, syrup. Both spellings are correct and both are equally acceptable. Note that in either pattern the adjective has only one *-p: syrupy, sirupy.*

sirynge. Misspelling of *syringe.*

sister-in-law. Hyphenated. Plural is *sisters-in-law.* (See HYPHENATING, 6A.)

site. See CITE, SITE.

sit-in. Hyphenated as a noun or adjective. (See HYPHENATING, 10A.)

SIX-. See HYPHENATING, 49D, E.

---

sixes. The plural of the number, when written as a word, requires no apostrophe. As a figure, the apostrophe is preferable, but may be omitted:

6's or *6s.* (See APOSTROPHE, USE OF, 2, 3.)

SIXTY-. See HYPHENATING, 49A.

---

sizable, sizeable. Both spellings correct, but the first is preferable. (See -ABLE, -EABLE, 2.)

skein. When sounded as *ay,* the spelling *-ei* is always correct. (See -IE, -EI, 6.)

skeptical. This spelling preferable to *sceptical,* which is, however, also correct. Same holds for other forms: *skeptic, sceptic; skepticism, scepticism;* etc.

ski. The plural of the noun is *skis.* The verb forms are spelled *skied, skiing;* and the performer is a *skier.*

skillful, skilful. Spelling with the double *-l* preferable, as in nouns *skillfulness, skilfulness.*

SKIN-

Adjective compounds mostly hyphenated (*skin-clad, skin-deep,* etc.), but *skintight* is written solid.

-SKIN

Noun compounds solid: *bearskin, calfskin, sheepskin,* etc.

-SKINNED

Adjective compounds hyphenated: *bare-skinned, thin-skinned,* etc.

---

sky. Plural is *skies.* (See -EYS, -IES, -YS, 3.)

SKY-

Noun compounds mainly solid: *skylight, skyline, skywriting,* etc. The color *sky blue,* as a noun, is separate, though hyphenated as an adjective preceding its noun (*sky-blue walls*).

Other adjectives are also hyphenated: *sky-high, sky-reaching,* etc.

---

slay (noun). Misspelling of *sleigh.*

sleazy. Not *sleezy.*

---

sleigh. When sounded as *ay,* the spelling *-ei* is always correct. (See -IE, -EI, 6.)

sleight (of hand). When sounded *eye,* the combination *-ei* is used, except when the following letter is an *-r.* (See -IE, -EI, 7.)

slier, sliest. Preferable to *slyer, slyest.* (See -IER, -IEST, 4.)

slily. See *slyly.*

sloop. See -OOP, -OUP, -UPE, 1.

SLOW-

Adjective compounds are hyphenated: *slow-motion, slow-moving, slow-witted,* etc.

---

slurred, slurring. Note the double *-r.* (See DOUBLING FINAL -R, 1.)

slyer, slyest. See *slier, sliest.*

slyly, slily. The former spelling is preferred. (See -LY, 3.)

slyness. In words of one syllable, such as *sly,* final *-y* is retained before *-ness.* (See -Y PLUS A SUFFIX, 7.)

smoky. Not *smokey.* Becomes *smokier, smokiest, smokily, smokiness* in derived forms.

smolder, smoulder. The shorter, modern spelling is preferable. (See -O, -OU, 1.)

smooth (verb). Not *smoothe.*

SNOW-

The following compound nouns are solid: *snowball, snowbank, snowberry, snowbird, snowbush, snowcap, snowdrift, snowdrop, snowfall, snowflake, snowplow, snowshed, snowshoe, snowstorm.*

Other noun compounds are two words: *snow line, snow pudding,* etc. *Snow-broth* is hyphenated.

Adjectives, too, are hyphenated: *snow-blind, snow-bound, snow-capped,* etc.

SOAP-

These noun compounds are solid: *soapbox, soapstone, soapsuds.*

These are separate: *soap bubble, soap flake, soap opera.*

SOAR, SORE

To *soar* is to rise or fly high, literally or figuratively; the noun has a corresponding meaning.

Sore is an adjective (That's his *sore* spot.) or a noun (A *sore* developed.) with a variety of common meanings.

sociable. -Able is the correct suffix after the letter *i*-. (See -ABLE, -IBLE, 3.)

sodder. Misspelling of *solder*.

SOFT-

Adjective compounds are invariably hyphenated: *soft-boiled, soft-shelled, soft-spoken,* etc.

But *softgrained* and *softhearted* are solid.

The nouns *softball, softhead,* and *softwood* are solid. Others are written as two words (*soft coal, soft drink, soft soap,* etc.), except *soft-shell,* another term for *soft-shelled crab.*

The verbs *soft-pedal* and *soft-soap* are hyphenated.

solder. This, strange as it may look, is the word pronounced *sodder,* and is so spelled because it drives from the same Latin root that gives us *solid.*

soldier-statesman. Note the hyphen. (See HYPHENATING, 1.)

solicitor. Ends in *-or.* (See -ER, -OR, 5.)

soliloquize. Each *-l* is single.

soliloquy. The plural is *soliloquies.* (See -EYS, -IES, -YS, 3.)

solo. Plural is *solos.* (See PLURALIZING WORDS IN TERMINAL -O, 2.)

somber, sombre. First spelling preferable. (See -ER, -RE.)

sombrero. Plural is *sombreros.* (See PLURALIZING WORDS IN TERMINAL -O, 2.)

SOME-

As a pronoun or adverb, a compound with *some-* is a solid word. Otherwise, if *some* is clearly an adjective, two separate words are used.

SOLID—PRONOUN OR ADVERB

Somebody came in.

Somehow, I can't believe it. (always solid)

Someone is here.

Something is funny.

I'll go *sometime.*

Sometimes I wonder about you.

He's *somewhat* embarrassed. (always solid)

Somewhere I'll find you. (always solid)

SEPARATE—ADJECTIVE PLUS NOUN OR PRONOUN

She has *some body!* (i.e., quite a body!)

Some one of these books has what I want.

Some things are hard to understand.

This is *some time* to lose your head!

Some times are better than others.

Let's eat *some place.* (always separate)

See also ANY-; EVERY-; NO-.

somebody, some body. See SOME-.

somehow. Always one word. (See SOME-.)

someone, some one. See SOME-.

some place. Always two words. (See SOME-.)

somersault, summersault. The first spelling preferable. Other variant but acceptable forms: *somerset, summerset.*

something, some thing. See SOME-.

sometime, some time. See SOME-.

SOMETIME, SOMETIMES

Sometime means one time or another in the future, or at some vague or unknown time.

I'll do it *sometime,* I
don't know just when.
He arrived *sometime* last
night.

As an adjective, it also means *former,* as a *sometime governor of Connecticut.*

Sometimes means occasionally, every now and then, etc.

Sometimes I really worry
about you.
Sometimes he stays awake
all night.

---

someway, some way, someways. All these spellings acceptable for any possible meaning of the adverb. If *some way* means *some particular way,* as in *I'll find some way or other to do it,* the words must, of course, be separate.

somewhat. Always one word. (See SOME-.)

somewhere, somewheres. Good style avoids the final *-s* here and in words like *anywhere, nowhere,* etc. *Somewhere* is always a solid word. (See SOME-.)

somnolence, somnolent. Generally, but not always, *-l* is followed by *-ence* or *-ent,* rather than *-ance* or *-ant.* (See -ANCE, -ENCE, AFTER L-, 1, 3.)

son-in-law. Hyphenated. Plural is *sons-in-law.* (See HYPHENATING, 6A).

soprano. Plural is *sopranos;* in musical circles *soprani* is sometimes used. (See PLURALIZING WORDS IN TERMINAL -O, 2.)

sorcerer. Ends in *-er.* (See -ER, -OR, 1.)

sore. See SOAR, SORE.

soubrette. Ends in *-ette.* (See -ET, -ETTE, 3.)

sought. The pattern is *-ought.* (See -AUGHT, -OUGHT, 1.)

sourbraten. Misspelling for *sauerbraten.*

sourkraut. Misspelling for *sauerkraut.*

sovereign, sovereignty. Note the *-ei* combination. (See -IE, -EI, 10.)

sow (verb). See SEW, SOW.

spaded. Incorrect past tense of *spay.* Proper form: *spayed.*

spaghetti. Note the *-h* and double *-t.*

spayed, spaying. Since the terminal *-y* of *spay* follows a vowel, it does *not* change to *-i* before a suffix. (See -Y PLUS A SUFFIX, 9.)

specially. The adverbial ending *-ly* is added to the adjective *special,* hence the double *-l.* (See -LY, -ALLY, 4.)

spectator. Ends in *-or.* (See -ER, -OR, 5.)

specter, spectre. The former spelling preferable. (See -ER, -RE.)

spectrum. The plural is either *spectra* or *spectrums.* (See PLURALIZING WORDS IN TERMINAL -UM, 1.)

speculator. Ends in *-or.* (See -ER, -OR, 5.)

speed-up. Hyphenated as a noun, separate as a verb.

spittoon. Double *-t.*

splendor, splendour. The first spelling is American, the second British. (See -OR, -OUR, 1.)

spongy. The *-e* of *sponge* is dropped before the suffix *-y.* (See -Y, -EY, 1.)

sponsor. Ends in *-or.* (See -ER, -OR, 5.)

spoof. The plural is *spoofs.* (See PLURALIZING WORDS IN TERMINAL -F OR -FE, 2.)

spoonful. The plural is *spoonfuls.* (See PLURALIZING WORDS IN TERMINAL -FUL.)

spryly. Not *sprily.* (See -LY, 3.)

spy. Verb forms are *spied, spies, spying;* noun plural is *spies.* (See -EYS, -IES, -YS, 3; -Y PLUS A SUFFIX, 1.)

squirrel. Double *-r.*

staccato. Double *-c,* one *-t.*

stadium. The plural *stadiums* is commoner than *stadia*. (See PLURAL-IZING WORDS IN TERMINAL -UM, 2.)

staff. For plural see PLURALIZING WORDS IN TERMINAL -F OR -FE, 4F.

stagy, stagey. Equally acceptable spellings. (See -Y, -EY, 1, 2.)

stanch, staunch. These spellings theoretically are interchangeable, but *stanch* is generally used for the verb (*stanch* the flow of blood), *staunch* for the adjective (*staunch* support).

stand-in. Hyphenated as a noun. (See HYPHENATING, 10A.)

standpoint. Solid word. (See- POINT.)

state-wide. Hyphenated.

STATIONERY, STATIONARY

Spell it *stationery* when you mean *paper* (note the -*er* in both words) and other writing materials; *stationary* when you mean *standing* (note the -*a* in both words), fixed, not movable, etc. For instance: *blue stationery, a small stationery store, a piece of stationery; stationary walls, keep the ruler stationary.*

statuary. Most words with both a primary and secondary accent end in -*ary* rather than -*ery*. (See -ARY, -ERY, 1, 2.)

statuette. Ends in -*ette*. (See -ET, -ETTE, 3.)

staunch. See *stanch*.

stay-at-home. Hyphenated as a noun or adjective. (See HYPHENATING, 10A.)

stay-out. Hyphenated as a noun. (See HYPHENATING, 10A.)

steadiness. The -*y* of *steady* changes to -*i* before -*ness*. (See -Y PLUS A SUFFIX, 6.)

STEAM-

Adjectives are hyphenated (*steam-filled, steam-heated*, etc.), except for *steamtight*, which is solid.

Nouns are generally two words (*steam fitter, steam shovel*, etc.), except for *steamboat, steampipe,* and *steamship,* which are solid.

The verb *steam-roller* is hyphenated.

---

stein. When sounded *eye,* the combination -*ei* is used, except when the following letter is an -*r*. See -IE, -EI, 7.)

STEP-, IN RELATIONSHIPS. See HYPHENATING, 6.

---

stepped-up. Hyphenated when used as an adjective preceding the noun. (See HYPHENATING, 11.)

stevedore. Not *stevadore*.

stickle. Note the -*le* ending. (See -ICKLE, -ICKEL.)

stigma. For plural see PLURALIZING WORDS IN TERMINAL -A, 6.

stiletto. Note the single -*l* and, as in so many words of Italian derivation, the double -*t*. The plural is either *stilettos* or *stilettoes,* the former preferable. (See PLURALIZING WORDS IN TERMINAL -O, 5.)

stimulant. One of the few words ending in -*ant,* rather than -*ent,* after *l*-. (See -ANCE, -ENCE, AFTER L-, 3.)

stimulus. Not *stimulous*. For plural, see PLURALIZING WORDS IN TERMINAL -US, 10.

stingy. Not *stingey*. Forms are *stingier, stingiest, stinginess.* (*Stingy* may also mean capable of stinging—*stingy* insects—and is then pronounced STING-ee, but the spelling is the same.)

stirred, stirrer, stirring. Note the double -*r* in these derived forms of *stir.* (See DOUBLING FINAL -R, 1.)

stirrup. Note the double -*r,* though *sirup* has only one -*r*.

stomach-ache. Hyphenated. (See HYPHENATING, 1.)

STONE-

Adjectives are hyphenated: *stone-faced, stone-blind, stone-broke, stone-deaf*, etc., but *stonehearted* is solid.

The following noun compounds are solid: *stonecutter, stonemason, stoneware, stonework.* Others are written separate.

stone's throw. Note the apostrophe. (See APOSTROPHE, USE OF, 4.)

stony. The *-e* of stone is dropped before the suffix *-y.* Derived forms are *stonier, stoniest, stonily, stoniness.* (See -Y, -EY, 1.)

stonyhearted. Solid word.

stoop, stoup. See -OOP, -OUP, -UPE, 3D.

STOP-

The following nouns are written solid: *stopcock, stopgap, stopover.* Others are separate (*stop light, stop sign, stop watch*, etc.).

stopped, stopper, stopping. Final *-p* of *stop* is doubled before a suffix beginning with a vowel. (See DOUBLING FINAL -P, 1.)

STORE-

These nouns are solid: *storehouse, storekeeper, storekeeping, storeroom.* Others are two words: *store sign, store teeth*, etc.

-STORE

The following are written solid: *bookstore, drugstore.*

Others are generally two words: *cigar store, shoe store*, etc.

storey. See *story.*

STORM-

Adjectives are hyphenated (*storm-drenched, storm-tossed*, etc.), except *stormbound* and *stormproof*, written solid.

Nouns are generally two words (*storm cellar, storm window*, etc.), except *stormwind*, which is solid.

-STORM

Nouns are solid: *hailstorm, rainstorm, windstorm*, etc.

story, storey. The first is the American spelling for each of the levels of a building, the second is British. The American plural is therefore *stories,* the British *storeys.* (See -EYS, -IES, -YS, 3.)

storybook. Solid word.

storyteller. Solid word.

stoup, stoop. See -OOP, -OUP, -UPE, 3D.

STRAIGHT-

Hyphenated in adjective compounds (*straight-edged, straight-line, straight-out, straight-sided*, etc.).

But the following adjectives are solid: *straightaway, straightforward.*

The nouns *straightaway* (of a track) and *straightedge* (i.e., a ruler) are solid. Others are two words: *straight angle, straight face*, etc.

STRAIGHT, STRAIT

Straight is an adjective (a *straight* line, etc.), or, as a noun, a combination of cards in poker or the straight part of a racecourse.

Strait is a noun (often in the plural, *straits*) meaning a narrow body of water or distressed circumstances. As a rarely used adjective, it means distressing or difficult; *straitened* is more common in this usage.

Strait is the spelling used in *strait jacket* and *strait-laced.*

strait jacket. Not *straight jacket.*

strait-laced. Not *straight-laced.*

STRANGE-
Adjective compounds are hyphenated: *strange-looking, strange-sounding,* etc.

stratagem. Not *strategem,* despite the spelling of *strategy.*

strategy. Not *stratagy.*

stratum. The plural is either *strata* or *stratums.* (See PLURALIZING WORDS IN TERMINAL -UM, 1.)

-STROKE
Noun compounds are solid: *backstroke, sunstroke, upstroke,* etc.

STRONG-
Adjective compounds are hyphenated: *strong-arm, strong-backed, strong - minded, strong - smelling, strong-willed,* etc. But *stronghearted* is solid.
The verb *strong-arm* is hyphenated.
Strongbox, stronghold, and *strongroom* are solid nouns; *strong drink* is written separate.

stubbornness. *Stubborn* plus *-ness,* hence the double *-n.* (See -NESS AFTER N-.)

stucco. Double *-c.*

studio. Plural is *studios.* (See PLURALIZING WORDS IN TERMINAL -O, 3.)

stupefy. One of only five nontechnical verbs in English that end in *-efy.* The noun, correspondingly, is spelled *stupefaction,* again with an *-e* preceding the *-f;* other forms are *stupefied, stupefactive, stupefacient,* etc.

SUB-
Compounds with *sub-* are written solid unless the root starts with a capital letter: *subcellar, subclass, subdivision, subirrigate, subnormal, sub-Adriatic,* etc.

subconscious. Like *conscience, conscious,* etc., this word too has that typical *-sci* combination.

submitted, submitting. Because *submit* is accented on the last syllable, the final *-t* is doubled before a suffix beginning with a vowel. (See DOUBLING FINAL -T, 2.)

subpoena, subpena. The former spelling is preferable. Derived forms are *subpoenaed* and *subpoenaing,* strange as they may look.

subsequent. Always *-ent,* not *-ant* after *qu-.* (See -ANCE, -ENCE, AFTER U-, 1.)

subservience, subservient. Most often, as here, *-ence* or *-ent,* rather than *-ance* or *-ant,* follows *i-.* (See -ANCE, -ENCE, AFTER I-, 1.)

subsidence. Almost always, with only a few exceptions, *-ence,* not *-ance,* follows a *d-.*

subsistence, subsistent. Note the *-ence, -ent* endings. (See -ANCE, -ENCE, AFTER T-, 3, 4.)

subterranean. Double *-r, -ean* suffix.

succeed. One of the only three words ending in *-ceed.* (See -CEED, -SEDE, -CEDE, 1.)

succor, succour. The second spelling is British. (See -OR, -OUR.)

succubus. Not *succubous.* (See -US, -OUS.)

succulence, succulent. Generally, but not always, *l-* is followed by *-ence* or *-ent,* rather than *-ance* or *-ant.* (See -ANCE, -ENCE, AFTER L-, 1, 3.)

succumb. Ends in silent *-b.*

suddenness. *Sudden* plus *-ness,* hence the double *-n.* (See -NESS AFTER N-.)

sufferance. Note the *-ance* ending. (See -ANCE, -ENCE, AFTER R-, 6.)

sufficient. The combination *-ie,* rather than *-ei,* is always used when the preceding *-c* has the sound of *sh.* (See -IE, -EI, 12.)

suffragette. Double *-f,* ends in *-ette.* (See -ET, -ETTE, 3.)

sugar. No -*h*.

sugar-coat (verb), **sugar-coating**. Hyphenated.

suggestible. If the root forms its noun by the immediate addition of -*ion* (*suggestion*), the correct ending is likely to be -*ible*. (See -IBLE, ABLE,- 2.)

suing. The -*e* of *sue* is dropped before -*ing*. (See DROPPED -E.)

SUITE, SUIT

A *suite* (pronounced SWEET) is used for:

(a) a group of attendants, servants, etc.—a *suite* of followers.

(b) a set of connected rooms—a four-room *suite*.

(c) a set of furniture—a bedroom *suite*.

(d) a musical composition—a *suite* for orchestra and piano.

Otherwise *suit* is the correct spelling for a wide variety of meanings (clothes, cards, dispute at law, etc.).

---

sullenness. *Sullen* plus -*ness*, hence the double -*n*. (See -NESS AFTER N-.)

summersault, summerset. See *somersault*.

sumptuous. Make sure to get in the -*p* before -*t*, and the -*u* before -*ous*. (See -UOUS.)

SUN-

Adjectives are hyphenated: *sunbaked, sun-drenched, sun-warmed*, etc.

Sunburned, sunfast, sunlighted, sunlit, sunproof, and *sunstruck* are the exceptions, all written solid.

Most noun compounds are solid: *sunbeam, sunrise, sunset, sunshade, sunup*, etc.

But the following nouns are separate words: *sun bath, sun dance, sun deck, sun god, sun lamp, sun parlor, sun tan*.

The verb *sun-bathe* is hyphenated; *sunburn* is solid.

---

sunderance. Ends in -*ance*. (See -ANCE, -ENCE, AFTER R-, 6.)

sunrise. Note the -*ise* ending, common to all words built on *rise* as a base. (See -ISE, 3.)

SUPER-

Compounds with *super-* are written solid unless the root starts with a capital letter: *superclass, supercool, superman*, etc.; *super-American*, etc.

---

supercede, superceed. Misspellings of *supersede*.

supereminence, supereminent. Somewhat more words end in -*ence*, -*ent*, after *n*-, than in -*ance*, -*ant*, these among others. (See -ANCE, -ENCE, AFTER N-, 1.)

superintendence, superintendent. Almost always, with only a few exceptions, -*ence* or -*ent*, not -*ance* or -*ant*, follows a *d*-. (See -ANCE, -ENCE, AFTER D-, 1.)

supersede. The only verb in English ending in -*sede*. (See -CEED, -SEDE, -CEDE, 2.)

superstition. Ends in -*ition*. (See -ICIOUS, -ITIOUS, 4.)

superstitious. Ends in -*itious*, not -*icious*. (See -ICIOUS, -ITIOUS, 3.)

supervise. Note the -*ise* ending, common to all words ending in -*vise*. (See -ISE, 2.)

supervisor. Ends in -*or*. (See -ER, -OR, 5.)

supoena. Misspelling of *subpoena*.

suppliance. Very occasionally, as here, -*ance*, not -*ence*, follows *i*-. (See -ANCE, -ENCE, AFTER I-, 2.)

supposition. Ends in -*ition*. (See -ICIOUS, -ITIOUS, 4.)

supposititious. Ends in -*itious*, not -*icious*. (See -ICIOUS, -ITIOUS, 3.)

suppress. Double -*p* here, and in all derived forms.

suppressible. If the root forms its noun by the immediate addition of -*ion* (*suppression*), the correct ending is likely to be -*ible*. (See -IBLE, -ABLE, 2.)

supprise. Misspelling of *surprise*.

sure. Not *shure*.

SURE-
Compounds are hyphenated: *sure-enough, sure-fire, sure-footed,* etc.

---

sureness, surety. The final -*e* of *sure* is retained before a suffix that starts with a consonant. (See RETAINED -E, 1.)

surfeit. Note the -*ei* combination. (See -IE, -EI, 9.)

surgeon. The -*e* keeps the -*g* "soft."

surmise. One of three words ending in -*mise* rather than -*mize*. (See -ISE, 5.)

surmountable. The ending is -*able*, not -*ible*. (See -ABLE, -IBLE, 1.)

surprise. Note the -*ise* ending, common to words ending in -*prise;* and make sure to get in that first -*r*, often omitted by careless spellers.

surveyor. Ends in -*or*. (See -ER, -OR, 5.)

survivor. Ends in -*or*. (See -ER, -OR, 5.)

susceptible. The ending is -*ible*, not -*able*. (See -IBLE, -ABLE, 1.)

suspension. Ends in -*ension*. (See -ENSION, -ENTION.)

suspicion. Note the uncommon ending, -*icion*.

suspicious. Ends in -*icious*, not -*itious*. (See -ICIOUS, -ITIOUS, 1.)

sustenance. One of a group of words ending in -*ance*, rather than -*ence*, after *n*-. (See -ANCE, -ENCE, AFTER N-, 3.)

SWEET-
Compound adjectives are hyphenated (*sweet-smelling, sweet-tem-*

pered, etc.), except for *sweethearted* and *sweetmouthed,* written solid.

Noun compounds are written separate (*sweet corn, sweet potato,* etc.) except for *sweetheart* and *sweetmeat,* written solid.

---

swimmer, swimming. Note the double -*m* in these derived forms of *swim.* (See DOUBLING FINAL -M, 1.)

swingeing. Note the -*e* preceding -*ing* when we refer to whipping. (See -NGE, 2.)

swoop. See -OOP, -OUP, -UPE, 1.

sy-. For many misspelled words that seem to start with this syllable, see PS-, S-.

-SY, -CY. See -CY, -SY.

Sybil. Correct for the girl's name, incorrect for *sibyl,* a fortuneteller. The proper name may also be spelled *Sibyl.*

sycophant. Not *sychophant*.

SYLLABICATING WORDS AT END OF A LINE

-able, 20
addresses, 4
-ance, 20
-ant, 20
-ary, 21
-cious, 20
compound words, 11
consonants between vowels, 7–10
contractions, 4
dates, 4
divide between syllables, 5
divide in middle of word, 6
dividing before or after -r, 18
double consonants, 7–9
-ence, -ency, 20
-ent, 20
-er, 23
-ery, 21
hyphenated compounds, 11
-ible, 20
-ive, 21

-ing, 20
-ity, 20
-ment, 20
monosyllables, 1
names, 4
number of letters before dividing, 3
one-letter division, 12, 14
one-syllable words, 1
-or, 22
-ory, 21
prefixes, 19
single consonant between vowels, 10
short words, 3
-sion, 20
suffixes, 20–23
-tious, 20
two consonants, 7
two-letter division, 13–14
when or where *not* to divide, 1–4; 12–17
where to divide, 5–11; 18–23
whole syllables, not to be divided, 2

Following are the more reliable principles for syllabicating words that run over from one line to the next. The most important rule is to keep such division to a minimum, typing a word solid on one line or the other wherever possible.

1. *Monosyllables.*

No matter how long, one-syllable words may not be divided. The following, for random example, must appear solid:

> brought (*not* brou-/ ght)
> rhythm (*not* rhy-/ thm)
> straight (*not* str-/ aight)
> thought (*not* thou-/ ght)
> weighed (*not* wei-/ ghed)

2. *Whole syllables.*

Never divide a whole syllable.

WRONG	RIGHT
confirm-/ ed	con-/ firmed
conscient-/ ious	consci-/ entious
courage-/ ous	coura-/ geous
intelligen-/ ce	intel-/ ligence
invent-/ ion	inven-/ tion
salaci-/ ous	sala-/ cious
survey-/ ed	sur-/ veyed

3. *Short words.*

Try not to divide words that con‚ tain fewer than seven letters. The following, again taking random examples, are preferably kept solid even though they have two or three syllables each:

> apple facing
> candy idea
> devil   moral
> eerie   radio

4. *Names, addresses, etc.*

Do not divide proper names, abbreviations, contractions, dates, numbers, addresses, etc. Avoid such absurdities, for example, as:

> John G. Da-/ vis
> Ph.-/ D.
> is-/ n't
> July 4, 19-/ 61
> 24-/ 96 Main Street
> 5,623,-/ 104

5. *Where to divide, 1.*

Divide words between syllables only, relying more or less on ear to tell you where the break occurs.

> blunt-/ ness (*not* bluntn-/ ess)
> frag-/ ment (*not* fragm-/ ent)
> match-/ less (*not* mat-/ chless)
> partic-/ ipate (*not* parti-/ cipate)
> tortu-/ ous (*not* tort-/ uous)

6. *Where to divide, 2.*

Divide preferably in or near the middle of a word.

> immi-/ gration (preferable to im-/ migration or immigra-/ tion)
> justi-/ fiability (preferable to justifiabil-/ ity or jus-/ tifiability)
> obso-/ lescence (preferable to ob-/ solescence)
> poison-/ ously (preferable to poi-/ sonously)
> revolu-/ tionary (preferable to rev-/ olutionary)

7. *Two consonants.*

Generally, if you are dividing at a place where two consonants occur between two vowels, break between the consonants. (In *symmetrical,* for example, *-mm* comes between the vowels *y-* and *-e*, *-tr* between *e-* and *-i;* the division is made between the *-m*'s, or between *t-* and *-r*.)

commen-/ tary	mus-/ tache
dod-/ dering	paren-/ tal
effec-/ tually	recol-/ lection
fragmen-/ tary	recom-/ mend
gut-/ tural	recom-/ pense
infor-/ mation	recon-/ noiter

8. *Double consonants, 1.*

If a final consonant has been doubled before a suffix (*beg—begging, occur—occurrence,* etc.), divide between the double consonants.

beg-/ garly	confer-/ ring
beg-/ ging	occur-/ rence
begin-/ ning	recur-/ rence
control-/ lable	repel-/ lent

9. *Double consonants, 2.*

But if the original word ended in a double consonant (*bluff, ebb, fall, pass, quaff, roll,* etc.), do not separate the two consonants.

bluff-/ ing	pass-/ ing
ebb-/ ing	quaff-/ ing
fall-/ ing	roll-/ ing

10. *Consonant between vowels.*

When a single consonant occurs between two vowels (for example, the *-v* in *unfavorable*), does it close the preceding syllable or open the next syllable?

Both, depending on the first of the two vowels.

If this first vowel is short (*-a* as in *-at; -e* as in *bet; -i* as in *bit; -o* as in *hot; -u* as in *but*), it usually attracts the consonant to the end of its own syllable, especially if that syllable is accented.

confed-/ eration (*not* confe-/ deration)
devel-/ opment (*not* deve-/ lopment)
inhib-/ iting (*not* inhi-/ biting)
inval-/ uable (*not*

inva-/ luable)
optom-/ etrist (*not* opto-/ metrist)
retal-/ iate (*not* reta-/ liate)

On the other hand, if the preceding vowel is long or obscure, the consonant generally starts the next syllable.

fa-/ tality (*not* fat-/ ality)
inhi-/ bition (*not* inhib-/ ition)
opto-/ metric (*not* optom-/ etric)
perse-/ verance (*not* persev-/ erance)
secu-/ rity (*not* secur-/ ity)
unfa-/ vorable (*not* unfav-/ orable)
unsea-/ sonable (*not* unseas-/ onable)

11. *Compound words.*

Separate hyphenated compounds at the hyphen, rather than anywhere else.

cross-/ question (*not* cross-ques-/ tion)
good-/ tempered (*not* good-tem-/ pered)
letter-/ perfect (*not* letter-per-/ fect)
runner-/ up (*not* run-/ ner-up)
self-/ respect (*not* self-re-/ spect)
stomach-/ ache (*not* stom-/ ach-ache)

12. *One-letter division.*

Never divide a word so that the first part has only one letter.

WRONG	RIGHT
a-/ rithmetic	arith-/ metic
e-/ conomic	eco-/ nomic
e-/ normous	enor-/ mous
i-/ conographic	icono-/ graphic
i-/ dealistic	ideal-/ istic
o-/ pening	open-/ ing

13. *Two-letter division.*

Avoid, if possible, breaking a word so that the first part has only two letters.

UNDESIRABLE	PREFERABLE
ac-/ company	accom-/ pany
bi-/ ographical	bio-/ graphical
Ca-/ tholicism	Cathol-/ icism
de-/ sirous	desir-/ ous
fa-/ natical	fanat-/ ical

14. *One or two letters at end.*

Avoid dividing a word in such a fashion that only one or two letters are carried over to the next line.

WRONG	RIGHT
accompan-/ y	accom-/ pany
ammoni-/ ac	ammo-/ niac
enormous-/ ly	enor-/ mously
occasion-/ al	occa-/ sional
periodical-/ ly	peri-/ odically
public-/ ly	pub-/ licly
reconsid-/ er	recon-/ sider
shovel-/ er	shov-/ eler
uneducat-/ ed	unedu-/ cated

15. *Confusing division, 1.*

Try not to end a line with part of a word that may be misconstrued or mispronounced. For example:

aver-/ (age)—looks like the verb *aver*

her-/ (bivorous)—looks like the feminine possessive pronoun

his-/ (tory)—looks like the masculine possessive pronoun

medal-/ lion)—will be mispronounced *meddle*

me-/ (diation)—looks like the objective pronoun

the-/ (ology)—looks like the definite article

16. *Confusing division, 2.*

Try not to carry over to the next line part of a word that may be misconstrued or mispronounced.

(aver-/) *age*—is this the word *age?*

(dande-/) *lion*—king of the beasts?

(gradu-/) *ate*—past tense of eat?

(his-/) *tory*—not a whig?

(inciden-/) *tally*—a score?

(inconden-/) *sable*—the color or the fur?

(medal-/) *lion*—again, our friend Leo?

(prov-/) *able*—having *ability?*

(sun-/) *dry*—opposite of *wet?*

(vege-/) *table*—a piece of furniture?

17. *Confusing division, 3.*

It is considered bad form, also, to break a word in such a way that the first part is itself a full word, as in *be-/* ginning, *far-/* ing, *he-/* roic, *in-/* formative, *out-/* rage, *sum-/* marize, *sun-/* dry, etc.

18. *-R.*

If *-r* follows *a-* or *e-*, let it *end*, not begin, a syllable.

gener-/ ality, *not* gene-/ rality

infer-/ ence, *not* infe-/ rence

inter-/ esting, *not* inte-/ resting

invar-/ iable, *not* inva-/ riable

19. *Prefixes.*

A standard prefix should not be divided; make your break *after* the prefix if this is close to the middle of the word.

ambi-/ dextrous, *not* am-/ bidextrous

ante-/ cedent, *not* an-/ tecedent

counter-/ sign, *not* coun-/ tersign

extra-/ dition, *not* ex-/ tradition

inter-/ view, *not* in-/ terview

preter-/ natural, *not* pre-/ ternatural

20. *Suffixes, 1.*

Generally, though not always, a standard suffix, such as *-able, -ible, -ance, -ant, -cious, -ence, -ency, -ent, -ing, -ity, -ment, -sion, -tion, -tious,* etc., may stand by itself when you make your division, particularly so if the root is a full word in its own right, or a full word from which final *-e* has been dropped. (But see *-ary, -ery, -ive, -ory,* Section 21.)

deliver-/ ance	persist-/ ent
depend-/ ence	preten-/ sion
elocu-/ tion	preten-/ tious
devil-/ ish	prevent-/ able
embarrass-/ ment	resist-/ ible
frivol-/ ity	return-/ ing
loqua-/ cious	

21. *Suffixes, 2.*

On the other hand, the suffixes *-ary, -ery, ive,* and *-ory* usually attract a preceding consonant.

elu-/ sive	regenera-/ tive
elu-/ sory	respira-/ tory
indica-/ tive	secre-/ tary
mili-/ tary	secre-/ tive
milli-/ nery	

22. *-Or.*

The suffix *-or* generally attracts the preceding consonant to its syllable.

RIGHT	WRONG
avia-/ tor	aviat-/ or
impos-/ tor	impost-/ or
protec-/ tor	protect-/ or

23. *-Er.*

The suffix *-er* is usually in a syllable by itself, but dividing *banish-er, bargain-er, gossip-er,* etc., as indicated runs counter to the rule that the second part of a divided word should contain at least three letters (Sections 12–14). Break the words above as *ban-/ isher, bar-/ gainer, gos-/ siper.*

---

syllable. Not *sillable.*

syllabus. For plural see PLURALIZING WORDS IN TERMINAL -US, 13.

SYMBOLS IN COMPOUNDS. See HYPHENATING, 52.

---

symmetry. Double *-m* in this word and all derived forms.

symposium. The plural is *symposiums* or *symposia.* (See PLURALIZING WORDS IN TERMINAL -UM, 2.)

symptom. Watch the *-p.*

synagogue, synagog. The longer spelling is preferable. (See -OGUE, -OG, 1.)

syncopate. Not *synchopate.*

synchronize. Note the *-h.*

synonym. There are two *-y*'s in this word, and also in the adjective *synonymous.*

synopsis. Plural is *synopses.* (See PLURALIZING WORDS IN TERMINAL -IS.)

syphon. See *siphon.*

syringe. Not *sirynge.*

syrup, syrupy. See *sirup.*

syzygy. A term in astronomy, this odd word, with its succession of *-y*'s,

could be said to have no vowels, except that *-y* is a vowel when sounded like *-i.*

T

(Rules for double *-t.* See DOUBLING FINAL -T.)

T-, PT-. See PT-, T-.

TABLE-

These noun compounds are solid words: *tablecloth, tablefellow, tableland, tablemate, tablespoon, tablespoonful, tableware.*

Others are written separate: *table linen, table talk,* etc.

---

tableau. The plural is *tableaux.* (See PLURALIZING WORDS IN TERMINAL -EAU, 1.)

tableau vivant. Plural is *tableaux vivants.*

tablespoonful. The plural is *tablespoonfuls.* (See PLURALIZING WORDS IN TERMINAL -FUL.)

taboo, tabu. The first is the more common spelling.

tabooed. This derived form of *taboo* is correctly spelled, although the three successive vowels may look strange at first. (See -OO, TERMINAL.)

taboret. Ends in *-et.* (See -ET, -ETTE, 4.)

tabu. See *taboo.*

TAIL-

Adjective compounds are hyphenated: *tail-wagging,* etc.

The following noun compounds are solid: *tailboard, tailgate, taillight, tailpiece, tailrace, tailspin, tailstock.*

Other noun compounds are written separate: *tail coat, tail wind,* etc.

-TAIL

Compounds with this word as suffix are solid: *foxtail, pigtail,* etc.

-TAILED

Adjective compounds are mostly hyphenated: *long-tailed, short-tailed,* etc.

However, these are solid: *bobtailed, dovetailed, drabbletailed, draggletailed, foxtailed, pigtailed.*

tailor. Ends in *-or.* (See -ER, -OR, 5.)

TAKE-

Nouns formed by suffixing a preposition to the verb *take* are generally hyphenated: *take-in, take-off, take-out, take-up.*

But *takedown,* noun or adjective, is solid.

-TAKE

Compound nouns formed by prefixing a preposition to *take* are solid: *intake, uptake,* etc.

talebearer. Solid word.

TALESMAN, TALISMAN

A *talesman* (pronounced TAILZm'n) is a person summoned to serve on a jury.

A *talisman* (pronounced (TALis-m'n) is a magic charm.

-TANCE, -TENCE. See -ANCE, -ENCE, AFTER T-.

tangible. The ending is *-ible* to keep the preceding *-g* "soft." (See -IBLE, -ABLE, 6.)

-TANT, -TENT. See -ANCE, -ENCE, AFTER T-.

tariff. Ends in *-riff,* not *-rrif.* Compare *sheriff.*

tarmigan. Misspelling of *ptarmigan.*

tarried, tarrier, tarries. The *-y* of *tarry* changes to *-i* before *-ed, -er,* or *-es.* (See -Y PLUS A SUFFIX, 1, 3.)

tarrif. Misspelling of *tariff.*

tastiness. The *-y* of *tasty* changes to *-i* before *-ness.* (See -Y PLUS A SUFFIX, 6.)

tatterdemalion. Note that the ending is *-ion,* not *-ian.*

tattletale. Solid word.

tattoo. Double *-t* in the middle, no matter whether the word means designs engraved in the skin or a signal on drums, bugle, etc. Plural is *tattoos.*

tattooed, tattooer, tattooing. These derived forms of *tattoo* are correctly spelled, although the three successive vowels may look strange at first. (See -OO, TERMINAL.)

taught. Note that the pattern is *-aught.* (See -AUGHT, -OUGHT, 1.)

tawdry. Not *taudry.*

tawny. Not *tauny.*

TAX-

Taxpayer and *taxpaying* are solid noun compounds; *tax assessment, tax rate* and other nouns are written separate.

Taxpaying is a solid adjective compound; others are hyphenated preceding their nouns: *tax-exempt, tax-free, tax-supported,* etc.

TEA-

Most noun compounds are separate words: *tea ball, tea dance, tea wagon,* etc.

However, the following are solid: *teaberry, teabox, teacake, teacup, teacupful, teahouse, teakettle, teamaker, teapot, tearoom, teaspoon, teaspoonful, teataster, teatime, teaware.*

TEAM, TEEM

A *team* is a group of people (or animals, as *horses,* etc.) engaged in a co-operative endeavor. The verb *team* reflects the same idea—let's *team* up.

Teem, a verb only, means to be full, crowded, etc., or to rain very hard—the place *teemed* with beatniks; it's *teeming* out, etc.

---

teammate. Solid word.

teamwork. No hyphen. (See HYPHENATING, 3A.)

TEAR-

Tear- (from the eye) is hyphenated to the next word in adjective compounds: *tear-filled, tear-stained,* etc.

Noun compounds like *tear bomb* or *tear gas* are written separate; *teardrop* is solid; *tear-jerker* is hyphenated.

---

teaspoonful. The plural is *teaspoonfuls.* (See PLURALIZING WORDS IN TERMINAL -FUL.)

technique, technic. The use of *technic* as a synonym of *technique* is now rare.

teem. See TEAM, TEEM.

teen-age, teen-ager. Hyphenated. (See HYPHENATING, 49C.)

temperament. Note the *-a,* sometimes ignored in pronunciation, after the *r-.*

temperance. Note the *-ance* ending. (See -ANCE, -ENCE, AFTER R-, 6.)

temperant. There is no such word, though it looks as if it should be the adjective form of *temperance.* Correct word: *temperate.*

temperate. Not *temperant.*

tempestuous. There is a *-u* before *-ous.* (See -UOUS.)

temporary. Most words with both a primary and secondary accent end in *-ary* rather than *-ery.* (See -ARY, -ERY, 1, 2.)

TEN-. See HYPHENATING, 49D, E.

---

tenancy, tenant. End in *-ancy, -ant,* not *-ency, -ent.*

tendency. Not *tendancy.*

tenement. Not *tenament.*

tens. The plural of the number, when written as a word, requires no apostrophe. As a figure, the apostrophe is preferable, but may be omitted: *10's* or *10s.* (See APOSTROPHE, USE OF, 2, 3.)

tension. Ends in *-ension.* (See -ENSION, -ENTION.)

tenuous. A *-u* precedes *-ous.* (See -UOUS.)

termagant. "Hard" *-g,* hence *-ant.* (See -ANCE, -ENCE, AFTER G-, 2.)

terminus. For plural see PLURALIZING WORDS IN TERMINAL -US, 11.

terodactyl. Misspelling of *pterodactyl.*

terrible. The ending is *-ible.* (See IBLE, -ABLE, 1.)

tertiary. Ends in *-ary.* (See -ARY, -ERY, 1.)

tessellate, tessellation. Double *-l* in all forms.

tetanus. Not *tetanous.* (See -US, -OUS.)

tête-à-tête. All three accents, plus two hyphens, needed in this French import.

tetralogy. Note that the ending is *-alogy,* not *-ology.* (See -ALOGY, -OLOGY.)

Teusday. Misspelling of *Tuesday.*

than, then. The only possible confusion occurs in a combination like *No sooner had he entered than we all began to eat,* in which *than,* not *then,* is used, as this is a comparison similar to *He's no taller than his brother.*

thaught. Misspelling of *thought.*

theater, theatre. The former spelling is preferable. (See -ER, -RE.)

theif. Misspelling of *thief.*

THEIR, THEY'RE, THERE

Their is possessive only.

Have they taken *their* coats?

They said *their* good-bys and left.

They're is a contraction of *they are.*

They're impossible.

They're late again.

There is the correct spelling for other uses.

Are *there* any left?

He's over *there.*

There are over 180,000,000 people in this country today.

---

theirs. The word is never written with an apostrophe.

then, than. See *than, then.*

therapeutics. Note that it's *-peu,* not *-pue.*

there. See THEIR, THEY'RE, THERE.

THERE-

Note that the second *-e* is retained in solid compounds like *thereabout, thereabouts, thereafter, thereagainst, thereat, thereby, therefor, therefore, therefrom, therein, thereinafter, thereinto, thereof, thereon, thereto, theretofore, thereunder, thereunto, thereupon, therewith,* and *therewithal.*

THEREFORE, THEREFOR

Therefore means *consequently, for that reason,* etc.

He's tall; *therefore* he can reach it.

Therefor means *for which, for it, for them,* etc.

His answers, and the reasons *therefor,* are hard to understand.

---

there'll. Contraction of *there will.* (See APOSTROPHE, USE OF, 1.)

there's. Contraction of *there is.* (See APOSTROPHE, USE OF, 1.)

thesaurus. Not *thesaurous.* (See -US, -OUS.)

thesis. Plural is *theses.* (See PLURAL-

IZING WORDS IN TERMINAL -IS.)

they're. Contraction of *they are.* (See APOSTROPHE, USE OF, 1; THEIR, THEY'RE, THERE.)

thief. *-I* before *-e* except after *c-;* plural is *thieves.* (See -IE, -EI, 1.)

thier. Misspelling of *their.*

THIRD-. See HYPHENATING, 51.

THIRTY-. See HYPHENATING, 49.

---

thisis. Misspelling of *phthisis.*

thorough, thoro. See -OUGH, -O.

thoroughfare, thorofare. See -OUGH, -O.

though, tho. See -OUGH, -O.

thought. The pattern is *-ought.* (See -AUGHT, -OUGHT, 1.)

THREE-. See HYPHENATING, 49D, E.

---

threes. The plural of the number, when written as a word, requires no apostrophe. As a figure, the apostrophe is preferable, but may be omitted: *3's* or *3s.* (See APOSTROPHE, USE OF, 2, 3.)

threshold. Only one *-h* after the *s-.*

through, thru. See -OUGH, -O.

thruway. Official spelling for a super-highway. (See -OUGH, -O.)

THUNDER-

Adjectives are hyphenated (*thunder-free, thunder-voiced,* etc.), except *thunderstricken* and *thunderstruck,* both solid.

Nouns are solid: *thunderbolt, thunderstorm,* etc.

---

tickle. Note the *-le* ending. (See -ICKLE, -ICKEL.)

tidbit, titbit. First spelling preferable.

TIDE-

Adjectives are hyphenated: *tide-covered, tide-swept,* etc.

Nouns are solid: *tideland, tidewater,* etc.

-TIDE

Compounds are solid: *Christmastide, eventide, yuletide,* etc.

tie. The participle is spelled *tying.* (See -IE to -Y.)

TIE-

Compound nouns formed by *tie* and a preposition are hyphenated: *tie-in, tie-up,* etc.

The nouns *tieback* and *tiepin* are solid; others are two words: *tie bar, tie clip,* etc.

TIGHT-

Adjectives are hyphenated: *tight-belted, tight-fitting, tight-lipped,* etc., but *tightfisted* is solid.

Nouns are mostly solid: *tightrope, tightwad, tightwire,* etc., but *tight squeeze* is two words.

-TIGHT

The following adjectives are solid: *airtight, gastight, oiltight, raintight, skintight, smoketight, steamtight, watertight, windtight.*

These are hyphenated: *dust-tight, fire-tight, storm-tight.*

till. The shortened form of *until* spelled only this way, not *'til* (except in poetry) or *til.*

TIME-

Adjective compounds are hyphenated (*time-honored, time-tested,* etc.), except the following, written solid: *timesaving, timeserving, timeworn.*

Noun compounds are written separate (*time deposit, time limit, time out, time study,* etc.), except the following, written solid: *timecard, timekeeper, timepiece, timeserver, timeserving, timetable, timework.*

-TIME

Compounds with this suffix are solid: *bedtime, mealtime, wartime,* etc.

timpani. The kettledrums in an orchestra. This is the plural of the Italian word *timpano.* Equally popular is the spelling *tympani.*

TIN-

Adjective compounds are hyphenated: *tin-covered, tin-plated,* etc.

Most noun compounds are two words: *tin cup, tin foil, tin plate,* etc.

But *tinman, tinsman, tinsmith, tintype, tinware,* and *tinwork* are solid.

Tin-pan alley is hyphenated, as is also the verb *to tin-plate.*

ting-a-ling. *Hyphenated.*

TINGE, TWINGE

Tinge, noun or verb, refers to color, shade, tint, trace (of color, odor, flavor, etc.), and so on.

Twinge, again noun or verb, refers to a sudden pain, or to a pang or qualm, as of conscience. Use *tinge,* not *twinge,* for a slight amount. The *-ing* forms are *tingeing* and *twinging.*

tingeing, tinging. The former is the preferable spelling of the participle of *tinge.*

tinker's damn, tinker's dam. Either spelling, the first preferable, the second used by those who hesitate to write *damn.*

tintinnabulation. This word and all related forms have a double *-n* before the first *-a;* also, one *-b.*

tip-off. Hyphenated as a noun. (See HYPHENATING, 10.)

tipped, tipping. Final *-p* of *tip* is doubled before a suffix beginning with a vowel. (See DOUBLING FINAL -P, 1.)

tiptoe. Solid word.

tiptoed, tiptoer, tiptoeing. These derivatives of the verb *tiptoe* are correctly spelled; note that terminal *-e* is retained before *-ing,* dropped before *-ed* and *-er.* (See -OE, TERMINAL, 7.)

tiptop. Solid word.

tire, tyre. The second is the British spelling for what goes on the wheel of a vehicle.

tiro. See *tyro.*

'tis (poetic). Contraction of *it is.* (See APOSTROPHE, USE OF, 1.)

tisic. Misspelling of *phthisic.*

titbit. See *tidbit.*

titillate. The verb and all derived forms have a single *-t* and double *-l* in the middle, and is similar in pattern to *oscillate, vacillate,* etc.

TITLES, RANK, etc. See HYPHENATING, 5, 7, 8.

TO, TWO, TOO. See TWO, TOO, TO.

---

tobacco. One *-b,* two *-c*'s; plural is *tobaccos.* (See PLURALIZING WORDS IN TERMINAL -O, 2.)

toccata. Two *-c*'s; one *-t* after the first *a-.*

today, to-day. Solid spelling is preferable. (See HYPHENATING, 3A.)

toed. Note the single *-e.* (See -OE, TERMINAL, 5.)

toe dance. Two words as a noun, hyphenated (*toe-dance*) as a verb. (See HYPHENATING, 4.)

toeing. Note that terminal *-e* of *toe* is retained before *-ing.* (See -OE, TERMINAL, 5.)

toilet, toilette. The bathroom is spelled *toilet* only; the process of dressing (making one's *toilette*) is preferably spelled with the double *-t* and the *-e,* and is then accented on the

final syllable. (See -ET, -ETTE, 2, 4.)

tolerable. Since *-a* is the corresponding vowel in another form of the word (*tolerate*), the correct ending is *-able.* (See -ABLE, -IBLE, 5.)

tolerance, tolerant. End in *-ance* and *-ant.* (See -ANCE, -ENCE, AFTER R-, 10.)

tomaine. Misspelling of *ptomaine.*

tomato. Plural is *tomatoes.* (See PLURALIZING WORDS IN TERMINAL -O, 1.)

tomorrow, to-morrow. Former spelling preferable. (See HYPHENATING, 3A.)

tone-deaf. Hyphenated.

tonight, to-night. Solid word preferable. (See HYPHENATING, 3A.)

tonsillitis. Two *-l*'s here, and in all related forms.

TOO, TWO, TO. See TWO, TOO, TO.

TOOTH-

Toothache, toothbrush, and *toothpick* are solid; *tooth paste, tooth powder,* and other noun compounds are written separate.

-TOOTHED

Compounds are hyphenated: *eventoothed, sharp-toothed,* etc.

TOP-

Adjective compounds are mostly hyphenated: *top-drawer, top-flight, top-heavy,* etc.

But *toplofty, topmost,* and *top-notch* are solid.

The following noun compounds are solid: *topcoat, topknot, topsail, topsoil.* Others are separate (*top hat, top sergeant,* etc.).

The noun *top-dressing* and the verb *top-dress* are hyphenated.

-TOP

Compounds are solid: *flattop, hilltop, housetop,* etc.

tornadoes, tornados. The former is the preferable plural; both are correct. (See PLURALIZING WORDS IN TERMINAL -O, 4.)

torpedo. Plural is *torpedoes.* (See PLURALIZING WORDS IN TERMINAL -O, 1.)

torrefy. One of only five nontechnical verbs in English that end in *-efy.* The noun, correspondingly, is spelled *torrefaction,* again with an *-e* preceding the *-f.* (See -IFY, -EFY, 2.)

torso. Plural is *torsos.* (See PLURALIZING WORDS IN TERMINAL -O, 2.)

tortuous. Note the *-u* before *-ous.* (See -UOUS.)

TORTUROUS, TORTUOUS

The first word, as its spelling indicates, refers to torture or agonizing pain; the second means twisting, winding, full of turns, as a road or passage; or deceitful or devious, as a person, his words, etc.

---

tossup. Solid as a noun, separate (*toss up*) as a verb.

totally. Note the double *-l,* since the adverbial suffix *-ly* is added to the adjective *total.* (See -LY, 7.)

touch and go. Separate words as a noun, hyphenated as an adjective (*touch-and-go*).

touch-up. Hyphenated as a noun or adjective, separate as a verb.

TOUGH-

Adjective compounds are hyphenated (*tough-talking,* etc.), except *toughhearted,* which is solid.

---

tought. Misspelling of *taught.*

toupee. Double *-e.*

tourniquet. Ends in *-et.* (See -ET, -ETTE, 4.)

toward, towards. Use only the first spelling as an *adjective;* use either

form as a *preposition.* (See -ARD, -ARDS.)

TOWN-

Hyphenated in adjective compounds: *town-bred,* etc.

Separate in noun compounds: *town hall, town house,* etc.

TOWNS-

Compounds are solid: *townsfolk, townspeople,* etc.

---

towpath, towrope. Solid nouns.

traceable. The *-e* of *trace* is retained before *-able* in order to preserve the original "soft" pronunciation of the preceding *-c.* (See -CEABLE.)

tractor. Ends in *-or.* (See -ER, -OR, 5.)

TRADE-, TRADES-

Noun compounds are separate (*trade route, trade school,* etc.), except the following, which are solid: *tradesfolk, tradesman, tradespeople, tradeswoman.*

Hyphenated are *trade-in* (noun), *trade-last, trade-mark* (noun or verb), *trade-union* (adjective). *Trademark* may also be written solid, and *trade-union,* as a noun, may also be hyphenated.

---

trafficked, trafficker, trafficking. The *-k* must be inserted in the derived forms of *traffic* in order to preserve the original pronunciation of final *-c.* (See -C, -CK, 1.)

traitor. Ends in *-or.* (See -ER, -OR, 5.)

tranquilize, tranquilizer. Because *tranquil* is not accented on the last syllable, final *-l* is *not* doubled before a suffix beginning with a vowel. Double *-l* forms are acceptable, but single *-l* forms are preferable. (See DOUBLING FINAL -L, 2.)

tranquillity, traniquility. Double *-l* is preferable. (See DOUBLING FINAL -L, 4.)

TRANS-

Compounds are solid words, unless the root starts with a capital, in which case a hyphen is required: trans-American, trans-Asiatic, etc.

However, *transatlantic* and *transpacific* are solid words, the *-a* and *-p* small letters.

---

transcend. Note the *-c*, as in *ascend, descend*, etc.

transcendence, transcendent. End in *-ence, -ent*, not *-ance, -ant*. (See -ANCE, -ENCE, AFTER D-, 1.)

transient. Note the *-ie* combination. (See -IE, -EI, 11.)

translator. Ends in *-or*. (See -ER, -OR, 5.)

transmissible. When the root ends in *-miss*, the correct ending is *-ible*. (See -IBLE, -ABLE, 4.)

transmittal, transmitted, transmitting. Because *transmit* is accented on the last syllable, the final *-t* is doubled before a suffix beginning with a vowel. (See DOUBLING FINAL -T, 2.)

transship. No hyphen. (See HYPHENATING, 3A.)

traveled, traveler, traveling. Because *travel* is *not* accented on the last syllable, final *-l* is *not* doubled before a suffix beginning with a vowel. Double *-l* forms are acceptable, but single *-l* forms are far preferable. (See DOUBLING FINAL -L, 2.)

travelogue, travelog. The longer spelling is preferable. (See -OGUE, -OG, 1.)

trespass. Single *-s* in the middle, double *-s* at the end. This pattern holds for all derivatives: *trespassed, trespasser, trespasses, trespassing*, etc.

tributary, tributory. See -ARY, -ORY, 3E.

trickle. Note the *-le* ending. (See -ICKLE, -ICKEL.)

TRIPLE-. See HYPHENATING, 48B.

TROCHE, TROCHEE

A *troche* (one *-e*, pronounced TRO-kee) is a medicated lozenge; a *trochee* (two *-e's*, same pronunciation) is a metrical foot in poetry.

---

troop, troupe. See -OOP, -OUP, -UPE, 3E.

trooper, trouper. See -OOP, -OUP, -UPE, 3E.

troupe, trouper. See -OOP, -OUP, -UPE, 3E.

trousseau. The plural is either *trousseaux* or *trousseaus*. (See PLURALIZING WORDS IN TERMINAL -EAU, 2.)

truculence, truculent. Generally, though not always, *-l* is followed by *-ence* or *-ent*, rather than *-ance* or *-ant*. (See -ANCE, -ENCE, AFTER L-, 1, 3.)

truly. The *-e* of *true* has been dropped before the adverbial suffix *-ly*. (See -LY, 9.)

truthteller, truthtelling. Solid words.

tryout. Solid word as a noun or adjective, separated as a verb.

tsar. See *czar*.

T square. No hyphen.

Tuesday. Not *Teusday*.

tumor, tumour. The first spelling is American, the second British. (See -OR, -OUR, 1.)

tumultuous. Note the *-u* before *-ous*. (See -UOUS.)

turbulence, turbulent. Generally, though not always, *-l* is followed by *-ence* or *-ent*, rather than *-ance* or *-ant*. (See -ANCE, -ENCE, AFTER L-, 1, 3.)

turf. For plural see PLURALIZING WORDS IN TERMINAL -F OR -FE, 4G.

turgescence, turgescent. Note the *-sc*. (See -ESCE, -ESCENT, -ESCENCE, 3.)

TURN-

Compounds are mostly solid (*turncoat, turntable,* etc.), including nouns formed by combining the verb with a preposition (*turnabout, turnover, turnup*).

The following are hyphenated as nouns or adjectives: *turn-about-face, turn-in, turn-out.*

tutelage. Ends in -*age.*
tutor. Ends in -*or.* (See -ER, -OR, 5.)
tutti-frutti. Hyphenated, and both parts with a double -*t,* and ending in -*i.*
twaddle, twattle. The former spelling is more common—both correct.
'twas (poetic). Contraction of *it was.* (See APOSTROPHE, USE OF, 1.)
twattle. See *twaddle.*
'twere (poetic). Contraction of *it were.* (See APOSTROPHE, USE OF, 1.)

TWENTY-. See HYPHENATING, 49.

TWICE-

All adjective compounds are hyphenated before their nouns: *twice-blessed, twice-removed, twice-told,* etc.

'twill (poetic). Contraction of *it will.* (See APOSTROPHE, USE OF, 1.)
twinge. See TINGE, TWINGE.
twinging. The participle of *twinge.* (See -NGE.)

TWO-. See HYPHENATING, 49D, E.

TWO, TOO, TO

Two is the number.
We have *two* hands, *two* feet, *two* ears.
Too means either *also* or *excessively.*
He's coming *too.*
He, *too,* is rich.
She's *too* happy to sit still.

That's much *too* expensive.
To is used in other instances, and is a preposition.
He walked *to* his office every morning.
I'll leave it all *to* you.
I'm trying *to* understand you.

twos. The plural of the number, when written as a word, requires no apostrophe. As a figure, the apostrophe is preferable, but may be omitted: 2's or 2s. (See APOSTROPHE, USE OF, 2, 3.)
tying. Participle of *tie,* -*ie* changing to -*y* before -*ing.* (See -IE TO -Y.)
tympani. See *timpani.*

TYPE-

Common compounds are solid: *typescript, typesetter, typewrite, typewriter,* etc.

typhus, typhous. *Typhus* is the noun, the disease itself; *typhous* is the adjective designating or referring to the disease.
tyranny. This word and all related forms except *tyrant* have one -*r,* two -*n*'s: *tyrannical, tyrannize,* etc.
tyre. See *tire.*
tyro. Plural is *tyros.* May also be spelled *tiro,* but rarely is.
tzar. See *czar.*

U

-UANCE, -UENCE. See -ANCE, -ENCE, AFTER U-.

-UANT, -UENT. See -ANCE, -ENCE, AFTER U-.

U-boat. Compounds with single-letter prefixes almost always are hyphenated, the letter capitalized. *T square* and *U bolt* are exceptions. (See HYPHENATING, 52.)

ultimatum. The plural is either *ultimata* or *ultimatums.* (See PLU-RALIZING WORDS IN TER-MINAL -UM, 1.)

ULTRA-
Compounds are solid (*ultraconservative, ultrahigh frequency, ultramodern,* etc.) unless the root starts with a capital letter (*ultra-American, ultra-English,* etc.).

ululate. No double *-l*'s in this verb or any of its derived forms.

umbrageous. The *-e* of *umbrage* is retained before *-ous* to keep the *-g* "soft."

UN-. See HYPHENATING, 19.

unacceptable. Note that the ending is *-able.* (See -ABLE, -IBLE, 1.)

unanimous. Note the single *-n*'s, and the *-i* before the *-m,* as also in the noun *unanimity.*

unavailable. Note that the ending is *-able.* (See -ABLE, -IBLE, 1.)

unavoidable. Note the *-able* ending. (See -ABLE, -IBLE, 1.)

unaware, unawares. The adjective is spelled without the *-s* (he was *unaware*), the adverb either way (he was caught *unaware* or *unawares*).

unbreakable. Note the *-able* ending. (See -ABLE, -IBLE, 1.)

uncalled-for. Hyphenated when used as an adjective preceding the noun. (See HYPHENATING, 11.)

UNCO-. See HYPHENATING, 15.

unconscious. Note the *-sci* combination.

unconscionable. Ends in *-able.* (See -ABLE, -IBLE, 7.)

unctuous. Note the *-u* before *-ous;* related nouns are *unctuosity* and *unction.*

undependable. The ending is *-able.* (See -ABLE, -IBLE, 1.)

UNDER-
All compounds are solid (*underage, underfoot, underhung, undergraduate, underrate,* etc.), even when the root starts with *r-.*

undesirable. Not *undesireable.* (See -ABLE, -EABLE, 1.)

undulant. One of the few words ending in *-ant,* rather than *-ent,* after *l-.* (See -ANCE, -ENCE, AFTER L-, 3.)

UNEQUIVOCAL, UNEQUIVOCABLE
The *second* of these two words exists only in the imaginations of writers who are unsuccessfully searching for the first. (*Unequivocal* is the negative of *equivocal,* which means purposely ambiguous or vague, misleading or evasive. When someone speaks *unequivocally,* he is clear and explicit, and leaves no room for even the slightest misunderstanding.

unevenness. *Uneven* plus *-ness,* hence the double *-n.* (See -NESS, AFTER N-.)

unfreer, unfreest. Two *-e*'s only, even though it's *unfree* plus *-er, -est.* (See -EER.)

unfriendly. Note the *-ie* combination. (See -IE, -EI, 13.)

unguent. Note the *-u* after the *g-.*

unheard-of. Hyphenated when used as an adjective preceding the noun. (See HYPHENATING, 11.)

unhoped-for. Hyphenated when used as an adjective preceding the noun. (See HYPHENATING, 11.)

unintelligible. The ending is *-ible* to keep the preceding *-g* "soft." (See -IBLE, -ABLE, 6.)

unlooked-for. Hyphenated when used as an adjective preceding the noun. (See HYPHENATING, 11.)

unnavigable. Only the *-able* ending

will keep the preceding -g "hard." (See -ABLE, -IBLE, 6.)

unpredictable. Note that the ending is *-able*, not *-ible*. (See -ABLE, -IBLE, 1.)

unprincipled. Not *unprincipaled*. (See PRINCIPAL, PRINCIPLE.)

unprofitable. Note the *-able* ending. (See -ABLE, -IBLE, 1.)

unrepentant. *-Ant* is slightly more common than *-ent* after *t-*. (See -ANCE, -ENCE, AFTER T-, 2.)

unskillful, unskilful. Preferably spelled with a double *-l*.

untaught. Note that the pattern is *-aught*. (See -AUGHT, -OUGHT.)

until. One *-l*, though *till* has two. (See -IL, -ILL, 5.)

untought. Misspelling of *untaught*.

-UOUS

Some people gaily ignore the first *-u* in the endings of the following words. Keep this important letter both in the spelling and pronunciation.

arduous	mellifluous
assiduous	presumptuous
conspicuous	strenuous
contemptuous	sumptuous
contiguous	superfluous
continuous	tempestuous
disingenuous	tenuous
fatuous	tortuous
impetuous	tumultuous
incestuous	unctuous
incongruous	vacuous
inconspicuous	virtuous
ingenuous	voluptuous
innocuous	

UP-

Compounds are invariably solid: *upborne, upgrowth, upstream, uptake*, etc.

Up-bow, a term in music, is hyphenated. *Up-to-date* is hyphenated if it is clearly an adjective, especially preceding its noun.

See also HYPHENATING, 2.

-UP

Most nouns formed from a verb plus *up* are solid: *breakup, blowup, windup,* etc.

The nouns *line-up, make-up, tie-up,* and *write-up* are hyphenated.

-UPE, -OOP, -OUP. See -OOP, -OUP, -UPE.

uprise. Note the *-ise* ending, common to all words built on *rise* as a base. (See -ISE, 3.)

upside-down. Hyphenated when preceding its noun (*upside-down* attitude), otherwise not (the table was *upside down*). (See HYPHENATING, 2.)

up-to-date. Hyphenated if clearly an adjective, especially before its noun. (See HYPHENATING, 2.)

upward, upwards. Use only the first spelling as an *adjective;* use either form as an *adverb*. (See -ARD, -ARDS.)

-US, -OUS

Hundreds of *adjectives* have the terminal *-ous* (*adventurous, dangerous,* etc.), so it is almost irresistibly tempting to end certain *nouns* the same way. However, the following are spelled *-us*, not *-ous*.

abacus	nucleus
angelus	octopus
animus	omnibus
caduceus	phosphorus
calculus	platypus
cumulus	radius
esophagus	sarcophagus
hippopotamus	stimulus
impetus	succubus
incubus	syllabus
nautilus	terminus
See also -UOUS.	

usable. Drop final *-e* of *use* before adding *-able*. (See -ABLE, -EABLE, 1.)

used to, use to. The correct pattern for frequent past action is *used to* (he *used to* come every day), not *use to.* However, in the negative and interrogative (I didn't *use to,* did you *use to?*), *use to* is correct.

useful. The final *-e* of *use* is retained before a suffix that starts with a consonant. (See RETAINED -E, 1.)

using. The final *-e* of *use* is dropped before a suffix that starts with a vowel. (See DROPPED -E.)

usurer. Note the *-er* ending. (See -ER, -OR, 1.)

utterance. Ends in *-ance.* (See -ANCE, -ENCE, AFTER R-, 6.)

V

vacillate. One *-c,* double *-l* in the verb and all derived forms.

vacuous. One *-c,* since it is built on the same root as *vacant, vacate,* etc. Noun is *vacuity,* again one *-c.*

vacuum. *Vacant* of everything—note the single *-c* in both words. And remember to double the *-u* by pronouncing the word carefully—VAC-u-um.

vail. See VALE, VEIL, VAIL.

VAIN, VANE, VEIN

Vain is the adjective meaning futile, useless, conceited, etc. It is also a noun in the phrase *in vain.*

A *vane* is an indicator (as in *weather vane*) or the flat part of a feather.

Vein, as a noun, is (a) a blood vessel, (b) the rib of a leaf or insect's body, (c) a fissure or crack in rock, etc., (d) a quality or strain, as *vein* of humor, jealousy, etc. As a verb, it has corresponding meanings.

vainness. *Vain* plus *-ness,* hence the double *-n.* (See -NESS AFTER N-.)

VALE, VEIL, VAIL

Vale is the poetic term for valley.

Veil, noun or verb, refers to something that covers or conceals.

Vail is an archaic word, and hence no longer seen in print; it is also an obsolete spelling of *veil.*

valedictorian. Note the *-e* following *l-.*

valeted, valeting. Because *valet* is *not* accented on the last syllable, final *-t* is *not* doubled before a suffix beginning with a vowel. (See DOUBLING FINAL -T, 3.)

valleys. A word like *valley,* ending in *-ey,* is pluralized by the simple addition of *-s.* (See -EYS, -IES, -YS, 1.)

valor, valour. The first spelling is American, the second British. (See -OR, -OUR, 1.)

valuable. Drop final *-e* of *value* before adding *-able.* (See -ABLE, -EABLE, 1.)

-VANCE, -VENCE. See -ANCE, -ENCE, AFTER V-.

vane. See VAIN, VANE, VEIN.

vanilla. One *-n,* double *-l.* Though sometimes pronounced *vinella,* never spelled that way.

-VANT, -VENT. See -ANCE, -ENCE, AFTER V-.

vapor, vapour. The first spelling is American, the second British. (See -OR, -OUR, 1.)

variance, variant. Very occasionally, as here, *-ance, -ant,* not *-ence, -ent,* follows *i-.* (See -ANCE, -ENCE, AFTER I-, 2.)

variegate. Despite the *-a* following *i-* in *variant, variation,* etc., in *variegate* and all derived forms *-e* follows *i-.*

veil. When sounded as *ay,* the spelling *-ei* is always correct. See also VALE, VEIL, VAIL. (See -IE, -EI, 6.)

vein. Again, *-ei.* (See -IE, -EI, 6; VAIN, VANE, VEIN.)

velure. One *-l.*

VENAL, VENIAL

Venal means characterized by, or open to, corruption, bribery, or purchase—*venal* public officials, for example. The noun is *venality.*

Venial means excusable or forgivable—*venial* sin, error, etc. The noun is *veniality.*

vendor. Ends in *-or.* (See -ER, -OR, 5.)

venerable. Since *-a* is the corresponding vowel in a related form (*venerate*), the correct ending is *-able.* (See -ABLE, -IBLE, 5.)

vengeance. The *-e* keeps the preceding *g-* "soft."

venial. See VENAL, VENIAL.

ventilator. Ends in *-or.* (See -ER, -OR, 5.)

VERB COMPOUNDS WITH PREPOSITIONS. See HYPHENATING, 11.

vertebra. Plural is *vertebrae,* or, less commonly, *vertebras.* (See PLURALIZING WORDS IN TERMINAL -A, 1.)

vertex. For plural see PLURALIZING WORDS IN TERMINAL -X, 1.

-VES, -FS, -FES. See PLURALIZING WORDS IN TERMINAL -F OR -FE.

veteran. The second *-e* is sometimes ignored in pronunciation, but must appear in spelling.

veto. Plural is *vetoes.* (See PLURALIZING WORDS IN TERMINAL -O, 1.)

vexatious. One of a few words ending in *-atious,* rather than *-acious.* (See -ACIOUS, -ACEOUS, -ATIOUS, 3.)

vibrator. Ends in *-or.* (See -ER, -OR, 5.)

VICE-. See HYPHENATING, 7.

vichyssoise. Note that the single *-s* comes at the end.

vicious. No *-s* before the *c-.* Indirectly a derivative of *vice,* which should get you started on the correct spelling.

victor. Ends in *-or.* (See -ER, -OR, 5.)

victuals. Strange as it may look, this is the word pronounced VITTLES. From Latin *victus,* part of a verb meaning *to live.*

vie. The participle is spelled *vying.* (See -IE to -Y.)

viel. Misspelling of *veil.*

vien. Misspelling of *vein.*

viewpoint. Solid word. (See -POINT.)

vigilance, vigilant. Here *-ance* or *-ant,* rather than *-ence* or *-ent,* follows *l-.* (See -ANCE, -ENCE, AFTER L-, 3.)

vignette. Ends in *-ette.* (See -ET, -ETTE, 3.)

vigor, vigour. The first spelling is American, the second British. (See -OR, -OUR, 1.)

vilify. To call someone *vile* names, hence only one *-l.*

villain. Double *-l* here.

vinegar. Note the *-e.*

vinella. Misspelling of *vanilla.*

violable. Since *-a* is the corresponding vowel in a related form (*violate*), the correct ending is *-able.* (See -ABLE, -IBLE, 5.)

violator. Ends in *-or.* (See -ER, -OR, 5.)

violence, violent. Generally, though not always, *l-* is followed by *-ence* or *-ent,* rather than *-ance* or *-ant.* (See -ANCE, -ENCE, AFTER L-, 1, 3.)

violoncello. Note the *-o* after *-l,* despite the temptation to imitate the pattern of *violin.* The plural, by the way, simply adds an *-s: violoncellos.*

(See PLURALIZING WORDS IN TERMINAL -O, 2.)

viragoes, viragos. The former is the preferable plural; both are correct. (See PLURALIZING WORDS IN TERMINAL -O, 4.)

viridescent. Note the *-sc* and single *-r.* (See -ESCE, -ESCENT, -ESCENCE, 3.)

virtuoso. Plural is *virtuosos* or *virtuosi.* (See PLURALIZING WORDS IN TERMINAL -O, 2.)

virtuous. A *-u* precedes the *-ous.* (See -UOUS.)

virulence, virulent. Generally, though not always, *l-* is followed by *-ence* or *-ent,* rather than *-ance* or *-ant.* (See -ANCE, -ENCE, AFTER L-, 1, 3.)

viscera. The *-c* is silent in pronunciation, but should not be invisible in spelling.

viscious. Common misspelling of *vicious.*

viscous. This word, pronounced VISS-kus, means thick and sticky; it is also one of the common misspellings of *vicious.*

visible. Ends in *-ible.* (See -IBLE, -ABLE, 1.)

visited, visiting. Because *visit* is *not* accented on the last syllable, final *-t* is *not* doubled before a suffix beginning with a vowel. (See DOUBLING FINAL -T, 3.)

visitor. Ends in *-or.* (See -ER, -OR, 5.)

vitamin, vitamine. The second spelling is now rare and should be avoided.

vittles. Loose spelling of *victuals,* often seen in ads.

vocabulary. Ends in *-ary.* (See -ARY, -ERY, 1.)

vocal cords. See CORD, CHORD.

voluptuous. Note the *-u* before *-ous.* (See -UOUS.)

vortex. For plural see PLURALIZING WORDS IN TERMINAL -X, 1.

V-shaped. Compounds with single-letter prefixes are usually hyphenated. (See HYPHENATING, 52.)

vulnerable. Ends in *-able.* (See -ABLE, -IBLE, 7.)

vying. Participle of *vie, -ie* changing to *-y* before *-ing.* (See -IE TO -Y.)

W

wageable. The *-e* of *wage* is retained before *-able.* (See -GEABLE.)

waif. The plural is *waifs.* (See PLURALIZING WORDS IN TERMINAL -F OR -FE, 2.)

wail. See WALE, WHALE, WAIL.

waive. See WAVE, WAIVE.

waiver. See WAVER, WAIVER.

WALE, WHALE, WAIL

A *wale* is a ridge, etc., in cloth. It is also a raised mark left on the skin by a blow, in which instance it may also be called a *wheal* or a *welt.*

Whale is the spelling for the sea mammal and hence for the word in expressions like *a whale of a party,* etc.; also for the verb meaning to beat or whip, as in *whale the tar out of him.*

A *wail* is a loud cry of grief or pain. Also a verb with similar meaning.

WALK-

The following noun compounds are solid: *walkaway, walkout, walkover.*

The following are hyphenated as nouns or adjectives: *walkie-talkie, walk-on, walk-up.*

-WALK

Compounds are solid: *boardwalk, catwalk,* etc.

WALL-

The following noun compounds are solid: *wallboard, walleye, wallflower, wallpaper*. Others are written separate.

Adjective compounds, with the exception of the solid *walleyed*, are hyphenated: *wall-climbing, wall-encircled*, etc.

walloped, walloper. Single *-p* in these derived forms since the accent does *not* fall on the last syllable of *wallop*. (See DOUBLING FINAL -P, 4.)

walnut. Not *wallnut*.

wantonness. *Wanton* plus *-ness*, hence the double *-n*. (See -NESS AFTER N-.)

WAR-

The following noun compounds are solid: *warfare, warmaker, warmaking, warmonger, warplane, warship, wartime*.

Others are written separate: *war cry, war head, war horse*, etc. Adjective compounds are hyphenated: *war-ridden, war-weary*, etc.

-WARE, -WEAR

Nouns referring to utensils, implements, etc., end in *-ware: chinaware, giftware, hardware*, etc.

Nouns referring to clothing end in *-wear: footwear, neckwear, sportswear*, etc.

WARM-

Adjective compounds are mostly hyphenated (*warm-blooded, warm-colored*, etc.), except *warmhearted*, which is solid.

WARRANTEE, WARRANTY

The first spelling is only for the person to whom a *warranty* is given. For all other meanings the word ends in *-y*.

warrantor. Ends in *-or*. (See -ER, -OR, 5.)

warranty. See WARRANTEE, WARRANTY.

warrior. Ends in *-or*. (See -ER, -OR, 5.)

WASH-, WASHED-

Noun compounds are invariably solid: *washcloth, washday, washout, washroom, washtub*, etc. The aeronautical term *wash-in* is hyphenated.

Adjective compounds with *washed-* are invariably hyphenated when preceding the noun: *washed-out, washed-up*, etc.

wasp-waisted. Hyphenated, but the noun *wasp waist* is two words.

WASTE-

Noun compounds largely separate (*waste can, waste collector, waste pipe*, etc.), except the following, written solid: *wastebasket, wasteland, wastepaper*.

Adjective compounds are hyphenated: *waste-producing, waste-saving*, etc.

wasteful. The final *-e* of *waste* is retained before a suffix that starts with a consonant. (See RETAINED -E, 1.)

wasting. The final *-e* of *waste* is dropped before a suffix that starts with a vowel. (See DROPPED -E.)

WATCH-

Compounds are largely two words (*watch dial, watch pocket, watch repair*, etc.), except the following, written solid: *watchcase, watchdog, watchmaker, watchmaking, watchman, watchtower, watchword*.

WATER-

The following compound nouns are solid: *waterbuck, watercourse, watercraft, waterfall, waterfinder, waterfowl, waterman, watermark, watermelon, waterscape, watershed, waterside, waterspout, waterway, waterweed, waterworks.*

Other nouns are two words: *water buffalo, water pipe,* etc.

Water glass and *water line,* preferably two words, may also be written solid: *waterglass, waterline.*

Water-colorist is hyphenated, as also are verb compounds: *water-jacket, water-ski, water-soak, water-wave,* etc., except *waterproof,* which is solid.

Adjectives are mostly hyphenated (*water-cooled, water-front, water-soluble,* etc.), except the following, which are solid: *waterproof, watertight, waterworn.*

-WATER

Noun compounds are mostly solid: *dishwater, firewater, limewater,* etc. *Rose water* is two words.

WAVE, WAIVE

Wave, as a verb, means to swing back and forth, up and down, etc., as a flag *waving* in the breeze; to signal, as *wave* your hand; to be or make wavy, as *waved* her hair; etc. *Wave* is, of course, also a noun.

Waive is a verb only, meaning give up voluntarily (*waived* all rights), not insist on, or put off to a later time. The noun is *waiver.*

WAVER, WAIVER

To *waver* is to swing back and forth, be indecisive, fluctuate, etc. The noun has corresponding meanings.

Waiver is a noun only—the act of giving up, or a written statement relinquishing some right, privilege, etc., as a *waiver* of immunity, claims, etc.

See also WAVE, WAIVE.

waylaid. Not *waylayed.* (See -AYED, -AID, 3.)

WEAK-

Adjective compounds are hyphenated (*weak-eyed, weak-kneed, weak-minded,* etc.), except *weakhearted,* which is solid.

weak-lunged. See *-lunged.*

-WEAR. See -WARE, -WEAR.

weariful. See *wearisome.*

weariness. The *-y* of *weary* changes to *-i* before *-ness.* (See -Y PLUS A SUFFIX, 6.)

wearisome. The *-y* of *weary* changes to *-i* before *-ful* and *-some.* (See -Y PLUS A SUFFIX, 8A.)

WEATHER-

Noun compounds are mostly written separate (*weather gauge, weather map,* etc.), except for the following solid words: *weatherboard, weathercock, weatherglass, weatherman.*

Adjective compounds are mostly hyphenated (*weather-beaten, weather-bound, weather-tight,* etc.), except for the following solid forms: *weatherproof, weatherworn.*

The verb *weatherproof* is solid; *weather-strip* is hyphenated.

WEATHER, WHETHER

The first spelling is a noun referring to climate, or is a verb.

It's nasty *weather.*

They *weathered* the storm.

Whether is a conjunction—he didn't say *whether* he could come.

Wednesday. Pronounced WENS-day, but spelled only as shown.

weekday. No hyphen. (See HYPHENATING, 3A.)

weekend, week-end, week end. All forms correct, but the solid form preferable whether noun, verb, or adjective. (See HYPHENATING, 3A.)

weigh. When sounded as *ay*, the spelling *-ei* is always correct (See -IE, -EI, 6.)

weight. Again, *-ei*. (See -IE, -EI, 6.)

weir. Note the *-ei* combination; this is an exception to the rule of *-i* before *-e* except after *c-*. (See -IE, -EI, 4.)

weird. Again, as in *weir*, an exception. (See -IE, -EI, 4.)

welcome. One *-l*.

welfare. One *-l*.

WELL-. See HYPHENATING, 30.

we'll. Contraction of *we will* or *we shall*. (See APOSTROPHE, USE OF, 1.)

wellcome. Misspelling of *welcome*.

wellfare. Misspelling of *welfare*.

well-off, well off. Either spelling may be used when the phrase functions adjectivally.

Wensday. Misspelling of *Wednesday*.

we're. Contraction of *we are*. (See APOSTROPHE, USE OF, 1.)

werewolf. The plural is *werewolves*. (See PLURALIZING WORDS IN TERMINAL -F OR -FE, 1.)

wet. See WHET, WET.

wet-nurse. Hyphenate only when a verb. (See HYPHENATING, 4.)

whale. See WALE, WHALE, WAIL.

wharf. For plural see PLURALIZING WORDS IN TERMINAL -F OR -FE, 4H.

wheal. See WALE, WHALE, WAIL.

WHERE-

Note that final *-e* of *where* is retained in the following solid compounds: *whereabouts, whereas, whereat, whereby, wherefore, wherefrom, wherein, whereinto, whereof, whereon, wheresoever, whereto, whereunto, whereupon, wherever, wherewith, wherewithal.*

wherefor. Means *for which*, but is rarely used; should not be confused with *wherefore*, which means *for what reason*, etc.

where's. Contraction of *where is*. (See APOSTROPHE, USE OF, 1.)

WHET, WET

To *whet*, as a verb, means to sharpen or stimulate—to *whet* the edge, *whet* one's appetite or curiosity, etc.

Wet, as a verb, is never used with these meanings, but only in the sense of making wet, damp, watery, etc.

whether. See WEATHER, WHETHER.

whimsy, whimsey. The first spelling is preferable and is pluralized as *whimsies*. The plural of *whimsey* is *whimseys*. (See -EYS, -IES, -YS.)

whinny. The forms are *whinnies, whinnied, whinnying.* Not to be confused with *whiny.* (See -Y PLUS A SUFFIX, 1.)

whiny. Given to *whining*, as a *whiny* child. Forms are *whinier, whiniest, whininess.* (See -IER, -IEST.)

whippersnapper. Not *wippersnapper*.

whipped, whipping. Final *-p* of *whip* is doubled before a suffix beginning with a vowel. (See DOUBLING FINAL -P, 1.)

whirred, whirring. Note the double *-r* in these derived forms of *whir*. (See DOUBLING FINAL -R, 1.)

whisk broom. It *whisks* away dirt, hence, not *wisk broom*.

whiskey, whisky. See -Y, -EY, 4.

WHITE-

Adjective compounds are hyphenated: *white-collar, white-faced, white-hot*, etc.

Noun compounds are mostly written separate: *white elephant, white feather, white gold*, etc.

The following common noun compounds are solid: *whitebeard, white-*

*cap, whitefish, whitesmith, white-
wash, whitewood.*
The verb *whitewash* is also solid.

-WHITE
Adjective compounds are hyphenated: *lily-white, snow-white,* etc.

WHOLE-
Adjective compounds are hyphenated (*whole-souled, whole-wheat,*
etc.), except *wholehearted,* which
is solid.
Noun compounds are invariably
two words: *whole blood, whole milk,*
etc.

wholly. Though an exception to the
general rule, final *-e* of *whole* is
dropped before the suffix *-ly.* (See
RETAINED -E, 2.)
whoop. See -OOP, -OUP, -UPE, 1.
who're. Contraction of *who are.* (See
APOSTROPHE, USE OF, 1.)

WHO'S, WHOSE
Who's means *who is; whose* is the
possessive of *who.*
Who's coming tonight?
Whose book is it?
The man *whose* name I've for-
gotten is the only one *who's* not
here.

WIDE-
Adjective compounds are mostly
hyphenated when preceding nouns:
wide-awake, wide-eyed, wide-open,
etc.
Widespread, however, meaning
prevalent, etc., is solid.

wiegh. Misspelling of *weigh.*
wier. Misspelling of *weir.*
wierd. Misspelling of *weird.*
wife. The plural is *wives.* (See PLU-
RALIZING WORDS IN TER-
MINAL -F OR -FE, 1.)

-WIFE
Noun compounds are solid: *fish-
wife, housewife,* etc.

WILD-
Adjective compounds are hyphenated when preceding their nouns:
wild-eyed, wild-spirited, etc.
Noun compounds are invariably
two words: *wild boar, wild rose,
wild West,* etc.
However, *wildcat, wildfire,* and
wildwood are solid. *Wild cat* may
also be written separate, and *wild
flower* and *wild fowl,* preferably
two words, may also be written solid.

willful, wilful. The former spelling,
double *-l,* is preferable. Note that
the ending, however, is only *-ful,*
not *-full;* hence the noun is *willful-
ness* or *wilfulness,* the adverb *will-
fully* or *wilfully.*
will-o'-the-wisp. Hyphenated. (See
HYPHENATING, 10A.)
wily. The adverb is *wilily,* the noun
wiliness, the comparative *wilier,* the
superlative *wiliest.* (See -IER,
-IEST; -Y PLUS A SUFFIX, 5, 6.)

WIND-
Adjective compounds mostly hyphenated: *wind-blown, wind-driven,
wind-swept,* etc.
Windproof and *windtight* are
solid.
Noun compounds are mostly solid:
*windbag, windbreaker, windfall,
windstorm,* etc.
The following common noun
compounds are two words: *wind
gap, wind gauge, wind scale.*

windowpane. Solid word.
window-shop. Hyphenated as a verb.
windup. Solid when a noun.

WINE-
Adjective compounds are hyphenated: *wine-growing, wine-red,* etc.

Noun compounds are mostly separate (*wine cask, wine cup, wine merchant,* etc.), except the following, which are solid: *winebibber, winebibbing, wineglass, winegrower, winegrowing, wineshop, wineskin.* The name for an American apple, *Winesap,* is also solid.

WINTER-

Adjective compounds are hyphenated: *winter-fed, winter-grown,* etc.

The following words are solid: *winterberry, winterbourne, winterfeed* (verb), *wintergreen, wintertide, wintertime.*

winy. Refers to *wine;* not to be confused with *whiny,* from *whine.*

wippersnapper. Misspelling of *whippersnapper.*

wisdom. Though an exception to the general rule, final *-e* of *wise* is dropped before the suffix *-dom.* (See RETAINED -E, 2.)

wisk broom. Misspelling of *whisk broom.*

withhold. Note the double *-h,* since this is a combination of *with* plus *hold*—unlike *threshold,* which has only one medial *-h.*

wizened. One *-z.*

woebegone, wobegone. The latter is a variant spelling, correct but uncommon. (See -OE, TERMINAL, 6.)

woeful, woful. The second spelling correct but uncommon. (See -OE, TERMINAL, 6.)

wolf. The plural is *wolves.* (See PLURALIZING WORDS IN TERMINAL -F OR -FE, 1.)

WOMAN-, -WOMAN

Woman-hater and *woman-suffragist* are hyphenated, as are compound adjectives (*woman-hating,* etc.), except *womanlike* and *womanproof.*

Woman suffrage and *women's rights* are written separate.

-Woman as a suffix is written solid with its root: *Frenchwoman, horsewoman,* etc. The same rule applies to *-women.*

WONDER-

Adjective compounds are hyphenated: *wonder-stricken, wonder-struck, wonder-working.*

Wonder-worker is hyphenated, but *wonderland* and *wonderwork* are solid.

won't. Contraction of *will not.* (See APOSTROPHE, USE OF, 1.)

WOOD-

Adjective compounds are hyphenated: *wood-block, wood-eating, wood-wind,* etc.

The following noun compounds are solid: *woodchuck, woodcock, woodcraft, woodcraftsman, woodcut, woodcutter, woodcutting, woodland, woodlander, woodman, woodpecker, woodpile, woodshed, woodsman, woodwork, woodworker, woodworking, woodworm.*

The noun *wood-note* is hyphenated; other noun compounds are separate (*wood engraver, wood winds,* etc.).

-WOOD

This suffix is written solid with its root: *boxwood, gumwood, hardwood,* etc.

WOODEN-

Hyphenated in adjective compounds (*wooden-faced, wooden-legged,* etc.), except *woodenheaded,* written solid.

Woodenhead and *woodenware* are solid nouns; *wooden horse* and *wooden Indian* are two words.

woolen, woollen. In this word one *-l* is the preferred form, two *-l*'s also correct. But see *woolly, wooly.*

wooley, woolley. Misspellings of *woolly.*

woolly, wooly. In this word two -*l*'s preferred, one -*l* also correct. Hence the noun is *woolliness* preferred, also *wooliness*. But see *woolen*.

-WORD

Most compounds with the suffix -*word* are solid: *byword, catchword, crossword, password,* etc. *Blend-word* is hyphenated; *curse word* and *cuss word* are written separate.

WORK-

Most noun compounds are solid: *workday, workhouse, workman, workout, workshop,* etc. *Work-up,* however, is hyphenated; *work horse* and *work sheet* are written separate.

Adjective compounds preceding their nouns are hyphenated: *work-weary, work-worn,* etc. But *workaday* and *workmanlike* are solid.

-WORK

Noun compounds are solid: *footwork, homework, masterwork,* etc.

-WORKER

Compounds are solid: *fieldworker, steelworker,* etc.

WORKING-

Workingman and *workingwoman* are solid if a title is clearly meant (i.e., a manual or industrial worker). If *working* is more likely an adjective to describe a girl, man, or woman who works for a living, use separate words: *working girl, working man, working woman.*

Other nouns (*working capital, working class, working papers,* etc.) are two words.

Adjective compounds are hyphenated: *working-class, working-day,* etc.

WORLD-, WORLDLY-

Adjective compounds are hyphenated: *world-shattering, world-wide, worldly-wise,* etc.

Noun compounds are two words: *world power, world series, world war,* etc.

WORM-, -WORM

Adjective compounds with *worm-* are hyphenated: *worm-eaten, worm-riddled,* etc.

Wormhole is a solid noun; *worm fence* and *worm gear* are separate.

Noun compounds ending in -*worm* are solid: *angleworm, earthworm, flatworm, silkworm,* etc.

-WORN

Adjective compounds ending in -*worn* are largely solid: *careworn, shopworn, timeworn, toilworn,* etc.

Tide-worn and *work-worn* are hyphenated. *Well-worn* is hyphenated when it *precedes* its noun, separate in the predicate (the dress is *well worn*).

---

worried, worries. The -*y* of *worry* changes to -*i* in these forms. (See -Y PLUS A SUFFIX, 1.)

worrier. The -*y* of *worry* changes to -*i* before -*er*. (See -Y PLUS A SUFFIX, 3.)

worriment. The -*y* of *worry* changes to -*i* before -*ment*. (See -Y PLUS A SUFFIX, 6.)

worrisome. The -*y* of *worry* changes to -*i* before -*some*. (See -Y PLUS A SUFFIX, 8A.)

WORSE-, WORST-

Adjective compounds preceding nouns are hyphenated: *worse-governed, worst-governed, worse-timed, worst-timed,* etc.

---

worshiped, worshipers, worshiping. Single -*p* in all derived forms of *worship,* since the accent does *not* fall on the last syllable. (See DOUBLING FINAL -P, 4.)

worth-while. Always hyphenated, no matter how used; the noun is *worthwhileness.*

-WORTHY

All adjective compounds are solid: *airworthy, noteworthy, seaworthy,* etc.

wouldn't. Contraction of *would not.* (See APOSTROPHE, USE OF, 1.)
would've. Contraction of *would have.* (See APOSTROPHE, USE OF, 1.)
wound. Whether rhyming with *mooned* as a noun, or with *hound* as a verb, the spelling is the same.

-WOVEN

Adjective compounds are hyphenated: *hand-woven, loose-woven, tight-woven,* etc.

wraith. Not *raith.*
wrap. See RAP, WRAP.
wraught. Misspelling of *wrought.*
wrier, wriest. May not be spelled *wryer, wryest.* (See -IER, -IEST, 5.)
wrily. Misspelling of *wryly.*
wriness. Misspelling of *wryness.*
wring. See RING, WRING.

WRIST-

Wristband is solid; *wrist pin* and *wrist watch* are separate.

wrought. The pattern is *-ought.* (See -AUGHT, -OUGHT, 1.)
wryer, wryest. Misspellings of *wrier, wriest.*
wryly. It is not spelled *wrily.* (See -LY, 3.)
wryness. In words of one syllable, such as *wry,* final *-y* is unchanged before *-ness.* (See -Y PLUS A SUFFIX, 7.)

X

Xanthippe. The wife of Socrates; hence any nagging, shrewish woman. Note the *-h.*

X-ray. Compounds with single-letter prefixes generally are hyphenated. (See HYPHENATING, 52.)
xylophone. The vowel after *l-* is *-o.*

Y

-Y, -EY

1. Generally, before adding *-y* to a word ending in *-e* preceded by a consonant (*stone, bone,* etc.), drop the final *-e.*

bone—bony   stage—stagy
sponge—spongy   stone—stony

2. *Cagey* is somewhat commoner than *cagy,* though both are correct; *homey* is preferable to *homy;* and *stagey* is an equally acceptable variant of *stagy.*

3. *Holey* (i.e., full of holes) is written with the *-e* retained in order to distinguish it from *holy* (pious, sacred, etc.).

4. *Whisky* and *whiskey* are interchangeable as correct spellings; as a matter of trade custom, however, domestic brands are generally written *whiskey;* imports, especially from Scotland, are *whisky.* The plural of *whisky* is *whiskies,* of *whiskey* is *whiskeys.*

-Y PLUS A SUFFIX

If a word ends in *-y,* adding a suffix may, or may not, require changing *-y* to *-i.* The following principles apply.

If -y is preceded by one or more consonants.

1. Change *-y* to *-i* before *-ed* to form the past, or *-es* to form the third person singular present, of the verb.

accompany—accompanied,
  accompanies
apply—applied, applies
busy—busied, busies

carry—carried, carries
copy—copied, copies
cry—cried, cries
defy—defied, defies
deny—denied, denies
dry—dried, dries
marry—married, marries
rely—relied, relies
simplify—simplified, simplifies
spy—spied, spies
tarry—tarried, tarries
whinny—whinnied, whinnies
worry—worried, worries

2. Similarly, to form the *plural* by adding *-es; lady—ladies; sky—skies;* etc. (See -EYS, -IES, -YS, 3.)

3. Again, before *-er* as a suffix denoting *one who* or *that which.*

  carry—carrier
  copy—copier
  cry—crier
  defy—defier
  tarry—tarrier
  worry—worrier

4. As also before *-er* and *-est* to form the comparative and superlative degrees of an adjective: *lively, livelier, liveliest,* etc. (See -IER, -IEST.)

5. And before adding *-ly* to words of *more than one syllable.* (For words of one syllable, such as *dry,* see -LY, 3, 4.)

  busy—busily
  heavy—heavily
  lucky—luckily
  ready—readily
  steady—steadily
  weary—wearily

6. Also before adding *-ness* or *-ment* to words of more than one syllable.

 accompany—accompaniment
 crazy—craziness
 happy—happiness
 hardy—hardiness
 hazy—haziness
 heavy—heaviness
 lazy—laziness

poky—pokiness
ready—readiness
silly—silliness
steady—steadiness
tasty—tastiness
weary—weariness
worry—worriment

7. But in words of only one syllable, keep the *-y* before *-ness.*

  dry—dryness
  shy—shyness
  sly—slyness
  wry—wryness

8. Before *-ing* the *-y* necessarily remains.

 accompany—accompanying
 cry—crying
 deny—denying
 dry—drying

8A. before *-ful* and *-some, -y* changes to *-i.*

beautiful	pitiful
bountiful	plentiful
dutiful	weariful
fanciful	wearisome
merciful	worrisome

If -y is preceded by a vowel.

9. Retain *-y* (with many exceptions noted later) before any suffix.

allay—allayed, allayer, allaying
betray—betrayed, betrayer,
 betraying, betrayment
boy—boyish
bray—brayed, braying
coy—coyly, coyness
decay—decayed, decaying
delay—delayed, delaying
destroy—destroyed, destroyer,
 destroying
dismay—dismayed, dismaying
disobey—disobeyed, disobeying
display—displayed, displaying
enjoy—enjoyed, enjoying,
 enjoyment
essay—essayed, essaying
gray—grayed, grayer, graying,
 grayly, grayness
hay—hayed, haying
key—keyed, keying, keys
pay—payer, paying

play—played, player, playing
pray—prayed, prayer, praying
prey—preyed, preyer, preying
spay—spayed, spaying
stray—strayed, straying
survey—surveyed, surveying, surveyor
sway—swayed, swaying
valley—valleys

10. The important exceptions are:
gay—*gaily* is preferred to *gayly;* and *gaiety* to *gayety.*
lay—past tense is *laid.*
money—though the plural *moneys* is preferable, *monies* is common and in good repute.
pay—past tense is *paid.*
say—past tense is *said.*
See also -AYED, -AID; -EYS, -IES, -YS; -IER, -IEST; -LY.

---

yeoman. Not *yoeman.*

yodel, yodle. The first spelling is preferable.

yodeler, yodeller, yodler. All these spellings are correct, but the first is preferable.

yoeman. Misspelling of *yeoman.*

yoga, yogi. The system is preferably spelled *yoga,* though some people write and say it *yogi.* The practitioner, on the other hand, is a *yogi,* or, rarely, a *yogin.*

yogurt, yoghurt. Spell it either way. Sometimes, though very rarely, it's even spelled *yohourt.*

YOKE, YOLK

Yoke is a harness, something that literally or figuratively links or connects, the symbol of slavery, etc. It may also be used as a verb.

Yolk is the yellow of the egg.

YOUR, YOU'RE

Your is possessive only.
Have you had *your* bath?
Do you like *your* mother-in-law?
You're is a contraction of *you are.*
You're a real character.
You're playing gin with us tonight, aren't you?

-YS, -IES, -EYS. See -EYS, -IES, -YS.

-YZE, -IZE. See -IZE, -YZE.

Z

zany. Not *zaney.*

zar. Misspelling of *czar.*

zephyr. Note the *-yr.*

zeros, zeroes. The former is the preferable plural; both are correct. (See PLURALIZING WORDS IN TERMINAL -O, 5.)

zincked, zincking, zincky. The *-k* must be inserted in the derived forms of *zinc* in order to preserve the original pronunciation of final *-c.* (See -C, -CK, 1.)

zwieback. Although from the German *zwei,* twice, and *backen,* baked, the combination in English is *-ie.* (See -IE, -EI, 4.)